AUSTIN A55 Mk.11   AUSTIN A60
RILEY 4/68 & 4/72

Owner's Workshop Manual

by John H. Haynes

Models Covered

1489 c. c. AUSTIN A55 Mk. II Cambridge Saloon – January 1959 to September 1961

1489 c. c. AUSTIN A55 Mk. II Cambridge Countryman – September 1960 to September 1961

1489 c. c. RILEY 4/68 Saloon – April 1959 to September 1961

1622 c. c. AUSTIN A60 Cambridge Saloon – October 1961 on

1622 c. c. AUSTIN A60 Cambridge Countryman – October 1961 on

1622 c. c. RILEY 4/72 – October 1961 on

2542/004

SBN 900550 04 X

HAYNES PUBLISHING GROUP
SPARKFORD YEOVIL SOMERSET ENGLAND
distributed in the USA by
HAYNES PUBLICATIONS INC
861 LAWRENCE DRIVE
NEWBURY PARK
CALIFORNIA, 91320
USA

ACKNOWLEDGEMENTS

It would not have been possible to produce such a detailed work without the generous assistance of the British Motor Corporation. who, through supplying us with all the technical data, procedures, and line illustrations requested have made a considerable contribution to the accuracy of this manual.

Thanks are due to Castrol Ltd. , for the lubrications chart; to the Champion Spark Plug Company Ltd.; to Motor ; to Mr. J. Mead, and Mr. G. Fursey. Special thanks are due to Mr. L. Tooze whose co-operation, experience and advice was of great help in the compilation of photographs for this manual; and to the many enthusiastic private owners who have come forward to give details of the methods and procedures adopted to get round the more unusual job.

Although every care has been taken to ensure all the data in this manual is correct, bearing in mind that manufacturers' current practice is to make small alterations and design changes without reclassifying the model, no liability can be accepted for damage, loss or injury caused by any errors or omissions in the information given.

PHOTOGRAPHIC CAPTIONS
& CROSS REFERENCES

For ease of reference this book is divided into numbered chapters, sections and paragraphs. The title of each chapter is self explanatory. The sections comprise the main headings within the chapter. The paragraphs appear within each section.

The captions to the majority of photographs are given within the paragraphs of the relevant section to avoid repetition. These photographs bear the same number as the sections and paragraphs to which they refer. The photograph always appears in the same Chapter as its paragraph. For example if looking through Chapter Ten it is wished to find the caption for photograph 9.4 refer to section 9 and then read paragraph 4.

To avoid repetition once a procedure has been described it is not normally repeated. If it is necessary to refer to a procedure already given this is done by quoting the original Chapter, section and sometimes paragraph number.

The reference is given thus; Chapter No./Section No. Para. No. For example Chapter 2, section 6 would be given as : Chapter 2/6. Chapter 2, Section 6, paragraph 5 would be given as Chapter 2/6.5. If more than one section is involved the reference would be written : Chapter 2/6 to 7 or where the section is not consecutive 2/6 and 9. To refer to several paragraphs within a section the reference is given thus : Chapter 2/6. 2 and 4.

To refer to a section within the same Chapter the Chapter number is usually dropped. Thus if a reference in a Chapter 4 merely reads 'see section 8', this refers to section 8 in that same Chapter.

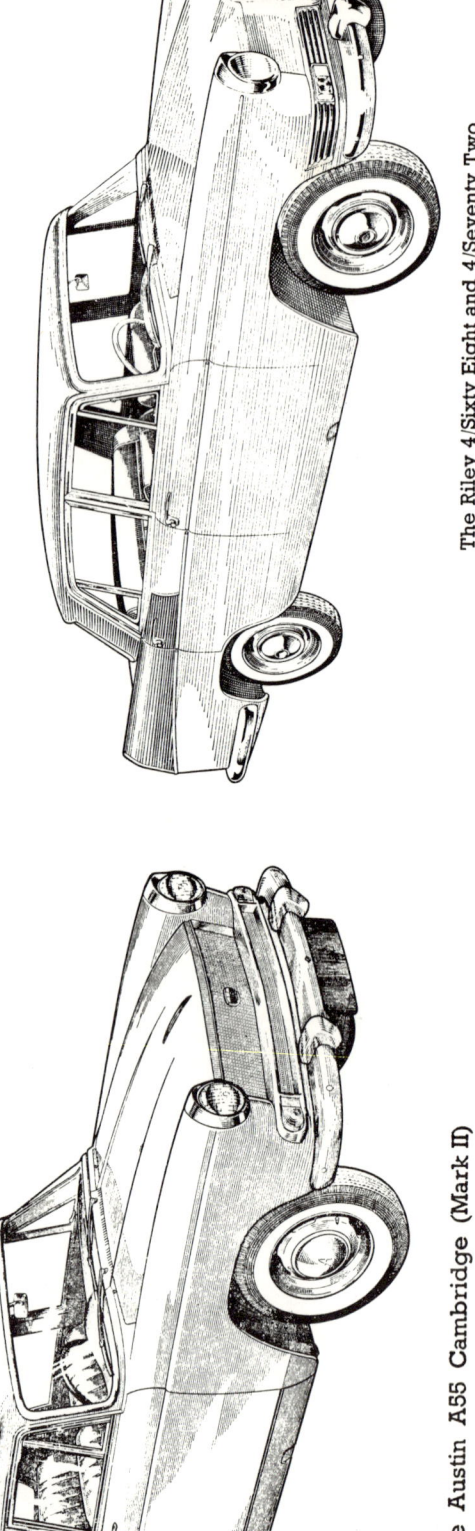

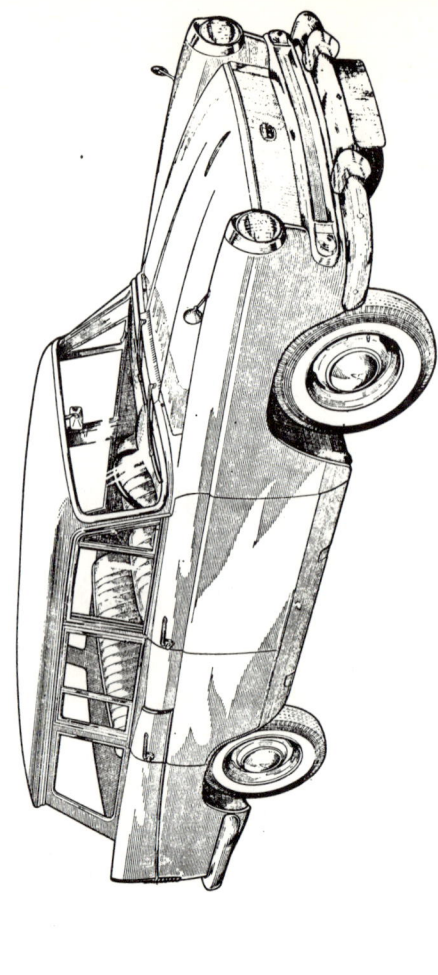

The Riley 4/Sixty Eight and 4/Seventy Two

THE AUSTIN CAMBRIDGE A55 (Mk. II) COUNTRYMAN

The Austin A55 Cambridge (Mark II)

THE AUSTIN CAMBRIDGE A60 SALOON

4

CONTENTS

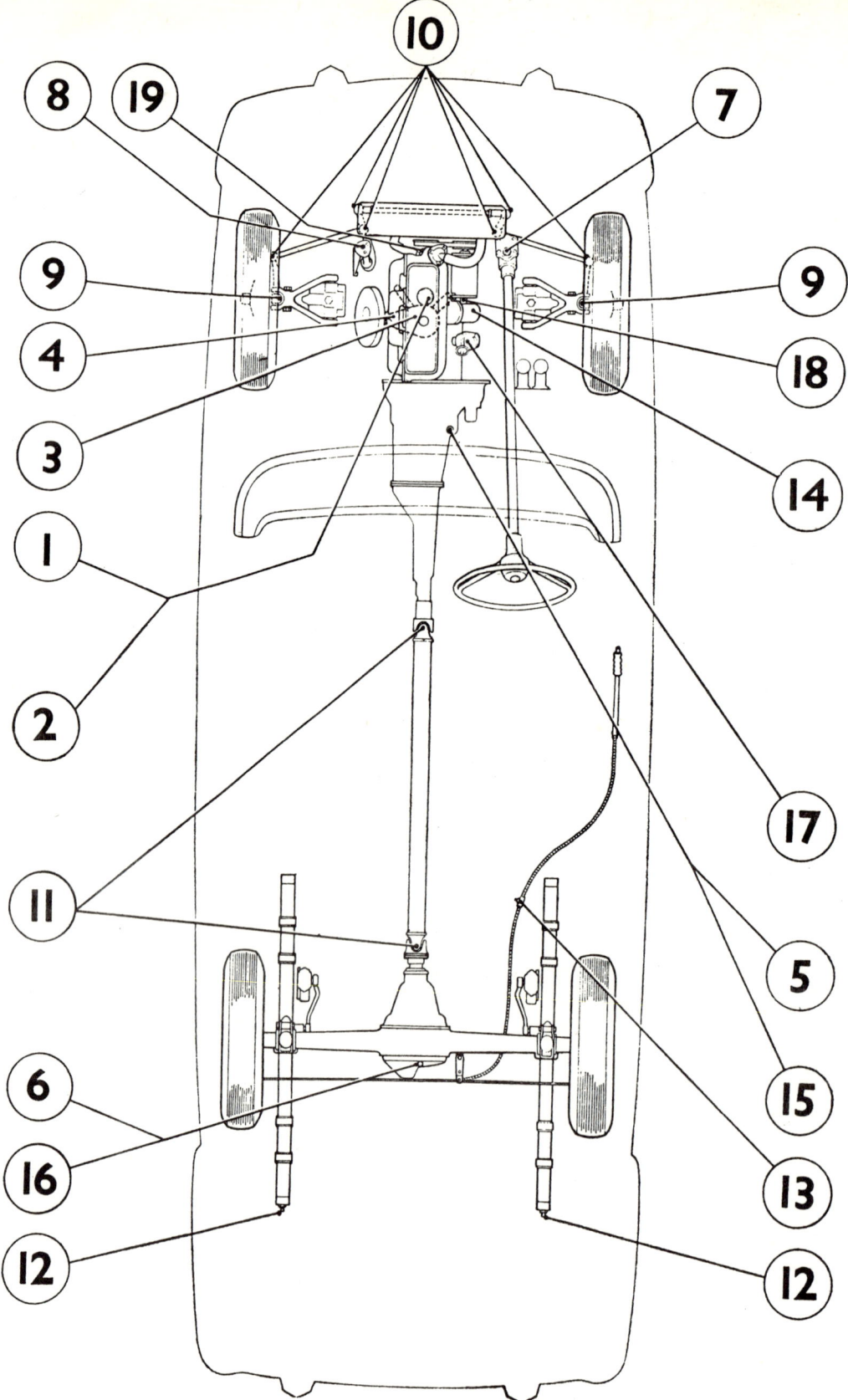

KEY TO LUBRICATION CHART

1 **Engine** oil filler orifice—Castrolite.   2 Drain and refill sump once every 6,000 miles—Castrolite.   3 Air cleaner (oil bath type)—Castrolite.   4 Carburetter dashpot/s—Castrolite.   5 Gearbox—Castrolite.   6 Rear axle—Castrol Hypoy   7 Steering box—Castrol Hypoy.   8 Steering idler—Castrol Hypoy.   9 Swivel and Fulcrum pins—Castrolease L.M.   10 Steering joints—Castrolease L.M.   11 P r o p e l l e r shaft—Castrolease L M   12 Leaf spring shackles—Castrolease L.M   13 Hand brake c a b l e—Castrolease L.M.   14 Oil filter—New element every 6,000 miles.   15 Gearbox—Drain and refill every 6,000 miles.   16 Rear axle—Drain and refill every 6,000 miles.   17 Distributor—Castrolite and Castrolease L M   18 Dynamo—Castrolite.   19 Water pump—Castrolease L.M.

INTRODUCTION

This is a manual for do-it-yourself minded A55, A60, Riley 4/68 and 4/72 enthusiasts. It shows how to maintain these cars in first class condition and how to carry out repairs when components become worn or break. Regular and careful maintenance is essential if maximum reliability and minimum wear are to be achieved.

The step-by-step photographs show how to deal with the major components and in conjunction with the text and exploded illustrations should make all the work quite clear - even to the novice who has never previously attempted the more complex job.

Although these cars are hardwearing and robust it is inevitable that their reliability and performance will decrease as they become older. Repairs and general reconditioning will become necessary if the car is to remain roadworthy. Early models requiring attention are frequently bought by the more impecunious motorist who can least afford the repair prices charged in garages, even though these prices are usually quite fair bearing in mind overheads and the high cost of capital equipment and skilled labour.

It is in these circumstances that this manual will prove to be of maximum assistance, as it is the ONLY workshop manual written from practical experience specially to help A55, A60, Riley 4/68 and 4/72 owners.

Manufacturer's official manuals are usually splendid publications which contain a wealth of technical information. Because they are issued primarily to help the manufacturers, authorised dealers and distributors they tend to be written in very technical language, and tend to skip details of certain jobs which are common knowledge to garage mechanics. Owner's workshop manuals are different as they are intended primarily to help the owner. They therefore go into many of the jobs in great detail with extensive photographic support to ensure everything is properly understood so that the repair is done correctly.

Owners who intend to do their own maintenance and repairs should have a reasonably comprehensive tool kit. Some jobs require special service tools, but in many instances it is possible to get round their use with a little care and ingenuity. For example, a $3\frac{1}{2}$ in. diameter jubilee clip makes a most efficient and cheap piston ring compressor.

Throughout this manual ingenious ways of avoiding the use of special equipment and tools are shown. In some cases the proper tool must be used. Where this is the case a description of the tool and its correct use is included.

When a component malfunctions repairs are becoming more and more a case of replacing the defective item with an exchange rebuilt unit. This is excellent practice when a component is thoroughly worn out, but it is a waste of good money when overall the component is only half worn, and requires the replacement of but a single small item to effect a complete repair. As an example, a non-functioning dynamo can frequently be repaired quite satisfactorily just by fitting new brushes.

A further function of this manual is to show the owner how to examine malfunctioning parts; determine what is wrong, and then how to make the repair.

Given the time, mechanical do-it-yourself aptitude, and a reasonable collection of tools, this manual will show the enthusiastic owner how to maintain and repair his car really economically.

ROUTINE MAINTENANCE

The maintenance instructions listed below are basically those recommended by the manufacturer. They are supplemented by additional maintenance tasks which, through practical experience, the author recommends should be carried out at the intervals suggested.

The additional tasks are indicated by an asterisk, and are primarily of a preventative nature in that they will assist in eliminating the unexpected failure of a component due to fair wear and tear.

The levels of the engine oil, radiator cooling water, windscreen washer water, and the battery electrolyte, also the type pressures, should be checked weekly, or more frequently if experience dictates this necessary. If not checked at home it is advantageous to regularly use the same garage for this work.

NOTE. It is recommended that when a monograde or single viscosity oil is used in the engine, the oil is changed at interva's of 3,000 miles irrespective of local conditions. Modern multigrade oil such as Castrol GTX need only be changed at intervals of 6,000 miles.

3,000 miles

EVERY 3,000 MILES (or every 3 months if 3,000 miles not exceeded). :-

1. Unscrew the top/s of the carburettor dash-pot/s, lift out the damper assembly and top up with Castrolite or a similar S.A.E. 30 oil to within ½ in. of the top of the pot/s. Oil the carburetter controls. See Fig. 1.

2. Fill a grease gun with Castrolease L.M. or a similar recommended multi-purpose grease and thoroughly lubricate the following through the appropriate grease nipple, which should be first wiped clean. Give 3-4 strokes of the grease gun to:-

a) The front suspension, upper and lower swivel pin bushes and the lower swivel pin. (A useful tip is to jack up the front of the car so the grease penetrates more easily). The ball joints on the steering drag link, track rod, and steering arm (6 nipples on each side of the car). See Fig. 2. NOTE on later models the ball joints are sealed for life so there are only three nipples on each side of the front suspension to attend to. Total No. of nipples to grease - 12 early cars, 6 later cars.

b) The universal joints on the front and rear of the propeller shaft (early cars only). Total No. of nipples to grease - 2. See Fig. 3.

c) The handbrake cable. See Fig. 4. Total No. of grease nipples to grease - 1.

d) The rear spring shackle lubrication nipples (early models only). See Fig. 5. Total No. of nipples to grease - 2.

3. On cars fitted with oil bath type air cleaners drain and wash out the cleaner bowl and refill with Castrolite or similar. See Chapter 3, page 64 for further details.

4. Check that the level of the hydraulic fluid inside the brake (2) and clutch (1) master cylinders is up to the level marked on the outside of the reservoirs and top up with Castrol Girling Brake Fluid Amber as necessary. See Fig. 6.

5. Adjust the front and rear brakes as described on page 132. Check the hoses and pipes for loose joints, or leaks or wear caused by the suspension or tyres rubbing against the flexible piping. See page 134 for further details.

6. Wash the bodywork and chromium fittings and clean out the interior. *

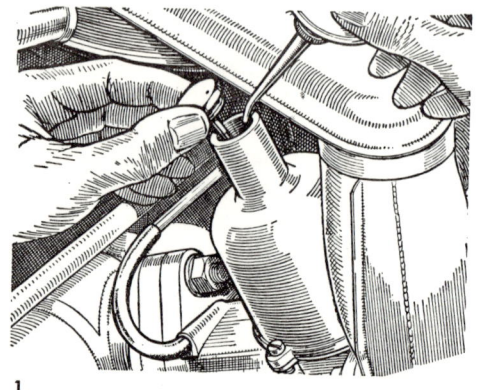

1

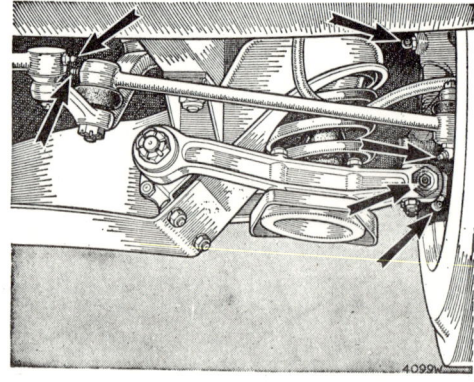

2

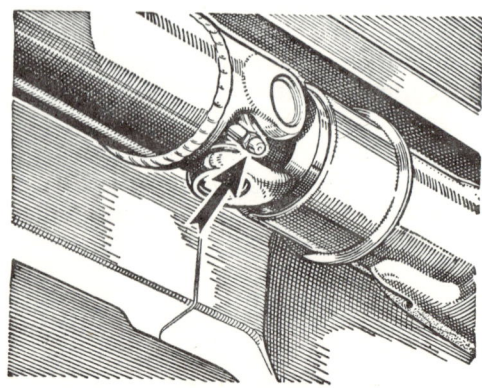

3

7. Check that all the lights are functioning correctly and replace blown bulbs as necessary.* Check the headlamp alignment if either unit is disturbed.

8. Lubricate with S.A.E. 20 oil the door hinges bonnet lock operating mechanism, and the safety catch.

9. Lubricate the boot catch and hinges with an S.A.E. 20 oil.

10. Check the battery cell specific gravity readings, and clean the terminals. See page 143 for details.

11. Lubricate the dynamo rear bearing. See page 145 for details. NOTE If wished this task need only be performed once every 6,000 miles, but once every 3,000 miles is to be preferred in the author's experience.

12. Examine the fan belt and adjust as necessary. See page 145.

13. Remove the plug 'A' (in Fig. 7) from the steering box and top up with S.A.E. 90 gear oil till the level is flush with the bottom of the filler hole. NOTE that the plug is in the position 'B' on later models.

14. Remove the square-headed plug (arrowed in Fig. 8) and top up with S.A.E. 90 gear oil to the bottom of the filler hole.

6,000 miles

EVERY 6,000 MILES (or every 6 months if 6,000 miles is not exceeded).

1. Run the engine until it has reached its normal working temperature. Then drain the oil from the sump by undoing the drain plug (arrowed in Fig. 9). Undo the filter and renew the element as described on page 33. The component parts of the engine oil filter are replaced in the order shown in Fig. 10. (1. Retaining clip. 2. Pressure plate. 3. Felt washer. 4. Steel washer. 5. Pressure spring. 6. Rubber washer). Refill the sump with 7½ pints of Castrolite or equivalent.

2. Perform all the maintenance tasks listed for the 3,000 miles service.

3. Check the condition of the heater and cooling system hoses and replace as necessary.*

4. Lubricate with engine oil the pivot point of the brake and clutch pedal shafts.*

5. Check the fuel lines and the union joints for leaks and replace defective parts as necessary.*

6. Remove and clean the filters in the carburetter/s and fuel pump where these are fitted.*

7. Check and adjust the valve rocker clearances. See page 49 for further details.

8. Remove the distributor cap, pull off the rotor arm and apply three drops of engine oil to the head of the large screw in the centre of the distributor. See 'B' in Fig. 11.

9. Allow three drops of oil past the cam to the automatic timing mechanism. See 'A' in Fig. 11.

10. Lubricate the four-sided cam by smearing a faint trace of grease over it. See 'C' in Fig. 12.

11. Apply a tiny spot of oil to the moving con-

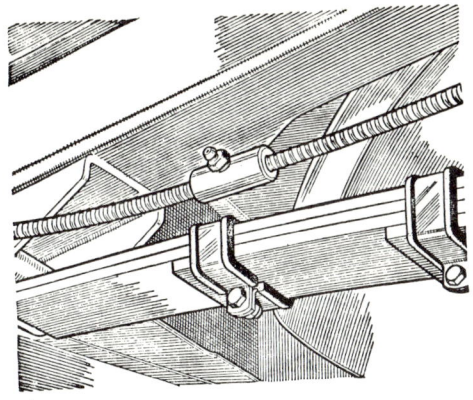

4

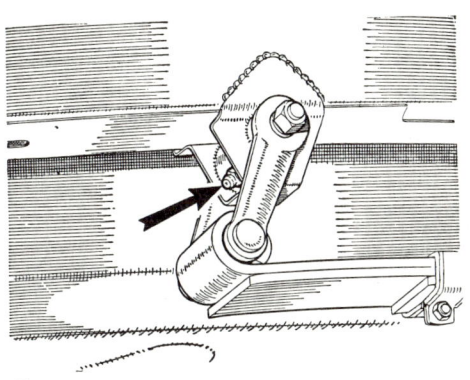

5

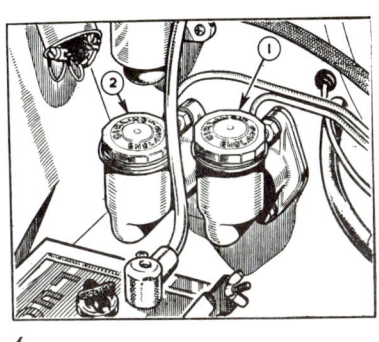

6

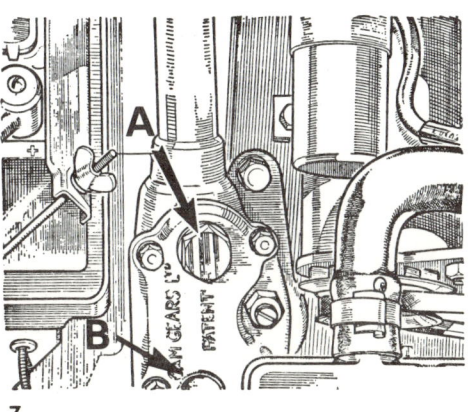

7

tact breaker pivot pin. See 'D' in Fig. 12. Any excess might get on the points and cause misfiring.

12. Check the condition of the contact breaker points, clean and regap them, and if necessary fit a new set and check the timing and advance and retard mechanism. See page 86 for further details.

13. Check the level of the oil in the gearbox (Fig. 13) and replenish with Castrolite as necessary as described on page 107. Remove the combined oil filler and level plug from the rear axle, (see Fig. 14) and top up with Castrol Hypoy. After topping up allow sufficient time for any excess to drain. See page 126 for further details.

14. Adjust the carburetter slow running and tune if necessary. See page 74 for details. *

15. Examine the exhaust system for holes and leaks and replace defective components as necessary. *

16. Wax polish the body and also the chromium plating. Force wax polish into any joints in the bodywork to help prevent rust formation. *

17. Balance the front wheels to eliminate steering vibration as necessary. *

18. Check and adjust the steering toe-in of the front wheels. See page 170 for further details.

19. Check the suspension nuts, and the steering nuts for tightness.

20. If wished, change over the tyres to equalise wear and inspect the walls for damage. *

21. Lubricate the washer round the wheelbase spindle with several drops of glycerine.

22. Clean and adjust the sparking plugs as described on page 93.

23. On models fitted with paper air cleaner elements fit new elements as described on page 64.

12,000 miles

EVERY 12,000 MILES (or once every 12 months if 12,000 miles not exceeded).

1. Perform all the maintenance tasks listed for the 6,000 mile service. In addition carry out the following operations:-

2. Remove the carburetter float chamber, empty any sediment present, check the condition of the needle valve, clean and refit.

3. Remove the speedometer cable, clean, and lightly lubricate the inner cable with Castrol-ease L.M. or similar. When reassembling the inner cable should be withdrawn approximately 8 in. and the surface grease wiped off. This is so none will work its way into the speedometer head.

4. Steam clean the underside of the body and clean the engine and engine compartment. *

5. Remove the sparking plugs, and fit new ones, correctly gapped.

6. Inspect the ignition leads for cracks and perishing and replace as necessary. *

7. Remove the brake drums, blow out the dust, and inspect the linings for wear. See page 134

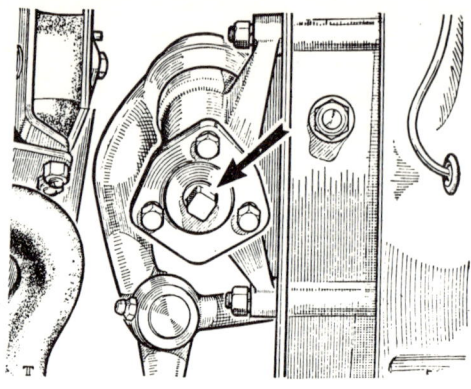

8

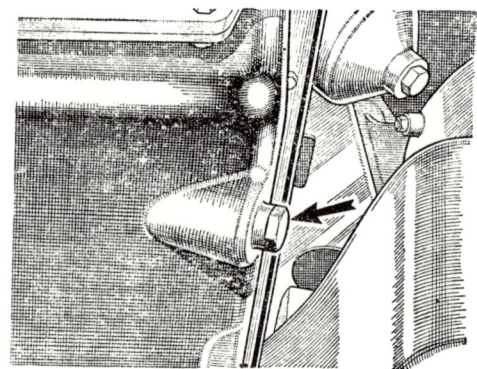

9

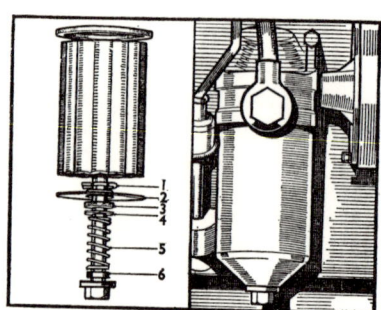

10

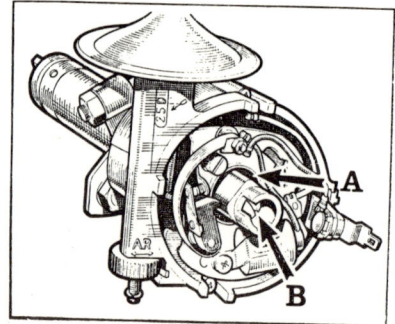

11

for further details. *

8. Examine the dynamo brushes, replace them if worn, and clean the commutator. See page 156 for further details.

9. Renew the windscreen wiper blades. *

10. Check the headlamp bulbs and renew them if slightly blackened or if the element sags.

11. On later models fitted with a crankcase closed circuit breathing system, change the engine oil filler cap and clean the crankcase breather valve. All the metal parts can be washed in petrol. The diaphragm should be cleaned with detergent or methylated spirits. See Fig. 1.20 on page 51.

12. Lubricate the water pump. To do this unscrew the oiling plug behind the pulley wheel and grease sparingly with Castrolease L.M. Replace the plug. If the pump squeaks a few teaspoonfuls of hydraulic fluid in the cooling system will silence the carbon sealing ring. Fig. 15 refers.

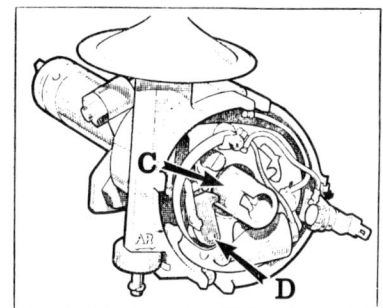

12

24,000 miles

EVERY 24,000 MILES

1. In addition to the maintenance tasks listed previously, carry out the following operations:-

2. Drain and refill the gearbox and rear axle to remove any small metal particles with which the oil may now be contaminated. *

3. Examine the ball joints and hub bearings for wear and replace as necessary. See page 166 for details. *

4. Check the tightness of the battery earth lead on the bodywork. *

5. Renew the condenser in the distributor. See page 89 for details. *

6. Remove the starter motor, examine the brushes, replace as necessary, and clean the commutator and starter drive. Please see page 150 for details.

7. Test the cylinder compressions, and if necessary remove the cylinder head, decarbonise, grind the valves and fit new valve springs. See pages 26, 38, and 41 for details. *

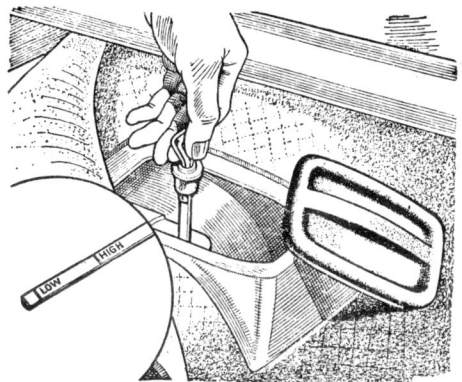

13

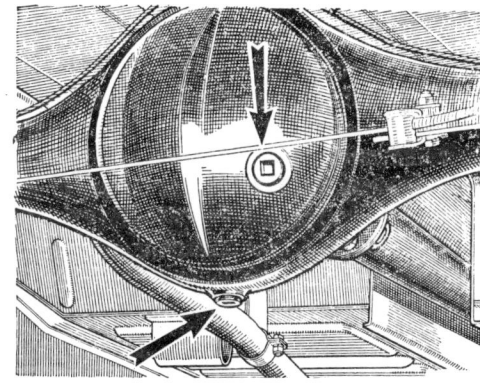

14

40,000 miles

1. Drain the brake fluid from the hydraulic system. Renew all the rubber seals and flexible hoses. Examine the brake pistons and their bores for scratches and renew as necessary. Refill the system and bleed the brakes. See Chapter 9, page 131 for details.

15

RECOMMENDED LUBRICANTS

Component	Engine/Gearbox and Carburetter	Steering Gearbox, Idler, and Rear Axle (Hypoid Gears)		Grease Points	Upper Cylinder Lubrication	Automatic Transmission
Climatic conditions	All temperatures above −18°C. (0°F.)*	All conditions down to −12°C. (10°F.)	Arctic consistently below −12°C. (10°F.)	All conditions	All conditions	All conditions
BP	Visco-Static Super Visco-Static 10W/40	Gear Oil S.A.E. 90 E.P.	Gear Oil S.A.E. 80 E.P.	Energrease L. 2	Upper Cylinder Lubricant	Automatic Transmission Fluid Type A
SHELL	Shell Super Motor Oil	Shell Spirax 90 E.P.	Shell Spirax 80 E.P.	Shell Retinax A	Shell Upper Cylinder Lubricant	Shell Donax T. 6
FILTRATE	Filtrate 10W/30 Multigrade	Filtrate E.P. Gear 90	Filtrate E.P. Gear 80	Filtrate Super Lithium Grease	Filtrate Petroyle	A.T.F. Type A
STERNOL	Sternol W.W. Multigrade 10W/40	Ambroleum E.P. 90	Ambroleum E.P. 80	Ambroline L.H.T.	Sternol Magikoyl	Sternol Lynx Type A
DUCKHAM'S	Q. 5500	Duckham's Hypoid 90	Duckham's Hypoid 80	Duckham's L.B. 10 Grease	Duckham's Adcoid Liquid	Nolmatic A.T.F. Type A
CASTROL	Castrolite	Castrol Hypoy	Castrol Hypoy Light	Castrolease L.M.	Castrollo	Castrol T.Q.
ESSO	Esso Extra Motor Oil 10W/30	Esso Gear Oil G.P. 90/140 or G.P. 90	Esso Gear Oil G.P. 80	Esso Multipurpose Grease H	Esso Upper Cylinder Lubricant	Esso Automatic Transmission Fluid
MOBIL	Mobiloil Special 10W/30 Mobiloil Super 10W/40	Mobilube G.X. 90	Mobilube G.X. 80	Mobilgrease M.P.	Mobil Upperlube	Mobil A.T.F. 200

Approval is also given to BP Super Visco-Static 20W/50, Shell X-100 Multigrade 20W/50, Sternol WW Multigrade 20W/50, Castrol XL, Duckham's Q. 20/50, Esso Extra Motor Oil 20W/40, Filtrate 20W/50, Mobiloil 20W/50, Mobiloil Special 20W/40 oil, for temperatures down to −12°C. (10°F.) and to monograde or single-viscosity conventional lubricants supplied by companies listed in this chart.

*For temperatures below −18°C. (0°F.) use Multigrade S.A.E. 5W/20 oil.

CHAPTER ONE

ENGINE

CONTENTS

CHAPTER ONE

SPECIFICATIONS

The engine originally fitted to the Austin A55 Mk. II was of 1489 c. c. and was designated type 15A or 15AMW. The power unit in the Riley 4/68 was virtually identical but made use of twin S. U. carburetters and was known as the type 15RB. When in October 1961 the A60 and the Riley 4/72 were introduced the cubic capacity was increased to 1622 c. c. and the engines were known as the 16AMW and the 16RA respectively.

ENGINE SPECIFICATIONS & DATA 1489 c. c. - SINGLE AND TWIN CARBURETTER MODELS

Engine - General

Type	4 cylinder in line O. H. V. operated	
Bore	2. 875 in. (73. 025 mm.)	
Stroke	3. 5 in. (88. 9 mm.)	
Cubic Capacity	90. 88 cu. in. (1489 c. c.)	
Compression Ratio: H. C.	8. 3 to 1 High Compression	
L. C.	7. 2 to 1 Low Compression	
Compression Pressure	Single S. U.	Twin S. U.
High compression ratio	137 lb/sq.in. at 2,100 r.p.m.	140 lb/sq.in. at 3,300 r.p.m.
Low compression ratio	127 lb/sq.in. at 2,000 r.p.m.	–
Torque		
High compression ratio	82. 5 lb.ft. at 2,100 r. p. m.	85 lb.ft. at 3,300 r.p.m.
Low compression ratio	77. 0 lb.ft. at 2,000 r. p. m.	–
Maximum B. H. P.		
High compression ratio	50. 5 at 4,400 r.p.m.	68 at 5,400 r. p. m.
Low compression ratio	48. 0 at 4,200 r.p.m.	–
Engine Idle Speed - Optimum	500 r. p. m.	
Firing Order	1, 3, 4, 2	
Location of No. 1 cylinder...	Next to radiator	
Engine mountings	3 - one each side of the engine 1 under gearbox	

Camshaft and Camshaft Bearings

Camshaft Drive	From crankshaft by double roller chain
Camshaft Bearings	Three - white metal replaceable liners
Camshaft Journal diameter:	
Front	1. 78875 to 1. 78925 in. (45. 424 to 45. 437 mm.)
Centre	1. 72875 to 1. 72925 in. (43. 910 to 43. 923 mm.)
Rear	1. 62275 to 1. 62325 in. (41. 218 to 41. 230 mm.)

ENGINE

Camshaft bearings internal diameter
after reaming in position in block

Front	1.79025 to 1.79075 in. (45.472 to 45.485 mm.)
Centre	1.73025 to 1.73075 in. (43.948 to 43.961 mm.)
Rear	1.62425 to 1.62475 in. (41.256 to 41.269 mm.)
Diametrical clearance	.001 to .002 in. (.0254 to .0508 mm.)
Endfloat	.003 to .007 in. (.076 to .178 mm.)
Timing Chain	3/8 in. (9.25 mm.) pitch by 52 pitches
End thrust	Taken by locating plate

Connecting Rods & Big & Little End Bearings

Type	Angular split big end, split clamp small end
Length between centres	6.5 in. (165.1 mm.)
Big end bearings - Type	Shell
Big end bearings - Material	Steel backed copper-lead
Big end bearings - Length	.995 to 1.005 in. (25.2 to 25.52 mm.)
Big end bearings - Clearance	.001 to .0027 in. (.0254 to .068 mm.)
Endfloat on crankpin	.008 to .012 in. (.20 to .30 mm.)
Undersizes available	-.010, -.020, -.030 and -.040 ins.
	(-.254, -.508, -.762, -1.016 mm.)

Crankshaft & Main Bearings

Main journal diameter	2.0005 to 2.001 in. (50.813 to 50.825 mm.)
Crankpin journal diameter	1.8759 to 1.8764 in. (47.648 to 47.661 mm.)
Crankshaft end thrust	Taken by thrust washers at centre main bearing
Endfloat	.002 to .003 in. (.051 to .076 mm.)
Main bearings	Three shell type
Bearing material	Steel backed white metal
Bearing length	1.375 in. (34.925 mm.)
Diametrical clearance	.001 to .0027 in. (.0254 to .068 mm.)
Undersizes available	-.010, -.020, -.030 and -.040 ins.
	(-.254, -.508, -.762, -1.016 mm.)

Cylinder Block

Type	Cylinder cast integral with top half of crankcase
Water jackets	Full length
Oversize bores: First	.010 in. (.254 mm.)
Max.	.040 in. (1.016 mm.)

Cylinder Head

Type	Cast iron with vertical valves
Port arrangements	Inlet & exhaust ports on same side
No. of ports: Exhaust	2 separate and one siamised
No. of ports: Inlet	2 siamised
Combustion chamber capacity	39.2 c.c. (2.4 cu. in.) with valves fitted

Gudgeon Pins

Type	Semi-floating. Held by clamp bolt
Fit in piston	Free push fit at 20°C (68°F)
Outer diameter	.6869 to .6871 in. (17.447 to 17.452 mm.)

Lubrication System

Type	Pressure and splash. Wet sump
Oil filter	Full flow. Tecalemit or Purolator
Capacity Oil Filter	1 pint. (1.2 U.S. pint. .57 litre)
Sump Capacity	7½ pints (4.2 litre, 9 U.S. pints)
Oil pump - Type	Hobourn-Eaton or eccentric rotor
Pump capacity	3¼ gallons a minute @ 2,000 r.p.m.
Oil pressure relief valve opens ...	75 lb/sq. in. (5.27 kg./cm2.). Twin S.U. models
...	50 lb/sq. in. (3.52 kg./cm2.). Single S.U. models

Relief valve spring - Length fitted ...	2.156 in. (54.77 mm.) at 16 lb. load. Twin S.U. models
...	2.156 in. (54.77 mm.) at 13½ lb. load. Single S.U. models
Relief valve spring - Length free ...	3 in. (76.2 mm.). Twin S.U. models.
...	2.859 in. (72.638 mm.) Single S.U. models.
Oil pump pumping rate	3¼ gal./min. at 1,000 r.p.m. (pump)
Normal oil pressure - Idling	15 lb/sq. in. (All models)
Normal oil pressure at 3,000 r.p.m. ..	60 to 75 lb/sq. in. (Twin S.U. models)
...	40 to 50 lb/sq. in. (Single S.U. models)

Pistons
Twin S.U. models

Type	Anodized aluminium alloy - Solid skirt
No. of rings	4. 3 compression, 1 oil control
Clearance of top of skirt	.0035 to .0042 in. (.0889 to .1067 mm.)
Clearance of bottom of skirt	.0017 to .0023 in. (.0432 to .0584 mm.)

Single S.U. models

Type	Anodized aluminium alloy - Split skirt
No. of rings	4. 3 compression, 1 oil control
Clearance of top of skirt	.0022 to .0034 in. (.0559 to .0863 mm.)
Clearance of bottom of skirt	.0006 to .0014 in. (.0152 to .0355 mm.)

Piston Rings

Top compression ring	Plain
2nd & 3rd compression rings	Tapered
Top ring width (Twin S.U. models) ...	.0615 to .0625 in. (1.562 to 1.587 mm.)
(Single S.U. models) ..	.0771 to .0781 in. (1.95 to 1.98 mm.)
Ring thickness (All 4 rings)	.119 to .126 in. (3.02 to 3.20 mm.)
Fitted gap (All 4 rings)	.008 to .013 in. (.20 to .33 mm.)
Oil control ring - type	Slotted scraper
Oil control ring - width	.1552 to .1562 in. (3.94 to 3.99 mm.)
Oil control ring - groove clearance ...	.0018 to .0038 in. (.046 to .096 mm.) (Twin S.U's)
...	.0016 to .0036 in. (.040 to .091 mm.) (Single S.U's)
Compression rings - groove clearance	.0015 to .0035 in. (.038 to .089 mm.)

Tappets

Type	Barrel with spherical base
Outside diameter	.81125 to .81175 in. (20.605 to 20.618 mm.)
Length	2.293 to 2.303 in. (58.25 to 58.5 mm.)
Clearance in block	.0005 to .00175 in. (.013 to .050 mm.)

Rocker Gear

Length of Rocker Shaft	14 1/32 in. (356 mm.)
Diameter	.624 to .625 in. (15.85 to 15.87 mm.)
Rocker arm bore	.7485 to .7495 in. (19.01 to 19.26 mm.)
Rocker arm bush - Inside diameter ...	.6255 to .626 in. (15.8 to 15.9 mm.)
Ratio	1.4 to 1

Valves
Twin S.U. models

Head diameter - Inlet	1.500 to 1.505 in. (38.10 to 38.23 mm.)
Head diameter - Exhaust	1.281 to 1.286 in. (32.54 to 32.67 mm.)

Single S.U. models

Head diameter - Inlet	1.370 to 1.375 in. (34.89 to 34.92 mm.)
Head diameter - Exhaust	1.182 to 1.187 in. (30.02 to 30.16 mm.)

All models

Valve seat angle - Inlet & Exhaust ...	45½°
Stem diameter - Inlet	.3422 to .3427 in. (8.68 to 8.69 mm.)
Exhaust	.3417 to .3422 in. (8.66 to 8.661 mm.)
Stem to guide clearance - Inlet ...	.0015 to .0025 in. (.0381 to .0762 mm.)
Exhaust	.002 to .003 in. (.0508 to .0778 mm.)
Valve lift - Inlet & Exhaust	.312 in. (7.925 mm.)
Valve stem to rocker arm clearance ..	.015 in. (.38 mm.) cold

ENGINE

Valve Guides

Length Inlet (Early Cars) ... ... 1⁷⁄₈ in. (47.63 mm.)
Length Exhaust ... ... 2¹³⁄₆₄ in. (55.95 mm.)
Outside diameter - Inlet & Exhaust ... .5635 to .5640 in. (14.30 to 14.32 mm.)
Inside diameter - Inlet & Exhaust ... .3442 to .3447 in. (8.73 to 8.74 mm.)
Fitted height above head - Inlet & Exhaust .625 in. ± .016 in. (16 ± .40 mm.)

Valve Timing

Inlet valve: Opens	5° B.T.D.C.)	Check with
Closes	45° A.B.D.C.)	.021 in. (.53 mm.)
Exhaust valve: Opens	40° B.B.D.C.)	rocker clearance
Closes	10° A.T.D.C.)	

Valve Springs

Twin S. U. Models

Type ... ... Double springs per valve
Free length inner ... ... 1³¹⁄₃₂ in. (50 mm.)
Free length outer ... ... 2³⁄₆₄ in. (52 mm.)
Fitted length inner ... ... 1⁷⁄₁₆ in. (36.5 mm.)
Fitted length outer ... ... 1⁹⁄₁₆ in. (39.7 mm.)
No. of working coils ... ... 6½ inner. 4½ outer
Pressure - valve open ... ... 155 lb. (70.3 kg.)
Pressure - valve closed ... ... 90½ lb. (41.1 kg.)

Single S. U. Models

Type ... ... Single spring per valve
Free length... ... ... 2¹⁄₆₄ in. (51.2 mm.)
No. of working coils ... ... 4½.
Pressure - valve open ... ... 130 lb. (59 kg.)
Pressure - valve closed ... ... 77.5 lb. (35.1 kg.)
Fitted length - valve open ... ... 1¹³⁄₆₄ in. (30.6 mm.)
Fitted length - valve closed ... ... 1¹⁷⁄₃₂ in. (38.9 mm.)

TORQUE WRENCH SETTINGS

Big End Bolts ... ... 35 to 40 lb.ft. (4.8 to 5.5 kg.m.)
Carburetter stud nuts ... ... 2 lb.ft. (.28 kg.m.)
Clutch to flywheel bolts... ... ... 25 to 30 lb.ft. (3.4 to 4.1 kg.m.)
Cylinder head nuts... ... ... 40 lb.ft. (5.5 kg.m.)
Cylinder tappet chest bolts ... ... 2 lb.ft. (.28 kg.m.)
Distributor clamp bolt (nut trapped) ... 4.16 lb.ft. (.57 kg.m.)
Distributor clamp nut (bolt trapped) ... 2.5 lb.ft. (.35 kg.m.)
Flywheel securing bolts... ... ... 40 lb.ft. (5.5 kg.m.)
Gudgeon pin clamp bolt ... ... 25 lb.ft. (3.4 kg.m.)
Main bearing nuts ... ... 70 lb.ft. (9.7 kg.m.)
Manifold nuts ... ... 15 lb.ft. (2.1 kg.m.)
Oil filter centre bolt ... ... 15 lb.ft. (2.1 kg.m.)
Oil pump to crankcase ... ... 14 lb.ft. (1.9 kg.m.)
Rear plate ⁵⁄₁₆ in. bolts ... ... 20 lb.ft. (2.8 kg.m.)
Rear plate ³⁄₈ in. bolts ... ... 30 lb.ft. (4.2 kg.m.)
Rocker bracket nuts ... ... 25 lb.ft. (3.4 kg.m.)
Rocker cover nuts ... ... 4 lb.ft. (.56 kg.m.)
Sump to crankcase... ... ... 6 lb.ft. (.8 kg.m.)
Timing cover ¼ in. bolts ... ... 6 lb.ft. (.8 kg.m.)
Timing cover ⁵⁄₁₆ in. bolts ... ... 14 lb.ft. (1.9 kg.m.)
Water outlet elbow nuts... ... ... 8 lb.ft. (1.1 kg.m.)
Water pump to crankcase ... ... 17 lb.ft. (2.3 kg.m.)

CHAPTER ONE

ENGINE SPECIFICATIONS & DATA 1622 c.c. – SINGLE AND TWIN CARBURETTER MODELS

The engine specifications and data are identical to the 1489 c.c. type except for the differences listed below

Engine - General

Bore	3 in. (76.2 mm.)
Stroke	3.5 in. (88.9)
Cubic Capacity	1622 c.c. (99.1 cu. in.)

Compression Pressure   Single S.U.   Twin S.U.

H.C. Engines	138 lb/sq.in @ 2,100 r.p.m.	136 lb/sq.in. @ 2,500 r.p.m.
L.C. Engines	128 lb/sq.in. @ 2,000 r.p.m.	

Torque

H.C. Engines	90 lb/ft. @ 2,100 r.p.m.	89 lb/ft. @ 2,500 r.p.m.
L.C. Engines	83 lb/ft. @ 2,000 r.p.m.	

Maximum B.H.P.

H.C. Engines	63 @ 4,500 r.p.m.	71.5 @ 5,000 r.p.m.
L.C. Engines	60 @ 4,200 r.p.m.	

Crankshaft & Main Bearings

Minimum regrind diameter	1.96 in. (49.78 mm.). Main journals
Minimum regrind diameter	1.835 in. (46.61 mm.). Crankpins
Main bearings - Type...	Steel backed copper lead.
Main bearings - Length	1.25 in. (31.75 mm.)

Cylinder Head

Combustion chamber capacity	43.0 c.c. (2.64 cu. in.)

Gudgeon Pins

Fit in piston	.0001 to .00035 in. (.0025 to .009 mm.)
Fit in connecting rod	.0001 to .0006 in. (.0025 to .0150 mm.)
Outer diameter of pin	.75 in. (19.05 mm.)

Pistons

Type	Anodized aluminium alloy - Solid skirt
Clearance at top of skirt (Single S.U.)	.0022 to .0034 in. (.0559 to .0863 mm.)
Clearance at bottom of skirt	.0015 to .0021 in. (.038 to .053 mm.)
Clearance at top of skirt (Twin S.U.)	.0035 to .0042 in. (.0889 to .1067 mm.)

Valves   Single S.U. models

Head diameter - Inlet	1.500 to 1.505 in. (38.10 to 38.23 mm.)
Head diameter - Exhaust	1.281 to 1.286 in. (32.54 to 32.67 mm.)

Valve Springs   Twin S.U. models

Free length - outer spring...	$1\frac{59}{64}$ in. (48.8 mm.)
Valve spring pressure - valve open ...	165 lb. (74.85 kg.) (Inner 50 lb. Outer 115 lb.)
Valve spring pressure - valve closed	92 lb. (31.62 kg.) (Inner 30 lb. Outer 62 lb.)

Valve Timing   Single S.U. models

Inlet Valve:	Opens	T.D.C. B.T.D.C.
	Closes	50° A.B.D.C.
Exhaust Valve:	Opens	35° B.B.D.C.
	Closes	15° A.T.D.C.

ENGINE

1. GENERAL DESCRIPTION

The engine is a four-cylinder, overhead valve type. It is supported by rubber mountings in the interests of silence and lack of vibration, longitudinal movement being controlled by a stay-rod fitted between the gearbox and the gearbox crossmember.

Two valves per cylinder are mounted vertically in the cast iron cylinder head and run in pressed in valve guides. They are operated by rocker arms, pushrods and tappets from the camshaft which is located at the base of the cylinder bores in the left-hand side of the engine. The correct valve stem to rocker arm pad clearance can be obtained by the adjusting screws in the ends of the rocker arms.

The cylinder head has all five inlet and exhaust ports on the left-hand side. Cylinders 1 and 2 share a siamised inlet port and also cylinders 3 and 4. Cylinders 1 and 4 have individual exhaust ports and cylinders 2 and 3 share a siamised exhaust port.

The cylinder block and the upper half of the crankcase are cast together. The bottom half of the crankcase consists of a pressed steel sump.

The pistons are made from anodised aluminium alloy with split or solid skirts. Three compression rings and a slotted oil control ring are fitted. The gudgeon pin is retained in the little end of the connecting rod by a pinch bolt. Renewable lead-indium, or lead-tin big end bearings are fitted.

At the front of the engine a duplex chain drives the camshaft via the camshaft and crankshaft chain wheels.

The chain is tensioned automatically by a Reynolds spring operated, hydraulically assisted rubber slipper tensioner which presses against the side of the duplex chain thus avoiding any lash or rattle.

The camshaft is supported by three steel-backed white metal bearings which can be renewed when worn. Endfloat is controlled by a bi-metal locating plate positioned between the rear of the camshaft chain wheel and the camshaft front bearing.

The statically and dynamically balanced forged steel crankshaft is supported by three renewable main bearings. Crankshaft endfloat is controlled by four semi-circular thrust washers, two of which are located on either side of the centre main bearing.

The centrifugal water pump and radiator cooling fan are driven together with the dynamo from the crankshaft pulley wheel by a rubber/fabric belt. The distributor is mounted towards the rear of the right-hand side of the cylinder block and advances and retards the ignition timing by mechanical and vacuum means. The distributor is driven at half crankshaft speed by a short shaft and skew gear from a skew gear on the camshaft.

The oil pump is located in the crankcase and is driven by a short shaft from the skew gear on the camshaft.

Attached to the end of the crankshaft by six bolts is the flywheel to which is bolted the 8in. diameter Borg & Beck clutch. Attached to the engine end plate is the gearbox bellhousing.

2. ROUTINE MAINTENANCE

1. Once a week, or more frequently if necessary, remove the dipstick and check the engine oil level which should be at the 'MAX' mark. Top up the oil in the sump with the recommended grade (see page 12 for details). On no account allow the oil to fall below the 'MIN' mark on the dipstick.

2. Every 6,000 miles run the engine till it is hot; place a container with a capacity of at least 8 pints under the drain plug in the sump; undo and remove the drain plug; and allow the oil to drain for at least ten minutes. At the same time renew the oil filter element as described in Section 24.

3. Clean the drain plug, ensure the washer is in place, and return the plug to the sump, tightening the plug firmly. Refill the sump with 7½ pints of the recommended grade of oil (see page 12 for details).

4. In very hot or dusty conditions, or in cold weather with much slow stop/start driving, with much use of the choke, it is beneficial to change the engine oil every 3,000 miles.

3. MAJOR OPERATIONS WITH ENGINE IN PLACE

The following major operations can be carried out to the engine with it in place in the body frame:-

1. Removal and replacement of the cylinder head assembly.
2. Removal and replacement of the sump.
3. Removal and replacement of the big end bearings.
4. Removal and replacement of the pistons and connecting rods.
5. Removal and replacement of the timing chain and gears.
6. Removal and replacement of the camshaft.
7. Removal and replacement of the oil pump.

NOTE To gain access to the front sump bolts it is necessary to undo the front engine mountings, and lift the engine with lifting tackle an inch or two. Lifting tackle should therefore be to hand for operations 2, 3, 4, and 7.

CHAPTER ONE

4. MAJOR OPERATIONS WITH ENGINE REMOVED

The following major operations can be carried out with the engine out of the body frame and on the bench or floor:-
1. Removal and replacement of the main bearings.
2. Removal and replacement of the crankshaft.
3. Removal and replacement of the flywheel.

5. METHODS OF ENGINE REMOVAL

There are two methods of engine removal. The engine can either be removed complete with gearbox, or the engine can be removed without the gearbox by separation at the gearbox bellhousing. Both methods are described.

6. ENGINE REMOVAL WITHOUT GEARBOX

1. Practical experience has proved that the engine can be removed easily in about 4 hours (less with experience) by adhering to the following sequence of operations.
2. Open the bonnet and prop it up to expose the engine and ancilliary components (see photo). Turn on the water drain taps found at the bottom of the radiator and on the side of the cylinder block. N.B. Do not drain the water in your garage or the place where you will remove the engine if receptacles are not at hand to catch the water.
3. Disconnect the battery by removing the earth lead. (Positive). See photograph.
4. Remove bonnet after undoing the securing nuts. Two pairs of hands are better than one when lifting the bonnet off as it is easy to damage it if care is not taken. Disconnect the pipe to the vacuum servo unit (if fitted).
5. Remove the radiator and radiator hoses as described in Chapter 2/6.
6. Undo the knurled securing nut in the centre of the coil and pull off the H.T. lead. Flip back the clips which hold the distributor cap to the distributor body, pull the H.T. leads off the plugs and remove the distributor cap from the engine. (The cap is made from plastic and is therefore fragile and easily broken while the engine is being lifted out).
7. Pull the two leads from the Lucar connectors on the rear of the dynamo as shown in the photograph, and tuck the leads back out of the way.
8. Undo the clip holding the small rubber pipe to the top of the front air cleaner (twin carburetter models); undo the nuts and spring washers holding the air cleaners to the carburetter intake flanges and lift the air cleaners off. (See photograph). On single carburetter models remove the wing nut from the centre of the air cleaner and then free the air cleaner base

from the carburetter.
9. Take off the carburetter/s and the heat shield as described in Chapter 3/5, but leave the inlet and exhaust mainfolds in place as they make useful handles when manoeuvring the engine about. Tape over the inlet manifold orifices to prevent accidental ingress of foreign objects. Remove the fan belt and undo the bolts holding the dynamo in place. Lift off the dynamo as shown.
10. Undo the nuts and bolts which hold the exhaust manifold clamp to the exhaust downpipe.
11. On models fitted with a rev. counter undo the knurled nut holding the rev. counter drive in place as shown.
12. Working underneath the car free the exhaust pipe front clamp so the exhaust pipe can be tied out of the way.
13. While under the car undo the long bolt (arrowed) which holds the oil cleaner bowl in position. The bowl will be full of oil and care should be taken when lifting it off.
14. Undo and carefully remove the water temperature gauge sender unit from the base of the thermostat housing. Bend the cable back gently.
15. Pull the leads from their Lucar connector tabs on the coil, as shown, and to give adequate room for engine removal disconnect and remove the coil and its bracket from the front engine mounting.
16. Undo the clip holding the heater unit water hose to the heater control as shown and pull the hose off its locating pipe.
17. Loosen the nut which locks the heater control inner cable to the control unit and pull the cable out of its housing. (See photograph).
18. Undo the clip holding the lower hose to the heater motor as shown and pull the hose off the short pipe to the motor.
19. Undo the clip holding the top hose to the heater motor (see photograph) and pull the hose away from the motor.
20. Undo the nut (arrowed) securing the oil pressure gauge union (where fitted) to the rear of the block and tuck the flexible pipe out of the way.
21. Place a sling round the engine or preferably fit the special BMC lifting hook under the front rocker cover securing nut, and take the weight on suitable lifting tackle. Alternatively remove the rocker cover and place the lifting hook round the rocker shaft. Place a jack under the gearbox as shown.
22. Undo the two rear, one front and one side bolts on each of the engine mountings (See Fig. 1.1) and take off the two nuts on the inner face

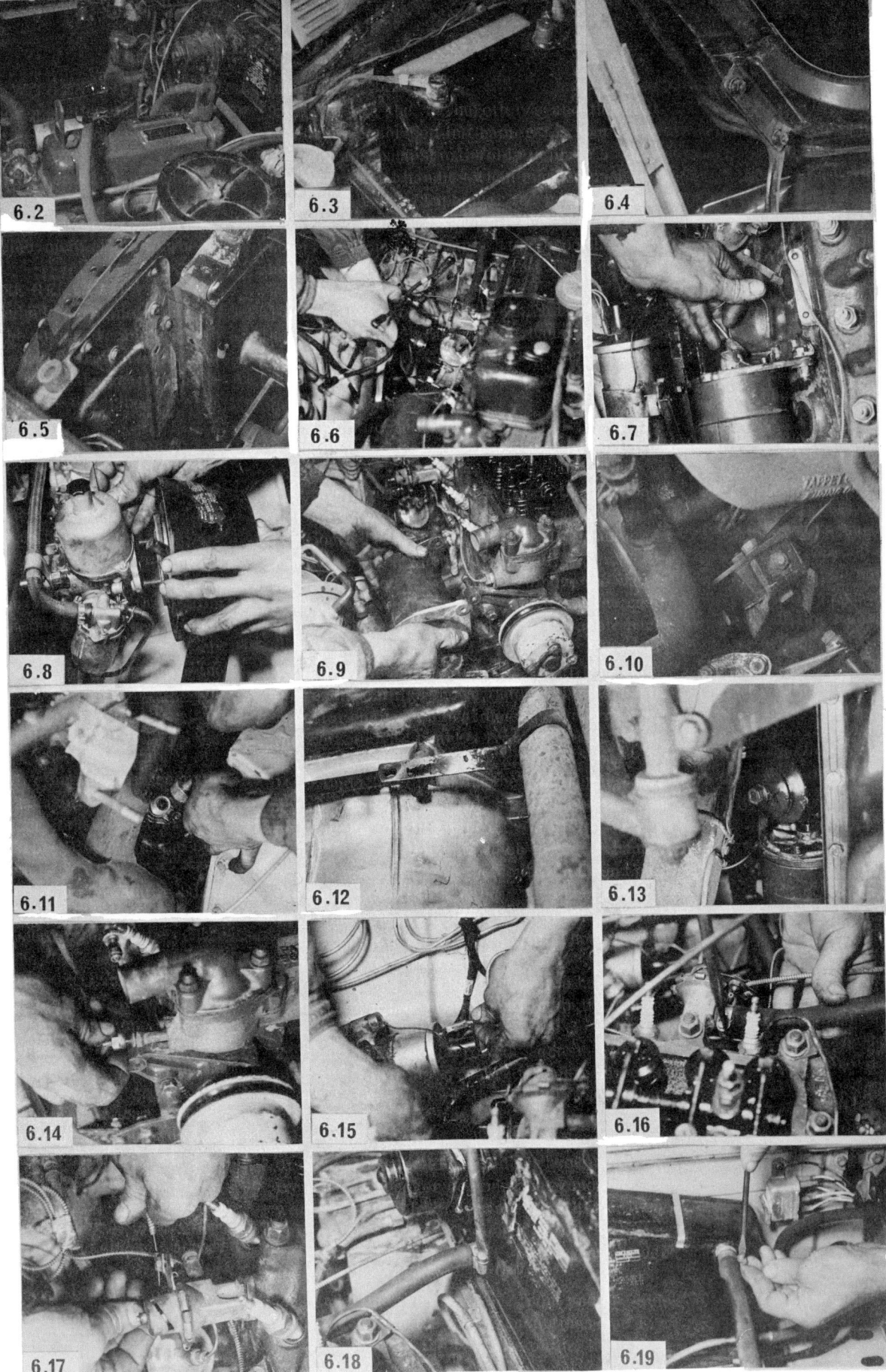

of each mounting. It will now be possible to move the mountings sufficiently to separate them from the engine.

23. Note that the front mountings may have been shimmed. If shims are fitted they must be replaced when the engine is returned into position.

24. Remove the starter motor by undoing the two bolts which hold it in place and the nut which holds the starter motor cable to the terminal on the starter. Undo the nuts and bolts securing the engine end plate to the bellhousing. Shown are the nuts and bolts under the car.

25. Slightly raise the engine, and the jack, and pull the engine forwards and up until the clutch is free from the first motion shaft in the gearbox. It is important that no excess load is placed on the clutch drive straps so take great care at this stage. Once clear of the bellhousing pull the engine forwards tilting the front further upwards to clear the front crossmember and wind the engine out of the car.

7. ENGINE REMOVAL WITH GEARBOX

1. Undo the drain plug and drain the oil from the gearbox. Free the starter cable from the starter motor.

2. Follow the instructions in section 6.1 to 23 which describes how to prepare the engine for removal.

3. From inside the driving compartment slacken the locknut on the gearlever and undo the gearlever knob as shown. Ensure the gearbox is in neutral.

4. Undo the Phillips screws which hold the chrome ring in position on the rubber gaiter at the base of the gearlever. (See photograph).

5. Remove the ring and pull the gaiter off the top of the gearlever. This exposes the ball spring cover and the circlip which holds it in place. (See photograph).

6. With a pair of long nosed pliers press the ends of the circlip together and remove the circlip from the remote control housing as shown.

7. Then remove the ball spring cover and the spring, lifting them off the top of the gearlever as shown.

8. The gearlever can now be lifted from the car. (See photograph).

9. On cars fitted with the steering column gear change take off the selector control rod from its lever on the gearbox.

10. Then remove the change speed rod from its lever.

11. Remove the exhaust pipe support from the gearbox (where fitted) and tie the exhaust pipe out of the way.

12. From under the car undo the knurled nut which holds the speedometer drive to the side of the gearbox and pull the cable out of the way (see photograph).

13. Mark the rear axle and propeller shaft rear flanges as shown to ensure replacement in the same relative position.

14. With the aid of two spanners undo the four nuts, bolts, and spring washers holding the flanges together. (See photograph).

15. Remove the bolts, separate the flanges, and allow the propeller shaft to drop slightly (See photograph).

16. To remove the propeller shaft simply pull it rearwards.

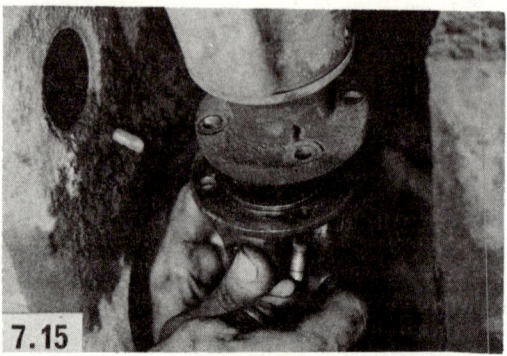

7.15

17. Undo and remove the nut and spring washer holding the rear block to the engine tie-rod which runs through the removable gearbox crossmember.

18. Lift off the rear block.

19. Undo the six bolts and lockwashers which hold the crossmember in place under the gearbox.

20. With the aid of a universally jointed socket spanner undo the nuts and spring washers which hold the gearbox mounting rubbers to the crossmember.

21. Pull the crossmember off each of the gearbox mounting blocks in turn and lower it from the car.

22. Undo the two bolts and lockwashers which hold the clutch slave cylinder to the side of the bellhousing.

23. Pull the slave cylinder away at the same time pulling the push rod (which can be left attached to the clutch release arm) out of its rubber boot as shown. Tie the slave cylinder back out of the way.

24. Make a final check to ensure all connections have been undone, especially if auxilliary equipment has been fitted, and then carefully lift the engine and gearbox up out of the car. The gearbox is a close fit in the front of the propeller shaft tunnel.

25. It will be necessary to lift the engine and gearbox out at a fairly steep angle.

26. To separate the engine from the gearbox bellhousing undo the nuts and bolts which hold the bellhousing to the engine endplate.

27. The gearbox is then easily separated from the engine.

8. DISMANTLING THE ENGINE - GENERAL

1. It is best to mount the engine on a dismantling stand, but as this is frequently not available, then stand the engine on a strong bench so as to be at a comfortable working height. Failing this, it can be stripped down on the floor.

2. During the dismantling process the greatest care should be taken to keep the exposed parts free from dirt. As an aid to achieving this aim, it is a very sound scheme to thorough-ly clean down the outside of the engine, removing all traces of oil and congealed dirt.

3. A good grease solvent such as 'Gunk' will make the job much easier, as, after the solvent has been applied and allowed to stand for a time, a vigorous jet of water will wash off the solvent and all the grease and filth. If the dirt is thick and deeply embedded, work the solvent into it with a wire brush.

4. Finally wipe down the exterior of the engine with a rag and only then, when it is quite clean should the dismantling process begin. As the engine is stripped, clean each part in a bath of paraffin or petrol.

5. Never immerse parts with oilways in paraffin, i.e. the crankshaft, but to clean wipe down carefully with a petrol dampened rag. Oilways can be cleaned out with pipe cleaners. If an air

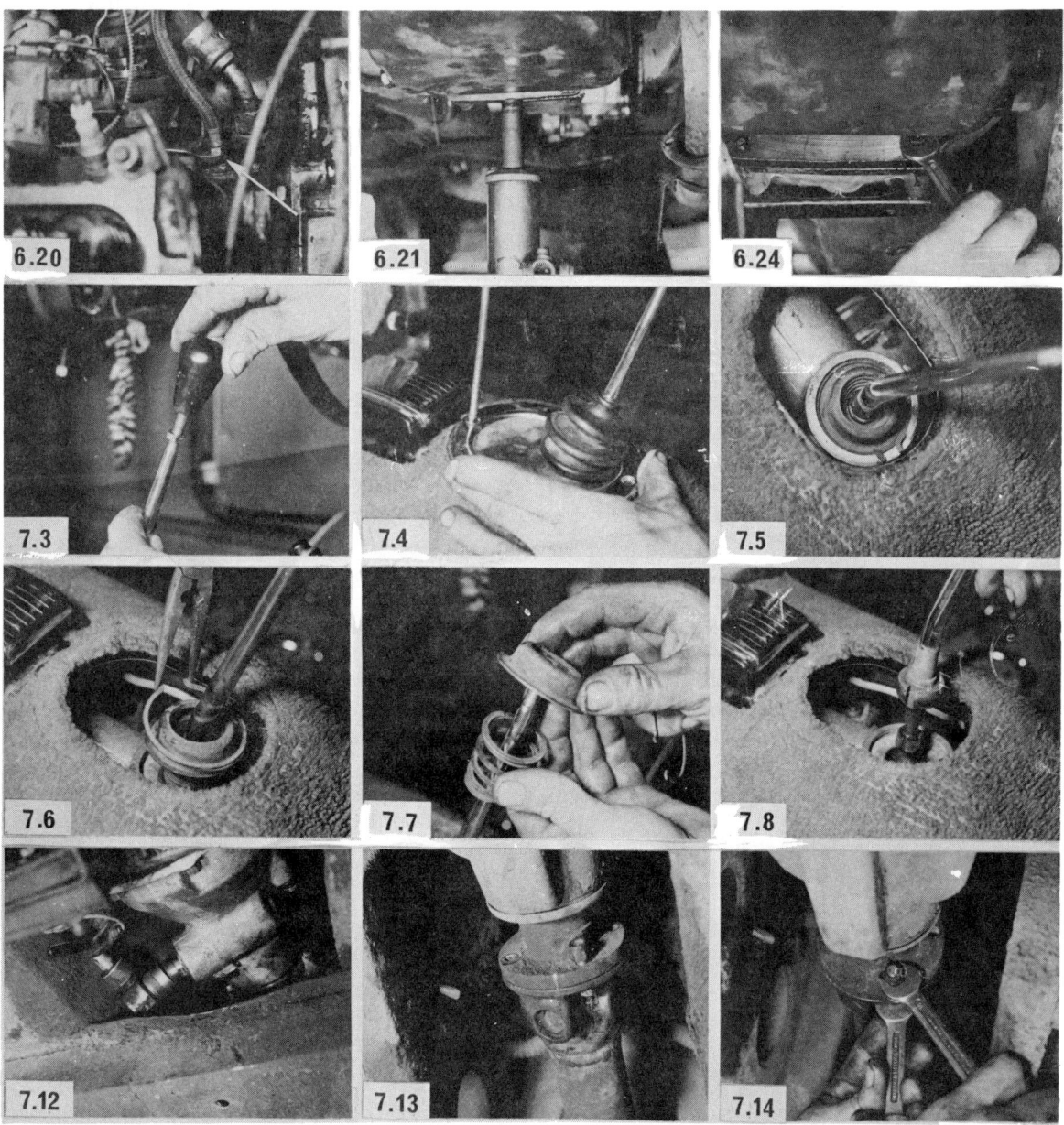

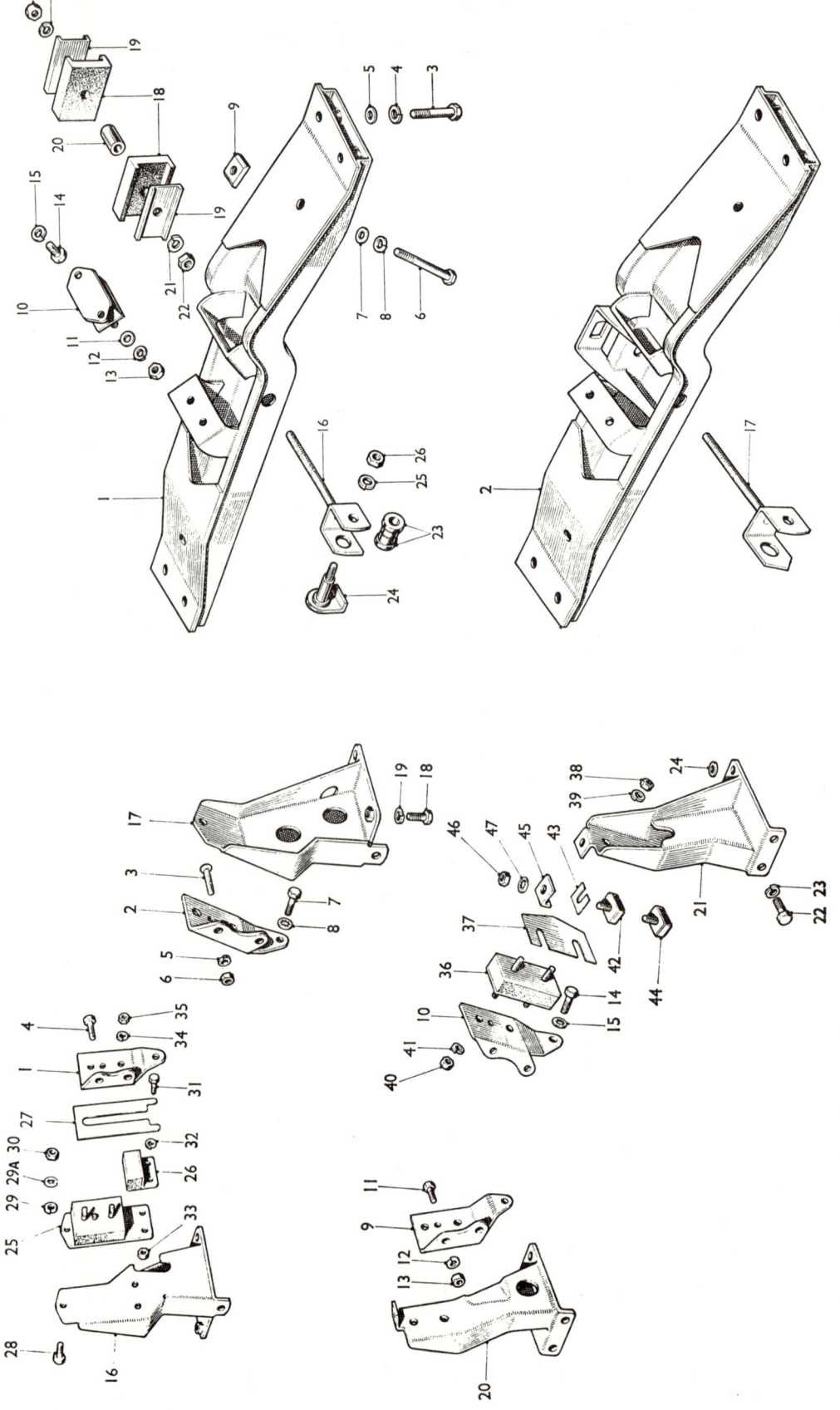

Fig. 1.2. EXPLODED VIEW OF THE GEARBOX CROSSMEMBER MOUNTING

1 Rear mounting cross member. 2 Rear mounting cross member fitted to automatics. 3 Bolt. 4 Spring washer. 5 Plain washer. 6 Bolt. 7 Plain washer. 8 Spring washer. 9 Nut. 10 Gearbox on rear engine mounting. 111 Plain washer. 12 Spring washer. 13 Nut. 14 Bolt. 15 Spring washer. 16 Engine steady stay. 17 Engine steady stay for automatics. 18 Buffer steady stay. 19 Buffer plate. 20 Distance tube. 21 Spring washer 22 Nut. 23 Gearbox rear extension bush. 24 Steady pin. 25 Spring washer. 26 Nut.

Fig. 1.1. EXPLODED VIEW OF THE ENGINE MOUNTINGS

1 R.H. engine support bracket. 2 L.H. engine support bracket. 3 Bolt. 4 Bolt. 5 Spring washer. 6 Nut. 7 Bolt. 8 Shakeproof washer. 9 R.H. engine support bracket (later models). 10 L.H. engine support bracket (later models). 11 Bolt. 12 Spring washer. 13 Nut. 14 Bolt. 15 Shakeproof washer. 16 R.H. engine mounting bracket. 17 L.H. engine mounting bracket. 18 Bolt. 19 Spring washer. 20 R.H. engine mounting bracket (later models). 21 L.H. engine mounting bracket (later models). 22 Bolt. 23 Spring washer. 24 Plain washer. 25 Engine mounting. 26 Mounting buffer. 27 Mounting shim. 28 Bolt. 29 Spring washer. 30 Nut. 31 Bolt. 32 Spring washer. 33 Nut. 34 Spring washer. 35 Nut. 36 Engine mounting (later models). 37 Mounting shim (later models). 38 Nut. 39 Spring washer. 40 Nut. 41 Spring washer. 42 Mounting buffer. 43 Mounting buffer shim. 44 Mounting buffer (later models). 45 Locking buffer plate. 46 Nut. 47 Shakeproof washer.

line is present all parts can be blown dry and the oilways blown through as an added precaution.

6. Re-use of old engine gaskets is a false economy and can give rise to oil and water leaks, if nothing worse. To avoid the possibility of trouble after the engine has been reassembled always use new gaskets throughout.

7. Do not throw the old gaskets away as it sometimes happens that an immediate replacement cannot be found and the old gasket is then very useful as a template. Hang up the old gaskets as they are removed on a suitable hook or nail.

8. To strip the engine it is best to work from the top down. The sump provides a firm base on which the engine can be supported in an upright position. When the stage where the sump must be removed is reached, the engine can be turned on its side and all other work carried out with it in this position.

9. Wherever possible, replace nuts, bolts and washers finger-tight from wherever they were removed. This helps avoid later loss and muddle. If they cannot be replaced then lay them out in such a fashion that it is clear from where they came.

9. REMOVING ANCILLIARY ENGINE COMP - ONENTS

Before basic engine dismantling begins it is necessary to strip it of ancilliary components and these are as follows:

Closed circuit breathing system (Later Engines).

Exhaust emission control equipment (Later Engines).

Dynamo.

Distributor.

Thermostat.

Inlet manifold and carburetters.

Exhaust manifold.

It is possible to strip all these items with the engine in the car if it is merely the individual items that require attention. Presuming the engine to be out of the car on the bench, starting on the right-hand side of the unit, follow the procedure described below:-

1. Remove the closed circuit breathing by undoing the three retaining clips, and remove the exhaust emission control equipment where fitted.

2. Slacken off the dynamo retaining bolts and remove the unit with its support brackets.

3. To remove the distributor first disconnect the manifold vacuum advance/retard pipe which leads from the small securing clip on the cylinder head. Unscrew the clamp bolt at the base of the distributor and lift the distributor away

from its base plate and drive shaft.

4. Remove the thermostat cover by releasing the three nuts and spring washers which hold it in position and then remove the gasket and thermostat unit.

5. Inlet manifolds and carburetter/s. Moving to the left-hand side of the engine, remove the inlet manifold complete with carburetter/s if this item has not already been removed, by unscrewing the brass nuts and washers holding the manifolds to the cylinder head.

6. The engine is now stripped of all ancilliary components and is ready for major dismantling to begin.

10. CYLINDER HEAD REMOVAL - ENGINE ON BENCH

1. With the engine out of the car and standing on its sump on the bench or on the floor remove the cylinder head as follows:-

2. Unscrew the two rocker cover bolts and lift the rocker cover and gasket away.

3. Unscrew the rocker pedestal nuts (four) and the eleven main cylinder head nuts half a turn at a time in the order shown in the Fig. 1.3. When all the nuts are no longer under tension they may be screwed off the cylinder head one at a time.

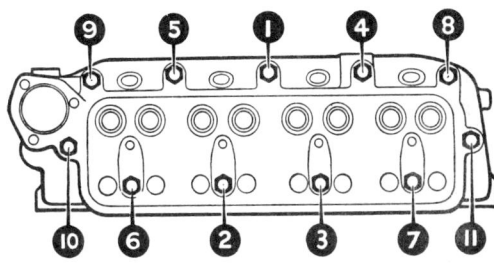

Fig. 1.3 The order in which to tighten or loosen the cylinder head nuts.

4. Remove the rocker assembly complete, and place it on one side.

5. Remove the push rods, keeping them in the relative order in which they were removed. The easiest way to do this is to push them

through a sheet of thick paper or thin card in the correct sequence.

6.   The cylinder head can now be removed by lifting upwards. If the head is jammed, try to rock it to break the seal. Under no circumstances try to prise it apart from the block with a screwdriver or cold chisel as damage may be done to the faces of the head or block. If the head will not readily free, turn the engine over by the flywheel as the compression in the cylinders will often break the cylinder head joint. If this fails to work, strike the head sharply with a plastic headed hammer, or with a wooden hammer, or with a metal hammer with an intersposed piece of wood to c u s h i o n the blows. Under no circumstances hit the head directly with a metal hammer as this may cause the iron casting to fracture. Several sharp taps with the h a m m e r at the same time pulling upwards should free the head. Lift the head off and place on one side.

11.   CYLINDER HEAD REMOVAL - ENGINE IN CAR
     To remove the cylinder head with the engine still in the car the following additional procedure to that above must be followed. This procedure should be carried out before that listed in section 10.

1.   Disconnect the battery by removing the lead from the positive terminal. (Negative terminal on later cars).

2.   Drain the water by turning the taps at the base of the radiator, and at the bottom left-hand corner of the cylinder block.

3.   Loosen the clip at the thermostat housing end on the top water hose, and pull the hose from the thermostat housing pipe.

4.   Remove the heater/demister unit inlet hose by releasing the clip securing it to the cylinder head (on cars with heater/demister units).

5.   Remove the air cleaners, the S.U. carburetter/s and the heat shield, as described in Chapter 3/5, and undo the   bolts and nuts holding the exhaust manifold to the exhaust down pipe. Leave the inlet and exhaust manifolds in place as they provide useful leverage when removing the cylinder head.

6.   The procedure is now the same as for removing the cylinder head when on the bench. One tip worth noting is that should the cylinder head refuse to free easily, the battery can be reconnected up, and the engine turned over on the solenoid switch. Under no circumstances turn the ignition on unless the wire to the pump is disconnected, and ensure that the distributor cap is removed as otherwise the engine might fire.

Fig. 1.4   EXPLODED VIEW OF THE MAIN STATIC ENGINE COMPONENTS.

1 Block assembly. 2 Plug for core hole. 3 Plug for oil gallery. 4 Taper plug for block oil hole. 5 Plug for oil relief valve hole. 6 Blanking plug. 7 Stud for cylinder head (long). 8 Stud for cylinder head (short). 9 Stud for main bearing cap. 10 Nut for bearing cap stud. 11 Spring washer for bearing cap stud. 12 Stud for oil pump (long). 13 Stud for oil pump (short). 14 Joint for front and rear main bearing cap. 15 Oil gauge pipe union. 16 Washer for union. 17 Dowel for gearbox mounting plate. 18 Water drain tap. 19 Fibre washer. 20 Dust cap. 21 Oil level indicator. 22 Oil level indicator tube. 23 Block side rear cover with elbow. 24 Block side front cover. 25 Joint—cover to block. 26 Screw—cover to block. 27 Washer for screw. 28 Cylinder block vent pipe with clip. 29 Manifold drain tube bracket. 30 Stud—bracket to block. 31 Spring washer for stud. 32 Nut for stud. 33 Grommet—drain tube bracket. 34 Cylinder head. 35 Plug for oil hole. 36 Rocker bracket stud (short). 37 Rocker bracket stud (long). 38 Nut for bracket stud. 39 Washer for bracket stud. 40 Spring washer for bracket stud. 41 Joint to block. 42 Nut for cylinder head stud. 43 Washer for cylinder head stud. 44 Stud for exhaust manifold. 45 Nut for stud. 46 Washer for stud. 47 Rocker gear cover. 48 Cap with cable. 49 Joint. 50 Cap nut for cover. 51 Bush for cap nut (rubber). 52 Cup washer for cap nut. 53 Washer for cap nut. 54 Nut—pump to block. 55 Spring washer for pump stud. 56 Washer for pump stud. 57 Oil pressure relief valve. 58 Spring. 59 Cap. 60 Fibre washer for cap. 61 Sump. 62 Joint—sump to block. 63 Drain plug. 64 Washer for drain plug. 65 Screw—sump to block. 66 Shakeproof washer. 67 Water outlet elbow. 68 Joint. 69 Stud for water outlet elbow. 70 Nut for stud. 71 Washer for stud. 72 Thermostat. 73 Joint. 74 Thermal transmitter. 75 Water pump body. 76 Plug for pump oil filler hole. 77 Washer for plug. 78 Spindle with vane and bearing. 79 Wire—bearing retaining. 80 Pulley. 81 Fan and water pump pulley hub. 82 Joint—water pump to block. 83 Screw—water pump to block (long). 84 Screw—water pump to block (short). 85 Spring washer for screw. 86 Fan blade. 87 Screw—fan blade to pulley. 88 Spring washer for screw. 89 Belt. 90 Cylinder block cover—front. 91 Felt. 92 Joint to front mounting plate. 93 Screw to mounting plate. 94 Screw. 95 Washer for screw. 96 Spring washer for screw. 97 Screw. 98 Front mounting plate. 99 Joint—front plate to block. 100 Screw—front plate to block. 101 Spring washer for screw. 102 Rear mounting plate. 103 Joint—rear plate to block. 104 Screw—rear plate to block. 105 Spring washer. 106 Distributor housing. 107 Screw—housing to block. 108 Screw—distributor to housing. 109 Ignition control pipe. 110 Olive (carburetter end). 111 Olive (distributor end). 113 Tube nut. 114 Clip—pipe to cylinder head. 115 Bolt for vacuum pipe. 116 Nut for bolt. 117 Spring washer. 118 Vacuum pipe bracket. 119 Blanking plug. 120 Washer for plug. 121 Oil filter pipe.

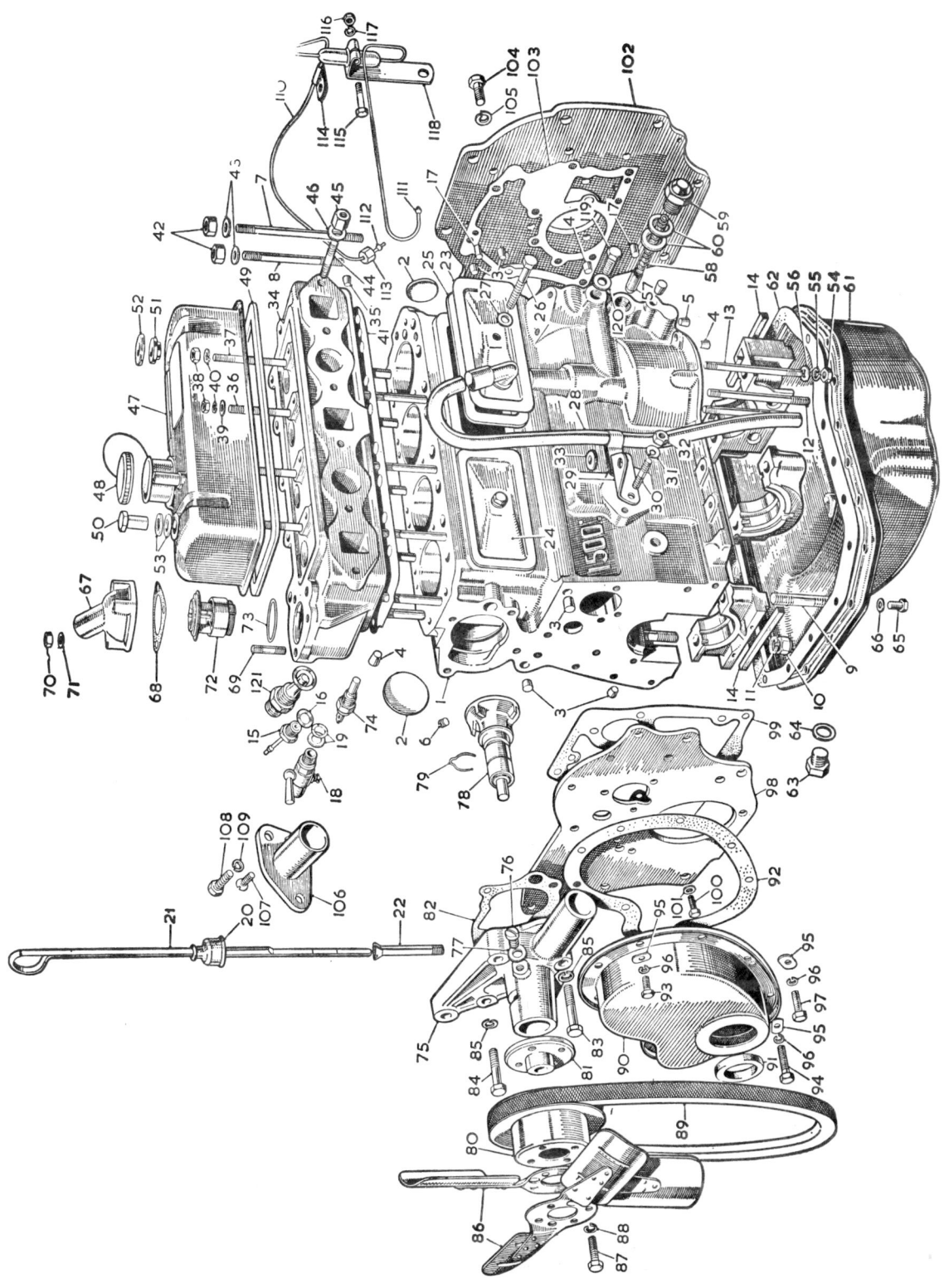

12. VALVE REMOVAL

1. The valves can be removed from the cylinder head by the following method. With a pair of pliers remove the spring circlips holding the two halves of the split tapered collets together. Compress each spring in turn with a valve spring compressor until the two halves of the collets can be removed. Release the compressor and remove the spring, shroud, and valve.

2. If, when the valve spring compressor is screwed down, the valve spring retaining cap refuses to free and expose the split collet, do not continue to screw down on the compressor as there is a likelihood of damaging it.

3. Gently tap the top of the tool directly over the cap with a light hammer. This will free the cap. To avoid the compressor jumping off the valve spring retaining cap when it is tapped, hold the compressor firmly in position with one hand.

4. Slide the rubber oil control seal off the top of each valve stem and then drop out each valve through the combustion chamber.

5. It is essential that the valves are kept in their correct sequence unless they are so badly worn that they are to be renewed. If they are going to be kept and used again, place them in a sheet of card having eight holes numbered 1 to 8 corresponding with the relative positions the valves were in when fitted. Also keep the valve springs, washers, etc. in the correct order.

13. VALVE GUIDE REMOVAL

If it is wished to remove the valve guides they can be removed from the cylinder head in the following manner. Place the cylinder head with the gasket face on the bench and with a suitable hard steel punch drift the guides out of the cylinder head.

14. DISMANTLING THE ROCKER ASSEMBLY

1. To dismantle the rocker assembly, release the rocker shaft locating screw, remove the split pins, flat washers, and spring washers from each end of the shaft and slide from the shaft the pedestals, rocker arms, and rocker spacing springs.

2. From the end of the shaft undo the plug which gives access to the inside of the rocker which can now be cleaned of sludge etc. Ensure the rocker arm lubricating holes are clear.

15. TIMING COVER, GEARS & CHAIN REMOVAL

The timing cover, gears, and chain can be removed with the engine in the car providing the radiator, radiator surround and fan belt are removed. The procedure for removing the timing cover, gears and chain is otherwise the same irrespective of whether the engine is in the car or on the bench, and is as follows:-

1. Bend back the locking tab of the crankshaft pulley locking washer under the crankshaft pulley retaining bolt, and with a large spanner remove the bolt and locking washer.

2. Placing two large screwdrivers behind the camshaft pulley wheel at 180° to each other, carefully lever off the wheel. It is preferable to use a proper pulley extractor if this is available, but large screwdrivers or tyre levers are quite suitable, providing care is taken not to damage the pulley flange.

3. Remove the woodruff key from the crankshaft nose with a pair of pliers and note how the channel in the pulley is designed to fit over it. Place the woodruff key in a glass jam jar as it is a very small part and can easily become lost.

4. Unscrew the bolts holding the timing cover to the block. NOTE that three different sizes of bolt are used, and that each bolt makes use of a large flat washer as well as a spring washer.

5. Pull off the timing cover and gasket.

6. With the timing cover off, take off the oil thrower. NOTE that the concave side faces forward. Take out the bottom plug from the chain tensioner, fit a $\frac{1}{8}$ in. Allen key in the cylinder and turn the key clockwise until the slipper head is pulled right back and locked behind the limit head.

7. Bend back the locking tab on the washer under the camshaft retaining nut and unscrew the nut noting how the locking washer locating tag fits in the camshaft gearwheel keyway.

8. To remove the camshaft and crankshaft timing wheels complete with chain, ease each wheel forward a little at a time levering behind each gearwheel in turn with two large screwdrivers at 180° to each other. If the gearwheels are locked solid then it will be necessary to use a proper gearwheel and pulley extractor, and if one is available this should be used anyway in preference to screwdrivers. With both gearwheels safely off, remove the woodruff keys from the crankshaft and camshaft with a pair of pliers and place them in the jam jar for safe keeping. Note the number of very thin packing washers behind the crankshaft gearwheel and remove them very carefully.

16. CAMSHAFT REMOVAL

The camshaft can be removed with the engine in place in the car, or with the engine on the bench. If the camshaft is to be removed with the engine in the car, the radiator, radiator surround and fan belt must be removed after the

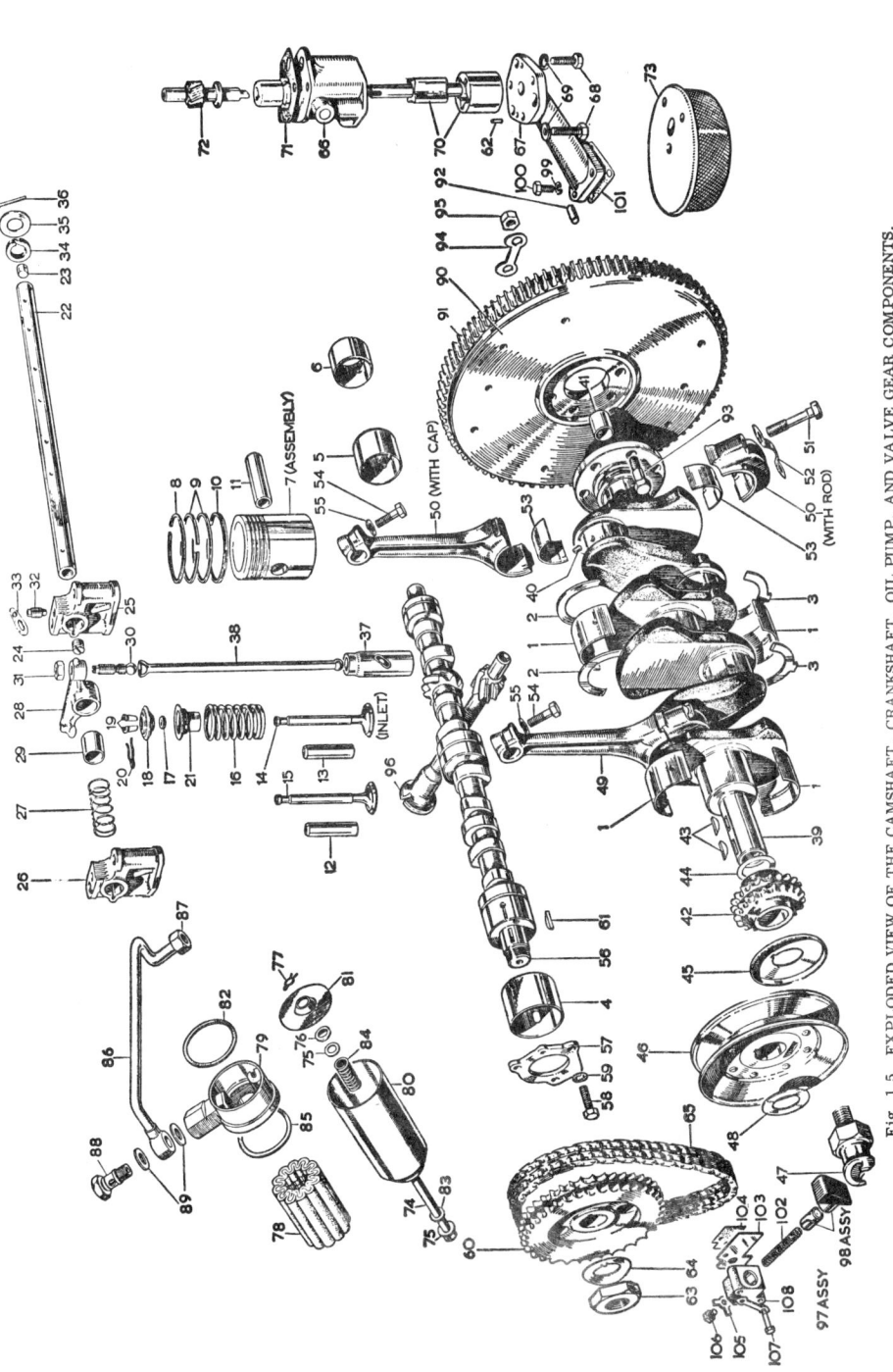

Fig. 1.5 EXPLODED VIEW OF THE CAMSHAFT, CRANKSHAFT, OIL PUMP, AND VALVE GEAR COMPONENTS.

1 Crankshaft main bearing. 2 Upper thrust washer. 3 Lower thrust washer. 4 Front camshaft bearing liner. 5 Centre camshaft bearing liner. 6 Rear camshaft bearing liner.
7 Piston assembly. 8 Compression ring—top. 9 Compression ring—second and third. 10 scraper ring. 11 Gudgeon pin. 12 Exhaust valve guide. 13 Inlet valve guide.
14 Inlet valve. 15 Exhaust valve. 16 Spring. 17 Packing ring. 18 Spring cup. 19 Valve cotter. 20 Circlip for cotter. 21 Guide shroud. 22 Valve rocker shaft.
23 Plain plug. 24 Screwed plug. 25 Bracket with tapped hole. 26 Plain bracket. 27 Spring. 28 Valve rocker. 29 Rocker bush. 30 Adjusting screw. 31 Locknut for screw.
32 Locating screw. 33 Screw locating plate. 34 Spring washer (D/C). 35 Washer for rocker. 36 Split pin. 37 Tappet. 38 Push-rod. 39 Crankshaft. 40 Oil restrictor.
41 First motion shaft bush. 42 Timing gear. 43 Key for gear and pulley. 44 Gear packing washer. 45 Oil thrower (front). 46 Pulley. 47 Nut for starting handle dog.
48 Nut locking washer. 49 Rod and cap (Nos. 1 and 3). 50 Rod and cap (Nos. 2 and 4). 51 Set screw for cap. 52 Cap set screw locking plate. 53 Connecting rod bearing.
54 Spring washer for clamp set screw. 55 Camshaft. 56 Nut for camshaft. 57 Locking plate. 58 Screw—plate to block. 59 Shakeproof washer for plate screw.
60 Timing gear. 61 Key for gear. 62 Dowel for pump body. 63 Nut locking washer. 64 Nut locking washer. 65 Oil pump body. 66 Oil pump body. 67 Cover. 68 Screw—
cover to body. 69 Spring washer for cover screw. 70 Shaft with rotors. 71 Joint to block. 72 Driving spindle. 73 Oil strainer. 74 Centre-bolt. 75 Washer. 76 Felt washer.
77 Circlip. 78 Element. 79 Oil filter head assembly. 80 Container. 81 Pressure plate. 82 Joint washer—filter head to block. 83 Sealing washer (bottom). 84 Spring.
85 Joint washer—container to filter head. 86 Oil pipe. 87 Nut for nipple. 88 Screw for banjo union. 89 Washer for screw. 90 Flywheel. 91 Starter ring. 92 Dowel for clutch.
93 Bolt—crankshaft to flywheel. 94 Locking plate for bolt. 95 Nut for bolt. 96 Distributor drive spindle. 97 Timing chain tensioner. 98 Slipper head and cylinder. 99 Spring
washer for screw. 100 Screw—pump cover to strainer. 101 Joint to oil strainer. 102 Spring. 103 Body backplate. 104 Joint. 105 Lock washer for plug. 106 Plug for body.
107 Bolt—tensioner to block. 108 Lock washer.

29

cooling system has been drained. The inlet and exhaust manifolds, rocker gear, pushrods and tappets must also be removed, together with the revolution indicator drive where the mechanical rev. counter is fitted. The timing cover, gears and chain, must be removed as described in Section 15. It is also necessary to remove the distributor drive gear as described in Section 17. With the drive gear out of the way, proceed in the following manner:-

1. Remove the three bolts and spring washers which hold the camshaft locating plate to the block. The bolts are normally covered by the camshaft gearwheel.

2. Remove the plate. The camshaft can now be withdrawn. Take great care to remove the camshaft gently, and in particular ensure that the cam peaks do not damage the camshaft bearings as the shaft is pulled forward.

17. DISTRIBUTOR DRIVE REMOVAL

To remove the distributor drive with the sump still in position it is first necessary to remove one of the tappet cover bolts. With the distributor and the distributor clamp plate already removed, this is achieved as follows:-

1. Unscrew the single retaining bolt and lockwasher to release the distributor housing.

2. With the distributor housing removed, if the sump is still in position screw into the end of the distributor drive shaft a $\frac{5}{16}$ in. U.N.F. bolt. A tappet cover bolt is ideal for this purpose. The drive shaft can then be lifted out, the shaft being turned slightly in the process to free the shaft skew gear from the camshaft skew gear.

3. If the sump has already been removed then it is a simple matter to push the drive shaft out from inside the crankcase.

18. SUMP, PISTON, CONNECTING ROD & BIG END BEARING REMOVAL

1. The sump, pistons, and connecting rods can be removed with the engine still in the car or with the engine on the bench. If in the car, proceed as for removing the cylinder head with the engine in the car, as described in Section 11. If on the bench proceed as for removing the cylinder head with the engine in this position, as described in Section 10. The pistons and connecting rods are drawn up out of the top of the cylinder bores.

2. With suitable lifting tackle attached to a lifting hook on the front cylinder head stud, free the bolts from the two front engine mountings and raise the engine an inch or two so as to gain access to the front sump bolts.

3. Remove the 19 bolts and washers holding the sump in position. Remove the sump and the sump gasket.

4. Undo the two bolts which hold the oil strainer pick up pipe to the oil pump and remove the strainer and pipe.

5. Knock back with a cold chisel the locking tabs on the big end retaining bolts, and remove the bolts and locking tabs.

6. Remove the big end caps one at a time, taking care to keep them in the right order and the correct way round. Also ensure that the shell bearings are also kept with their correct connecting rods and caps unless they are to be renewed. Normally, the numbers 1 to 4 are stamped on adjacent sides of the big end caps and connecting rods, indicating which cap fits on which rod and which way round the cap fits. If no numbers or lines can be found then with a sharp screwdriver scratch mating marks across the joint from the rod to the cap. One line for connecting rod No. 1, two for connecting rod No. 2, and so on. This will ensure there is no confusion later as it is most important that the caps go back in the correct position on the connecting rods from which they were removed.

7. If the big end caps are difficult to remove they may be gently tapped with a soft hammer

8. To remove the shell bearings, press the bearing opposite the groove in both the connecting rod, and the connecting rod caps and the bearings will slide out easily.

9. Withdraw the pistons and connecting rods upwards and ensure they are kept in the correct order for replacement in the same bore Refit the connecting rod caps and bearings to the rods if the bearings do not require renewal to minimise the risk of getting the caps and rods muddled.

19. GUDGEON PIN

1. To remove the gudgeon pin to free the piston from the connecting rod, it is merely necessary to remove the little end bolt and lockwasher. With the bolt removed the gudgeon pin should push out through either side of the piston.

2. If the pin shows reluctance to move, then on no account force it out, as this could damage the piston. Immerse the piston in a pan of boiling water for three minutes. On removal the expansion of the aluminium should allow the gudgeon pin to slide out easily.

3. Make sure the pins are kept with the same piston for ease of refitting.

20. PISTON RING REMOVAL

1. To remove the piston rings, slide them carefully over the top of the piston, taking care

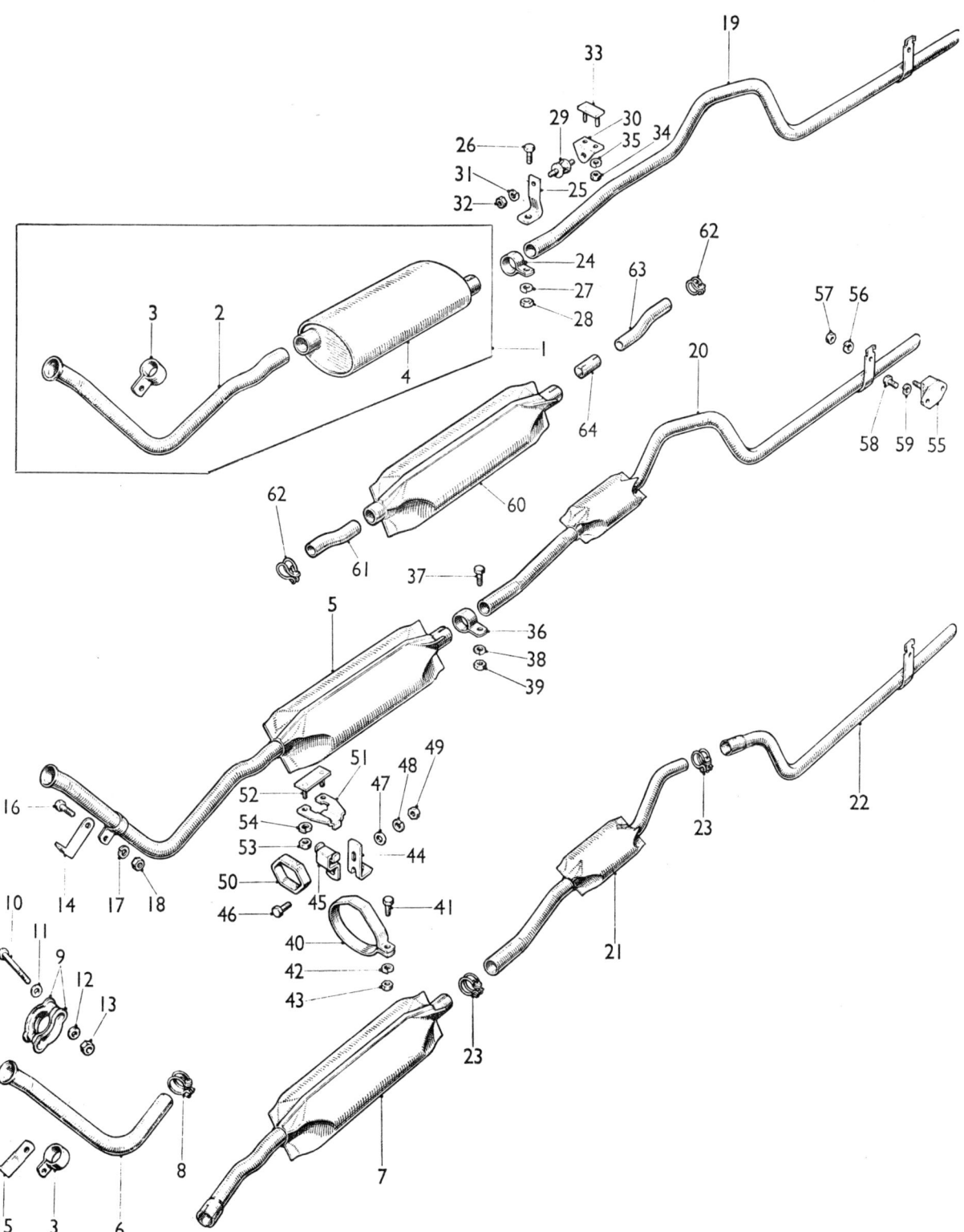

Fig. 1.6 EXPLODED VIEW OF THE THREE EXHAUST SYSTEMS ANY ONE OF WHICH MAY BE FITTED.

1 Front pipe and silencer assembly (early models). 2 Front pipe. 3 Clip. 4 Silencer. 5 Front pipe and silencer (later models). 6 Front pipe. 7 Front silencer (later models). 8 Clip. 9 Exhaust pipe to manifold clamp. 10 Bolt. 11 Washer. 12 Washer. 13 Nut. 14 Bracket. 15 Bracket. 16 Screw. 17 Spring washer. 18 Nut. 19 Tail pipe. 20 Rear exhaust pipe and silencer. 21 Rear silencer. 22 Rear tail pipe. 23 Clip. 24 Clip. 25 Mounting bracket. 26 Bolt. 27 Spring washer. 28 Nut. 29 Rubber mounting bracket. 30 Bracket. 31 Spring washer. 32 Nut. 33 Plate. 34 Nut. 35 Spring washer. 36 Clip. 37 Screw. 38 Spring washer. 39 Nut. 40 Strap. 41 Bolt. 42 Spring washer. 43 Nut. 44 Link. 45 Retainer. 46 Bolt. 47 Plain washer. 48 Spring washer. 49 Nut. 50 Rubber mounting. 51 Bracket. 52 Plate. 53 Nut. 54 Spring washer. 55 Rear tail pipe rubber mounting. 56 Spring washer. 57 Nut. 58 Bolt. 59 Spring washer. 60 Silencer (rationalized mo-
60 Silencer. 61 Adaptor. 62 Clip. 63 Rear adaptor. 64 Connecting sleeve.

not to scratch the aluminium alloy. Never slide them off the bottom of the piston skirt. It is very easy to break the iron piston rings if they are pulled off roughly so this operation should be done with extreme caution. It is helpful to make use of an old hacksaw blade, or better still, an old .020 in. feeler gauge.

2. Lift one end of the piston ring to be removed out of its groove and insert the end of the feeler gauge under it.

3. Turn the feeler gauge slowly round the piston and as the ring comes out of its groove apply slight upward pressure so that it rests on the land above. It can then be eased off the piston with the feeler gauge stopping it from slipping into any empty grooves if it is any but the top piston ring that is being removed.

21. FLYWHEEL & ENGINE END PLATE REMOVAL & REPLACEMENT

Having removed the clutch (see Chapter 5/5) the flywheel and engine end plate can be removed. It is only possible for this operation to be carried out with the engine out of the car.

1. Bend back the locking tabs from the six bolts which hold the flywheel to the flywheel flange on the rear of the crankshaft.

2. Unscrew the bolts and remove them, complete with the three locking plates.

3. Lift the flywheel away from the crankshaft flange. NOTE - Some difficulty may be experienced in removing the bolts by the rotation of the crankshaft every time pressure is put on the spanner. The only answer is to lock the crankshaft in position while the bolts are removed. To lock the crankshaft a wooden wedge can be inserted between the crankshaft and the side of the block inside the crankcase.

4. The engine end plate is held in position by a number of bolts and spring washers of varying size. Release the bolts noting where different sizes fit and place them together to ensure none of them become lost. Lift away the end plate from the block complete with the paper gasket.

5. Flywheel replacement is described in Section 52. To replace the engine end plate first fit a new paper gasket in place on the rear of the block and hold it in place with jointing compound.

6. Remember to fit into its groove the square section cork which will fit into the bottom of the rear main bearing cap. If this is not done the plate will have to be removed later.

17. On some engines the end plate is fitted with an oil seal whose lip fits over the flange on the end of the crankshaft. Renew the seal and lubricate it to prevent heat scorch when the

engine is started.

8. Replace the end plate and the oil seal retaining plate, insert the securing bolts and pull up the tabs of the lockwashers. (See photograph)

21.8

22. CRANKSHAFT & MAIN BEARING REMOVAL

With the engine out of the car, drain the engine oil, remove the timing gears and remove the sump, the oil gauge filter, and suction pipe, and the big end bearings, pistons, flywheel and engine end plate as has already been described in Sections 15, 18, and 21. Removal of the crankshaft can only be attempted with the engine on the bench or floor.

1. Undo by one turn the nuts which hold the three main bearing caps in place.

2. Unscrew the nuts and remove them together with the washers.

3. Remove the two bolts and tab washer which hold the front main bearing cap against the engine front plate.

4. Remove the main bearing caps and the bottom half of each bearing shell, taking care to keep the bearing shells in the right caps.

5. When removing the centre bearing cap, NOTE the bottom semi-circular halves of the thrust washers, one half lying on either side of the main bearing. Lay them with the centre bearing along the correct side.

6. Slightly rotate the crankshaft to free the upper halves of the bearing shells and thrust washers which should now be extracted and placed over the correct bearing cap.

7. Remove the crankshaft by lifting it away from the crankcase.

23. LUBRICATION SYSTEM - DESCRIPTION

1. A forced feed system of lubrication is fitted with oil circulated round the engine from the sump below the block. The level of engine oil in the sump is indicated on the dipstick which is fitted on the right-hand side of the engine. It is marked to indicate the optimum level which is the maximum mark.

2. The level of oil in the sump, ideally, should not be above or below this line. Oil is replenished via the filler cap on the front of the rocker cover.

3. The eccentric rotor-type oil pump is bolted in the left-hand side of the crankcase and is driven by a short shaft from the skew gear on the camshaft which also drives the distributor shaft.

4. The pump is the non-draining variety to allow rapid pressure build-up when starting from cold.

5. Oil is drawn from the sump through a gauze screen in the oil strainer and is sucked up the pickup pipe and drawn into the oil pump. From the oil pump it is forced under pressure along a gallery on the right-hand side of the engine, and through drillings to the big end, main and camshaft bearings. A small hole in each connecting rod allows a jet of oil to lubricate the cylinder wall with each revolution.

6. From the camshaft front bearing oil is fed through drilled passages in the cylinder block and head to the front rocker pedestal where it enters the hollow rocker shaft. Holes drilled in the shaft allow for the lubrication of the rocker arms, and the valve stems and push rod ends.

7. This oil is at a reduced pressure to the oil delivered to the crankshaft bearings. Oil from the front camshaft bearing also lubricates the timing gears and the timing chain. Oil returns to the sump by various passages, the tappets being lubricated by oil returning via the push rod drillings in the block.

8. On all models a full-flow oil filter is fitted, and all oil passes through this filter before it reaches the main oil gallery. The oil is passed directly from the oil pump across the block to an external pipe on the right-hand side of the engine which feeds into the filter head.

24. OIL FILTER REMOVAL & REPLACEMENT

1. The full flow oil filter fitted to all engines is located three quarters of the way down the right-hand side of the engine towards the front.

2. It is removed by unscrewing the long centre bolt which holds the filter bowl in place. With the bolt released (use a $9/16$ A.F. spanner) carefully lift away the filter bowl which contains the filter and will also be full of oil. It is helpful to have a large basin under the filter body to catch the amount which is bound to spill.

3. Throw the old filter element away and thoroughly clean down the filter bowl, the bolts and associated parts with petrol and when perfectly clean wipe dry with a non-fluffy rag.

4. A rubber sealing ring is located in a groove round the head of the oil filter and forms an effective leak-proof joint between the filter head and the filter bowl. A new rubber sealing ring is supplied with each new filter element.

5. Carefully prise out the oil sealing ring from the locating groove. If the ring has become hard and is difficult to move take great care not to damage the sides of the sealing ring groove.

6. With the old ring removed, fit the new ring in the groove at four equidistant points and press it home a segment at a time as shown. Do not insert the ring at just one point and work round the groove pressing it home as, using this method, it is easy to stretch the ring and be left with a small loop of rubber which will not fit into the locating groove.

24.6

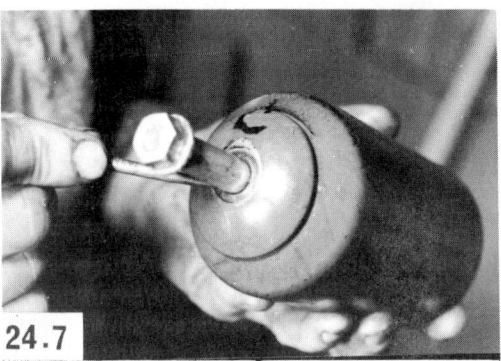

24.7

7. Reassemble the oil filter assembly by first passing up the bolt through the hole in the bottom of the bowl, and with a steel washer under the bolts head and a rubber or felt washer on top of the steel washer and next to the filter bowl as shown.

8. Slip the spring over the bolt inside the bowl as shown in the photograph.

9. Then fit the other steel washer and the remaining rubber or felt washer to the centre bolt as shown.

10. Fit the sealing plate over the centre bolt with the concave side facing the bottom of the bowl as shown.

11. Then slide the new element into the oil filter bowl. (See photograph).

12. With the bolt pressed hard up against the

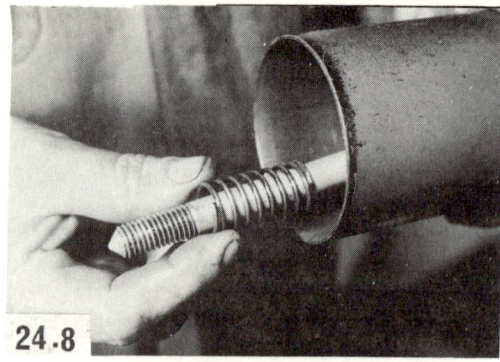

24.8

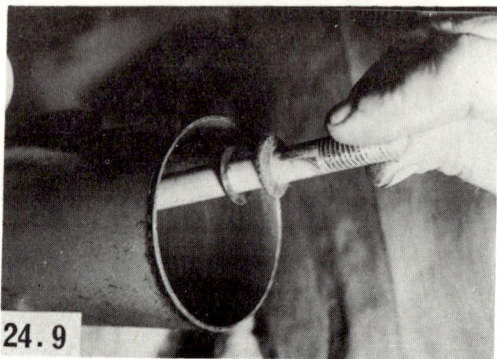

24.9

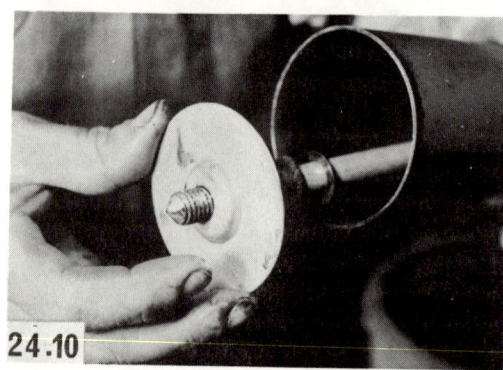

24.10

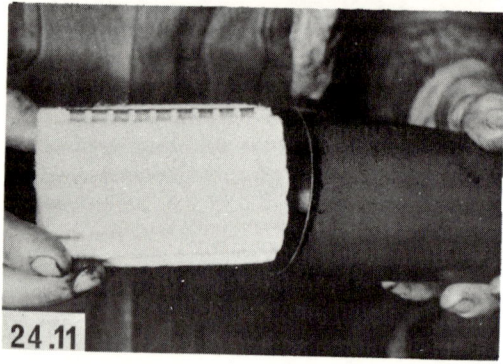

24.11

not offset and off the ring. If the bowl is not seating properly, rotate it until it is. Run the engine and check the bowl for leaks.

25. OIL PRESSURE RELIEF VALVE - REMOVAL & REPLACEMENT

1. To prevent excessive oil pressure - for example when the engine is cold - an oil pressure relief valve is built into the left-hand side of the engine at the rear just below the rev. counter drive take-off point.

2. The relief valve is identified externally by a large $^9/16$ in. domed hexagon nut. To dismantle the unit unscrew the nut and remove it, complete with the two fibre or copper sealing washers. The relief spring and the relief spring cup can then be easily extracted.

3. In position, the metal cup fits over the opposite end of the relief valve spring resting in the dome of the hexagon nut, and bears against a machining in the block. When the oil pressure exceeds 50 or 75 lb/sq. in. depending on the model, the cup is forced off its seat and the oil by-passes it and returns to the sump.

4. Check the tension of the spring by measuring its length. If it is shorter than 3 in. it should be replaced by a new spring. Reassembly of the relief valve unit is a reversal of the above procedure.

26. OIL PUMP - REMOVAL & DISMANTLING

1. Undo the nuts from the three studs which hold the oil pump to the crankcase and lift away the pump and its drive shaft, together with the pump gasket.

2. Undo the two bolts and spring washers holding the oil pump cover in place and pull the cover off the two dowels in the pump body which hold it in its correct position.

3. Pull out from the pump body the outer rotor and the inner rotor, together with the pump shaft.

27. TIMING CHAIN TENSIONER - REMOVAL & DISMANTLING

1. Remove the cover from the timing gears as described in Section 15 and lock the rubber tensioner in its fully retracted position as described in Section 15. 6.

2. Knock back the tabs of the joint lockwasher and undo the two bolts which hold the tensioner and its backplate to the engine.

3. Pull the rubber slipper together with the spring and plunger from the tensioner body. Fit the Allen key to its socket in the cylinder and, holding the slipper and plunger firmly, turn the key clockwise to free the cylinder and spring from the plunger.

filter bowl body (to avoid leakage) three quarter fill the bowl with engine oil.

13. Offer up the bowl to the rubber sealing ring and before finally tightening down the centre bolt, check that the lip of the filter bowl is resting squarely on the rubber sealing ring and is

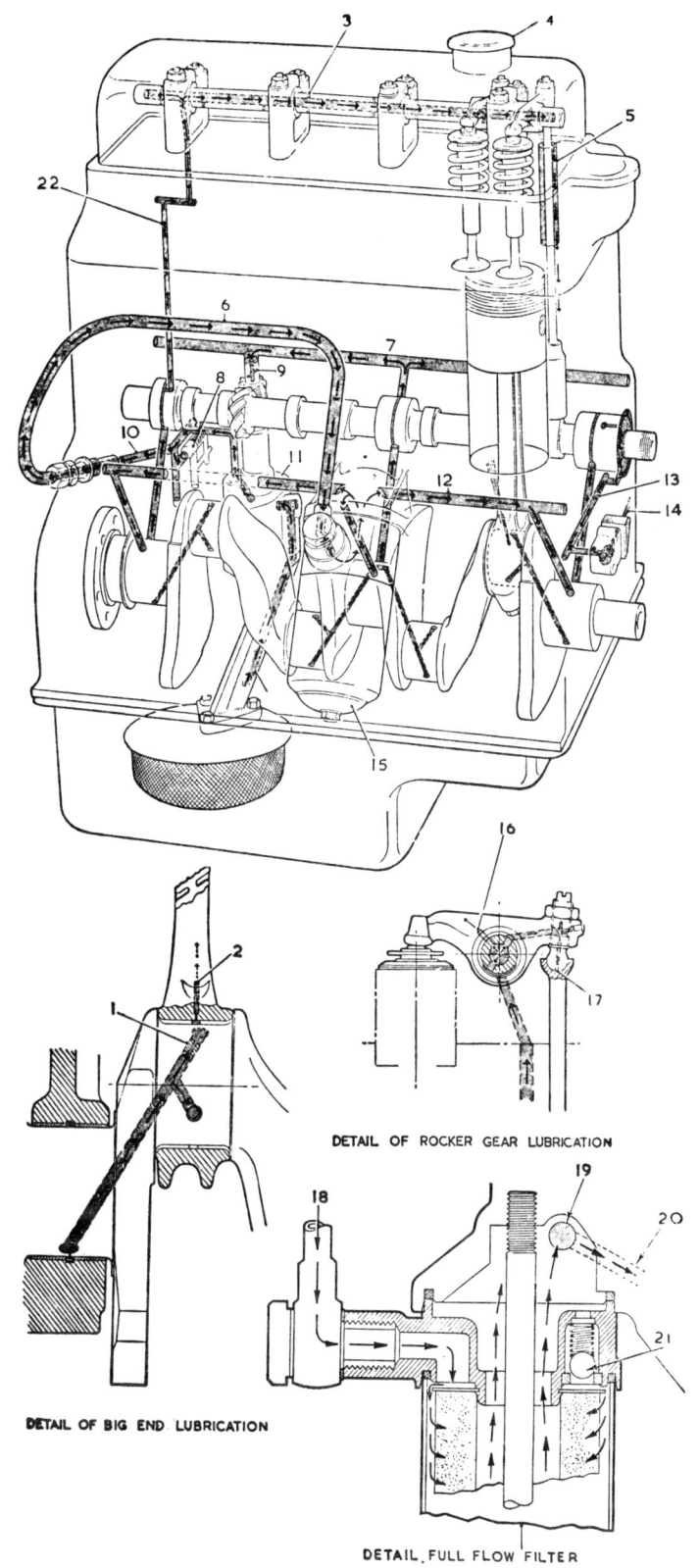

DETAIL OF ROCKER GEAR LUBRICATION

DETAIL OF BIG END LUBRICATION

DETAIL FULL FLOW FILTER

Fig. 1.7. EXPLODED VIEW OF THE ENGINE LUBRICATION SYSTEM

1 Restrictor. 2 Oil squirt to cylinder walls. 3 Rocker feed hole. 4 Oil filler. 5 Oil return to sump. 6 External pipe. 7 Low pressure gallery. 8 Relief valve. 9 Feed to gears. 10 Main feed. 11 Oil pump. 12 Main high pressure gallery. 13 Feed to chain tensioner. 14 Oil bleed to chain. 15 Full flow filter (see detail). 16 Oil bleed for valve stem tip. 17 Pressure feed to ball tip. 18 Inlet. 19 Oil gallery. 20 To main bearing. 21 Release bearing. 22 Feed to rocker gear (intermittent)

28. EXAMINATION & RENOVATION - GENERAL

With the engine stripped down and all parts thoroughly cleaned, it is now time to examine everything for wear. The following items should be checked and where necessary renewed or renovated as described in the following sections.

29. CRANKSHAFT EXAMINATION & RENOVATION

Examine the crankpin and main journal surfaces for signs of scoring or scratches. Check the ovality of the crankpins at different positions with a micrometer. If more than 0.001 in. out of round, the crankpins will have to be reground. It will also have to be reground if there are any scores or scratches present. Also check the journals in the same fashion. On highly tuned engines the centre main bearing has been known to break up. This is not always immediately apparent, but slight vibration in an otherwise normally smooth engine and a very slight drop in oil pressure under normal conditions are clues. If the centre main bearing is suspected of failure it should be immediately investigated by dropping the sump and removing the centre main bearing cap. Failure to do this will result in a badly scored centre main journal. If it is necessary to regrind the crankshaft and fit new bearings your local BMC garage or engineering works will be able to decide how much metal to grind off and the correct under-size shells to fit.

30. BIG END & MAIN BEARINGS - EXAMINATION & RENOVATION

Big end bearing failure is accompanied by a noisy knocking from the crankcase, and a slight drop in oil pressure. Main bearing failure is accompanied by vibration which can be quite severe as the engine speed rises and falls and a drop in oil pressure.

Bearings which have not broken up, but are badly worn will give rise to low oil pressure and some vibration. Inspect the big ends, main bearings, and thrust washers for signs of general wear, scoring, pitting, and scratches. The bearings should be mat grey in colour. With lead-indium bearings should a trace of copper colour be noticed the bearings are badly worn as the lead bearing material has worn away to expose the indium underlay. Renew the bearings if they are in this condition or if there is any sign of scoring or pitting.

The undersizes available are designed to correspond with the regrind sizes, i.e. -.010 bearings are correct for a crankshaft reground -.010 undersize. The bearings are in fact, slightly more than the stated undersize as running clearances have been allowed for during their manufacture.

Very long engine life can be achieved by changing big end bearings at intervals of 30,000 miles and main bearings at intervals of 50,000 miles, irrespective of bearing wear. Normally, crankshaft wear is infinitesimal and regular changes of bearings will ensure mileages of between 100,000 to 120,000 miles before crankshaft regrinding becomes necessary. Crankshafts normally have to be reground because of scoring due to bearing failure.

31. CYLINDER BORES- EXAMINATION & RENOVATION

The cylinder bores must be examined for taper, ovality, scoring and scratches. Start by carefully examining the top of the cylinder bores. If they are at all worn a very slight ridge will be found on the thrust side. This marks the top of the piston ring travel. The owner will have a good indication of the bore wear prior to dismantling the engine, or removing the cylinder head. Excessive oil consumption accompanied by blue smoke from the exhaust is a sure sign of worn cylinder bores and piston rings.

Measure the bore diameter just under the ridge with a micrometer and compare it with the diameter at the bottom of the bore, which is not subject to wear. If the difference between the two measurements is more than .006 in. then it will be necessary to fit special piston rings or to have the cylinders rebored and fit over-size pistons and rings. If no micrometer is available remove the rings from a piston and place the piston in each bore in turn about 3/4 in. below the top of the bore. If an 0.010 feeler gauge can be slid between the piston and the cylinder wall on the thrust side of the bore then remedial action must be taken. Oversize pistons are available in the following sizes:- +.010 in. (.254 mm.), +.020 in. (.508mm.), +.030 in. (.762 mm.), +.040 in. (1.016mm.)

These are accurately machined to just below these measurements so as to provide correct running clearances in bores bored out to the exact oversize dimensions.

If the bores are slightly worn but not so badly worn as to justify reboring them, then special oil control rings can be fitted to the existing pistons which will restore compression and stop the engine burning oil. Several different types are available and the manufacturers instructions concerning their fitting must be followed closely.

32. PISTONS & PISTON RINGS - EXAMINATION & RENOVATION

If the old pistons are to be refitted, carefully remove the piston rings and then thorough-

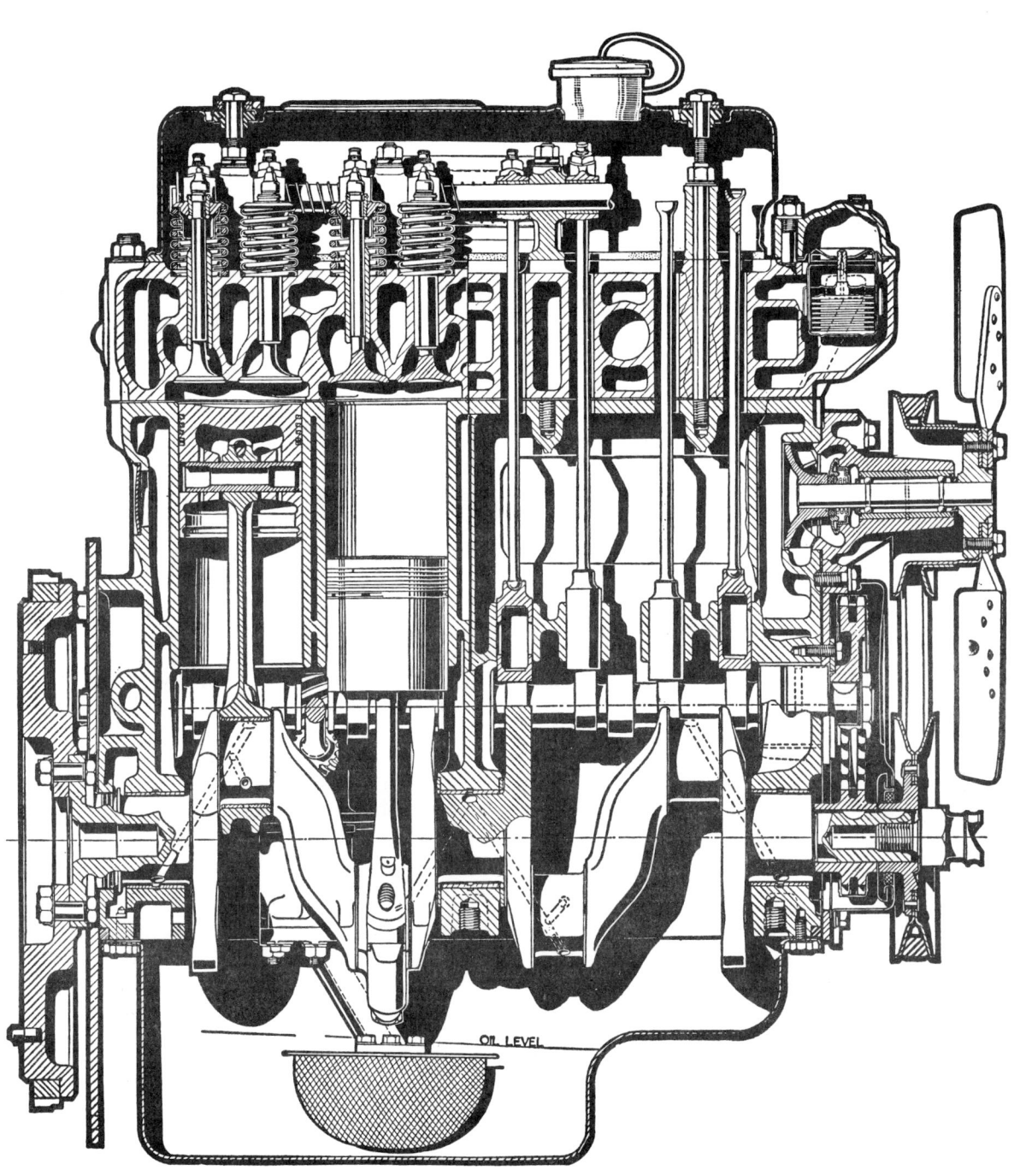

Fig. 1 . 8. A SECTIONED VIEW OF THE 1,489 c.c. ENGINE FITTED TO ALL MODELS UP TO 1961

ly clean them. Take particular care to clean out the piston ring grooves. At the same time do not scratch the aluminium in any way. If new rings are to be fitted to the old pistons then the top ring should be stepped so as to clear the ridge left above the previous top ring. If a normal but oversize new ring is fitted, it will hit the ridge and break, because the new ring will not have worn in the same way as the old, which will have worn in unison with the ridge.

Before fitting the rings on the pistons each should be inserted approximately 3 in. down the cylinder bore and the gap measured with a feeler gauge. This should be between .012 in. and .017 in. It is essential that the gap should be measured at the bottom of the ring travel, as if it is measured at the top of a worn bore and gives a perfect fit, it could easily seize at the bottom. If the ring gap is too small rub down the ends of the ring with a very fine file until the gap, when fitted, is correct. To keep the rings square in the bore for measurement line each up in turn by inserting an old piston in the bore upside down, and use the piston to push the ring down about 3 in. Remove the piston and measure the piston ring gap.

When fitting new pistons and rings to a rebored engine the piston ring gap can be measured at the top of the bore as the bore will not now taper. It is not necessary to measure the side clearance in the piston ring grooves with the rings fitted as the groove dimensions are accurately machined during manufacture. When fitting new oil control rings to old pistons it may be necessary to have the grooves widened by machining to accept the new wider rings. In this instance the manufacturers representative will make this quite clear and will supply the address to which the pistons must be sent for machining.

When new pistons are fitted, take great care to fit the exact size best suited to the particular bores in your engine. BMC go one stage further than merely specifying one size of piston for all standard bores. Because of very slight differences in cylinder machining during production it is necessary to select just the right piston for the bore. Five different sizes are available for the standard bore as well as the four oversize dimensions already shown.

Examination of the cylinder block face will show adjacent to each bore a small diamond shaped box with a number stamped in the metal. Careful examination of the piston crown will show a matching diamond and number. These are the standard piston sizes and will be the same for all four bores. If standard pistons are to be refitted or standard low compression pistons changed to standard high compression pistons, then it is essential that only pistons with the same number in the diamond are used. With larger pistons. the amount oversize is stamped in an ellipse in the piston crown.

On engines with tapered second and third compression rings, the top narrow side of the ring is marked with a 'T'. Always fit this side uppermost and carefully examine all rings for this mark before fitting.

33. CAMSHAFT & CAMSHAFT BEARINGS-EXAMINATION & RENOVATION

Carefully examine the camshaft bearings for wear. If the bearings are obviously worn or pitted or the metal underlay is showing through, then they must be renewed. This is an operation for your local BMC dealer or the local engineering works as it demands the use of specialised equipment. The bearings are removed with a special drift after which new bearings are pressed in, care being taken to ensure the oil holes in the bearings line up with those in the block. With a special tool the bearings are then reamered in position.

The camshaft itself should show no signs of wear, but, if very slight scoring on the cams is noticed, the score marks can be removed by very gentle rubbing down with a very fine emery cloth. The greatest care should be taken to keep the cam profiles smooth.

Fit the retaining plate and then the chainwheel to the end of the camshaft while it is out on the bench, and measure the endfloat between the thrust face of the camshaft front journal and the retaining plate. If more than .007 in. the retaining plate must be renewed.

34. VALVES & VALVE SEATS - EXAMINATION & RENOVATION

Examine the heads of the valves for pitting and burning, especially the heads of the exhaust valves. The valve seatings should be examined at the same time. If the pitting on valve and seat is very slight the marks can be removed by grinding the seats and valves together with coarse, and then fine, valve grinding paste. Where bad pitting has occured to the valve seats it will be necessary to recut them and fit new valves. If the valve seats are so worn that they cannot be recut, then it will be necessary to fit new valve seat inserts. These latter two jobs should be entrusted to the local BMC agent or engineering works. In practice it is very seldom that the seats are so badly worn that they require renewal. Normally, it is the valve that is too badly worn for replacement, and the owner can easily purchase a new set of valves and match them to the seats by valve grinding.

Valve grinding is carried out as follows:-

Smear a trace of coarse carborundum paste on the seat face and apply a suction grinder tool to the valve head. With a semi-rotary motion, grind the valve head to its seat, lifting the valve occasionally to redistribute the grinding paste. When a dull matt even surface finish is produced on both the valve seat and the valve, then wipe off the paste and repeat the process with fine carborundum paste, lifting and turning the valve to redistribute the paste as before. A light spring placed under the valve head will greatly ease this operation. When a smooth unbroken ring of light grey matt finish is produced, on both valve and valve seat faces, the grinding operation is completed.

Scrape away all carbon from the valve head and the valve stem. Carefully clean away every trace of grinding compound, taking great care to leave none in the ports or in the valve guides. Clean the valves and valve seats with a paraffin soaked rag then with a clean rag, and finally, if an air line is available, blow the valves, valve guides and valve ports clean.

35. TIMING GEARS & CHAIN - EXAMINATION & RENOVATION

Examine the teeth on both the crankshaft gear wheel and the camshaft gearwheel for wear. Each tooth forms an inverted 'V' with the gearwheel periphery, and if worn the side of each tooth under tension will be slightly concave in shape when compared with the other side of the tooth, i.e. one side of the inverted 'V' will be concave when compared with the other. If any sign of wear is present the gearwheels must be renewed.

Examine the links of the chain for side slackness and renew the chain if any slackness is noticeable when compared with a new chain. It is a sensible precaution to renew the chain at about 30,000 miles and at a lesser mileage if the engine is stripped down for a major overhaul. The actual rollers on a very badly worn chain may be slightly grooved.

36. TIMING CHAIN TENSIONER - EXAMINATION & RENOVATION

1. Thoroughly clean the component parts in petrol and clean out the oil holes in the slipper and spigot. If either of these holes become blocked slipper wear will increase considerably. After high mileages the slipper head is bound to be worn and must be renewed together with the cylinder assembly.

2. Check the bore of the adjuster body for ovality. If the diameter is more than .003 in. (.076 mm.) out of round at the bore mouth, then a new adjuster unit must be fitted.

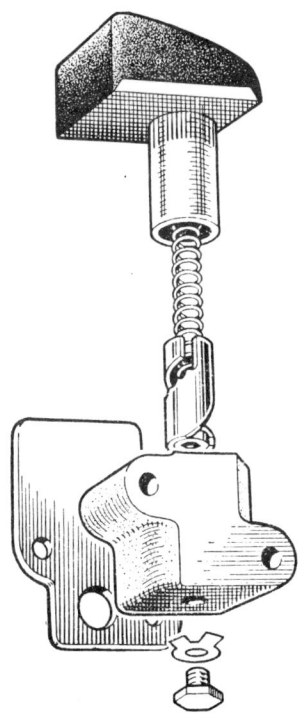

Fig. 1.9 Exploded view of the chain tensioner components.

37. ROCKERS & ROCKER SHAFT - EXAMINATION & RENOVATION

Remove the threaded plug with a screwdriver from the end of the rocker shaft and thoroughly clean out the shaft. As it acts as the oil passage for the valve gear also ensure the oil holes in it are quite clear after having cleaned them out. Check the shaft for straightness by rolling it on the bench. It is most unlikely that it will deviate from normal, but, if it does, then a judicious attempt must be made to straighten it. If this is not successful purchase a new shaft. The surface of the shaft should be free from any worn ridges caused by the rocker arms. If any wear is present, renew the shaft. Wear is only likely to have occured if the rocker shaft oil holes have become blocked.

Check the rocker arms for wear of the rocker bushes, for wear at the rocker arm face which bears on the valve stem, and for wear of the adjusting ball ended screws. Wear in the rocker arm bush can be checked by gripping the rocker arm tip and holding the rocker arm in place on the shaft, noting if there is any lateral rocker arm shake. If shake is present, and the arm is very loose on the shaft, remedial action must be taken. Forged rocker arms which have worn bushes may be taken to your local BMC agent or engineering works to have the old bush drawn out and a new bush fitted.

Check the tip of the rocker arm where it bears on the valve head for cracking or serious wear on the case hardening. If none is present reuse the rocker arm. Check the lower half of the ball on the end of the rocker arm adjusting screw. On high performance BMC engines wear on the ball and top of the pushrod is easily noted by the unworn 'pip' which fits in the small central oil hole on the ball. The larger this 'pip' the more wear has taken place to both the ball and the pushrod. Check the pushrods for straightness by rolling them on the bench. Renew any that are bent.

38. TAPPETS - EXAMINATION & RENOVATION

Examine the bearing surface of the tappets which lie on the camshaft. Any indentation in this surface or any cracks indicate serious wear and the tappets should be renewed. Thoroughly clean them out, removing all traces of sludge. It is most unlikely that the sides of the tappets will prove worn, but, if they are a very loose fit in their bores and can readily be rocked, they should be exchanged for new units. It is very unusual to find any wear in the tappets, and any wear present is likely to occur only at very high mileages.

39. FLYWHEEL STARTER RING - EXAMINATION & RENOVATION

If the teeth on the flywheel starter ring are badly worn, or if some are missing, then it will be necessary to remove the ring. This is achieved by splitting the ring with a cold chisel. The greatest care should be taken not to damage the flywheel during this process.

To fit a new ring heat it gently and evenly with an oxy-acetylene flame until a temperature of approximately 350°C is reached. This is indicated by a light metallic blue surface colour. With the ring at this temperature, fit it to the flywheel with the front of the teeth facing the flywheel register. The ring should be tapped gently down onto its register and left to cool naturally when the shrinkage of the metal on cooling will ensure that it is a secure and permanent fit. Great care must be taken not to overheat the ring, as if this happens the temper of the ring will be lost.

Alternatively, your local BMC agent or local engineering works may have a suitable oven in which the flywheel can be heated. The normal domestic oven will only give a temperature of about 250°C at the very most and, al-

though it may be just possible to fit the ring with it at this temperature, it is unlikely and no great force should have to be used.

40. OIL PUMP - EXAMINATION & RENOVATION

Thoroughly clean all the component parts in petrol and then check the rotor end float and lobe clearances in the following manner:-

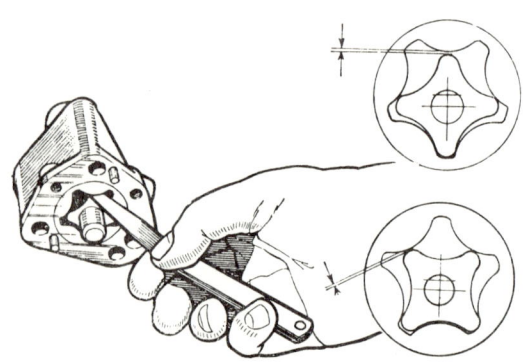

Fig. 1.10 Measure the lobe clearances with a feeler gauge in the positions indicated. The gaps should not exceed .006 ins.

Position the rotors in the pump and place the straight edge of a steel ruler across the joint face of the pump. Measure the gap between the bottom of the straight edge and the top of the rotors with a feeler gauge. If the measurement exceeds .005 in. (.127 mm.) then check the lobe clearances as described in the following paragraph. If the lobe clearances are correct then remove the dowels from the joint face of the pump body and lap the joint face on a sheet of plate glass.

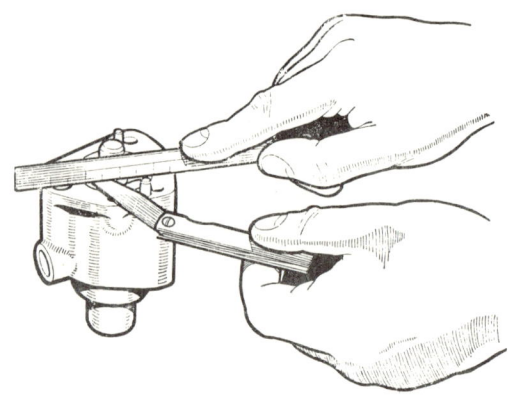

Fig. 1.11 Measuring the oil pump rotor end float with a straight edge and feeler gauge. Not more than .005 in. (.127 mm.) should be permitted.

Measure the gaps between the peaks of the lobes and the peaks in the pump body with a feeler gauge, and if the gap exceeds .010 in. (.254 mm.) then fit a replacement pump.

41. CYLINDER HEAD - DECARBONISATION

This can be carried out with the engine either in or out of the car. With the cylinder head off carefully remove with a wire brush and blunt scraper all traces of carbon deposits from the combustion spaces and the ports. The valve head stems and valve guides should also be freed from any carbon deposits. Wash the combustion spaces and ports down with petrol and scrape the cylinder head surface free of any foreign matter with the side of a steel rule, or a similar article

Clean the pistons and top of the cylinder bores. If the pistons are still in the block then it is essential that great care is taken to ensure that no carbon gets into the cylinder bores as this could scratch the cylinder walls or cause damage to the piston and rings. To ensure this does not happen, first turn the crankshaft so that two of the pistons are at the top of their bores. Stuff rag into the other two bores or seal them off with paper and masking tape. The waterways should also be covered with small pieces of masking tape to prevent particles of carbon entering the cooling system and damaging the water pump.

There are two schools of thought as to how much carbon should be removed from the piston crown. One school recommends that a ring of carbon should be left round the edge of the piston and on the cylinder bore wall as an aid to low oil consumption. Although this is probably true for early engines with worn bores, on later engines the thought of the second school can be applied; which is that for effective decarbonisation all traces of carbon should be removed.

If all traces of carbon are to be removed, press a little grease into the gap between the cylinder walls and the two pistons which are to be worked on. With a blunt scraper carefully scrape away the carbon from the piston crown, taking great care not to scratch the aluminium. Also scrape away the carbon from the surrounding lip of the cylinder wall. When all carbon has been removed, scrape away the grease which will now be contaminated with carbon particles, taking care not to press any into the bores To assist prevention of carbon build-up the piston crown can be polished with a metal polish such as Brasso. Remove the rags or masking tape from the other two cylinders and turn the crankshaft so that the two pistons which were at the bottom are now at the top. Place rag or masking tape in the cylinders which have been decarbonised and proceed as just described.

If a ring of carbon is going to be left round the piston then this can be helped by inserting an old piston ring into the top of the bore to rest on the piston and ensure that carbon is not accidentally removed. Check that there are no particles of carbon in the cylinder bores. Decarbonising is now complete.

42. VALVE GUIDES - EXAMINATION & RENOVATION

Examine the valve guides internally for wear. If the valves are a very loose fit in the guides and there is the slightest suspicion of lateral rocking, then new guides will have to be fitted. If the valve guides have been removed compare them internally by visual inspection with a new guide as well as testing them for rocking with the valves.

43. SUMP - EXAMINATION & RENOVATION

Thoroughly wash out the sump with petrol and then inspect the cork packings in the semicircular crankshaft seal housings. If they are at all flattened new ones should be fitted. Remove the old packing pieces, carefully pushing them right down into the grooves. Should the packing material stand out more than 1/16 in. above the sump flange it must be cut back to this figure.

44. ENGINE REASSEMBLY - GENERAL

To ensure maximum life with minimum trouble from a rebuilt engine, not only must everything be correctly assembled, but everything must be spotlessly clean, all the oilways must be clear, locking washers and spring washers must always be fitted where indicated and all bearing and other working surfaces must be thoroughly lubricated during assembly. Before assembly begins renew any bolts or studs the threads of which are in any way damaged, and whenever possible use new spring washers. Apart from your normal tools, a supply of clean rag, an oil can filled with engine oil (an empty plastic detergent bottle thoroughly cleaned and washed out, will invariably do just as well), a new supply of assorted spring washers, a set of new gaskets, and preferable a torque spanner, should be collected together.

45. CRANKSHAFT REPLACEMENT

Ensure that the crankcase is thoroughly clean and that all oilways are clear. A thin-twist drill is useful for cleaning them out. If possible, blow them out with compressed air.

Treat the crankshaft in the same fashion, and then inject engine oil into the crankshaft oilways.

Commence work on rebuilding the engine by replacing the crankshaft and main bearings:-

45.1

1. If the old main bearing shells are to be replaced, (a false economy unless they are virtually as new), fit the three upper halves of the main bearing shells to their location in the crankcase, after wiping the locations clean. See photograph.

2. NOTE that at the back of each bearing is a tab which engages in locating grooves in either the crankcase or the main bearing cap housings.

3. If new bearings are being fitted, carefully clean away all traces of the protective grease with which they are coated.

45.4

4. With the three upper bearing shells securely in place, wipe the lower bearing cap housings and fit the three lower shell bearings to their caps ensuring that the right shell goes into the right cap if the old bearings are being refitted. (See photograph).

5. Wipe the recesses either side of the centre main bearing which locate the upper halves of the thrust washers.

6. Generously lubricate the crankshaft journals and the upper and lower main bearing shells and carefully place the crankshaft in position.

7. Introduce the upper halves of the thrust washers (the halves without tabs) into their grooves either side of the centre main bearing, rotating the crankshaft in the direction towards the main bearing tabs (so that the main bearing shells do not slide out). At the same time feed the thrust washers into their locations with their oil grooves outwards away from the bearing.

45.8

8. Fit the main bearing caps in position ensuring they locate properly. The mating surfaces must be spotlessly clean or the caps will not seat correctly. (See photograph).

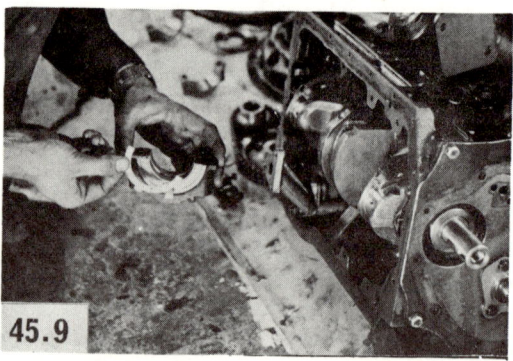

45.9

9. When replacing the centre main bearing cap ensure the thrust washers, generously lubricated, are fitted with their oil grooves facing outwards, and the locating tab of each washer is in the slot in the bearing cap as shown.

45.10

10. Replace the washers over the main bearing cap bolts and replace the main bearing cap nuts screwing them up finger-tight. (See photo).

11.   Test the crankshaft for freedom of rotation. should it be very stiff to turn or posses high spots a most careful inspection must be made, preferably by a qualified mechanic with a micrometer to get to the root of the trouble.   It is very seldom that any trouble of this nature will be experienced when fitting the crankshaft.

12.   Tighten the main bearing nuts to a torque of 70lb/ft. and recheck the crankshaft for freedom of rotation.   (See photograph).

45.12

46.   OIL PUMP - REASSEMBLY & REPLACEMENT

1.   Fit the outer rotor in the body of the pump so the champered end is at the driving end of the rotor pocket in the body of the pump.

2.   Replace the inner rotor together with the oil pump shaft and fill the pump with oil to thoroughly lubricate it.

3.   Fit the cover in position over the dowels on the joint face and use a new gasket. Replace and tighten the two securing nuts.   Check that the pump turns freely.

4.   Fit the pump and shaft to the crankcase using a new gasket and insert and tighten up the three nuts which hold the pump in place.

47.   PISTON & CONNECTING ROD REASSEMBLY

If the same pistons are being used, then they must be mated to the same connecting rod with the same gudgeon pin.   If new pistons are being fitted it does not matter which connecting rod they are used with, but, the gudgeon pins should be fitted on the basis of selective assembly.

This involves trying each of the pins in each of the pistons in turn and fitting them to the ones they fit best as is detailed below.

Because aluminium alloy, when hot, expands more than steel, the gudgeon pin may be a very tight fit in the piston when they are cold.   To avoid any damage to the piston it is best to heat it in boiling water when the pin will slide in easily.

Lay the correct piston adjacent to each connecting rod and remember that the same rod and piston must go back into the same bore. If new pistons are being used it is only necessary to ensure that the right connecting rod is placed in each bore.

To assemble the pistons to the connecting rods, proceed as follows:

1.   Locate the small end of the connecting rod in the piston, with the marking 'FRONT' on the piston crown towards the front of the engine, and the hole for the gudgeon pin bolt in the connecting rod towards the camshaft.

2.   NOTE the indentation in the centre of the gudgeon pin and insert the pin in the connecting rod so that the indentation lines up with the clamp bolt hole in such a way that the bolt will pass through without touching the gudgeon pin.

3.   For the gudgeon pin to fit correctly it should slide in three quarters of its travel quite freely and for the remaining quarter have to be tapped in with a plastic or wooden headed hammer, or the piston heated in water so the pin will slide in the remaining quarter easily.

4.   Fit a new spring washer under the head of the connecting rod bolt and screw it into position using a torque figure of 25 lb./ft.

48.   PISTON RING REPLACEMENT

1   Check that the piston ring grooves and oilways are thoroughly clean and unblocked. Piston rings must always be fitted over the head of the piston and never from the bottom.

2.   The easiest method to use when fitting rings is to wrap a .020 feeler gauge round the top of the piston and place the rings one at a time, starting with the bottom oil control ring, over the feeler gauge.

3.   The feeler gauge, complete with ring, can then be slid down the piston over the other piston ring grooves until the correct groove is reached. The piston ring is then slid gently off the feeler gauge into the groove.

4.   An alternative method is to fit the rings by holding them slightly open with the thumbs and both of your index fingers.   This method requires a steady hand and great care as it is easy to open the ring too much and break it.

49.   PISTON REPLACEMENT

The pistons, complete with connecting rods, can be fitted to the cylinder bores in the following sequence:-

1.   With a wad of clean rag wipe the cylinder bores clean.

2.   The pistons, complete with connecting rods, are fitted to their bores from above.

3.   As each piston is inserted into its bore ensure that it is the correct piston/connecting rod assembly for that particular bore and that the

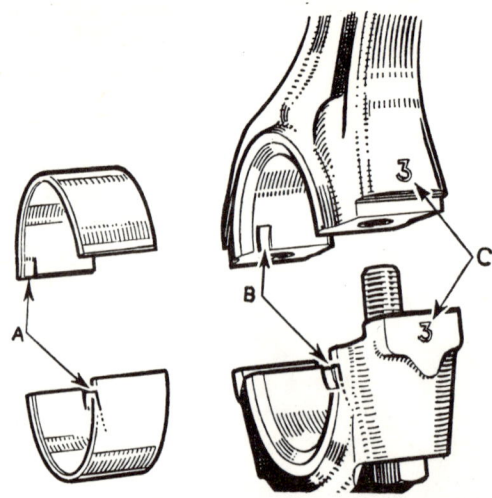

Fig. 1.12 The shell bearing tabs 'A' fit in the connecting rod grooves 'B'. Ensure the rod and bearing cap numbers 'C' correspond and note they also indicate the cylinder from which the rod was removed.

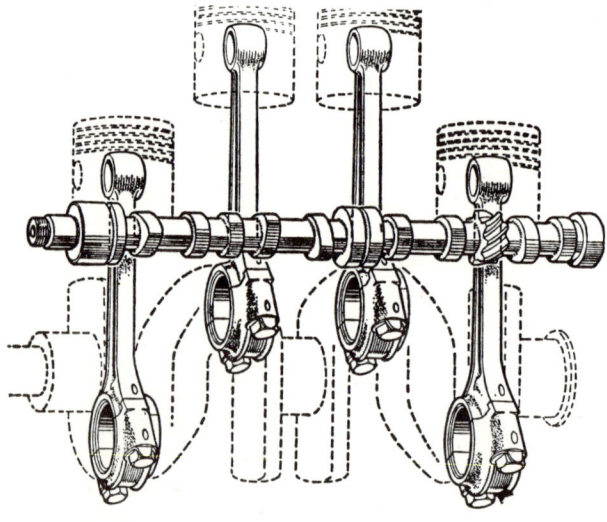

Fig. 1.13 Assemble the connecting rods with the offsets in the positions shown.

connecting rod is the right way round, and that the front of the piston is towards the front of the bore, i.e. towards the front of the engine.

4. The piston will only slide into the bore as far as the oil control ring. It is then necessary to compress the piston rings into a clamp and to gently tap the piston into the cylinder bore with a wooden or plastic hammer. If a proper piston ring clamp is not available than a suitable jubilee clip does the job very well.

50. CONNECTING ROD TO CRANKSHAFT RE-ASSEMBLY

As the big ends on the connecting rods are offset it will be obvious if they have been in-serted the wrong way round as they will not fit over the crankpins. The centre two connecting rods should be fitted with the offset part of the rods adjacent, and the connecting rods at each extremity of the engine should have the offset part of the rods facing outwards.

1. Wipe the connecting rod half of the big end bearing cap and the underside of the shell bearing clean, and fit the shell bearing in position with its locating tongue engaged with the corresponding groove in the connecting rod.

2. If the old bearings are nearly new and are being refitted then ensure they are replaced in their correct locations on the correct rods.

3. Generously lubricate the crankpin journals with engine oil, and turn the crankshaft so that the crankpin is in the most advantageous position for the connecting rod to be drawn onto it.

4. Wipe the connecting rod bearing cap and back of the shell bearing clean and fit the shell bearing in position ensuring that the locating tongue at the back of the bearing engages with the locating groove in connecting rod cap.

50.5

5. Generously lubricate the shell bearing and offer up the connecting rod bearing cap to the connecting rod. (See photograph).

6. Fit the connecting rod bolts with the one-piece locking tab u n d e r them and tighten the bolts with a torque spanner to 35 lb/ft. With a cold chisel or pair of pliers knock up the locking tabs against the bolt head.

7. When all the connecting rods have been fitted, rotate the crankshaft to check that everything is free, and that there are no high spots causing binding.

51. GAUZE STRAINER & SUCTION PIPE ASS-EMBLY

1. The gauze strainer and suction pipe should be thoroughly cleaned in petrol, and then blown dry with a compressed air line.

2. Reassembly consists of refitting the centre nut and bolt and the two delivery pipe flange bolts and then inserting and doing up the two bolts which hold it to the pump cover.

3. Do not forget to replace the distance tube and ensure the locating tongue on the side of the cover is correctly positioned.

52. FLYWHEEL REPLACEMENT

1. When replacing the flywheel it is import-andto ensure that it is placed in the correct relative position with the crankshaft.

2. To do this, turn the crankshaft until piston Nos. 1 and 4 are at the top of their bores and lock the crankshaft in this position with a wedge of wood between the crankshaft and the crank-case.

52.3

3. Wipe the mating surfaces of the crankshaft flange and flywheel clean, and then fit the fly-wheel so the marks '1/4' on the flywheel per-iphery are at the top. (See photograph).

4. Screw in the six nuts and bolts and locking plates and tighten the bolts to a torque of 40 lb/ft. Bend up the locking tabs on the locking plates and replace the clutch as described in Chapter 5/6.

53. SUMP REPLACEMENT

1. After the sump has been thoroughly cleaned, scrape all traces of the old sump gasket from the sump flange, and fit new main bearing cap oil seals if required.

2. Wipe c l e a n the inside of the crankcase, including the camshaft bearing surfaces. Th-oroughly clean and scrape the crankshaft to sump flange.

53.3

3. With a new sump gasket held lightly in pos-ition offer up the sump to the crankcase. (See photograph).

4. Bolt the sump in position with the large flat washer next t o the sump flange and the starred or spring washer under the bolt head.

5. Take care not to over-tighten the sump bolts as they strip their threads very easily. T h e correct torque that they should be tightened to is 6 lb/ft.

54. CAMSHAFT REPLACEMENT

1. With the sump in position the engine can be stood upright and the following operations, in-

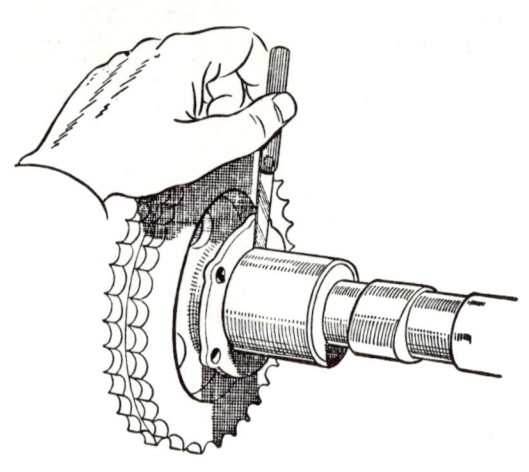

Fig. 1.14 The camshaft end float can be checked with a feeler gauge as shown.

cluding camshaft replacement, will be found easier with the engine in this position.

2. Wipe the camshaft bearing journals clean and lubricate them generously with engine oil.

3. Insert the camshaft into the crankcase gently, taking care not to damage the camshaft bearings with the cams.

4. With the camshaft inserted into the block as far as it will go, rotate it slightly to ensure the skew gear has mated with the oil pump drive.

5. Replace the camshaft locating plate and tighten down the three retaining bolts and washers.

55. TIMING GEARS, CHAIN TENSIONER, COVER REPLACEMENT

1. Before reassembly begins check that the packing washers are in place on the crankshaft nose. If new gearwheels are being fitted it may be necessary to fit additional washers (please see para. 7). These washers ensure that the crankshaft gearwheel lines up correctly with the camshaft gearwheel.

2. Replace the woodruff keys in their respective slots in the crankshaft and camshaft and ensure that they are fully seated. If their edges are burred they must be cleaned with a fine file.

3. Lay the camshaft gearwheels on a clean surface so that the two timing dots are adjacent to each other. Slip the timing chain over them and pull the gearwheels back into mesh with the chain so that the timing dots, although further apart, are still adjacent to each other. (See photograph).

55.3

4. Rotate the crankshaft so that the woodruff key is at top dead centre. (The engine should be standing upright on its sump).

5. Rotate the camshaft so that when viewed from the front the woodruff key is at two o'clock position.

6. Fit the timing chain and gearwheel assembly onto the camshaft and crankshaft, keeping the timing marks adjacent. If the camshaft and crankshaft have been positioned accurately it will be found that the keyways on the gearwheels will match the position of the keys, although it may be necessary to rotate the camshaft a fraction to ensure accurate lining-up of the camshaft gearwheel.

7. Press the gearwheels into position on the crankshaft and camshaft as far as they will go. NOTE If new gearwheels are being fitted they should be checked for alignment before being finally fitted to the engine. Place the gearwheels in position without the timing chain and place the straight edge of a steel ruler from the side of the camshaft gearteeth to the crankshaft gearwheel, as shown in Fig. 1.15, and measure the gap between the steel rule and the gearwheel. If a gap exists a suitable number of packing washers must be placed on the crankshaft nose to bring the crankshaft gearwheel onto the same plane as the camshaft gearwheel.

8. Next assemble the chain tensioner by inserting one end of the spring into the plunger and fit the other end of the spring into the cylinder as shown.

55.8

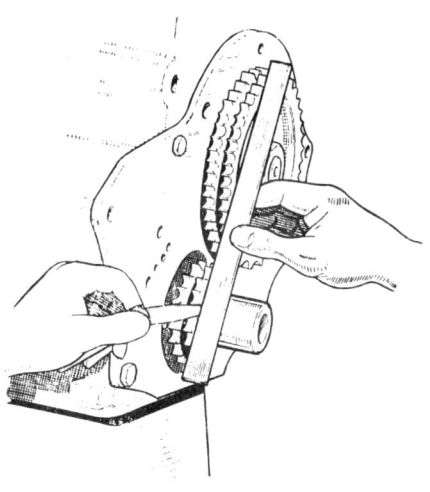

Fig. 1.15 Use the straight edge of a steel rule to line up the gearwheel teeth. Add shims to the thickness of the feeler gauge blade to the rear of the crankshaft gearwheel as necessary.

9. Compress the s p r i n g until the cylinder enters the plunger bore and ensure the peg in the plunger engages the helical slot. Insert and turn the Allen key clockwise until the end of the cylinder is below the peg and the spring is held compressed.

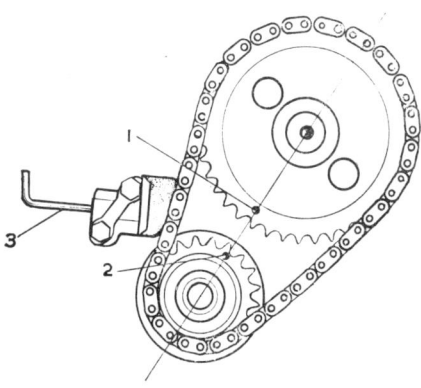

Fig. 1.16. To retract the chain tensioner turn the Allen key '3' clockwise. The engine timing is correct when the dimples '1' & '2' are in line with and adjacent to each other as shown.

10. Fit the backplate and secure the assembly to the cylinder block with the two bolts. Turn up the tabs of the lockwasher. (See photograph)

55.10

11. With the timing chain in position, the tensioner can now be relaxed. Insert the Allen key and turn it clockwise so the slipper head moves forward under spring pressure against the chain. Do not under any circumstances turn the key anti-clockwise or force the slipper head into the chain.

12. On early engines fit the oil thrower to the crankshaft nose with the concave side forward. Later models make use of a modified timing cover and oil thrower with an 'F' on its front face; i.e. this face must be furthest from the engine. On no account use a later oil thrower with an early cover or vice-versa.

55.13

13. Fit the locking washer to the camshaft gearwheel with its locating tab in the gearwheel keyway as shown.

55.14

14. Screw on the camshaft gearwheel retaining nut and tighten securely. (See photograph).

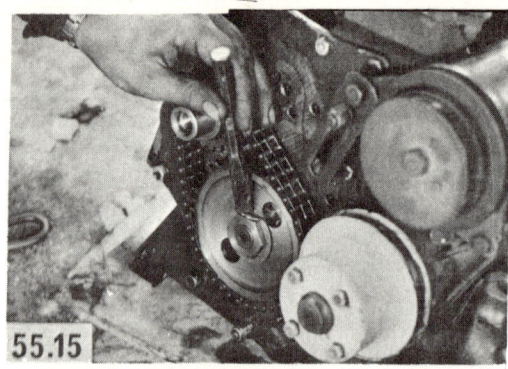

55.15

15. Bend up the locking tab of the locking washer to securely hold the camshaft retaining nut as shown.

16. Generously oil the chain and gearwheels.

55.17

17. Ensure the interior of the timing cover and the timing cover flange is clean and generously lubricate the oil seal in the timing cover. Then, with a new gasket in position, fit the timing cover to the block as shown.

18. Screw in the timing cover retaining bolts with the flat washer next to the cover flange and under the spring washer. The $\frac{1}{4}$ in. bolts should be tightened with a torque spanner to 6 lb/ft., and the $\frac{5}{16}$ in. bolts to 14 lb/ft.

55.19

19. Fit the crankshaft pulley to the nose of the crankshaft ensuring that the keyway engages with the woodruff key as shown.

20. Fit the crankshaft retaining bolt locking washer in position and screw on the crankshaft

pulley retaining dog. Tighten to a torque of 70 lb/ft.

56. VALVE & VALVE SPRING REASSEMBLY

To refit the valves and valve springs to the cylinder head, proceed as follows:-

1. Rest the cylinder head on its side, or if the manifold studs are still fitted, with the gasket surface downwards.

2. Fit each valve and valve spring in turn, wiping down and lubricating each valve stem as it is inserted into the same valve guide from which it was removed.

3. As each valve is inserted slip the oil control rubber ring into place just under the bottom of the cotter groove. (Use a new rubber ring if possible).

4. Move the cylinder head towards the edge of the work bench if it is facing downwards and slide it partially over the edge of the bench so as to fit the bottom half of the valve spring compressor to the valve head.

5. Slip the valve spring, shroud and cap over the valve stem.

6. With the base of the valve compressor on the valve head, compress the valve spring until the cotters can be slipped into place in the cotter grooves. Gently release the compressor and fit the circlip in position in the grooves in the cotters.

7. Repeat this procedure until all eight valves and valve springs are fitted.

57. ROCKER SHAFT REASSEMBLY

1. To reassemble the rocker shaft fit the split pin, flat washer, and spring washer at the rear end of the shaft and then slide on the rocker

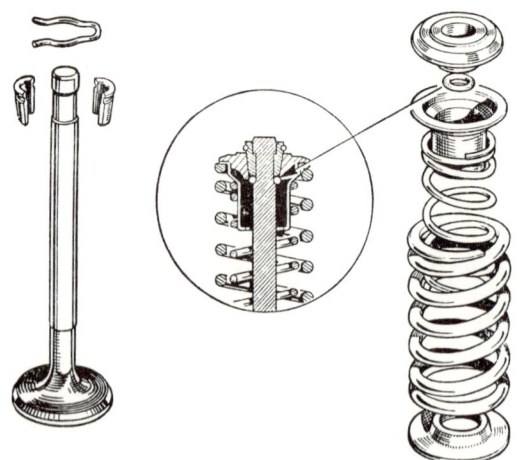

Fig. 1.17 The component parts of the valve assembly. Note how the valve packing ring fits in the bottom of the cotter groove.

arms, rocker shaft pedestals, and spacing springs in the same order in which they were removed.

2   With the front pedestal in position, screw in the rocker shaft locating screw and slip the locating plate into place. Finally, fit to the front of the shaft the spring washer, plain washer, and split pin, in that order.

58. TAPPET & PUSHROD REPLACEMENT

Generously lubricate the tappets internally and externally and insert them in the bores from which they were removed through the tappet chest.

With the cylinder head in position fit the pushrods in the same order in which they were removed. Ensure that they locate properly in the stems of the tappets, and lubricate the pushrod ends before fitment.

59. CYLINDER HEAD REPLACEMENT

After checking that both the cylinder block and cylinder head mating faces are perfectly clean, generously lubricate each cylinder with engine oil.

1.   Always use a new cylinder head gasket as the old gasket will be compressed and not capable of giving a good seal.

2.   Never smear grease on either side of the gasket as when the engine heats up the grease will melt and may allow compression leak to develop. Personally, I never like using gasket cement as if a new gasket is used and the head and block faces are true there should be no requirement for it. (The most successful racing engines seldom use gasket cement).

3.   The cylinder head gasket is marked 'FRONT' and 'TOP' and should be fitted in position according to the markings.

4.   With the gasket in position carefully lower the cylinder head onto the cylinder block.

5.   With the head in position fit the cylinder head nuts and washers finger tight to the seven cylinder head holding down studs, which remain outside the rocker cover. It is not possible to fit the remaining nuts to the studs inside the rocker cover until the rocker assembly is in position.

6.   Fit the pushrods as detailed in the previous section.

7.   The rocker shaft assembly can now be lowered over its eight locating studs. Take care that the rocker arms are the right way round. Lubricate the ball joints, and insert the rocker arm ball joints in the pushrod cups.

NOTE   Failure to place the ball-joints in the cups can result in the ball joints seating on the edge of a pushrod or outside it when the head

and rocker assembly is pulled down tight.

8.   Fit the four rocker pedestal nuts and washers, and then the four cylinder head stud nuts and washers which also serve to hold down the rocker pedestals. Pull the nuts down evenly, but without tightening them right up.

9.   When all is in position, the eleven cylinder head nuts and the four rocker pedestal nuts can be tightened down in the order shown in Fig. 1. 3 page 25. Turn the nuts a quarter of a turn a time and tighten the four rocker pedestal nuts to 25 lb/ft. and the nine cylinder head nuts to 40 lb/ft.

60. ROCKER ARM/VALVE ADJUSTMENT

1.   The valve adjustments should be made with the engine cold. The importance of correct rocker arm/valve stem clearances cannot be overstressed as they vitally affect the performance of the engine.

2.   If the clearances are set too open, the efficiency of the engine is reduced as the valves open late and close earlier than was intended. If, on the other hand the clearances are set too close there is a danger that the stems will expand upon heating and not allow the valves to close properly which will cause burning of the valve head and seat and possible warping.

3.   If the engine is in the car to get at the rockers it is merely necessary to remove the two holding down studs from the rocker cover, and then to lift the rocker cover and gasket away.

4.   It is important that the clearance is set when the tappet of the valve being adjusted is on the heel of the cam, (i.e. opposite the peak). This can be done by carrying out the adjustments in the following order, which also avoids

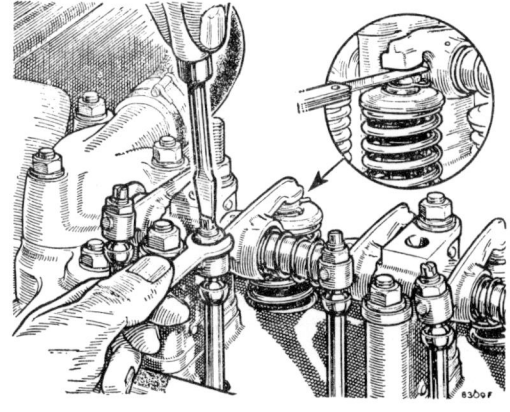

Fig. 1.18 Slip a .015 feeler gauge between the rocker arm pad and the valve stem head and adjust the arm as shown till it lightly nips the gauge blade.

turning the crankshaft more than necessary.

Valve fully open	Check & adjust
Valve No. 8	Valve No. 1
" " 6	" " 3
" " 4	" " 5
" " 7	" " 2
" " 1	" " 8
" " 3	" " 6
" " 5	" " 4
" " 2	" " 7

5. The correct valve clearance of .015 in. is obtained by slackening the hexagon locknut with a spanner while holding the ball pin against rotation with the screwdriver. Then, still pressing down with the screwdriver, insert a feeler gauge in the gap between the valve stem head and the rocker arm and adjust the ball pin until the feeler gauge will just move in and out without nipping. Then, still holding the ball pin in the correct position, tighten the locknut.

6. An alternative method is to set the gaps with the engine running, and although this may be faster it is no more reliable.

61. DISTRIBUTOR & DISTRIBUTOR DRIVE RE-PLACEMENT

It is important to set the distributor drive correctly as otherwise the ignition timing will be totally incorrect. It is easy to set the distributor drive in apparently the right position, but, exactly 180° out by omitting to select the correct cylinder which must not only be at T.D.C. but must also be on its firing stroke with both valves closed. The distributor drive should therefore not be fitted until the cylinder head is in position and the valves can be observed. Alternatively, if the timing cover has not been replaced, the distributor drive can be replaced when the dots on the timing wheels are adjacent to each other.

1. Rotate the crankshaft so that No. 1 piston is at T D C and on its firing stroke (the dots in the timing gears will be adjacent to each other). When No. 1 piston is at T.D.C. the inlet valve on No. 4 cylinder is just opening and the exhaust valve closing.

2. When the marks '1/4' on the flywheel are at T.D.C., or when the dimple on the crankshaft pulley wheel is in line with the pointer on the timing gear cover, then Nos. 1 and 4 pistons are at T.D.C.

3. Screw the tappet cover bolt into the head of the distributor drive (any 5/16 in. U.N.F. bolt will do).

4. Insert the distributor drive into its housing so that when fully home the slot in the top of the drive shaft is positioned between 8 and 2 o'clock with the smaller segment facing downwards. To

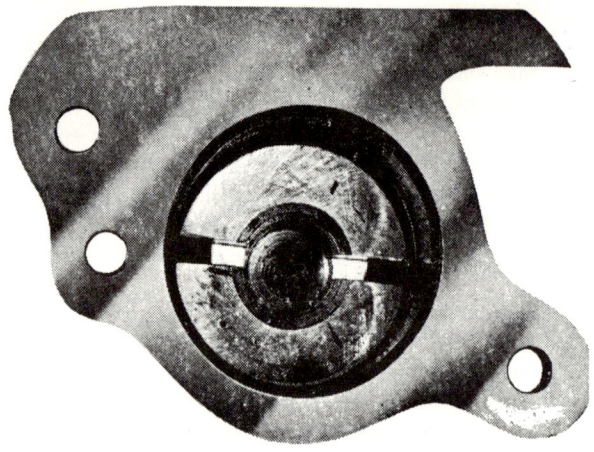

Fig. 1.19 Before replacing the distributor turn Nos. 1 & 4 piston to T.D.C. with the timing marks correctly aligned. Then insert the distributor drive shaft so the slot is in the position shown with the larger offset uppermost.

allow for the rotation of the distributor drive as its skew gear meshes with the skew gear on the camshaft, the drive should be positioned so as to take into account the anti-clockwise rotation of the shaft as it is pushed into place.

5. Remove the tappet cover bolt from the drive shaft.

6. Replace the distributor housing and lock it in position with the single bolt and lockwasher.

7. The distributor can now be replaced and the two securing bolts and spring washers which hold the distributor clamping plate to the distributor housing, tightened. If the clamp bolt on the clamping plate was not previously loosened and the distributor body was not turned in the clamping plate, then the ignition timing will be as previously. If the clamping bolt has been loosened, then it will be necessary to retime the ignition as described in Chapter 4/10.

62. FINAL ASSEMBLY

1. The rocker cover can now be fitted, using a new cork gasket. Fit the two tappet cover plates, using new gaskets, and tighten the tappet chest bolts to a torque of 2lb/ft. Do not exceed this figure or the covers will distort and leak oil. Reconnect the ancilliary components to the engine in the reverse order to which they were removed.

2. It should be noted that in all cases it is best to reassemble the engine as far as possible before refitting it to the car. This means that the inlet and exhaust manifolds, starter motor, water thermostat, oil filter, distributor, but not the carburetters or dynamo, should all be in position. Ensure that the oil filter is filled with engine oil, as otherwise there will be a delay in the oil reaching the bearings while the oil filter refills.

63. ENGINE REPLACEMENT

Although the engine can be replaced with one man and a suitable winch, it is easier if two are present. One to lower the engine into the engine compartment and the other to guide the engine into position and to ensure that it does not foul anything. Generally speaking, engine replacement is a reversal of the procedures used when removing the engine, (see Sections 6 and 7), but one or two added tips may come in useful.

1. Ensure all the loose leads, cables etc., are tucked out of the way. If not it is easy to trap one and so cause much additional work after the engine is replaced.

2. Fit the starter motor and oil filter before lowering the engine and gearbox into place.

3. After the dynamo has been replaced it is advisable to fit a new fan belt as shown. See Chapter 2/12 and 13 for further details.

4. When refitting the engine do not omit to insert the alignment plate between the mounting bracket and the mounting rubber. These plates or shims as they are sometimes known come in two thicknesses .036 in. (.91 mm.) and .048 in. (1.31 mm.). When the engine has been disturbed it may be necessary to fit a different plate. To ascertain this, loosen the nuts on the engine side of the mounting rubbers and rock the engine so it takes up its free position. Measure the gap between the engine and its mountings and then fit the necessary plates.

5. Remember to reconnect the earth strap and when replacing the engine and gearbox together make sure that the bracket for the tie bar faces the rear of the car and that the tie-rod is fitted through the bracket as the crossmember is lifted into place.

6. Finally, check that the drain taps are closed and refill the cooling system with water and the engine with the correct grade of oil. Start the engine and carefully check for oil or water leaks. There should be no oil or water leaks if the engine has been reassembled carefully, all nuts and bolts tightened down correctly, and new gaskets and joints used throughout.

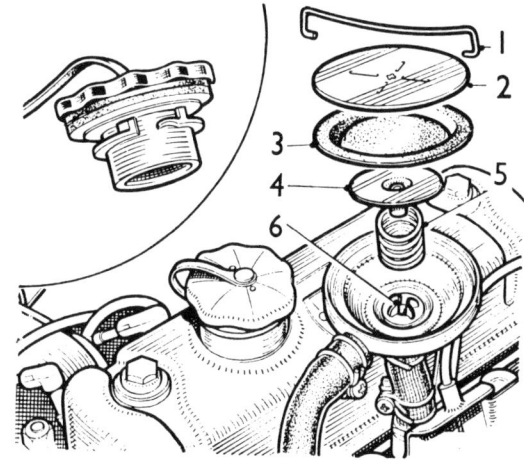

Fig. 1.20 COMPONENT PARTS OF THE CLOSED CIRCUIT BREATHING VALVE.
1 Spring clip. 2 Cover. 3 Diaphragm. 4 Metering lever.
5 Spring. 6 Cruciform guides.

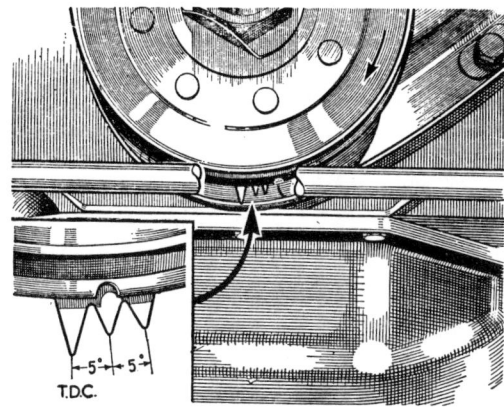

Fig. 1.21 When the small cut out in the pulley wheel periphery is in line with the longer pointer the engine is at T.D.C. Each of the smaller pointers indicate 5° advance. The inset shows the timing set at 5° B.T.D.C.

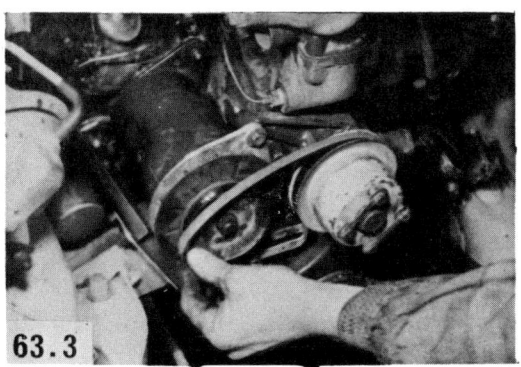

63.3

FAULT FINDING CHART

Cause	Trouble	Remedy
SYMPTOM:	ENGINE FAILS TO TURN OVER WHEN STARTER BUTTON PULLED	
No current at starter motor	Flat or defective battery	Charge or replace battery. Push-start car.
	Loose battery leads	Tighten both terminals and earth ends of earth lead.
	Defective starter solenoid or switch or broken wiring	Run a wire direct from the battery to the starter motor or by-pass the solenoid.
	Engine earth strap disconnected	Check and retighten strap.
Current at starter motor	Jammed starter motor drive pinion	Place car in gear and rock from side to side. Alternatively, free exposed square end of shaft with spanner.
	Defective starter motor	Remove and recondition.
SYMPTOM:	ENGINE TURNS OVER BUT WILL NOT START	
No spark at sparking plug	Ignition damp or wet	Wipe dry the distributor cap and ignition leads.
	Ignition leads to spark plugs loose	Check and tighten at both spark plug and distributor cap ends.
	Shorted or disconnected low tension leads	Check the wiring on the CB and SW terminals of the coil and to the distributor.
	Dirty, incorrectly set, or pitted contact breaker points	Clean, file smooth, and adjust.
	Faulty condenser	Check contact breaker points for arcing, remove and fit new.
	Defective ignition switch	By-pass switch with wire.
	Ignition leads connected wrong way round	Remove and replace leads to spark plugs in correct order.
	Faulty coil	Remove and fit new coil.
	Contact breaker point spring earthed or broken	Check spring is not touching metal part of distributor. Check insulator washers are correctly placed. Renew points if the spring is broken.
No fuel at carburettor float chamber or at jets	No petrol in petrol tank	Refill tank!
	Vapour lock in fuel line (In hot conditions or at high altitude)	Blow into petrol tank, allow engine to cool, or apply a cold wet rag to the fuel line.
	Blocked float chamber needle valve	Remove, clean, and replace.
	Fuel pump filter blocked	Remove, clean, and replace.
	Choked or blocked carburettor jets	Dismantle and clean.
	Faulty fuel pump	Remove, overhaul, and replace. Check CB points on S.U. pumps.
Excess of petrol in cylinder or carburettor flooding	Too much choke allowing too rich a mixture to wet plugs	Remove and dry sparking plugs or with wide open throttle, push-start the car.
	Float damaged or leaking or needle not seating	Remove, examine, clean and replace float and needle valve as necessary.
	Float lever incorrectly adjusted	Remove and adjust correctly.
SYMPTOM:	ENGINE STALLS & WILL NOT START	
No spark at sparking plug	Ignition failure - Sudden	Check over low and high tension circuits for breaks in wiring
	Ignition failure - Misfiring precludes total stoppage	Check contact breaker points, clean and adjust. Renew condenser if faulty.
	Ignition failure - In severe rain or after traversing water splash	Dry out ignition leads and distributor cap.
No fuel at jets	No petrol in petrol tank	Refill tank.
	Petrol tank breather choked	Remove petrol cap and clean out breather hole or pipe.
	Sudden obstruction in carburettor(s)	Check jets, filter, and needle valve in float chamber for blockage
	Water in fuel system	Drain tank and blow out fuel lines

ENGINE FAULT FINDING CHART

Cause	Trouble	Remedy
SYMPTOM:	ENGINE MISFIRES OR IDLES UNEVENLY	
Intermittent sparking at sparking plug	Ignition leads loose	Check and tighten as necessary at spark plug and distributor cap ends.
	Battery leads loose on terminals	Check and tighten terminal leads.
	Battery earth strap loose on body attachment point	Check and tighten earth lead to body attachment point.
	Engine earth lead loose	Tighten lead.
	Low tension leads to SW and CB terminals on coil loose	Check and tighten leads if found loose.
	Low tension lead from CB terminal side to distributor loose	Check and tighten if found loose.
	Dirty, or incorrectly gapped plugs	Remove, clean, and regap.
	Dirty, incorrectly set, or pitted contact breaker points	Clean, file smooth, and adjust.
	Tracking across inside of distributor cover	Remove and fit new cover.
	Ignition too retarded	Check and adjust ignition timing.
	Faulty coil	Remove and fit new coil.
Fuel shortage at engine	Mixture too weak	Check jets, float chamber needle valve, and filters for obstruction. Clean as necessary. Carburettor(s) incorrectly adjusted.
	Air leak in carburettor(s)	Remove and overhaul carburettor.
	Air leak at inlet manifold to cylinder head, or inlet manifold to carburettor	Test by pouring oil along joints. Bubbles indicate leak. Renew manifold gasket as appropriate.
Mechanical wear	Incorrect valve clearances	Adjust rocker arms to take up wear.
	Burnt out exhaust valves	Remove cylinder head and renew defective valves.
	Sticking or leaking valves	Remove cylinder head, clean, check and renew valves as necessary.
	Weak or broken valve springs	Check and renew as necessary.
	Worn valve guides or stems	Renew valve guides and valves.
	Worn pistons and piston rings	Dismantle engine, renew pistons and rings.
SYMPTOM:	LACK OF POWER & POOR COMPRESSION	
Fuel/air mixture leaking from cylinder	Burnt out exhaust valves	Remove cylinder head, renew defective valves.
	Sticking or leaking valves	Remove cylinder head, clean, check, and renew valves as necessary.
	Worn valve guides and stems	Remove cylinder head and renew valves and valve guides.
	Weak or broken valve springs	Remove cylinder head, renew defective springs.
	Blown cylinder head gasket (Accompanied by increase in noise)	Remove cylinder head and fit new gasket.
	Worn pistons and piston rings	Dismantle engine, renew pistons and rings.
	Worn or scored cylinder bores	Dismantle engine, rebore, renew pistons & rings.
Incorrect Adjustments	Ignition timing wrongly set. Too advanced or retarded	Check and reset ignition timing.
	Contact breaker points incorrectly gapped	Check and reset contact breaker points.
	Incorrect valve clearances	Check and reset rocker arm to valve stem gap.
	Incorrectly set sparking plugs	Remove, clean and regap.
	Carburation too rich or too weak	Tune carburettor(s) for optimum performance.
Carburation and ignition faults	Dirty contact breaker points	Remove, clean, and replace.
	Fuel filters blocked causing top end fuel starvation	Dismantle, inspect, clean, and replace all fuel filters.
	Distributor automatic balance weights or vacuum advance and retard mechanisms not functioning correctly	Overhaul distributor.
	Faulty fuel pump giving top end fuel starvation	Remove, overhaul, or fit exchange reconditioned fuel pump.

Cause	Trouble	Remedy
SYMPTOM:	EXCESSIVE OIL CONSUMPTION	
Oil being burnt by engine	Badly worn, perished or missing valve stem oil seals Excessively worn valve stems and valve guides Worn piston rings Worn pistons and cylinder bores Excessive piston ring gap allowing blow-by Piston oil return holes choked	Remove, fit new oil seals to valve stems. Remove cylinder head and fit new valves and valve guides. Fit oil control rings to existing pistons or purchase new pistons. Fit new pistons and rings, rebore cylinders. Fit new piston rings and set gap correctly. Decarbonise engine and pistons.
Oil being lost due to leaks	Leaking oil filter gasket Leaking rocker cover gasket Leaking tappet chest gasket Leaking timing case gasket Leaking sump gasket Loose sump plug	Inspect and fit new gasket as necessary. " " " " " " " " " " " " " " " " " " " " " " " " " " " " Tighten, fit new gasket if necessary.
SYMPTOM:	UNUSUAL NOISES FROM ENGINE	
Excessive clearances due to mechanical wear	Worn valve gear (Noisy tapping from rocker box) Worn big end bearing (Regular heavy knocking) Worn timing chain and gears (Rattling from front of engine) Worn main bearings (Rumbling and vibration) Worn crankshaft (Knocking, rumbling and vibration)	Inspect and renew rocker shaft, rocker arms, and ball pins as necessary. Drop sump, if bearings broken up clean out oil pump and oilways, fit new bearings. If bearings not broken but worn fit bearing shells. Remove timing cover, fit new timing wheels and timing chain. Drop sump, remove crankshaft, if bearings worn but not broken up, renew. If broken up strip oil pump and clean out oilways. Regrind crankshaft, fit new main and big end bearings.

CHAPTER TWO

COOLING SYSTEM

CONTENTS

SPECIFICATIONS

Type of System	Pressurised. Pump impeller and fan assisted
Thermostat Setting - Standard	64°C (147°F) early cars
Thermostat Setting - Cold Climates	82°C (180°F) all cars with single S.U.
Thermostat Setting - Standard	70°C (158°F) later cars with single S.U.
Thermostat Setting - Standard	82°C (180°F) later cars with twin S.U's
Thermostat Setting - Cold Climates	88°C (190°F) later cars with twin S.U's
Cooling System capacity - Early models	11½ pints (13.8 U.S. pints 6.5 litres)
Later models	9½ pints (11.4 U.S. pints 5.4 litres)
Pressure cap opens	7 lb. (3.175 kg.)
Tension of Fan Belt	½ in. (12.8 mm.) movement midway between dynamo and water pump pulley wheels
Type of Water Pump	Centrifugal
Water Pump drive	Belt from crankshaft pulley

1. GENERAL DESCRIPTION

The engine cooling water is circulated by a thermo-siphon, water pump assisted system, and the coolant is pressurised. This is to both prevent the loss of water down the overflow pipe with the radiator cap in position and to prevent premature boiling in adverse conditions.

The radiator cap is pressurised to 7lb/sq. in. and increases the boiling point to 225°F. If the water temperature exceeds this figure and the water boils, the pressure in the system forces the internal part of the cap off its seat, thus exposing the overflow pipe down which the steam from the boiling water escapes thus re-

lieving the pressure.

It is, therefore, important to check that the radiator cap is in good condition and that the spring behind the sealing washer has not weakened. Most garages have a special machine in which radiator caps can be tested.

The cooling system comprises the radiator, top and bottom water hoses, heater hoses (if heater/demister fitted), the impeller water pump, (mounted on the front of the engine it carries the fan blades and is driven by the fan belt), the thermostat and the two drain taps.

The system functions in the following fashion. Cold water in the bottom of the radiator circulates up the l o w e r radiator hose to the water pump where it is pushed round the water passages in the cylinder block, helping to keep the cylinder bores and pistons cool.

The water then travels up into the cylinder head and circulates round the combustion spaces and valve seats absorbing more heat, and then, when the engine is at its proper operating temperature, travels out of the cylinder head, past the open thermostat into the upper radiator hose and so into the radiator header tank.

The water travels down the radiator where it is rapidly cooled by the in-rush of cold air through the radiator core, which is created by both the fan and the motion of the car. The water, now cold, reaches the b o t t o m of the radiator, when the cycle is repeated.

When the e n g i n e is cold the thermostat (which is a valve which opens and closes according to the temperature of the water) maintains the circulation of the same water in the engine.

Only when the correct minimum operating temperature has been reached, as shown in the specification, does the thermostat begin to open, allowing water to return to the radiator.

2. ROUTINE MAINTENANCE

1. Check the level of the water in the radiator once a week or more frequently if necessary, and top up with a soft water (rain water is excellent) as required.

2. Once every 6,000 miles check the fan belt for wear and correct tension and renew or adjust the belt as necessary. (See Sections 12 and 13 for details).

3. Once every 12,000 miles unscrew the plug from the top of the water pump and press in by hand a little grease. Do not overgrease or the seal may be rendered inoperative. Replace the plug and screw down.

3. COOLING SYSTEM - DRAINING

1. With the car on level g r o u n d drain the system as follows:-

2. If the engine is cold remove the filler cap from the radiator by turning the cap anti-clockwise. If the engine is hot having just been run, then turn the filler cap very slightly until the pressure in the system has had time to disperse. Use a rag over the cap to protect your hand from escaping steam. If, with the engine very hot, the cap is released suddenly, the drop in pressure can result in the water boiling. With the pressure released the cap can be removed.

3. If anti-freeze is in the radiator drain it into a clean bucket or bowl for re-use.

4. Open the two drain taps. When viewed from the front the radiator drain tap is on the botto

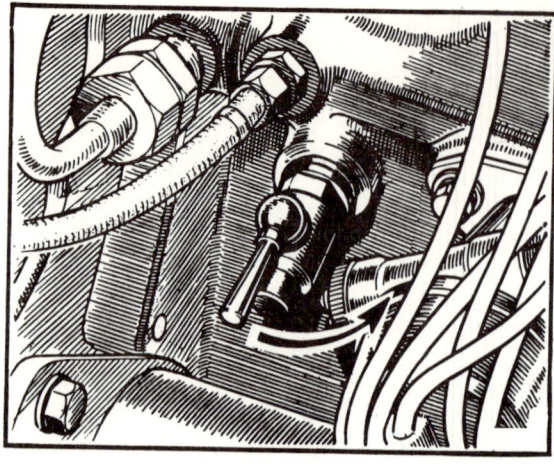

Fig. 2.1 The drain tap for the cylinder block is adjacent to the distributor on the right hand side of the engine.

right-hand side of the radiator, and the engine drain tap is halfway down the rear left-hand side of the cylinder block. A short length of rubber tubing over the radiator drain tap nozzle will assist draining the coolant into a container without splashing.

5. When the water has finished running, probe the drain tap orifices with a short piece of wire to dislodge any particles of rust or sediment which may be blocking the taps and preventing all the water draining out.

4. COOLING SYSTEM - FLUSHING

1. With time the cooling system will gradually lose its e f f i c i e n c y as the radiator becomes c h o k e d with rust scales, deposits from the water and other sediment. To clean the system out, remove the radiator cap and the drain tap and leave a hose running in the radiator cap orifice for ten to fifteen minutes.

Fig. 2.2 The radiator drain tap is on the bottom left hand side of the radiator as shown.

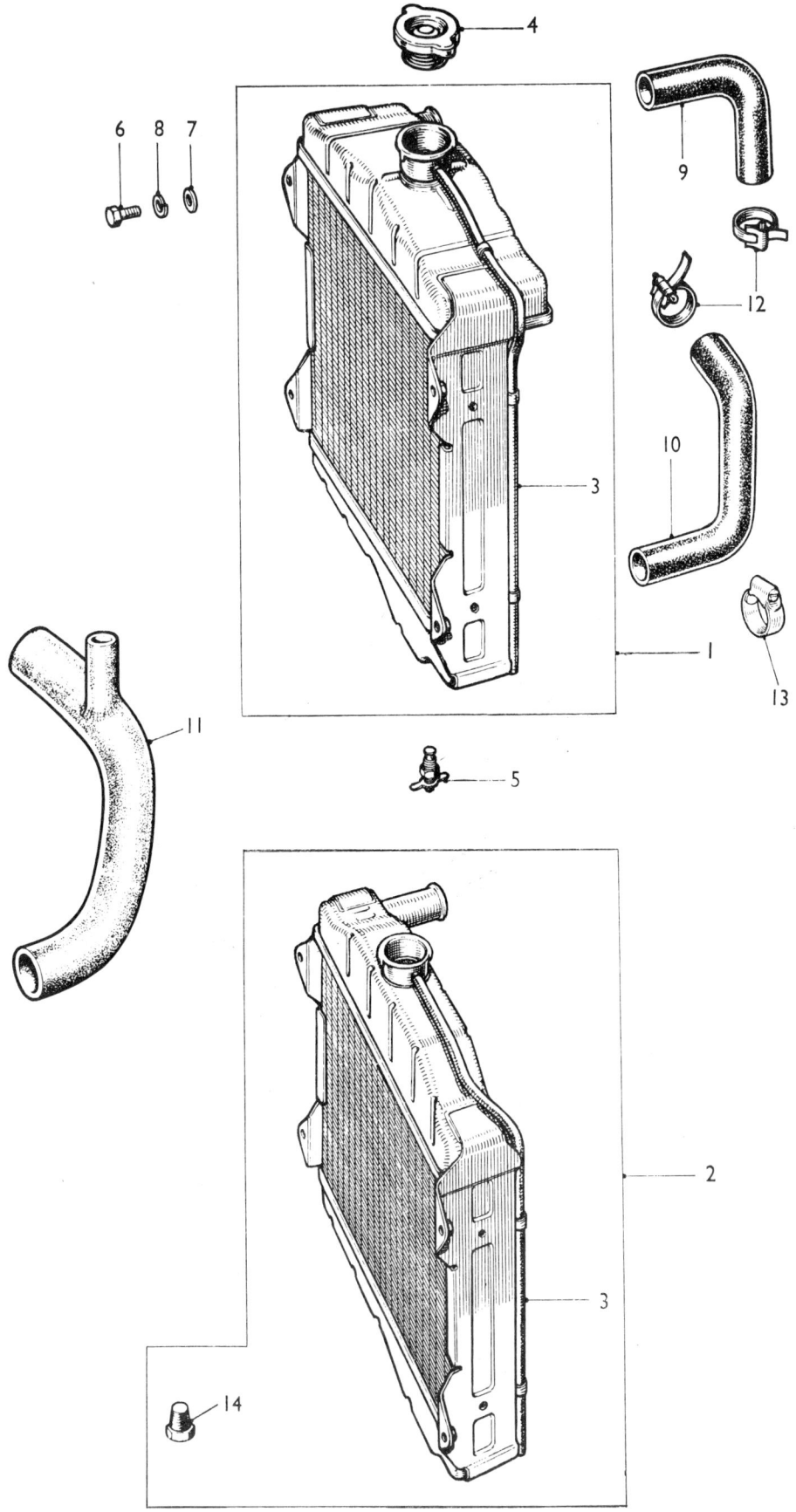

Fig. 2.3 COMPONENT PARTS OF BOTH TYPES OF RADIATOR AND HOSES.

1 Early type radiator. 2 Later type radiator. 3 Overflow pipe. 4 Radiator cap. 5 Drain tap. 6 Screw. 7 Plain washer.
8 Spring washer. 9 Top hose. 10 Bottom hose. 11 Alternative bottom hose used when heater/demister fitted. 12 Hose clip.
13 Jubilee hose clip. 14 Drain plug.

2. In very bad cases the radiator should be reverse flushed. This can be done with the radiator in position. The cylinder block tap is closed and a hose placed over the open radiator drain tap. Water, under pressure, is then forced up through the radiator and out of the header tank filler orifice.

3. The hose is then removed and placed in the filler orifice and the radiator washed out in the usual fashion.

5. COOLING SYSTEM - FILLING

1. Close the two drain taps.

2. Fill the system slowly to ensure that no air locks develop. If a heater is fitted, check that the valve to the heater unit is open, otherwise an air lock may form in the heater. The best type of water to use in the cooling system is rain water, so use this whenever possible.

3. Do not fill the system higher than within ½ in. of the filler orifice. Overfilling will merely result in wastage, which is especially to be avoided when anti-freeze is in use.

4. Only use anti-freeze mixture with a glycerine or ethylene base.

5. Replace the filler cap and turn it firmly clockwise to lock it in position.

6. RADIATOR REMOVAL, INSPECTION, CLEANING & REPLACEMENT

1. To remove the radiator first drain the cooling system as described in Section 2.

2. Then undo the jubilee clip which holds the top water hose to the thermostat pipe outlet.

3. Pull the top water hose off the thermostat elbow, and then undo the jubilee clip on the bottom hose and pull the end of the hose off the radiator.

4. Undo and remove the four bolts, spring and flat washers (two on either side of the radiator) which hold the radiator core in place.

5. Lift the radiator up out of the engine compartment.

6. With the radiator out of the car any leaks can be soldered up or repaired with a substance such as 'cataloy'. Clean out the inside of the radiator by flushing as detailed in the section before last. When the radiator is out of the car it is advantageous to turn it upside down for reverse flushing. Clean the exterior of the radiator by hosing down the radiator matrix with a strong jet of water to clear away road dirt, dead flies, etc.

7. Inspect the radiator hoses for cracks, internal or external perishing, and damage caused by overtightening of the securing clips. Replace the hoses as necessary. Examine the radiator hose securing clips and renew them if

they are rusted or distorted. The drain taps should be renewed if leaking, but ensure the leak is not because of a faulty washer behind the tap. If the tap is suspected try a new washer to see if this clears the trouble first.

8. Replacement is a straightforward reversal of the removal procedure.

7. THERMOSTAT REMOVAL, TESTING & REPLACEMENT

1. To remove the thermostat partially drain the cooling system (4 pints is enough), loosen the upper radiator hose at the thermostat elbow end and pull it off the elbow.

2. Unscrew the three set bolts and spring washers from the thermostat housing and lift the housing and paper gasket away. Take out the thermostat.

3. Test the thermostat for correct functioning by immersing it in a saucepan of cold water together with a thermometer.

4. Heat the water and note when the thermostat begins to open. The standard setting is 82°C, but in cold weather the thermostat should not open till 88°C.

5. Discard the thermostat if it opens too early Continue heating the water until the thermostat is fully open. Then let it cool down naturally. If the thermostat will not open fully in boiling water, or does not close down as the water cools, then it must be exchanged for a new one.

6. If the thermostat is stuck open when cold this will be apparent when removing it from the housing.

7. Replacing the thermostat is a reversal of the removal procedure. Remember to use a

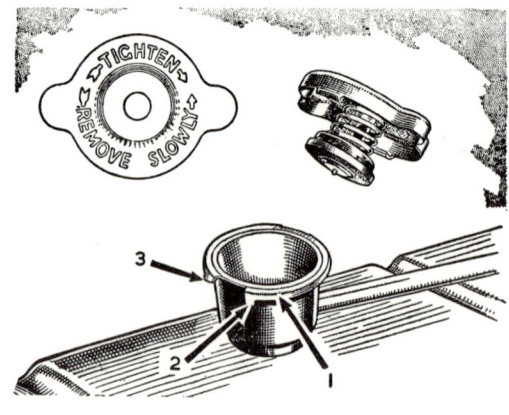

Fig. 2.3A. 1 Filler cap retaining cam. 2 Stop. 3 Safety catch

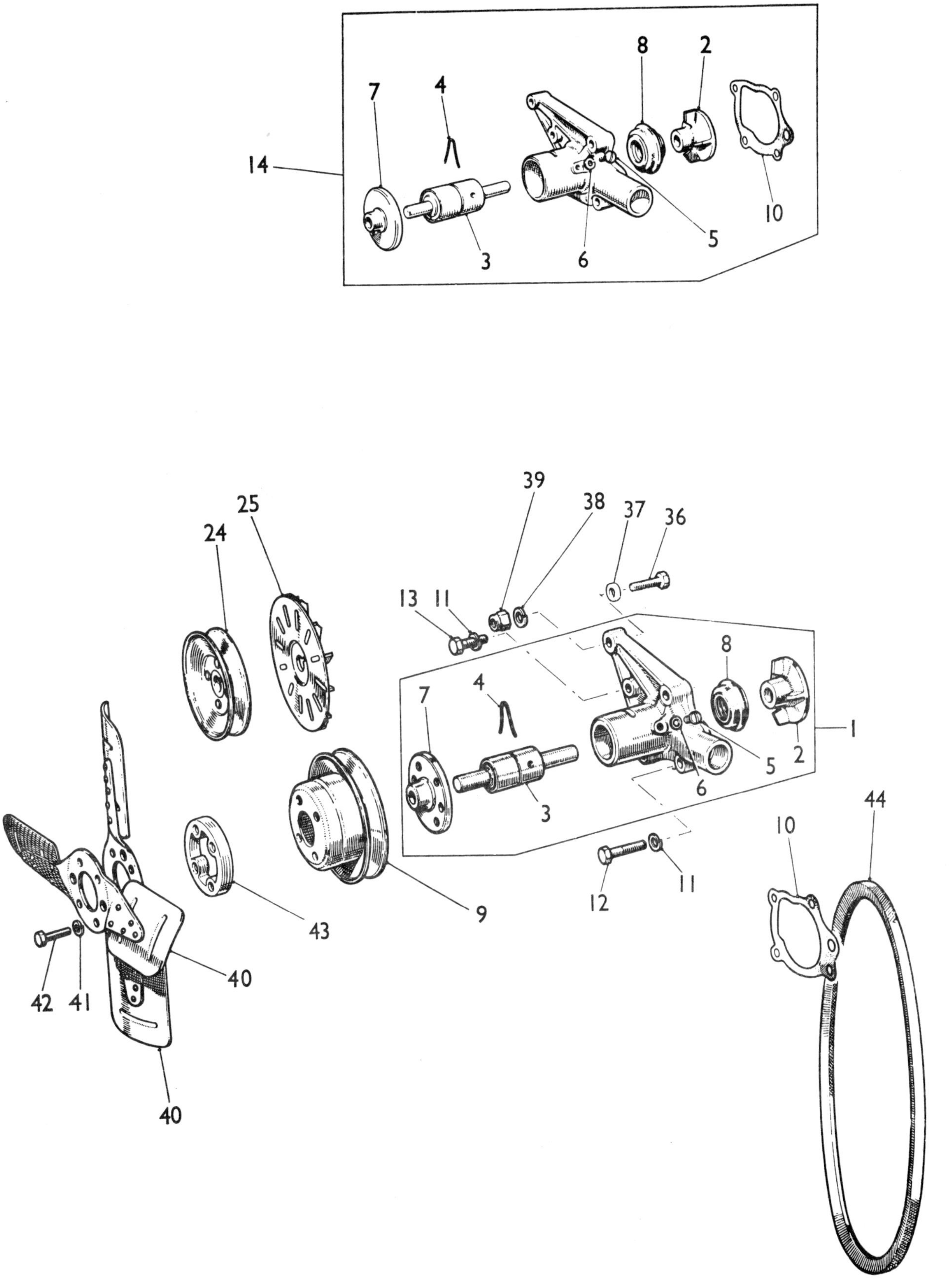

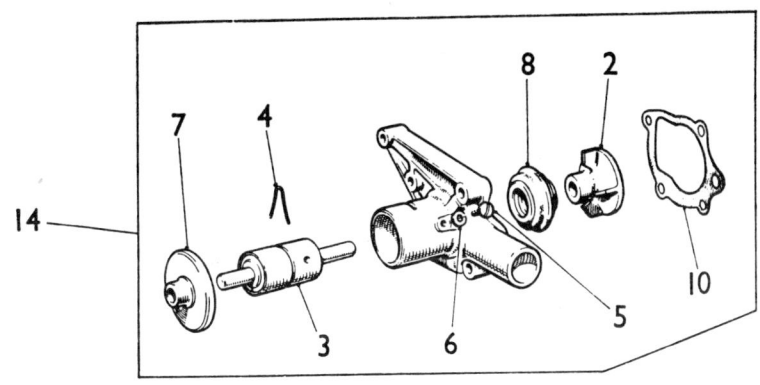

Fig. 2.4 EXPLODED VIEW OF THE WATER PUMP, PULLEY AND ASSOCIATED PARTS.

1 Water pump assembly. 2 Vane. 3 Bearing and spindle. 4 Locating wire. 5 Screw. 6 Fibre washer. 7 Pulley. 8 Seal.
9 Fan and water pump belt pulley. 10 Gasket. 11 Spring washer. 12 Bolt. 13 Bolt. 14 Water pump repair kit—component parts.
(Not pump body). 36 Bolt. 37 Plain washer. 38 Spring washer. 39 Locknut. 44 Fan belt.

new paper gasket between the thermostat housing elbow and the thermostat. Renew the thermostat elbow if it is badly eaten away.

8. WATER PUMP - REMOVAL & REPLACEMENT

1. Partially drain the cooling system as described in section 2 and then remove the radiator as described in Section 6.
2. Remove the dynamo as described in 10/8.
3. All numbers in brackets refer to Fig. 2.4. Undo the four bolts and spring washers (12, 11, 13, 11,) which hold the pump body (1) to the front of the cylinder block. Lift the combined fan and water pump away from the engine and remove the gasket (10).
4. Replacement is a straightforward reversal of the removal sequence. Note that the fan belt tension must be correct when all is reassembled. If the belt is too tight undue strain will be placed on the water pump and dynamo bearings, and if the belt is too loose it will slip and wear rapidly as well as giving rise to low electrical output from the dynamo.

9. WATER PUMP - DISMANTLING & REASSEMBLY

1. Remove the four bolts and spring washers which hold the fan blades and fan pulley in place. With these removed, pull or tap off the hub from the end of the spindle, taking great care not to damage it.
2. Then pull out the bearing retaining wire.
3. The spindle and bearing assembly are combined (and are only supplied on exchange as a complete unit), and should now be gently tapped out of the rear of the water pump.
4. The oil seal assembly and the impeller will also come out with the spindle and bearing assembly.

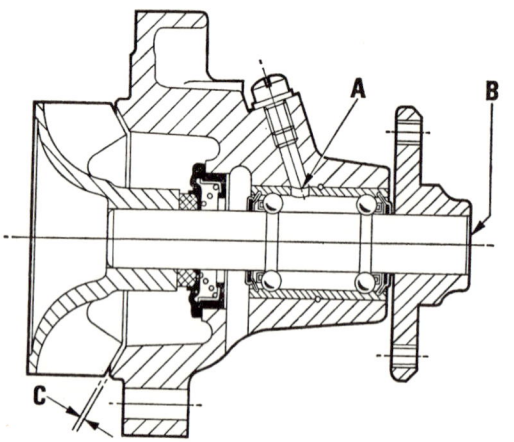

Fig. 2.5 Ensure the hole in the bearing 'A' aligns with the lubricating hole in the pump body. The end of the spindle should be flush with the face of the hub 'B'.

5. The impeller vane is removed from the spindle by judicious tapping and levering, or preferably, to ensure no damage and for ease of operation, with an extractor. The oil seal assembly can then be slipped off.

Reassembly of the water pump is a reversal of the above sequence. Three points should be noted which have not already been covered:-

a) If the oil seal assembly shows any sign of damage or wear it should be renewed, and the gasket between the water pump and the cylinder block should be renewed every time the pump is removed.

b) There is a small hole in the bearing body cover. When assembled it is vital that this hole lines up with the lubrication hole in the pump body. To check that this is so, prior to reassembly remove the greasing screw and check visually that the hole is in the correct position directly below the greasing aperture.

c) Regrease the bearing by pushing a small amount of grease into the greaser and then screwing in the greasing screw. Under no circumstances should grease be applied under pressure as it could ruin the efficiency of the oil seal.

10. ANTI-FREEZE MIXTURE

1. In circumstances where it is likely that the temperature will drop to below freezing it is essential that some of the water is drained and an adequate amount of ethylene glycol antifreeze such as Bluecol added to the cooling system.
2. If Bluecol is not available any antifreeze which conforms with specification B.S. 3151 or B.S. 3152 can be used. Never use an antifreeze with an alcohol base as evaporation is too high.
3. Bluecol anti-freeze with an anti-corrosion additive can be left in the cooling system for up to two years, but after six months it is advisable to have the specific gravity of the coolant checked at your local garage, and thereafter once every three months.
4. Listed below are the amounts of Bluecol which should be added to ensure adequate protection down to the temperature given.

Amount of A.F.	Protection to
2½ pints (1.4 litres)	-13°C (9°F)
3½ pints (2.0 litres)	-19°C (-2°F)
5 pints (2.8 litres)	-36°C (-33°F)

11. TEMPERATURE GAUGE - REMOVAL & REPLACEMENT

1. The temperature gauge comprises a thermal indicator, a wire protected pipe filled with mercury and a dial type of temperature gauge.
2. The gauge is held to the instrument panel

by a small bracket behind the dial body and this bracket must be released if it is wished to remove the gauge. The thermal indicator is secured to the radiator header tank with a gland nut. If the gauge ceases to function it is necessary to renew the complete assembly as a unit.

12 FAN BELT ADJUSTMENT

1. It is important to keep the fan belt correctly adjusted and although not listed by the manufacturer, it is considered that this should be a regular maintenance task performed every 6,000 miles.

2. If the belt is too loose it will slip, wear rapidly, and cause the dynamo and water pump to mal-function. If the belt is too tight the dynamo and water pump bearings will wear rapidly causing premature failure of these components.

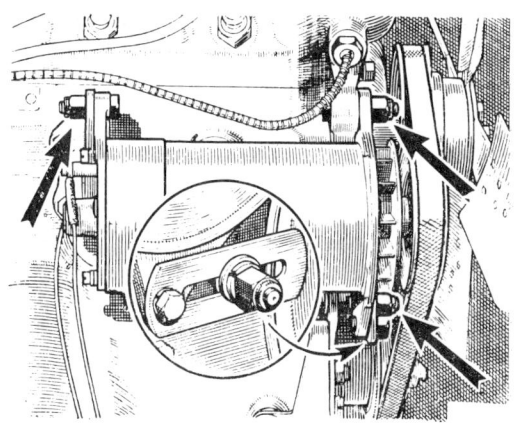

Fig. 2.6 The three bolts which must be loosened before the fan belt can be correctly tensioned.

3. The fan belt tension is correct when there is ½ in. of lateral movement at the midpoint position of the belt between the dynamo pulley wheel and the water pump pulley wheel.

4. To adjust the fan belt, slacken the dynamo securing bolts and move the dynamo either in or out until the correct tension is obtained. It is easier if the dynamo bolts are only slackened a little so it requires some force to move the dynamo. In this way the tension of the belt can be arrived at more quickly than by making frequent adjustments.

5. If difficulty is experienced in moving the dynamo away from the engine a long spanner placed behind the dynamo and resting against the block serves as a very good lever and can be held in this position while the dynamo bolts are tightened.

13. FAN BELT - REMOVAL & REPLACEMENT

1. If the fan belt is worn or has stretched unduly it should be replaced. The most usual reason for replacement is that the belt has broken in service. It is therefore recommended that a spare belt is always carried. Replacement is a reversal of the removal sequence, but as replacement due to breakage is the most usual operation, it is described below.

2. Loosen the two dynamo pivot bolts and the nut on the adjusting link and push the dynamo in towards the engine.

3. Slip the belt over the crankshaft, dynamo, and water pump pulleys.

4. Adjust the belt as described in the previous section and tighten the dynamo mounting nuts. NOTE After fitting a new belt it will require adjustment 250 miles later.

FAULT FINDING CHART

Cause	Trouble	Remedy
SYMPTOM:	OVERHEATING	
Heat generated in cylinder not being successfully disposed of by radiator	Insufficient water in cooling system	Top up radiator
	Fan belt slipping (Accompanied by a shrieking noise on rapid engine acceleration	Tighten fan belt to recommended tension or replace if worn.
	Radiator core blocked or radiator grill restricted	Reverse flush radiator, remove obstructions.
	Bottom water hose collapsed, impeding flow	Remove and fit new hose.
	Thermostat not opening properly	Remove and fit new thermostat.
	Ignition advance and retard incorrectly set (Accompanied by loss of power, and perhaps, misfiring)	Check and reset ignition timing.
	Carburettor(s) incorrectly adjusted (mixture too weak)	Tune carburettor(s).
	Exhaust system partially blocked	Check exhaust pipe for constrictive dents and blockages.
	Oil level in sump too low	Top up sump to full mark on dipstick.
	Blown cylinder head gasket (Water/steam being forced down the radiator overflow pipe under pressure)	Remove cylinder head, fit new gasket.
	Engine not yet run-in	Run-in slowly and carefully.
	Brakes binding	Check and adjust brakes if necessary.
SYMPTOM:	UNDERHEATING	
Too much heat being dispersed by radiator	Thermostat jammed open	Remove and renew thermostat.
	Incorrect grade of thermostat fitted allowing premature opening of valve	Remove and replace with new thermostat which opens at a higher temperature.
	Thermostat missing	Check and fit correct thermostat.
SYMPTOM	LOSS OF COOLING WATER	
Leaks in system	Loose clips on water hoses	Check and tighten clips if necessary.
	Top, bottom, or by-pass water hoses perished and leaking	Check and replace any faulty hoses.
	Radiator core leaking	Remove radiator and repair.
	Thermostat gasket leaking	Inspect and renew gasket.
	Radiator pressure cap spring worn or seal ineffective	Renew radiator pressure cap.
	Blown cylinder head gasket (Pressure in system forcing water/steam down overflow pipe	Remove cylinder head and fit new gasket.
	Cylinder wall or head cracked	Dismantle engine, dispatch to engineering works for repair.

CHAPTER THREE

FUEL SYSTEM AND CARBURATION

CONTENTS

SPECIFICATIONS

Carburetters

	S.U. HS2	S.U. HD4
Austin A55 MkII and A60 1489 & 1622 c.c. ...	Single S.U. HS2 semi down-draught	
Riley 4/68, 4/72 1489 & 1622 c.c....	Twin S.U. HD4 semi down-draught	
Individual specifications	S.U. HS2	S.U. HD4
Choke diameter	1$\frac{1}{4}$ in. (31.75 mm.)	1$\frac{1}{2}$ in. (38.10 mm.)
Jet size	.090 in. (2.29 mm.)	.090 in. (2.29 mm.)
Standard Needle (1489 c.c. models)	M	FU
Standard Needle with AUC 978 & AUC 979 carbs	GY	--
Rich Needle (1489 c.c. models)	AH2	FT
Weak Needle (1489 c.c. models)	EB	M9
Piston spring (1489 c.c. models)	Red	Red
Standard Needle (1622 c.c. models)	GX	HB
Rich Needle (1622 c.c. models)	M	FU
Weak Needle (1622 c.c. models)	GG	FK
Piston spring (1622 c.c. models)	Yellow	Red

Fuel Pump

Make & type 1489 c.c. models ...	Either S.U. electric PD or SP	
Individual specifications	PD	SP
Minimum delivery rate	45 pints/hr. (25.5 litres/hr.)	56 pints/hr. (31.8 litres/hr.).
Delivery pressure	2 to 3 lb/sq. in.	2 to 3.8 lb/sq. in.
Make & type 1622 c.c. models ...	Either S.U. electric SP or AUF 204	
Individual specifications	SP	AUF 200
Minimum delivery rate	56 pints/hr. (31.8 litres/hr.)	56 pints/hr. (31.8 litres/hr.).
Delivery pressure	2 to 3.8 lb/sq. in.	2 to 3.8 lb/sq. in.

Air Cleaner

All 1489 c.c. models	Oil bath air cleaner/silencer
All 1622 c.c. models	A.C. Delco or Tecalemit paper element type

Tank Capacity

All models 1489 & 1622 c.c.	10 gallons (12 U.S. gals. 45.4 litres).

1. GENERAL DESCRIPTION

The fuel system consists of a 10 gallon fuel tank mounted in the front of the boot (under the boot floor panel in Traveller/Countryman versions), either an S.U. PD, SP or AUF204 electric fuel pump mounted on the left-hand side of the boot (under a hinged flap at the rear of the boot in the Traveller/Countryman; either single or twin S.U. carburetters and the necessary fuel lines between the tank, pump and carburetter.

Early air cleaners were of the oil bath type which could be cleaned at specified intervals and the original element replaced Later cleaners make use of a disposable paper element and are easier to service.

2. ROUTINE MAINTENANCE

1. Once every 3,000 miles undo the hexagon caps on the dashpot/s and top them up to within 1/2 in. of the top with Castrolite or a similar S.A.E. 20 oil as shown under 'recommended lubricants' on page 12. Renew the oil in the oil bath type of air cleaner.
2. Once every 6,000 miles adjust the carburetter slow running and tune the carburetter/s if necessary. See section 15 for further details. Check the fuel lines and the union joints for leaks or weeping and replace defective washers as required.
3. Also every 6,000 miles renew the paper airfilter element/s and thoroughly clean the interior of the air cleaners. Remove the float chamber/s from the carburetter/s, empty away any sediment, check the condition of the needle valve, clean and reassemble. Remove and clean the filter/s in the carburetters and fuel pump where these are fitted.

3. AIR CLEANERS - REMOVAL, REPLACEMENT & MAINTENANCE

1. At intervals of 3,000 miles clean out the oil bath type of air cleaner and refill with fresh oil. At intervals of 6,000 miles clean out the dry type air cleaner and fit a new paper element.
2. To clean and service the oil bath type air cleaner follow the instructions given in sub. paras. 3 to 7. The instructions for the dry type air cleaner are given in sub. para. 8.
3. Referring to Fig. 3.2 slacken the clip (22) and free the breather pipe from the air cleaner body. Unscrew the clip (20 or 9A) which holds the air cleaner to the carburetter air cleaner manifold (19A or 14). Lift the complete air cleaner off at the same time moving it sideways to disengage the stud (8) from its rubber bush (11) and locating hole in the top of the steady bracket (10).
4. Undo the wing nut (4) (on later models a wing bolt is fitted) and lift off the top cover and element (2). Lift out the oil container (7), empty away the old oil, and scrape off the sludge in the bottom of the container (dust and dirt in the atmosphere trapped by the oil).
5. Thoroughly wash and clean the filter element and oil container in paraffin, and dry with an air line if available. Check the condition of the rubber gasket (3) and replace it if necessary.
6. Fill the container to the marked line with Castrolite or a similar 10W/30 oil, refit the element and top cover, and tighten the wing nut/bolt not omitting the washer (5).
7. There is no need to oil the element mesh before refitment as the inrush of air in through the oil will carry the latter up into the mesh. 50
8. On dry type air cleaners first obtain a new AC Delco or Tecalemit filter - they are not interchangeable, then free the breather pipe from the cleaner body by undoing the clip; undo the two bolts which hold the cleaner body to the carburetter air intake and the single bolt which holds the cleaner body against the steady stays, and pull off the air cleaner body to expose the

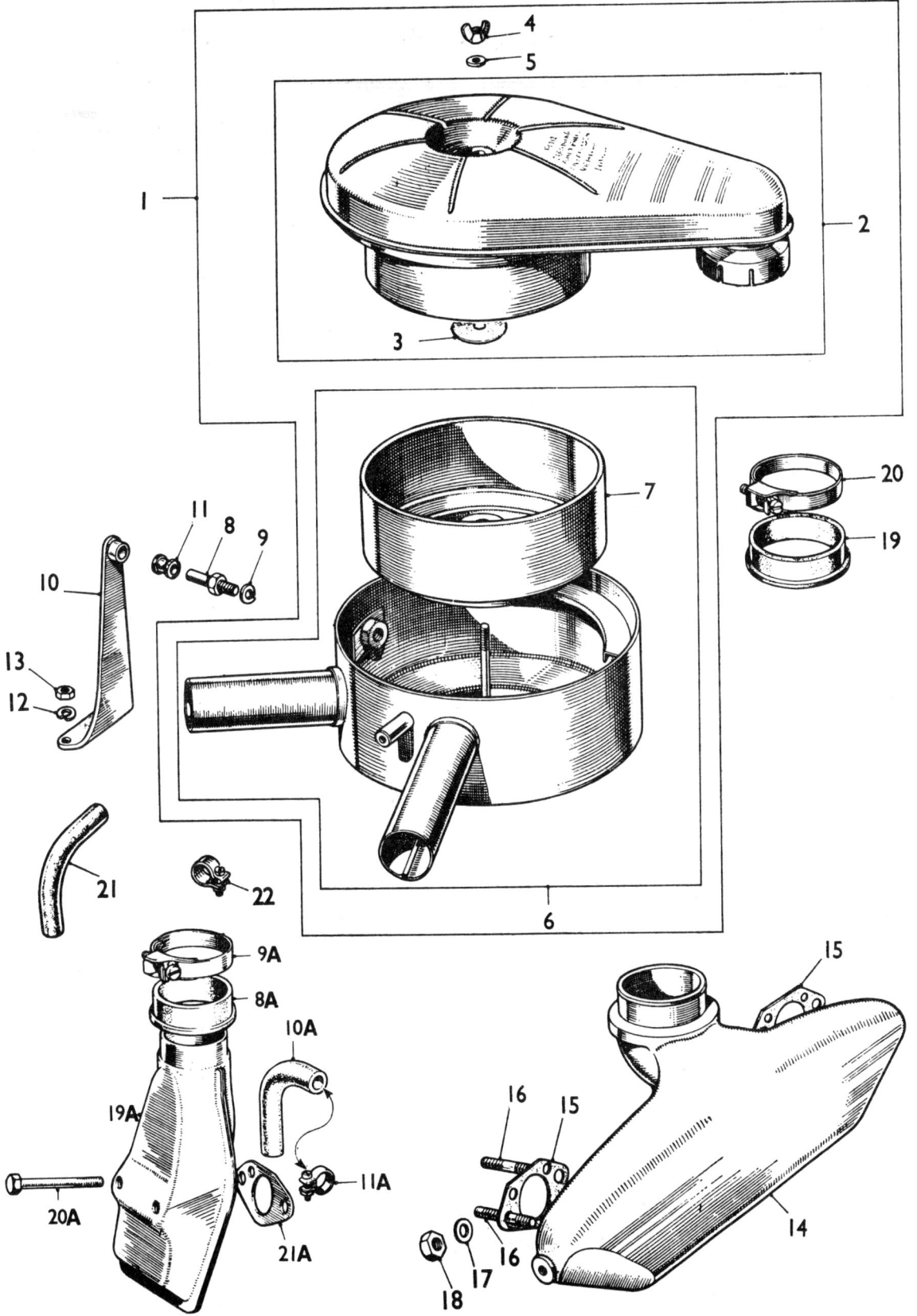

Fig. 3.1 EXPLODED VIEW OF THE OIL BATH TYPE OF AIR CLEANER/SILENCER

1 Complete oil bath air cleaner. 2 Element & elbow. 3 Rubber gasket. 4 Wing nut. 5 Washer. 6 Silencer assembly. 7 Oil container. 8 Cleaner to bracket locating stud. 9 Spring washer. 10 Steady bracket. 11 Rubber bush. 12 Spring washer. 13 Nut. 14 Air manifold (twin S. U's). 15 Gasket. 16 Stud. 17 Plain washer. 18 Nut. 19 Rubber grommet. 20 Clip. 21 Rubber air cleaner to rocker cover pipe. 22 Clip. 8A Rubber insulator. 9A Clip. 10A Rubber air cleaner to rocker cover pipe. 11A Clip. 19A Air cleaner to carburetter pipe (Single S. U. models) 20A Fixing bolt. 21A Pipe to carburetter gasket.

paper element and the base plate. Thoroughly clean out all traces of dust and reassemble, using a new paper element.

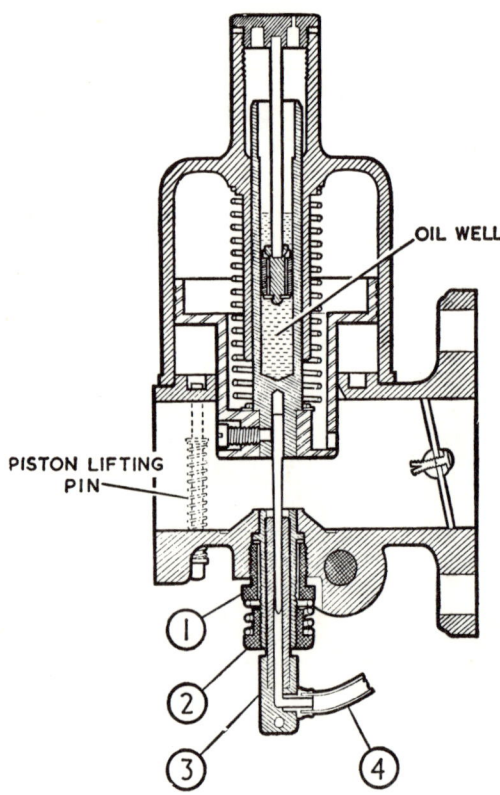

Fig. 3.3 SECTION VIEW OF THE HD4 CARBURETTER.
1 Jet locking nut. 2 Jet adjusting nut. 3 Jet head. 4 Feed tube from float chamber.

4   S.U. CARBURETTERS - DESCRIPTION

The variable choke S.U. carburetter is a relatively simple instrument and is basically the same irrespective of its size and type. It differs from most other carburetters in that instead of having a number of various sized fixed jets for different conditions, only one variable jet is fitted to deal with all possible conditions.

Air passing rapidly through the carburetter choke draws petrol from the jet so forming the petrol/air mixture, The amount of petrol drawn from the jet depends on the position of the tapered carburetter needle, which moves up and down the jet orifice according to engine load and throttle opening, thus effectively altering the size of the jet so that exactly the right amount of fuel is metered for the prevailing road conditions.

The position of the tapered needle in the jet is determined by engine vacuum. The shank of the needle is held at its top end in a piston which

slides up and down the dashpot in response to the degree of manifold vacuum. This is directly controlled by the position of the throttle.

With the throttle fully open, the full effect of inlet manifold vacuum is felt by the piston which has an air bleed into the choke tube on the outside of the throttle. This causes the piston to rise fully, bringing the needle with it. With the accelerator partially closed only slight inlet manifold vacuum is felt by the piston (although, of course, on the engine side of the throttle the vacuum is now greater), and the piston only rises a little, blocking most of the jet orifice with the metering needle.

To prevent the piston fluttering, and to give a richer mixture when the accelerator is suddenly depressed, an oil damper and light spring are fitted inside the dashpot.

The only portion of the piston assembly to come into contact with the piston chamber or dashpot is the actual central piston rod. All the other parts of the piston assembly, including the lower choke portion, have sufficient clearances to prevent any direct metal to metal contact which is essential if the carburetter is to work properly.

The correct level of the petrol in the carburetter is determined by the level of the float in the float chamber. When the level is correct the float rises and by means of a lever resting on top if it closes the needle valve in the cover of the float chamber. This closes off the supply of fuel from the pump. When the level in the float chamber drops as fuel is used in the carburetter the float sinks. As it does, the float needle comes away from its seat so allowing more fuel to enter the float chamber and restore the correct level.

5.   S.U. CARBURETTER/S - REMOVAL & REPLACEMENT

1. The photographs in this section are of the removal of the twin carburetter installation. NOTE that removal of the single S.U. is virtually identical, but that all connections are on the one instrument. Undo the clip which secures the breather pipe to the air cleaner and remove the air cleaner/s as described in section 3.

2. Undo the nut from the top of the float chamber/s to free the overflow pipe/s or pull off the rubber overflow pipe from the top of the float chamber.

3. Bend back the two halves of the split pin (arrowed) from the choke operating lever and pull the split pin out.

4. The choke return spring and pin can now be freed from the choke operating lever and tucked back out of the way.

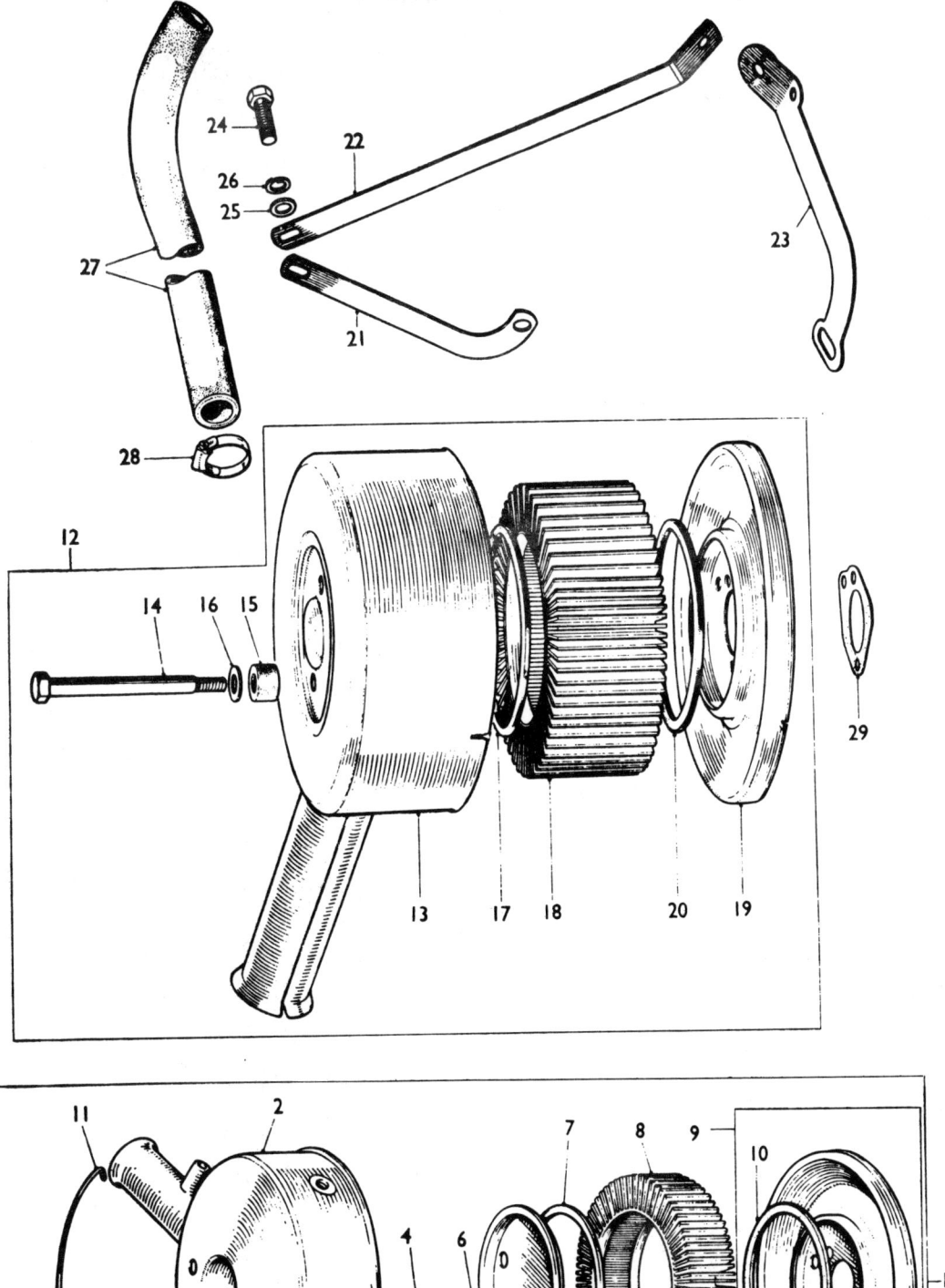

Fig. 3.3 EXPLODED VIEW OF THE PAPER ELEMENT TYPE OF AIR CLEANER/SILENCER

1. AC Delco air cleaner/silencer assembly. 2 Cover assembly. 3 Bolt. 4 Spring. 5 Seal. 6 Washer. 7 Rubber gasket. 8 Paper element. 9 Bottom plate assembly. 10 Rubber gasket. 11 Spring clip. 12 Alternative air cleaner/silencer. 13 Cover. 14 Bolt. 15 Seal. 16 Washer. 17 Rubber gasket. 18 Paper element. 19 Bottom plate assembly. 20 Rubber gasket. 21 Air cleaner steady **stay (front).** 22 Air cleaner steady stay (rear). 23 Stay. 24 Screw. 25 Plain washer. 26 Spring washer. 27 Rubber breather tube. 28 Clip. 29 Air cleaner to carburetter gasket.

5. To free the accelerator inner cable simply undo the nut which locks the cable in place on the pin in the actuating arm and then push the cable out of the pin as shown in the photograph.

6. With a small Phillips screwdriver undo the two clips from each end of the fuel pipe 'T' piece and pull off the fuel pipe hoses

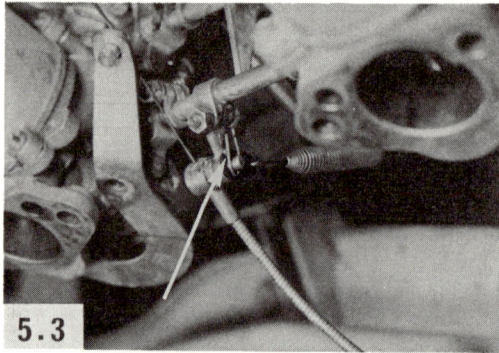

7. Disconnect the throttle return springs (see photograph).

8. Carefully pull off the rubber connection for the vacuum ignition control pipe from the top of the rear carburetter body as shown.

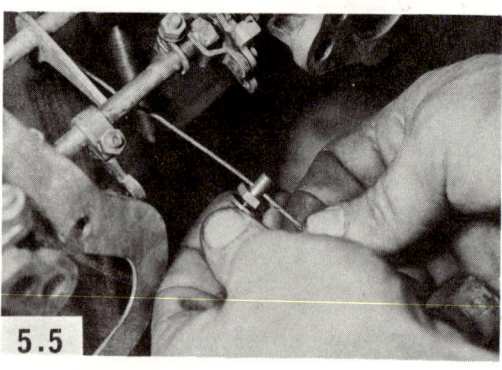

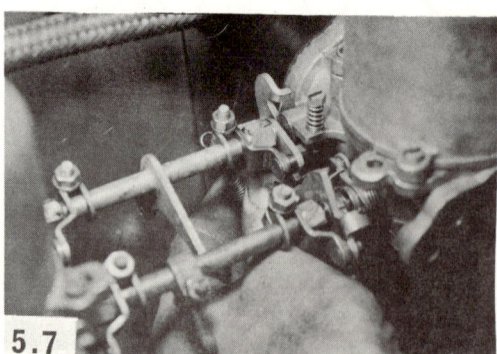

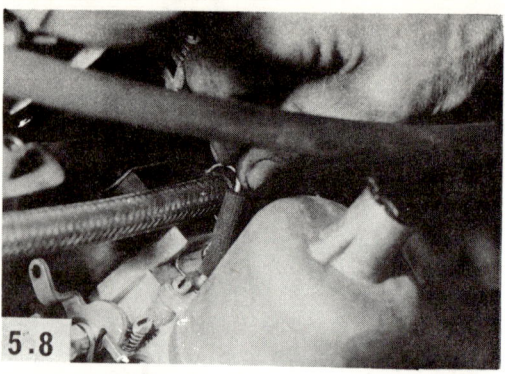

9. Undo the four nuts which hold the carburetter flanges to the studs which pass through the plastic composition blocks. Shown is the top front nut being removed.

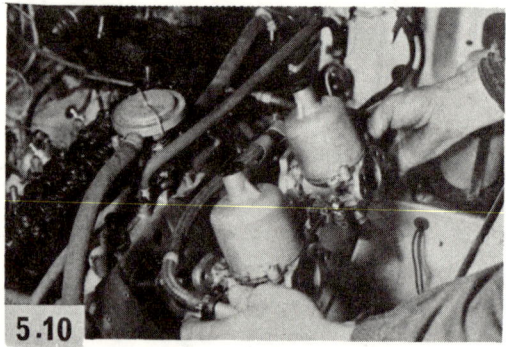

10. Carefully lift the twin carburetters off the engine together as shown.

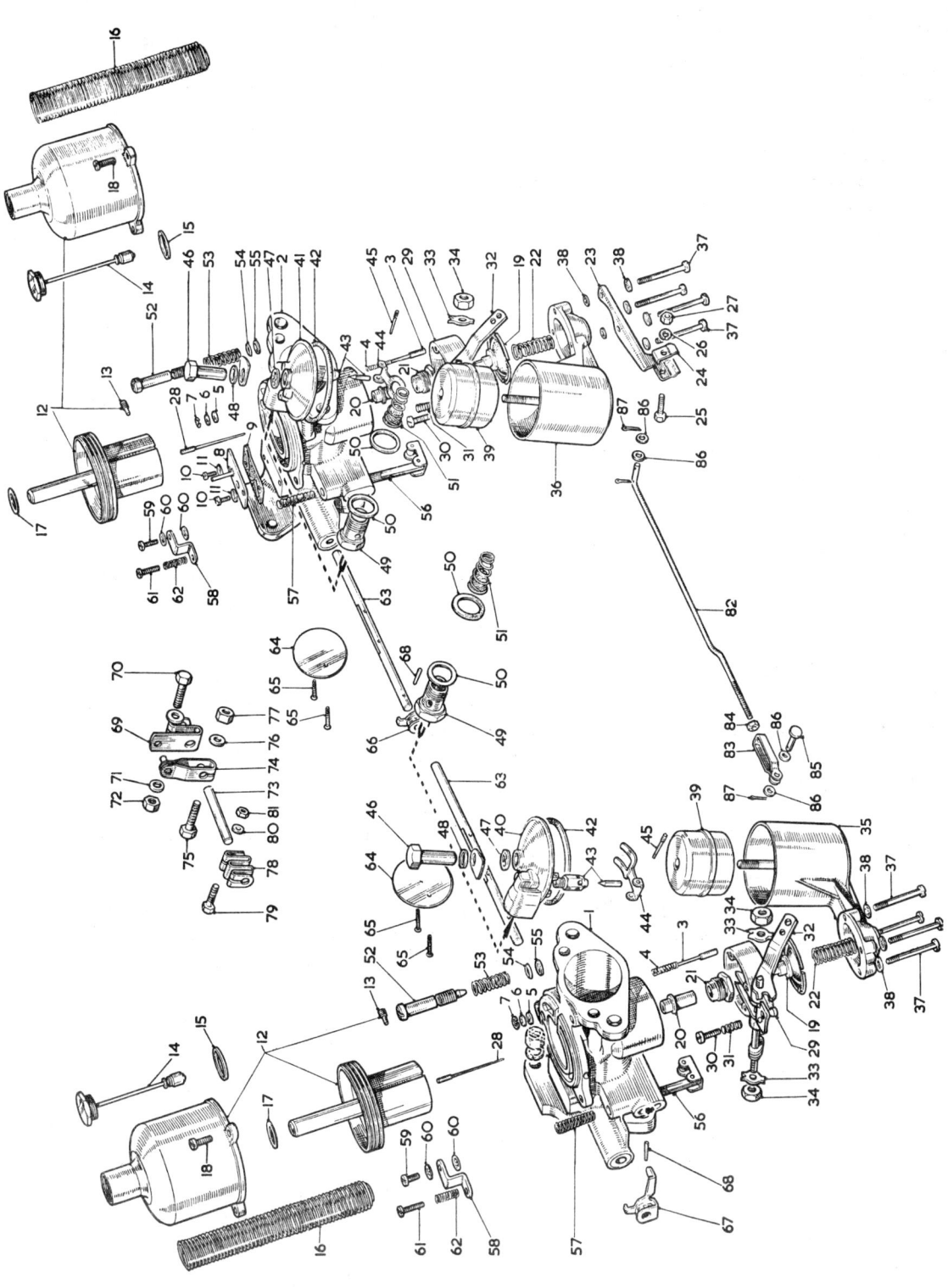

Fig. 3.4 EXPLODED VIEW OF THE TWIN S.U. CARBURETTERS FITTED TO HIGHER POWERED MODELS

1 Body assembly—front carburetter. 2 Body assembly—rear carburetter. 3 Pin—piston lifting. 4 Spring for lifting pin. 5 Washer (neoprene). 6 Washer (brass). 7 Circlip. 8 Adaptor assembly. 9 Gasket—adaptor to body. 10 Screw—adaptor to body. 11 Washer for screw. 12 Chamber and piston assembly. 13 Screw—needle locking. 14 Cap and damper assembly. 15 Washer for cap. 16 Spring—piston (red). 17 Washer (skid). 18 Screw. 19 Jet assembly. 20 Bearing—jet. 21 Screw—jet locking. 22 Spring—jet. 23 Bracket—anchor. 24 Clip. 25 Bolt. 26 Washer. 27 Nut. 28 Needle—jet. 29 Housing assembly—jet. 30 Screw—stop. 31 Spring—screw. 32 Lever—jet control. 33 Washer—shakeproof. 34 Nut—washer. 35 Chamber—float (front). 36 Chamber—float (rear). 37 Bolt—chamber fixing. 38 Washer for bolt. 39 Float. 40 Lid—float-chamber (front). 41 Lid—float-chamber (rear). 42 Washer for lid. 43 Needle and seat assembly. 44 Lever—hinged. 45 Pin—hinged lever. 46 Cap nut. 47 Washer—nut (fibre). 48 Washer—nut (aluminium). 49 Bolt—banjo. 50 Washer—banjo bolt. 51 Filter. 52 Valve—slow-running. 53 Spring-gland. 54 Washer (dished). 55 Gland (neoprene). 56 Cam shoe and rod assembly. 57 Spring—rod. 58 Plate—top. 59 Screw—plate retaining. 60 Shakeproof washer—screw. 61 Lever—coupling. 63 Spring—screw. 63 Spindle—throttle. 64 Disc—throttle. 65 Screw—disc to spindle. 66 Stop (rear carburetter). 67 Stop (front carburetter). 68 Pin—taper. 69 Lever—coupling. 70 Bolt. lever. 71 Plain washer—bolt. 72 Nut—bolt. 73 Rod—throttle connecting. 74 Lever—throttle. 75 Bolt—lever. 76 Plain washer—bolt. 77 Nut—bolt. 78 Coupling—bolt. 79 Bolt—coupling. 80 Washer—bolt. 81 Nut—bolt. 82 Rod—jet connecting. 83 Fork—rod. 84 Nut—rod. 85 Pin—link-fork. 86 Washer—plain. 87 Pin—split.

69

11.   With the carburetters removed take off the two gaskets as shown.

5.12

12   Then take off the two plastic composition blocks which act as distance pieces. (See photograph).

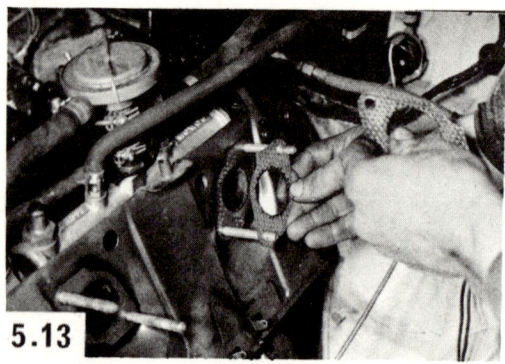

5.13

13.   Under the distance pieces are two further gaskets. Remove these as shown and put on one side pending replacement.

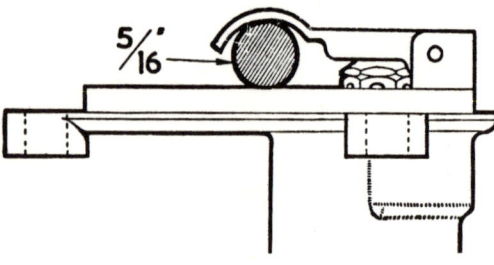

Fig. 3.5.   The method of setting the correct clearance of the float lever on early carburetter

14.   Finally pull off the heat shield.
15.   Note that behind the heat shield on the inlet manifold flanges are fitted two further gaskets.
16.   To replace the carburetters reverse the above procedure using new gaskets throughout. Ensure that the centre throttle return spring end eye is located between the throttle lever and the flat washer.

6.   S.U CARBURETTERS - DISMANTLING
      The S. U. carburetter with only two normally

5.15

moving parts - the throttle valve and the piston assembly - makes it a straightforward instrument to service, but at the same time it is a delicate unit and clumsy handling can cause much damage. In particular it is easy to knock the finely tapering needle out of true, and the greatest care snould be taken to keep all the parts associated with the dashpot scrupulously clean.
1.   Remove the oil dashpot plunger nut from the top of the dashpot.
2.   Unscrew the set screws holding the dashpot to the carburetter body, and lift away the dashpot, light spring, and piston and needle assembly.
3.   To remove the metering needle from the choke portion of the piston unscrew the sunken retaining screw from the side of the piston choke and pull out the needle. When replacing the needle ensure that the shoulder is flush with the underside of the piston.
4.   Release the float chamber from the carburetter by releasing the clamping bolt and sealing washers from the side of the carburetter base.
5.   Normally, it is not necessary to dismantle the carburetter further, but if because of wear or for some other reason it is wished to remove the jet, this is easily accomplished by removing the clevis pin holding the jet operating lever to the jet head, and then just removing the jet by extracting it from the base of the carburetter. The jet adjusting screw can then be unscrewed together with the jet adjusting screw locking spring.
6.   If the larger locking screw above the jet adjusting screw is removed, then the jet will have to be recentred when the carburetter is reassembled. With the jet screws removed it is a simple matter to release the jet bearing.
7.   To remove the throttle and actuating spindle release the two screws holding the throttle in position in the slot in the spindle, slide the throttle out of the spindle and then remove the spindle.

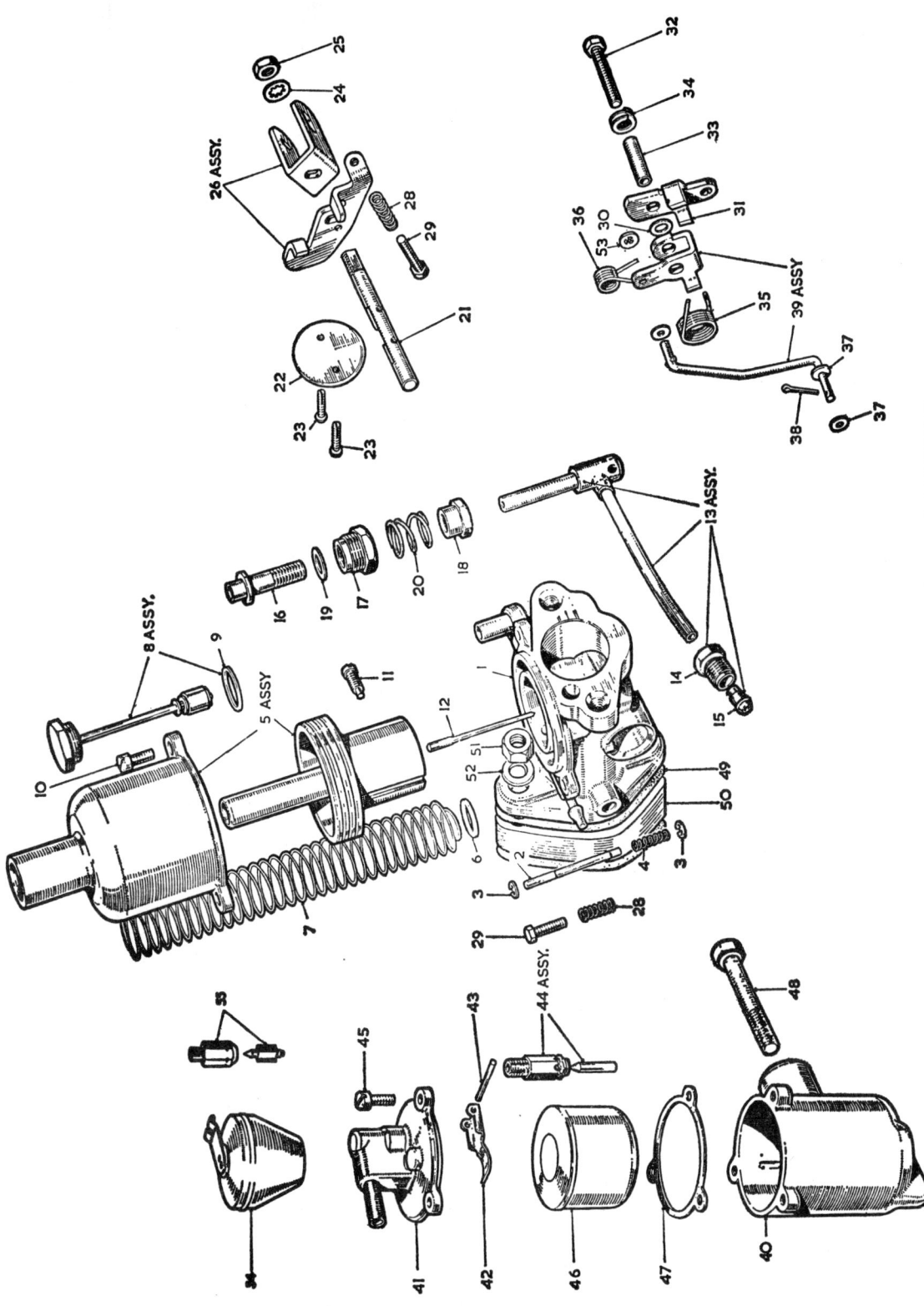

Fig. 3.6 EXPLODED VIEW OF THE SINGLE S.U. HS2 CARBURETTER

1 Body assembly. 2 Pin—piston lift. 3 Circlip. 4 Spring. 5 Chamber and piston assembly. 6 Washer—thrust. 7 Spring—piston (red). 8 Damper assembly—piston. 9 Washer for damper. 10 Screw—chamber to body. 11 Screw—needle locking. 12 Needle—jet. 13 Jet assembly. 14 Gland nut. 15 Nipple. 16 Bearing—jet. 17 Screw—jet. 18 Screw—jet adjusting. 19 Washer for jet bearing (brass). 20 Spring—jet adjusting. 21 Spindle—throttle. 22 Disc—throttle. 23 Screw for throttle. 24 Washer for spindle nut. 25 Nut for throttle spindle. 26 Lever assembly—throttle. 28 Spring—throttle stop screw. 29 Screw—lever stop. 30 Washer for cam lever. 31 Lever—cam. 32 Bolt—pivot. 33 Tube—pivot bolt. 34 Washer. 35 Spring—return. 36 Spring—return—cam lever. 37 Washer. 38 Pin—split. 39 Lever and rod assembly. 40 Chamber—float. 41 Lid assembly. 42 Lever—hinged. 43 Pin—hinged lever. 44 Needle and seat assembly. 45 Screw—lid to chamber. 46 Float. 47 Gasket—lid to chamber. 48 Bolt—chamber to body. 49 Joint washer. 50 Distance piece. 51 Nut for stud. 52 Washer. 53 Washer. 54 Float assembly (nylon). 55 Needle and seat assembly (later type).

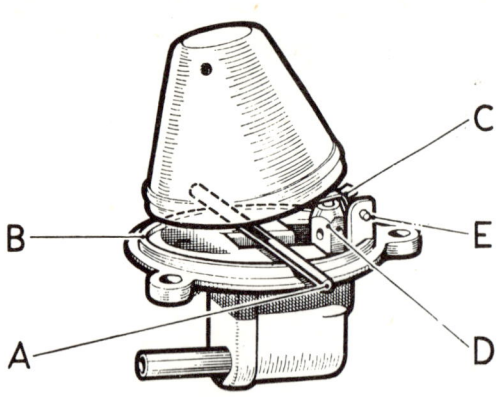

Fig. 3.7 THE COMPONENTS INVOLVED WHEN SETTING THE
NYLON FLOAT LEVEL.
A $\frac{1}{8}$ to $\frac{3}{16}$ in. (3.18 to 4.76 mm.) diameter bar. B. Machined
lip. C. Float lever resetting point. D. Needle valve assembly.
E. Hinge pin.

8.   Reassembly is a straightforward reversal of the dismantling procedure. It will be necessary to centre the jet. How to do this correctly is described in section 14.

7.   **S U. CARBURETTER FLOAT CHAMBER DISMANTLING, EXAMINATION & REASSEMBLY**
1.   To dismantle the float chamber, first disconnect the inlet pipe from the fuel pump at the top of the float chamber cover, if this has not already been done.
2.   Undo the three screws which hold the float chamber cover in position, and lift off the cover.
3.   If it is not wished to remove the float chamber completely and the carburetter is still attached to the engine, carefully insert a thin piece of bent wire under the float and lift the float out.
4.   To remove the float chamber from the carburetter body undo the bolt which runs horizontally through the carburetter.
5.   Make a careful note of the rubber grommets and washers and on reassembly ensure they are replaced in the correct order. If the float chamber is removed completely it is a simple matter to turn it upside down to drop the float out. Check that the float is not cracked or leaking. If it is, it must be repaired or renewed.
6.   The float chamber cover contains the needle valve assembly which regulates the amount of fuel which is fed into the float chamber.
7.   One end of the float lever rests on top of the float, rising and falling with it, while the other end pivots on a hinge pin which is held by two lugs. On the float cover side of the float lever is a needle which rises and falls in its brass seating according to the movement of the lever.

8.   With the cover in place the hinge pin is held in position by the walls of the float chamber. With the cover removed the pin is easily pushed out so freeing the float lever and the needle.
9.   Examine the tip of the needle and the needle seating for wear. Wear is present when there is a discernible ridge in the chamfer of the needle. If this is evident then the needle and seating must be renewed. This is a simple operation and the hexagon head of the needle housing is easily screwed out.
10.   Never renew either the needle or the seating without renewing the other part as otherwise it will not be possible to get a fuel tight joint.
11.   Clean the fuel chamber out thoroughly. Reassembly is a reversal of the dismantling procedure detailed above. Before replacing the float chamber cover, check that fuel level setting is correct.

8.   **S. U. CARBURETTER FLOAT CHAMBER FUEL LEVEL ADJUSTMENT**
1.   It is essential that the fuel level in the float chamber is always correct as otherwise excessive fuel consumption may occur. On reassembly of the float chamber check the fuel level before replacing the float chamber cover, in the following manner:-
2.   Invert the float chamber so that the needle valve is closed. It should now be just possible to place an $\frac{1}{8}$ in. (3.18 mm.) or $\frac{5}{16}$ in. diameter bar across the middle diameter of the machined float chamber lip parallel to the float lever hinge, so the face of the float lever just rests on the bar, when the float needle is held fully on its seating.
3.   If the bar lifts the lever or if the lever stands proud of the bar then it is necessary to bend the lever at the bifurcation point between the shank and the curved portion until the clearance is correct. Never bend the flat portion of the lever.

9.   **S. U. CARBURETTER EXAMINATION & REPAIR**
    The S.U. carburetter generally speaking is most reliable, but even so it may develop one of several faults which may not be readily apparent unless a careful inspection is carried out. The common faults the carburetter is prone to are:-
1.   Piston sticking.
2.   Float needle sticking.
3.   Float chamber flooding.
4.   Water and dirt in the carburetter.
    In addition the following parts are susceptible to wear after long mileages and as they vitally affect the economy of the engine should

be checked and renewed, w h e r e necessary, every 24,000 miles.

a) The Carburetter Needle. If this has been incorrectly assembled at some time so that it is not centrally located in the jet orifice, then the metering needle will have a tiny ridge worn on it. If a ridge can be seen then the needle must be renewed. S.U carburetter needles are made to very fine tolerances and should a ridge be apparent no attempt should be made to rub the needle down with fine emery paper. If it is wished to clean the needle it can be polished lightly with metal polish.

b) The Carburetter Jet. If the needle is worn it is likely that the rim of the jet will be damaged where the needle has been striking it. It should be renewed as otherwise fuel consumption will suffer. The jet can also be badly worn or ridged on the outside from where it has been sliding up and down between the jet bearings everytime the choke has been pulled out. Removal and renewal is the only answer here as well.

c) Check the edges of the throttle and the choke tube for wear. Renew if worn.

d) The washers fitted to the base of the jet, to the float chamber, and to the petrol inlet union may all leak after a time and can cause much fuel wastage. It is wisest to renew them automatically when the carburetter is stripped down.

e) After high mileages the float chamber needle and seat are bound to be ridged. They are not an expensive item to replace and should be renewed as a set. They should never be renewed separately.

10. S U CARBURETTERS - PISTON STICKING

1. The hardened piston rod which slides in the centre guide tube in the middle of the dashpot is the only part of the piston assembly (which comprises the jet needle, suction disc, and piston choke) that should make contact with the dashpot.

2. The piston rim and the choke periphery are machined to very fine tolerances so that they will not touch the dashpot or the choke tube walls.

3. After high mileages wear in the centre guide tube (especially on semi-downdraught S.U.s) may allow the piston to touch the dashpot wall. This condition is known as sticking.

4. If piston sticking is suspected or it is wished to test for this condition, rotate the piston about the centre guide tube at the same time sliding it up and down inside the dashpot.

5. If any portion of the piston makes contact with the dashpot wall then that portion of the wall must be polished with metal polish until clearance exists. In extreme cases, fine emery cloth can be used.

6. The greatest care should be taken to remove only the minimum amount of metal to provide the clearance, as too large a gap will cause air leakage and will upset the functioning of the carburetter.

7. Clean down the walls of the dashpot and the piston rim and ensure that there is no oil on them. A trace of oil may be judiciously applied to the piston rod.

8. If the piston is sticking under no circumstances try to clear it by trying to alter the tension of the light return spring.

11. S U CARBURETTERS - FLOAT NEEDLE STICKING

1. If the float needle sticks the carburetter will soon run dry and the engine will stop despite there being fuel in the tank.

2. The easiest way to check a suspected sticking float needle is to remove the inlet pipe at the carburetter, and turn on the ignition.

3. If fuel s p u r t s from the end of the pipe (direct it towards the ground or into a wad of cloth or jar), then the fault is almost certain to be a sticking float needle.

4. Remove the float chamber and dismantle the valve as detailed on page 72 and clean the housing and float chamber out thoroughly.

12. S.U. CARBURETTERS - FLOAT CHAMBER FLOODING

If fuel emerges from the small breather hole in the cover of the float chamber this condition is known as flooding. It is caused by the float chamber needle not seating properly in its housing; normally because a piece of dirt or foreign matter has become jammed between the needle and the needle housing. Alternatively the float may have developed a leak or be maladjusted so that it is holding o p e n the float chamber needle valve even though the chamber is full of petrol. Remove the float chamber cover, clean the needle assembly, check the setting of the float, and shake the float to verify if any petrol has leaked into it.

13. S.U. CARBURETTERS - WATER & DIRT IN CARBURETTER

1. Because of the size of the jet orifice, water or dirt in the carburetter is normally easily cleared.

2. If dirt in the carburetter is suspected lift the piston assembly and flood the float chamber. The normal level of fuel should be about $\frac{1}{16}$ in. below the top of the jet and on flooding the carburetter the fuel should well up out of the jet hole.

3. If very little or no petrol appears, start the engine (the jet is never completely blocked)

and with the throttle fully open, blank off the air intake. This will create a partial vacuum in the choke tube and help to suck out any foreign matter from the jet tube. Release the throttle as soon as the engine starts to race. Repeat this procedure several times, stop the engine, and then check the carburetter as detailed in the first paragraph

4.   If this has failed to do the trick then there is no alternative but to remove and blow out the jet.

14.   S.U. CARBURETTERS   JET CENTRING

1.   Remove the union holding the nylon feed tube to the base of the jet, together with the jet adjusting nut securing spring, after removing the link between the jet head and lever.

2.   Replace the jet and nylon feed tube and press them up under the head of the large hexagonal jet locking nut. Unscrew this nut slightly until the jet bearing can be turned.

3.   Remove the damper securing nut and damper from the top of the dashpot and push the piston assembly right down so that the metering needle enters fully into the jet.

4.   Tighten the jet locking nut and test the piston assembly to check that the needle is still quite free to slide in the jet orifice. On lifting the piston and then releasing it the piston should hit the inside jet bridge with a soft metallic click, and the intensity of the click should be the same whether the jet is in its normal position or is fully lowered.

5.   If the sound is different when the jet is fully lowered then the jet is not yet properly centralised and the process must be repeated.

15.   S.U. CARBURETTER - ADJUSTMENT & TUNING

1.   To adjust and tune the S.U. carburetter proceed in the following manner:- Check the colour of the exhaust at idling speed with the choke fully in.

2.   If the exhaust tends to be black, and the tailpipe interior is also black it is a fair indication that the mixture is too rich.

3.   If the exhaust is colourless and the deposit in the exhaust pipe is a very light grey it is likely that the mixture is too weak.

4.   This condition may also be accompanied by intermittent misfiring, while too rich a mixture will be associated with 'hunting'. Ideally the exhaust should be colourless with a medium grey pipe deposit.

5.   Once the engine has reached its normal operating temperature, disconnect the carburetters so each can be worked independently by slackening the nut on the folded metal clamp on the interconnecting shaft.

6.   Only two adjustments are provided on the S.U. carburetter. Idling speed is governed by the throttle adjusting screw, and the mixture strength by the jet adjusting screw. The S.U. carburetter is correctly adjusted for the whole of its engine revolution range when the idling mixture strength is correct.

7.   Idling speed adjustment is effected by the idling adjusting screw. To adjust the mixture set the engine to run at about 1,000 r.p.m. by screwing in the idling screw. Repeat this procedure for each instrument in turn.

8.   Check the mixture strength by lifting the piston of the carburetter approximately $\frac{1}{32}$ in. (8mm.) with a thin wire spoke or small screwdriver so as to disturb the airflow as little as possible, when if:

a)   the speed of the engine increases appreciably the mixture is too rich.

b)   the engine speed immediately decreases the mixture is too weak.

c)   the engine speed increases very slightly the mixture is correct.

9.   To enrich the mixture rotate the adjusting screw, which is the screw at the bottom of the

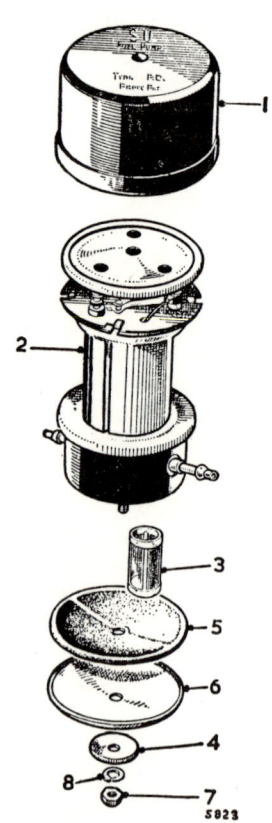

Fig. 3.8 EXPLODED VIEW OF THE PD PUMP
1 Top cover. 2 Pump body. 3 Filter. 4 Dished washer. 5 Cork gasket. 6 Cover-plate. 7 Nut. 8 Spring washer.

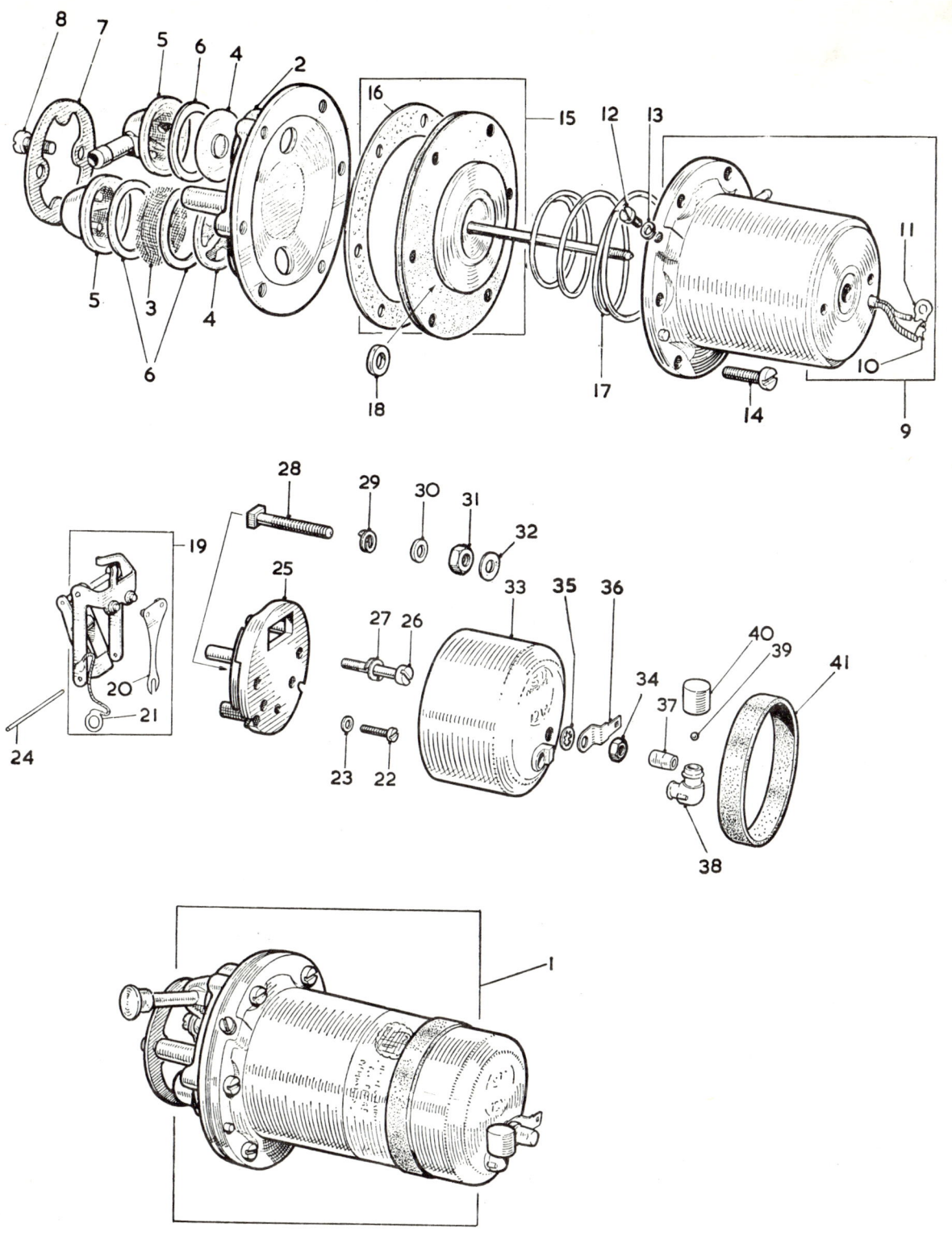

Fig. 3.9. EXPLODED VIEW OF THE A.U.F. TYPE FUEL PUMP

1 Pump assembly	9 Coil housing	17 Armature spring
2 Pump body	10 5 B.A. terminal tag	18 Roller
3 Filter	11 2 B.A. terminal tag	19 Rocker & blade
4 Valves	12 Earth screw	assembly
5 Inlet and outlet	13 Spring washer	20 Blade
nozzles	14 Screw	21 Tag terminal 2 B.A.
6 Sealing washer	15 Diaphragm	22 Blade screw
7 Clamp plate	16 Diaphragm sealing	23 Dished washer
8 Plate screw	washer	24 Contact breaker spindle

25 Pedestal	34 Cover nut
26 Screw	35 Shakeproof washer
27 Spring washer	36 Lucar connector
28 Terminal screw	37 Insulating sleeve
29 Spring washer	38 Ventilator valve
30 Lead washer	39 Valve ball
31 Recessed nut	40 Sealing ring
32 Washer	
33 End cover	

carburetter, in an anti-clockwise direction, i.e. downwards. To weaken the mixture rotate the jet adjusting screw in a clockwise direction, i.e. upwards. Only turn the adjusting screw a flat at a time and check the mixture strength between each turn. It is likely that there will be a slight increase or decrease in r.p.m. after the mixture adjustment has been made so the throttle idling adjusting screw should now be turned so that the engine idles at between 600 and 700 r.p.m.

16. **SYNCHRONISATION OF TWIN S U. CARB-URETTERS**

1. First ensure that the mixture is correct in each instrument. With twin S.U. carburetters, in addition to the mixture strength being correct for each instrument, the idling suction must be equal on both. It is best to use a vacuum synchronising device such as the Motor Meter synchro-tester. If this is not available, it is possible to obtain fairly accurate synchronisation by listening to the hiss made by the air flow into the intake throats of each carburetter.

2. The aim is to adjust the throttle butterfly disc so that an equal amount of air enters each carburetter. Loosen the screw on the folded clamp which connects the two throttle disc spindles. Listen to the hiss from each carburetter and if a difference in intensity is noticed between them, then unscrew the throttle adjusting screw on the other carburetter until the hiss from both the carburetters are the same.

3. With vacuum synchronisation device all that it is necessary to do is to place the instrument over the mouth of each carburetter in turn and adjust the adjusting screws until the reading on the gauge is identical for both carburetters.

4. Tighten the screw on the folded clamp to connect the throttle disc of the two carburetters together, at the same time holding down the throttle adjusting screws against their idling stops. Synchronisation of the two carburetters is now complete.

17. **S.U. FUEL PUMPS - DESCRIPTION**

1. The PD pump is fitted to pre-1962 models and the SP and AUF 204 to later models. The PD pump is unusual in that the diaphragm is operated by light mineral oil which is displaced by a metal plunger. The main part of the pump is therefore sealed, and the pump cannot be completely dismantled for repair.

2. The main portion comprises an oil filled brass tube which also contains a steel plunger with an insulated distance piece, a permanent magnet with two pole pieces and a coil spring. Each end of the tube is hermetically sealed by a diaphragm.

3. With the ignition off the plunger, magnet and pole pieces are at the bottom of their travel and the contacts closed because of the contact breaker rocker. On switching on the ignition the plunger, magnet and pole pieces move upwards magnetically. As the fluid in the brass tube is hermetically sealed the bottom diaphragm also moves upwards so sucking in fuel from the petrol tank through the inlet valve.

4. When the plunger is almost at the top of its stroke the rocker mechanism allows the contacts to open, so breaking the magnetic circuit. The plunger, magnet, and pole pieces are then forced down by the coil spring and the action of the lower diaphragm is reversed, which expels the fuel through the outlet valve to the carburetter. The points then close and the whole cycle is repeated.

5. The SP and AUF pumps are so similar it is quite possible that a non-standard one has been fitted on an exchange basis, and for this reason the differences between them will be listed in the text as they occur so that if a later type of pump has been fitted it will create no difficulty. The following can be taken to apply equally to both types of pump except where otherwise stated.

6. The S.U. 12-volt electric fuel pump consists of a long outer body casing housing and diaphragm, armature and solenoid assembly, with at one end the contact breaker assembly protected by a bakelite cover, and at the other end a short casting containing the inlet and outlet ports, filter, valves, and pumping chamber. The joint between the bakelite cover and the body casing is protected with a rubber sheath.

7. The pump operates in the following manner. When the ignition is switched on current travels from the terminal on the outside of the bakelite cover through the coil located round the solenoid core which becomes energised and acting like a magnet draws the armature towards it. The current then passes through the points to earth.

8. When the armature is drawn forward it brings the diaphragm with it against the pressure of the diaphragm spring. This creates sufficient vacuum in the pump chamber to draw in fuel from the tank through the fuel filter and non-return inlet valve.

9. As the armature nears the end of its travel a 'throw-over' mechanism operates which separates the points so breaking the circuit.

10. The diaphragm return spring then pushes the diaphragm and armature forwards into the pumping chamber so forcing the fuel in the chamber out to the carburetter through the non-return outlet valve. When the armature is nearly fully forward the throw over mechanism again functions, this time closing the

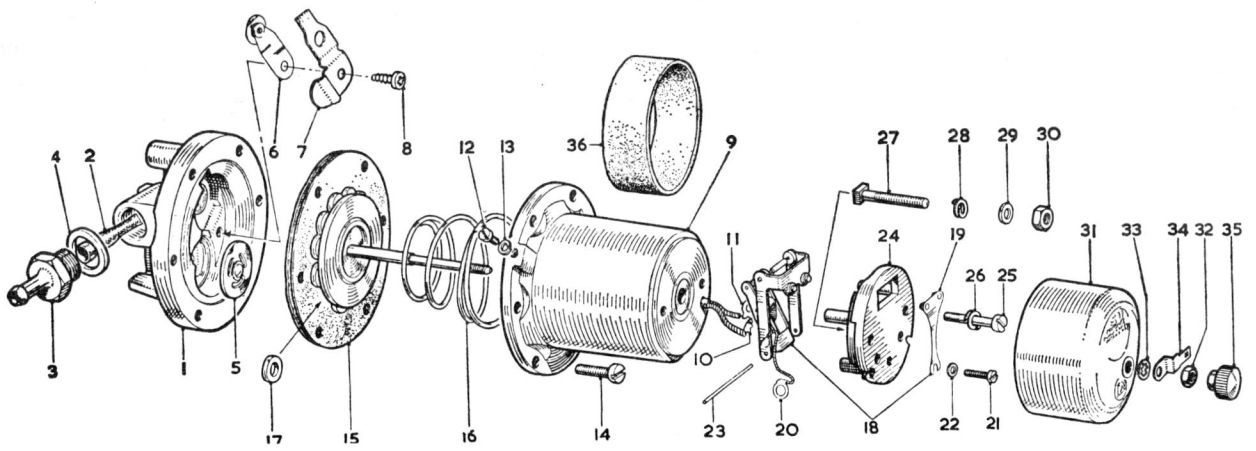

Fig. 3.10. AN EXPLODED VIEW OF THE SP-TYPE FUEL PUMP

1 Body	10 5 B.A. terminal tag	19 Blade	28 Spring washer
2 Filter	11 2 B.A. terminal tag	20 2 B.A. terminal tag	29 Lead washer for screw
3 Nozzle inlet	12 Earth screw	21 Screw for blade	30 Nut for screw
4 Washer for nozzle	13 Spring washer	22 Dished washer	31 End cover
5 Outlet valve	14 Housing to body screw	23 Spindle for contact breaker	32 Nut for cover
6 Inlet valve	15 Diaphragm assembly	24 Pedestal	33 Shakeproof washer
7 Valve retainer	16 Spring	25 Pedestal to housing screw	34 Lucar connector
8 Screw for retainer	17 Roller	26 Spring washer	35 Terminal knob
9 Coil housing	18 Rocker & blade	27 Screw for terminal	36 Rubber sleeve

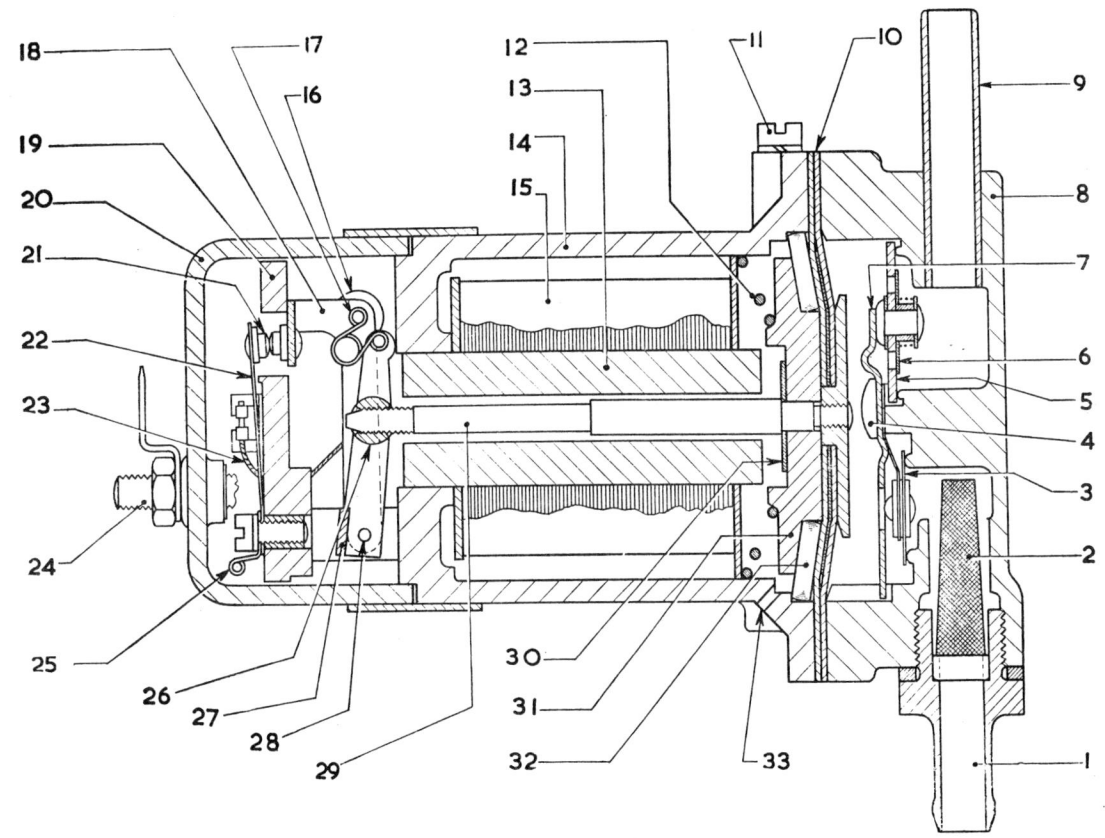

Fig. 3.11. A SECTIONED VIEW OF THE SP-TYPE FUEL PUMP

1 Feed nozzle	8 Body	15 Coil	22 Spring blade	29 Armature spindle
2 Filter	9 Outlet connection	16 Fibre rollers	23 Braided earth wire	30 Impact washer
3 Inlet valve	10 Diaphragm	17 Toggle spring	24 Terminal screw	31 Armature
4 Valve retainer screw	11 Earth screw	18 Outer rocker	25 Coil lead tag	32 Brass rollers
5 Carrier plate	12 Feed spring	19 Pedestal	26 Trunnion	33 Air vent
6 Delivery valve	13 Solenoid core	20 End cap	27 Inner rocker	
7 Valve retainer	14 Coil housing	21 Contact points	28 Rocker hinge pin	

77

points and re-energising the solenoid, so repeating the cycle.

18. S.U. FUEL PUMP - REMOVAL & REPLACEMENT

1. Disconnect the earth lead from the battery (Positive terminal).

2. The fuel pump is positioned behind the trim in the left-hand side of the boot in saloon models. Undo the screws in the trim cover to gain acces. In the Countryman/Traveller undo the two quick release screws and raise the hinged flat at the rear of the boot.

3. Disconnect the earth and the supply wires from their terminals on the pump body.

4. Prepare to squeeze the rubber portion of the petrol pipe leading from the tank with a mole wrench to ensure the minimum of fuel is lost.

5. Remove the fuel inlet and outlet pipes by undoing the union nuts or the clip screws.

6. Unscrew the bolts and spring washers which hold the pump bracket in position and remove the pump and bracket together.

7. Replacement of the pump is a reversal of the above process. Two particular points to watch are that:-

a) The fuel inlet and outlet pipes are connected up the right way round.

b) A good electrical earth connection is made.

19. S.U. FUEL PUMP - DISMANTLING

1. The filter and inlet and outlet arrangements differ between the three pumps and for this reason it is necessary to deal with them individually at this stage:-

a) Type SP. Remove the inlet nozzle by unscrewing it, and take out the filter from the inlet port. NOTE. The fibre washer under the nozzle head. The outlet nozzle is pressed into the end casting and cannot be removed.

b) Type AUF. Release the inlet and outlet nozzles, valves, sealing washers, and filter by unscrewing the two screws from the spring clamp plate which hold them all in place.

c) Type PD. The filter is at the bottom of the pump under the cover plate. To remove the cover plate undo the retaining nut, and take off the spring washer, dished washer, cover plate, and cover plate cork gasket. The bakelite cover can be removed from the top of the pump to give access to the contacts. It is not possible to dismantle the pump any further and the following instructions refer to the SP and AUF pumps only.

2. Mark the flanges adjacent to each other and separate the housing holding the armature and solenoid assembly from the pumping chamber casting, by unscrewing the six screws holding both halves of the pump together. Take great care not to tear or damage the diaphragm as it may stick to either of the flanges as they are separated. On the SP pump, remove the pan-headed screw which holds the valve retainer in place to the floor of the pumping chamber, and remove the retainer and the inlet and outlet valves which have already been removed on the AUF pump.

3. The armature spindle which is attached to the armature head and diaphragm is unscrewed anti-clockwise from the trunnion at the contact breaker end of the pump body. Lift out the armature, spindle, and diaphragm, and remove the impact washer from under the head of the armature. (This washer quietens the noise of the armature head hitting the solenoid core), and the diaphragm return spring.

4. Slide off the protective rubber sheath and unscrew the terminal nut, connector (where fitted), and washer from the terminal screw, and remove the bakelite contact breaker cover,

5. Unscrew the 5 B.A. screws which hold the contact spring blade in position and remove it with the blade and screw washer.

6. Remove the cover retaining nut on the terminal screw, and cut through the lead washer under the nut on the terminal screw with a pocket knife.

7. Remove the two bakelite pedestal retaining screws complete with spring washers which hold the pedestal to the solenoid housing, remove the braided copper earth lead, and the coil lead from the terminal screw.

8. Remove the pin on which the rockers pivot by pushing it out sideways and remove the rocker assembly. The pump is now fully dismantled. It is not possible to remove the solenoid core and coil and the rocker assembly must not be broken down, as it is only supplied on exchange as a complete assembly.

20. S.U. FUEL PUMP - INSPECTION & SERVICING

Although not given in the official manufacturers servicing charts, I consider it a very sound scheme to service the S.U. fuel pump every 12,000 miles to minimise the possibility of failure.

Remove the filter as has already been detailed and thoroughly clean it in petrol. At the same time clean the points by gently drawing a piece of thin card between them. Do this very carefully so as not to disturb the tension of the spring blade. If the points are burnt or pitted they must be renewed, and a new blade and rocker assembly fitted. The cork gasket

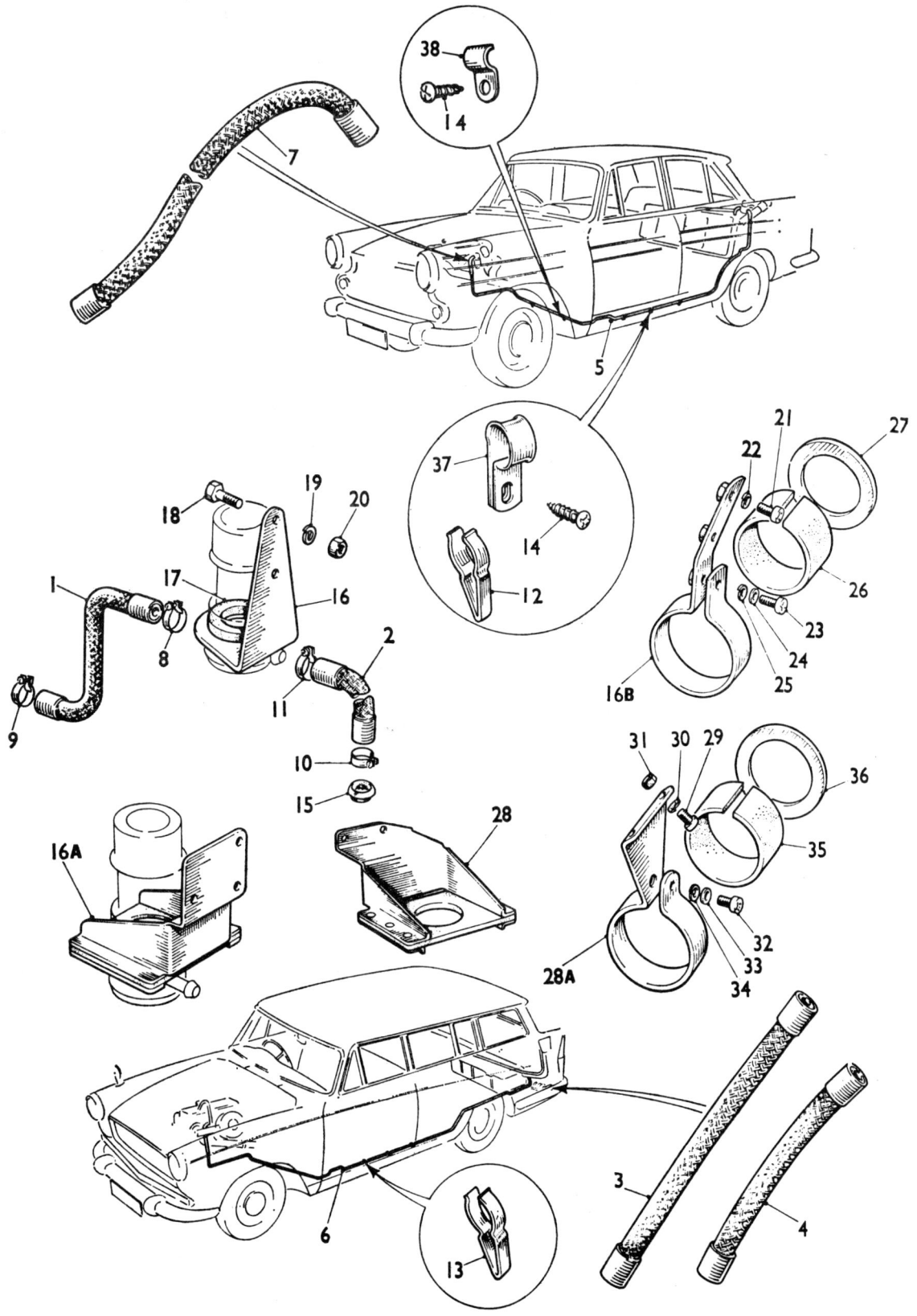

Fig. 3.12 EXPLODED VIEW OF THE FUEL PIPE LAYOUT AND FUEL PUMP BRACKETS

1 Flexible pipe (Tank to pump). 2 Flexible pipe from pump outlet. 3 Flexible pipe (Tank to pump—estate cars). 4 Pipe from pump outlet—estate cars). 5 Main fuel pipe—108 in. 6 Main fuel pipe—estate cars—155 in. 7 Flexible pipe to carburetter. 8 Clip. 9 Clip. 10 Flexible pipe to pipe clip. 11 Clip. 12 Clip. 13 Clip. 14 Screw. 15 Grommet. 16 Fuel pump mounting bracket. 16A Modified bracket. 16B Alternative bracket. 17 Ferrule. 18 Bolt. 19 Spring washer. 20 Nut. 21 Screw. 22 Spring washer. 23 Screw. 24 Plain washer. 25 Spring washer. 26 Strap. 27 Washer. 28 Fuel pump mounting bracket. 29 Bolt. 30 Spring washer. 31 Nut. 32 Screw. 33 Plain washer. 34 Spring washer. 35 Pump to mounting bracket strap. 36 Washer.

on the PD pump should be renewed as a matter of course. If this gasket leaks the pump will work rapidly and fuel starvation is likely. If, after having cleaned the contacts and the filter the PD pump still refuses to function, it should be exchanged for the later SP type complete with modified mounting bracket.

On any of the three pumps fuel starvation combined with rapid operations is indicative of an air leak on the suction side. To check whether this is so, undo the fuel line at the top of the float chamber, and immerse the end of the pipe in a jam jar half filled with petrol. With the ignition on and the pump functioning, should a regular stream of air bubbles emerge from the end of the pipe, air is leaking in on the suction side.

If the filter is coated with gum-like substance very like varnish, serious trouble can develop in the future unless all traces of this gum (formed by deposits from the fuel) are removed.

To do this, boil all steel and brass parts in a 20% solution of caustic soda, then dip them in nitric acid and clean them in boiling water. Alloy parts can be cleaned with a clean rag after they have been left to soak for a few hours in methylated spirits.

With the pump stripped right down, wash and clean all the parts thoroughly in paraffin and renew any that are worn, damaged, fractured, or cracked. Pay particular attention to the gaskets and diaphragm.

21. S.U. FUEL PUMP - REASSEMBLY

1. Fit the rocker assembly to the bakelite pedestal and insert the rocker pivot pin. The pin is case hardened and wire or any other substitute should never be used if the pin is lost.

2. Place the spring washer, wiring tag from the short lead from the coil, a new lead washer, and the nut on the terminal screw, and tighten the nut down.

3. Attach the copper earth wire from the outer rocker immediately under the head of the nearest pedestal securing screw, and fit the pedestal to the solenoid housing with the two pedestal securing screws and lockwashers. It is unusual to fit an earth-wire immediately under the screw head but in this case the spring washer has been found not to be a particularly good conductor.

4. Fit the lockwasher under the head of the spring blade contact securing screw, then the last lead from the coil, and then the spring blade so that there is nothing between it and the bakelite pedestal. It is important that this order

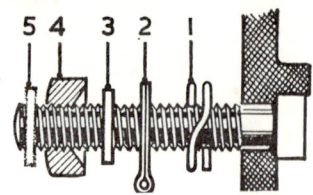

Fig. 3.13. The components of the terminal screw assembled in correct order. 1 Spring washer. 2 Wiring tag. 3 Lead washer. 4 Recessed nut. 5 Seal

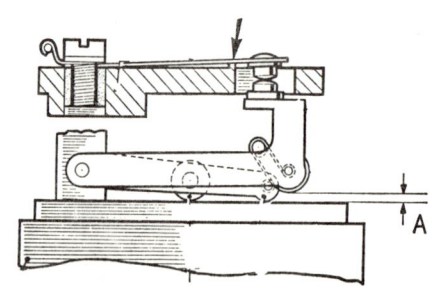

Fig. 3.14. The contact gap setting 'A' on early type rocker assemblies should be .030 in. (8 mm.)

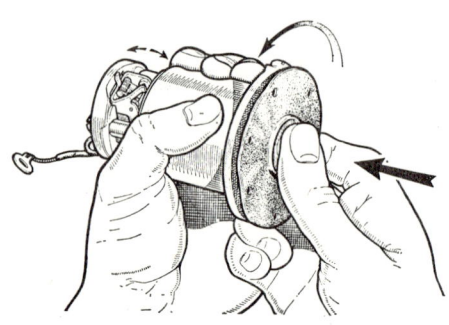

Fig. 3.15. Screw in the Diaphragm until rocker throw over stops

of assembly is adhered to. Tighten the screw lightly.

5. The static position of the pump when it is not in use is with the contact points making firm contact and this forces the spring blade to be bent slightly back. Move the outer rocker arm up and down and position the spring blade so that the contacts on the rocker or blade wipe over the centre line of the other points. When open the blade should rest against the small ledge on the bakelite pedestal just below the points. The points should come into contact with each other when the rocker is halfway forward. To check that this is correct press the middle of the blade gently so that it rests against the ridge with the points just having come into contact. It should now be possible to slide a .030 in. feeler gauge between the rocker rollers and the solenoid housing. If the clearance is not correct bend the tip of the blade very carefully until it is.

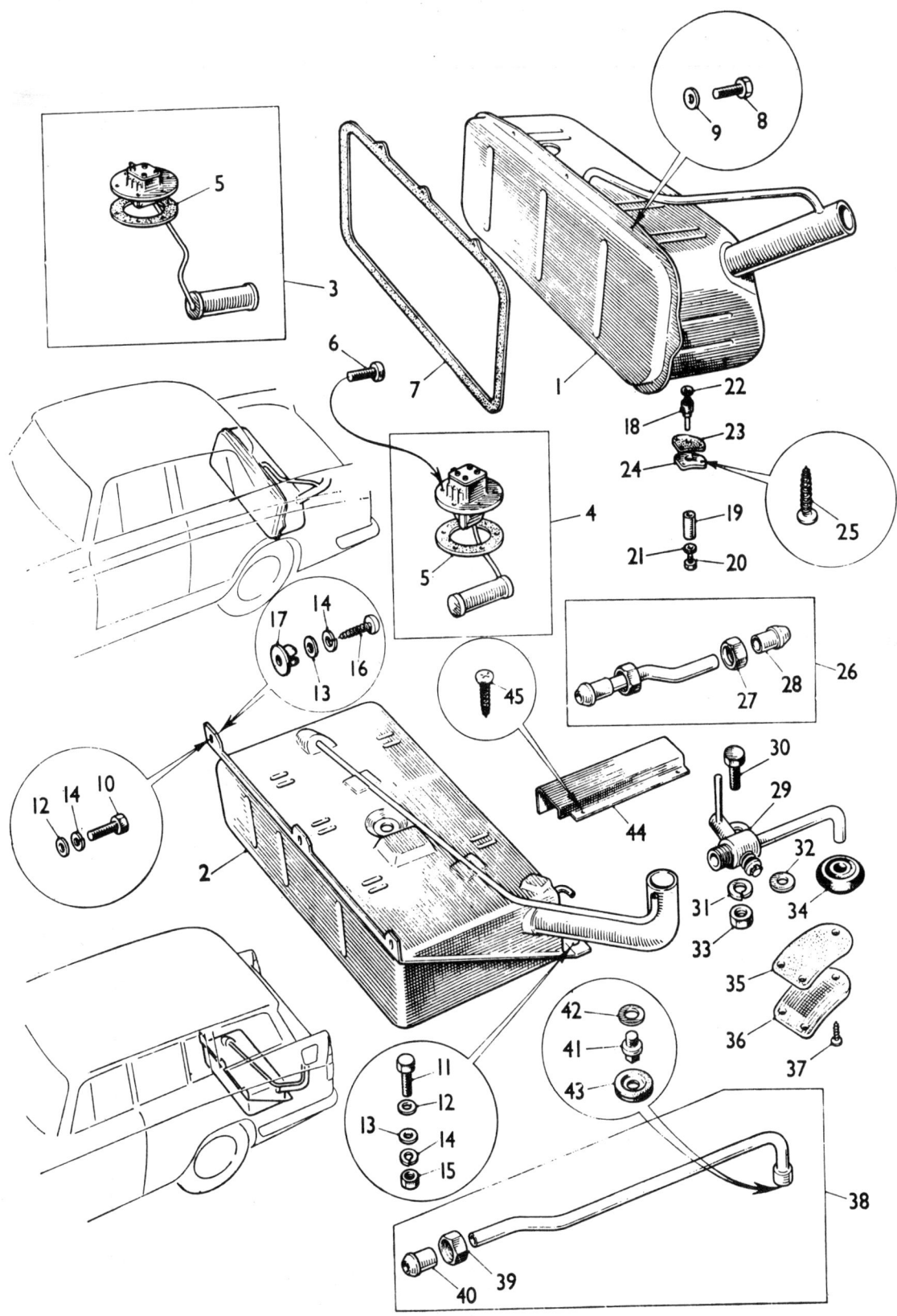

Fig. 3.16 EXPLODED VIEW OF THE FUEL TANKS AND ASSOCIATED COMPONENTS AS FITTED TO THE SALOON AND ESTATE CARS

1 Saloon fuel tank. 2 Estate car fuel tank. 3 Fuel gauge sender unit (saloons). 4 Fuel gauge sender unit (estate cars). 5 Washer. 6 Bolt. 7 Joint washer. 8 Bolt. 9 Plain washer. 10 Bolt. 11 Bolt. 12 Plain washer. 13 Plain washer. 14 Spring washer. 15 Nut. 16 Screw. 17 Nylon snap in nut. 18 Tank drain tap. 19 Drain pipe. 20 Drain pipe plug. 21 Seal. 22 Washer. 23 Pad. 24 Plate. 25 Screw. 26 Tank to drain tap pipe assembly. 27 Union nut. 28 Nipple. 29 Drain tap. 30 Bolt. 31 Spring washer. 32 Plain washer. 33 Nut. 34 Grommet. 35 Pad. 36 Sealing plate. 37 Screw. 38 Tank drain pipe assembly. 39 Union nut. 40 Nipple. 31 Drain pipe plug. 42 Drain pipe plug seal. 43 Grommet. 44 **Cover plate**. 45 Screw.

On the AUF and SP pumps with the outer rocker against the coil housing and the spring blade contact resting against the pedestal, the gap between the points should be .030 in.

6. Tighten down the blade retaining screw, and check that with AUF and SP models a considerable gap exists between the underside of the spring blade and the pedestal ledge, with the rocker contact bearing against the blade contact and the rocker fully forward in the normal static position. With the rocker arm down, ensure that the underside of the blade rests on the ledge of the pedestal. If not, remove the blade and very slightly bend it until it does.

7. Place the impact washer on the underside of the armature head, fit the diaphragm return spring with the wider portion of the coil against the solenoid body, place the brass rollers in position under the diaphragm and insert the armature spindle through the centre of the solenoid core, and screw the spindle into the rocker trunnion.

8. It will be appreciated that the amount the spindle is screwed into the rocker trunnion will vitally affect the functioning of the pump. To set the diaphragm correctly, turn the steel blade to one side, and screw the armature spindle into the trunnion until, if the spindle was screwed in a further sixth of a turn, the throw-over rocker would not operate the points closed to points open position. Now screw out the armature spindle four holes (2/3 of a turn) to ensure that wear in the points will not cause the pump to stop working. Turn the blade back into its normal position.

9. Reassembly of the valves, filters, and nozzles into the pumping chamber is a reversal of the dismantling process. Use new washers and gaskets throughout.

10. With the pumping chamber reassembled, replace it carefully on the solenoid housing, ensuring that the previously made mating marks on the flanges line up with each other. Screw the six screws in firmly.

11. Fit the bakelite cover and replace the shake-proof washer, lucar conductor, cover nut, and terminal knob to the terminal screw. Then, replace the terminal lead and cover nut, so locking the lead between the cover nut and the terminal nut. Assembly of all three types is now complete.

22. FUEL TANK, SALOON CAR MODELS - REMOVAL & REPLACEMENT
1. The fuel tank is located behind the rear seat at the front of the boot. Undo the self-tapping screws which hold the petrol tank trim cover in place in the front of the boot and remove the cover to gain access.
2. Disconnect the battery by removing the earth (positive lead).
3. Drain the contents of the tank into a suitable container and remove the drain plug/tap.
4. Loosen the clips on the filler neck rubber hose and free the hose from the petrol tank filler tube.
5. Disconnect the electrical lead to the fuel gauge sender unit and the earth lead and undo the fuel pipe union from the tank.
6. Undo the bolts which hold the flanges of the tank to the support brackets and lift the tank out through the boot.
7. Replacement is a straightforward reversal of the removal sequence.

23. FUEL TANK, COUNTRYMAN/TRAVELLER -
1. Disconnect the battery by removing the earth (positive lead).
2. The fuel tank is located under the floor at the rear of the car. Drain the contents of the tank into a suitable container after undoing the slotted drain plug/tap.
3. Undo the two bolts which hold the left-hand rear seat stop to the side of the body and remove the rear left-hand trim panel by prising it out carefully so freeing the snap-on connectors. Also remove the panel which covers the left-hand tail/stop lamp unit.
4. With the trim panel removed, access can be gained to the two clips on the fuel filler neck extension. Undo the clips and pull the extension piece off from outside the car.
5. Lift back the floor carpet at the rear, undo the four screws which hold the rear floor panel in place and remove the panel.
6. Disconnect the electrical lead and the earth lead to the fuel gauge sender unit; free the clips from the vent pipe and undo the union nut on the fuel pump flexible hose to separate the pump from the tank.
7. Undo the six bolts and spring washers from the petrol tank flanges and lift the tank out from inside the car.

24. FUEL TANK GAUGE SENDER UNIT - REMOVAL & REPLACEMENT
1. Disconnect the earth lead from the battery (positive terminal). Remove the front boot trim in the saloons, and the rear floor panel in the case of the Countryman/Traveller by undoing the securing screws.
2. The sender unit is located in the top panel of the petrol tank.
3. Disconnect the two gauge wires and undo the six screws which hold the sender unit to the tank.
4. Carefully lift the complete unit away making

FUEL SYSTEM AND CARBURATION

sure that the float lever is not bent or damaged in the process.

5. Replacement of the unit is a reversal of the above process. To ensure a fuel tight joint, scrape both the tank and sender gauge mating flanges clean, and always use a new joint gasket (Part No. 2H 1082).

25. FUEL TANK CLEANING

1. With time it is likely that sediment will collect in the bottom of the fuel tank. Condensation, resulting in rust and other impurities, will usually be found in the fuel tank of any car more than three or four years old.

2. When the tank is removed it should be vigorously flushed out and turned upside down, and if facilities are available, steam cleaned.

FAULT FINDING CHART

Cause	Trouble	Remedy
SYMPTOM:	FUEL CONSUMPTION EXCESSIVE	
Carburation and ignition faults	Air cleaner choked and dirty giving rich mixture Fuel leaking from carburettor(s), fuel pumps, or fuel lines Float chamber flooding Generally worn carburettor(s) Distributor condenser faulty Balance weights or vacuum advance mechanism in distributor faulty	Remove, clean and replace air cleaner. Check for and eliminate all fuel leaks. Tighten fuel line union nuts. Check and adjust float level. Remove, overhaul and replace. Remove, and fit new unit. Remove, and overhaul distributor.
Incorrect adjustment	Carburettor(s) incorrectly adjusted mixture too rich Idling speed too high Contact breaker gap incorrect Valve clearances incorrect Incorrectly set sparking plugs Tyres under-inflated Wrong sparking plugs fitted Brakes dragging	Tune and adjust carburettor(s). Adjust idling speed. Check and reset gap. Check rocker arm to valve stem clearances and adjust as necessary. Remove, clean, and regap. Check tyre pressures and inflate if necessary. Remove and replace with correct units. Check and adjust brakes.
SYMPTOM:	INSUFFICIENT FUEL DELIVERY OR WEAK MIXTURE DUE TO AIR LEAKS	
Dirt in system	Petrol tank air vent restricted Partially clogged filters in pump and carburettor(s) Dirt lodged in float chamber needle housing Incorrectly seating valves in fuel pump	Remove petrol cap and clean out air vent. Remove and clean filters. Remove and clean out float chamber and needle valve assembly. Remove, dismantle, and clean out fuel pump.
Fuel pump faults	Fuel pump diaphragm leaking or damaged Gasket in fuel pump damaged Fuel pump valves sticking due to petrol gumming	Remove, and overhaul fuel pump. Remove, and overhaul fuel pump. Remove, and thoroughly clean fuel pump.
Air leaks	Too little fuel in fuel tank (Prevalent when climbing steep hills) Union joints on pipe connections loose Split in fuel pipe on suction side of fuel pump Inlet manifold to block or inlet manifold to carburettor(s) gasket leaking	Refill fuel tank. Tighten joints and check for air leaks. Examine, locate, and repair. Test by pouring oil along joints - bubbles indicate leak. Renew gasket as appropriate.

CHAPTER FOUR

IGNITION SYSTEM

CONTENTS

SPECIFICATIONS

Coil … … … … … … … … … … … … Lucas LA 12
    Resistance at 20°C (68°F) in primary winding … 3.2 to 3.4 ohms (cold)
    Consumption – Ignition switched on … … … 3.6 amps at 15°C (60°F)
    At 2,000 r.p.m. … … … … … … … … 1.25 amps at 15°C (60°F)

Distributor … … … … … … … … … … Lucas 25 D4
    Contact Points gap setting … … … … … .014 to .016 in. (.35 to .40 mm.)
    Rotation of Rotor … … … … … … … Anti-clockwise
    Cam form … … … … … … … … … 4 cylinder high lift
    Automatic Advance … … … … … … … Centrifugal and Vacuum
    Contact Breaker Spring – Tension … … … 18 to 24 oz.
    Condenser capacity … … … … … … .18 to .24 microfarad

Sparking Plugs … … … … … … … … Champion N5
    Size … … … … … … … … … 14 mm. 3/4 in. (19.0 mm.) reach
    Plug electrode gap … … … … … … .024 to .026 in. (.625 to .660 mm.)
    Firing order … … … … … … … … 1, 3, 4, 2.

IGNITION SYSTEM

Distributor Identification & Performance 1489 c.c. single carburetter engines

	High Compression	Low Compression
Engine compression ratio	High Compression	Low Compression
Distributor Serial No.	40643 A/H	40624 A/H
Automatic advance commences (engine r.p.m.)	500 r.p.m.	900 r.p.m.
Vacuum advance commences...	5 in. (13 cm.) Hg	6 in. (15 cm.) Hg
Vacuum advance ceases (crankshaft degrees) ...	20° at 17 in.	16° at 14 in.
Maximum advance (crank degrees at engine r.p.m.)	24° at 4,800	34° at 4,200
Decelerating check (crank degrees at engine r.p.m.)	20° at 3,000	28° at 3,600
	14° at 2,260	20° at 2,800
	3° at 900	10° at 1,800
Static Ignition Timing	5° B.T.D.C.	T.D.C. *** fuel
		10° B.T.D.C. **** fuel .

Distributor Identification & Performance 1489 c.c. twin carburetter engines

Distributor Serial No.	40644 A/B
Automatic advance commences (engine r.p.m.) ...	700 r.p.m.
Vacuum advance commences...	6 in. (15 cm.) Hg
Vacuum advance ceases (crankshaft degrees) ...	16° at 14 in. (136 cm.) Hg
Maximum advance (crank degrees at engine r.p.m.)	28° at 2,800 r.p.m.
Decelerating check (crank degrees at engine r.p.m.)	20° at 2,000 r.p.m.
	15° at 1,600 r.p.m.
	8° at 1,000 r.p.m.
Static Ignition Timing	8° B.T.D.C.

Distributor Identification & Performance 1622 c.c. single carburetter engines

	High Compression	High Compression	Low Compression
Engine compression ratio	High Compression	High Compression	Low Compression
Distributor Serial No.	40822 A	40822 B	40821
Automatic advance commences	700 r.p.m.	750 r.p.m.	600 r.p.m.
Vacuum advance commences...	4 in. (10 cm.) Hg	4 in. (10 cm.) Hg.	7 in. (18 cm.) Hg
Vacuum advance ceases...	12° at 17 in.	12° at 17 in.	24° at 18 in.
Maximum advance (degrees/r.p.m.) ...	25° at 3,000	26° at 3,750	30° at 4,200
Decelerating check (degrees/r.p.m.) ...	20° at 2,400	26° at 3,700	30° at 4,200
	12° at 1,400	18° at 2,700	20° at 3,000
	8° at 1,100	10° at 1,400	4° at 1,000
Static Ignition Timing	5° B.T.D.C.	5° B.T.D.C.	6° B.T.D.C.
Stroboscopic Ignition Timing @ 600 r.p.m.	8° B.T.D.C.	8° B.T.D.C.	9° B.T.D.C.

Distributor Identification & Performance 1622 c.c. twin carburetter engines

Distributor Serial No.	40823 A
Automatic advance commences (engine r.p.m.) ...	700 r.p.m.
Vacuum advance commences...	6 in. (15 cm.) Hg
Vacuum advance ceases (crankshaft degrees) ...	24° at 16 in. (41 cm.) Hg

CHAPTER FOUR

Maximum advance (crank degrees at engine r.p.m.)   26° at 3,700 r.p.m.
Decelerating check (crank degrees at engine r.p.m.)   19° at 2,700 r.p.m.
6° at 1,000 r.p.m.
10° at 1,400 r.p.m.
6° at 1,000 r.p.m.
Static Ignition timing   .. ..   4° B.T.D.C.
Stroboscopic Ignition Timing @ 600 r.p.m.   ... ...   7° B.T.D.C.

1. GENERAL DESCRIPTION

In order that the engine can run correctly it is necessary for an electrical spark to ignite the fuel/air mixture in the combustion chamber at exactly the right moment in relation to engine speed and load. The ignition system is based on feeding low tension voltage from the battery to the coil where it is converted to high tension voltage. The high tension voltage is powerful enough to jump the sparking plug gap in the cylinders many times a second under high compression pressures, providing that the system is in good condition and that all adjustments are correct.

The ignition system is divided into two circuits. The low tension circuit and the high tension circuit.

The low tension (sometimes known as the primary) circuit consists of the battery, lead to the control box, lead to the ignition switch, lead from the ignition switch to the low tension or primary coil windings (terminal SW), and the lead from the low tension coil windings (coil terminal CB) to the contact breaker points and condenser in the distributor.

The high tension circuit consists of the high tension or secondary coil windings, the heavy ignition lead from the centre of the coil to the centre of the distributor cap, the rotor arm, and the sparking plug leads and sparking plugs.

The system functions in the following manner. Low tension voltage is changed in the coil into high tension voltage by the opening and closing of the contact breaker points in the low tension circuit. High tension voltage is then fed via the carbon brush in the centre of the distributor cap to the rotor arm of the distributor. The rotor arm revolves inside the distributor cap, and each time it comes in line with one of the four metal segments in the cap, which are connected to the sparking plug leads, the opening and closing of the contact breaker points causes the high tension voltage to build up, jump the gap from the rotor arm to the appropriate metal segment and so via the sparking plug lead to the sparking plug, where it finally jumps the spark plug gap before going to earth.

The ignition is advanced and retarded automatically, to ensure the spark occurs at just the right instant for the particular load at the prevailing engine speed.

The ignition advance is controlled both mechanically and by a vacuum operated system. The mechanical governor mechanism comprises two lead weights, which move out from the distributor shaft as the engine speed rises due to centrifugal force. As they move outwards they rotate the cam relative to the distributor shaft, and so advance the spark. The weights are held in position by two light springs and it is the tension of the springs which is largely responsible for correct spark advancement.

The vacuum control consists of a diaphragm, one side of which is connected via a small bore tube to the carburetter, and the other side to the contact breaker plate. Depression in the inlet manifold and carburetter, which varies with engine speed and throttle opening, causes the diaphragm to move, so moving the contact breaker plate, and advancing or retarding the spark. A fine degree of control is achieved by a spring in the vacuum assembly.

2. CONTACT BREAKER ADJUSTMENT

1. To adjust the contact breaker points to the correct gap, first pull off the two clips securing the distributor cap to the distributor body, and lift away the cap. Clean the cap inside and out with a dry cloth. It is unlikely that the four segments will be badly burned or scored, but if they are the cap will have to be renewed.

2. Push in the carbon brush located in the top of the cap once or twice to make sure that it moves freely.

3. Gently prise the contact breaker points open to examine the condition of their faces. If they are rough, pitted, or dirty, it will be necessary to remove them for resurfacing, or for replacement points to be fitted.

4. Presuming the points are satisfactory, or that they have been cleaned and replaced, measure the gap between the points by turning the engine over until the contact breaker arm is on the peak of one of the four cam lobes (arrowed).

5. A 0.015 in. feeler gauge should now just fit between the points.

6. If the gap varies from this amount, slacken the contact plate securing screw (arrowed).

2.4

2.6

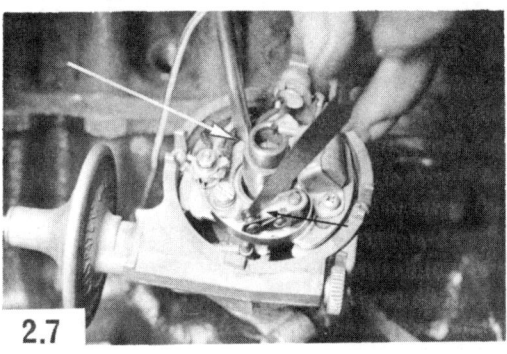

2.7

7.   Adjust the contact gap by inserting a screwdriver in the notched hole (arrowed) at the end of the plate. Turning clockwise to decrease and anti-clockwise to increase the gap. Tighten the s e c u r i n g screw and check the gap again (small arrow).

8.   Replace the rotor arm and distributor cap and clip the spring blade retainers into position.

3   REMOVING & REPLACING CONTACT BREAK-ER POINTS

1.   If the contact breaker points are burned, pitted or badly worn, they must be removed and either replaced, or their faces must be filed smooth.

2.   To remove the points unscrew the terminal nut and remove it together with the steel washer under its head. Remove the flanged nylon bush and then the condenser lead and the low tension

lead from the terminal pin. Lift off the contact breaker arm and then remove the large fibre washer from the terminal pin.

3.   The adjustable contact breaker plate is re-moved by unscrewing the one h o l d i n g down screw and removing it, complete with spring and flat washer.

4.   To reface the points, rub their faces on a fine carborundum stone, or on fine emery paper. It is important that the faces are rubbed flat and parallel to each other so that there will be com-plete face to face contact when the points are closed. One of the points will be pitted and the other will have deposits on it.

5.   It is necessary to completely remove the built-up deposits, but not necessary to rub the pitted point right down to the stage where all the pitting has disappeared, though obviously if this is done it will prolong the time before the operation of refacing the points has to be repeated.

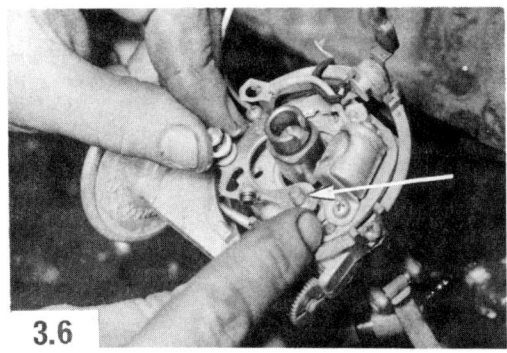

3.6

6.   To replace the points first position the ad-justable contact breaker plate over the terminal pin (arrowed, see photograph).

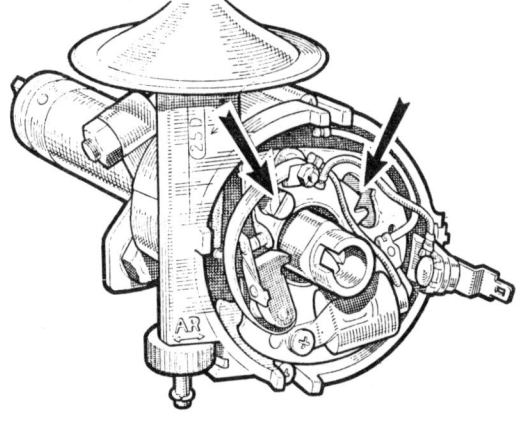

Fig. 4.1 Loosen the screw (arrowed) and by means of a screwdriver placed between the notches (arrowed) the points gap can be adjusted.

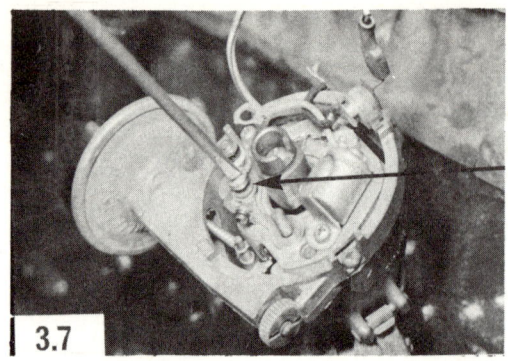

3.7

7. Secure the contact plate by screwing in the screw (arrowed) which should have a spring and a flat washer under its head.

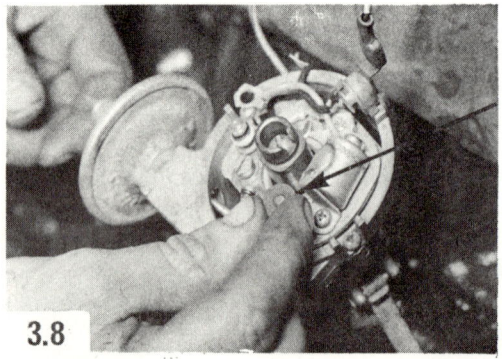

3.8

8. Then fit the fibre washer (arrowed) over the terminal pin.

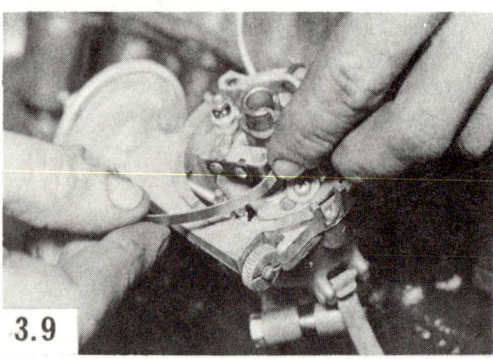

3.9

9. Next fit the contact breaker arm complete with spring over the terminal pin.

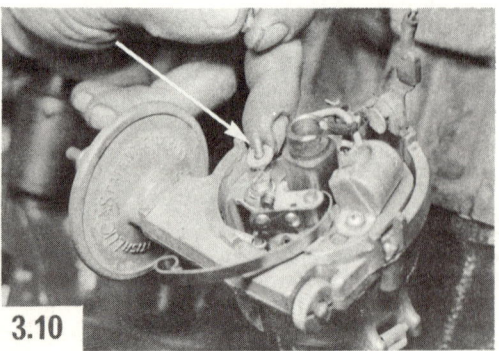

3.10

10. Drop the fibre washer over the terminal bolt (arrowed).

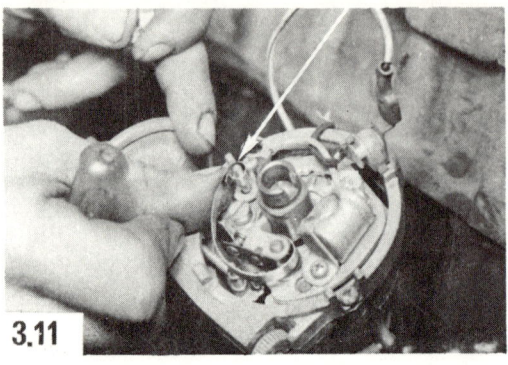

3.11

11. Then bend back the spring of the contact breaker arm and fit it over the terminal bolt (arrowed).

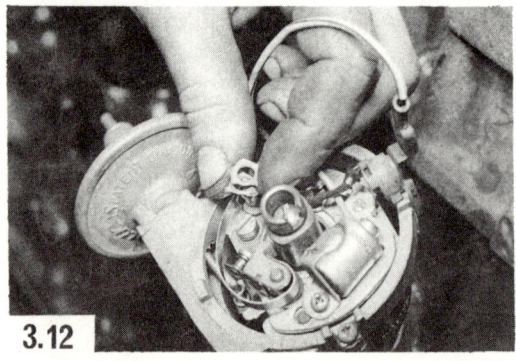

3.12

12. Place the terminals of the low tension lead and the condenser over the terminal bolt.

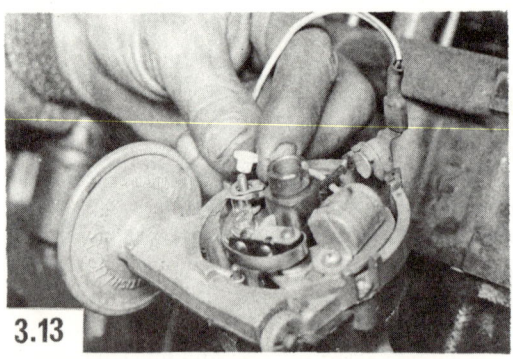

3.13

3.14

13.   Then fit the flanged nylon bush over the terminal bolt with the two leads immediately under its flange as shown.

14.   Next fit a steel washer and then a 'star' washer over the nylon bush. (See photograph).

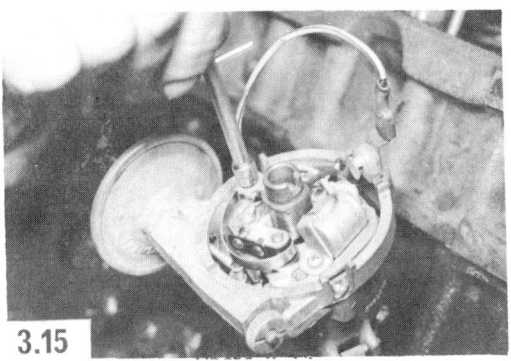

3.15

15.   Then fit the nut over the terminal bolt and tighten it down as shown.

16.   The points are now reassembled and the gap should be set as described in the previous section.

17.   Finally replace the rotor arm and then the distributor cap.

4.   CONDENSER REMOVAL, TESTING & REPLACEMENT

1.   The purpose of the condenser, (sometimes known as a capacitor) is to ensure that when the contact breaker points open there is no sparking across them which would waste voltage and cause wear.

2.   The condenser is fitted in parallel with the contact breaker points. If it develops a short circuit, it will cause ignition failure as the points will be prevented from interrupting the low tension circuit.

3.   If the engine becomes very difficult to start or begins to miss after several miles running and the breaker points show signs of excessive burning, then the condition of the condenser must be suspect. A further test can be made by separating the points by hand with the ignition switched on. If this is accompanied by a flash it is indicative that the condenser has failed.

4.   Without special test equipment the only sure way to diagnose condenser trouble is to replace a suspected unit with a new one and note if there is any improvement.

5.   To remove the condenser from the distributor, remove the distributor cap and the rotor arm. Unscrew the contact breaker arm terminal nut, and remove the nut, washer, and flanged nylon bush and release the condenser lead from the bush. Unscrew the condenser retaining screw from the breaker plate and remove the condenser. Replacement of the cond-

enser is simply a reversal of the removal process. Take particular care that the condenser lead does not short circuit against any portion of the breaker plate.

5.   DISTRIBUTOR LUBRICATION

1.   It is important that the distributor cam is lubricated with petroleum jelly at the specified mileages, and that the breaker arm, governor weights, and cam spindle, are lubricated with engine oil once every 1,000 miles. In practice it will be found that lubrication every 2,000 miles is adequate, though once every 1,000 miles is best.

2.   Great care should be taken not to use too much lubricant, as any excess that finds its way onto the contact breaker points could cause burning and misfiring.

3.   To gain access to the cam spindle, lift away the rotor arm. Drop no more than two drops of engine oil onto the screw head. This will run down the spindle when the engine is hot and lubricate the bearings.

4.   To lubricate the automatic timing control allow a few drops of oil to pass through the hole in the contact breaker base plate through which

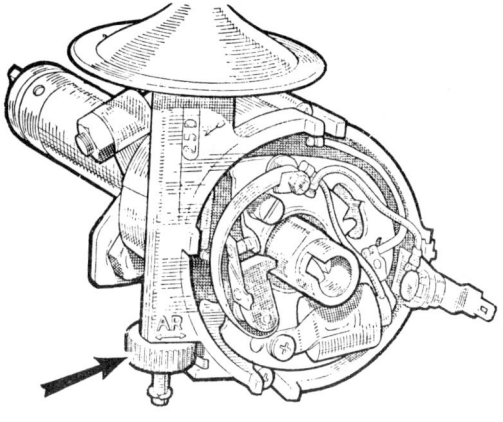

Fig. 4.2 The fine adjustment screw on the distributor.

the four sided cam emerges. Apply not more than one drop of oil to the pivot post and remove any excess.

6. DISTRIBUTOR REMOVAL & REPLACEMENT

1. To remove the distributor from the engine, start by pulling the terminals off each of the sparking plugs. Release the Lucar connector which holds the low tension lead to the terminal on the side of the distributor and unscrew the high tension lead retaining cap from the coil and remove the lead.

2. Unscrew the union holding the vacuum tube to the distributor vacuum housing.

3. Remove the distributor body clamp bolts which hold the distributor clamp plate to the engine and remove the distributor. NOTE if it is not wished to disturb the timing then under no circumstances should the clamp pinch bolt, which secures the distributor in its relative position in the clamp, be loosened. Providing the distributor is removed without the clamp being loosened from the distributor body, the timing will not be lost.

4. Replacement is a reversal of the above process providing that the engine has not been turned in the meantime. If the engine has been turned it will be best to retime the ignition. This will also be necessary if the clamp pinch bolt has been loosened.

7. DISTRIBUTOR DISMANTLING

1. With the distributor removed from the car and on the bench, remove the distributor cap and lift off the rotor arm. If very tight, lever it off gently with a screwdriver.

2. Remove the points from the distributor as described in section 3.

3. Remove the condenser from the contact breaker plate by releasing its securing screw.

4. Unhook the vacuum unit spring from its mounting pin on the moving contact breaker plate.

5. Remove the contact breaker plate.

6. Unscrew the two screws and lockwashers which hold the contact breaker base plate in position and remove the earth lead from the relevant screw. Remember to replace this lead on reassembly.

7. Lift out the contact breaker base plate.

8. NOTE the position of the slot in the rotor arm drive in relation to the offset drive dog at the opposite end of the distributor. It is essential that this is reassembled correctly as otherwise the timing may be 180° out.

9. Unscrew the cam spindle retaining screw, which is located in the centre of the rotor arm drive, and remove the cam spindle.

10. Lift out the centrifugal weights together with their springs.

11. To remove the vacuum unit, spring off the small circlip which secures the advance adjustment nut which should then be unscrewed. With the micrometer adjusting nut removed, release the spring and the micrometer adjusting nut lock spring clip. This is the clip that is responsible for the 'clicks' when the micrometer adjuster is turned, and it is small and easily lost as is the circlip, so put them in a safe place. Do not forget to replace the lock spring clip on reassembly.

12. It is only necessary to remove the distributor drive shaft or spindle if it is thought to be excessively worn. With a thin punch drive out the retaining pin from the driving tongue collar on the bottom end of the distributor drive shaft. The shaft can then be removed. The distributor is now completely dismantled.

8. DISTRIBUTOR INSPECTION & REPAIR

1. Check the points as described in section 3. Check the distributor cap for signs of tracking, indicated by a thin black line between the segments. Replace the cap if any signs of tracking are found.

2. If the metal portion of the rotor arm is badly burned or loose, renew the arm. If slightly burnt clean the arm with a fine file.

3. Check that the carbon brush moves freely in the centre of the distributor cover.

4. Examine the fit of the breaker plate on the bearing plate and also check the breaker arm pivot for looseness or wear and renew as necessary.

5. Examine the balance weights and pivot pins for wear, and renew the weights or cam assembly if a degree of wear is found.

6. Examine the shaft and the fit of the cam assembly on the shaft. If the clearance is excessive compare the items with new units, and renew either, or both, if they show excessive wear.

7. If the shaft is a loose fit in the distributor bush and can be seen to be worn, it will be necessary to fit a new shaft and bush. The single bush is simply pressed out. NOTE that before inserting a new bush, it should be stood in engine oil for at least 24 hours.

8. Examine the length of the balance weight springs and compare them with new springs. If they have stretched they must be renewed.

9. DISTRIBUTOR REASSEMBLY

1. Reassembly is a straight reversal of the dismantling process, but there are several points which should be noted in addition to those

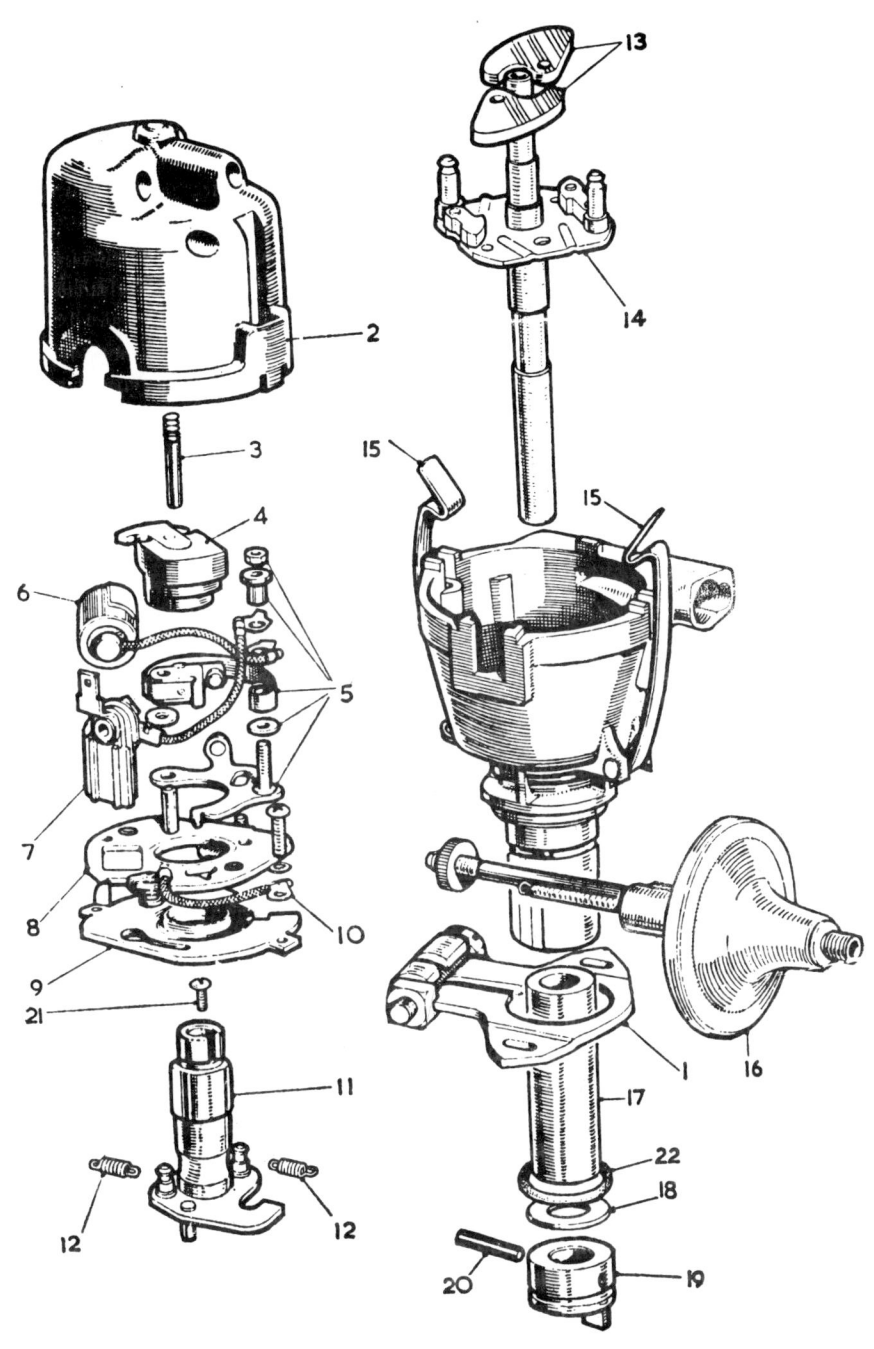

Fig. 4.3 EXPLODED VIEW OF THE DISTRIBUTOR.

1 Clamping plate. 2 Moulded cap. 3 Brush and spring. 4 Rotor arm. 5 Contacts. 6 Condenser. 7 Low tension terminal.
8 Moving contact breaker plate. 9 Contact breaker base plate. 10 Earth lead. 11 Cam. 12 Automatic advance spring. 13 Weight
assembly. 14 Shaft and action plate. 15 Cap retaining clips. 16 Vacuum unit. 17 Bush. 18 Thrust washer. 19 Driving dog.
20 Parallel pin. 21 Cam screw. 22 'O' ring oil seal.

already given in the section on dismantling.

2.   Lubricate with S. A. E. 20 engine oil the balance weights and other parts of the mechanical advance mechanism, the distributor shaft, and the portion of the shaft on which the cam bears, during assembly. Do not oil excessively but ensure these parts are adequately lubricated.

3.   On reassembling the cam driving pins with the centrifugal weights, check that they are in the correct position so that when viewed from above, the rotor arm should be at six o'clock position, and the small offset on the driving dog must be on the right.

4.   Check the action of the weights in the fully advanced and fully retarded positions and ensure they are not binding.

5.   Tighten the micrometer adjusting nut to the middle position on the timing scale.

6.   Finally, set the contact breaker gap to the correct clearance of .015 in.

10.   IGNITION TIMING

1.   If the clamp plate pinch bolt has been loosened on the distributor and the static timing lost, or if for any other reason it is wished to set the ignition timing, proceed as follows:-

2.   The static advance is checked at the exact moment of opening of the points with regards to the position of the dimple in the crankshaft pulley in relation to the pointers on the bottom of the timing gear cover case. The longest pointer indicates T. D. C. and each of the two shorter pointers indicate 5° B. T. D. C. and 10° B. T. D. C., respectively.

3.   Check the 'Ignition specification' for the correct position of the crankshaft pulley wheel when the points should be just beginning to open. This is shown as 'static setting'.

4.   Having determined whether your engine possesses a high or low compression ratio (by checking the engine number), turn the engine over so that No. 1 piston is coming up to T. D. C. on the compression stroke. (This can be checked by removing No. 1 sparking plug and feeling the pressure being developed in the cylinder, or by removing the rocker cover and noting when the valves in No. 4 cylinder are rocking, i. e. the inlet valve just opening and exhaust valve just closing. If this check is not made it is all too easy to set the timing 180° out, as both No. 1 and 4 cylinders come up to T. D. C. at the same time, but only one is on the firing stroke.

5.   Continue turning the engine until the dimple on the crankshaft pulley is in line with the correct timing mark on the timing cover, or is in the correct position with regards to the pointers.

6.   Remove the distributor cover, slacken off

the distributor body clamp bolt, and with the rotor arm pointing towards the No. 1 terminal (check this position with the distributor cap and lead to No. 1 sparking plug), insert the distributor into the distributor housing. The dog on the drive shaft should match up with the slot in the distributor driving spindle.

7.   Insert the two bolts holding the distributor in position.

8.   With the engine set in the correct position and the rotor arm opposite the correct segment for No. 1 cylinder, turn the advance/retard knob on the distributor until the contact points are just beginning to open. Eleven clicks of the knurled micrometer adjuster nut represent 1° of timing movement.

9.   If the range of adjustment provided by this adjuster is not sufficient, then, if the clamp bolt is not already slackened, it will be necessary to slacken it, and turn the distributor body half a graduation as marked on the adjusting spindle barrel. (Each graduation represents 5° timing movement or 55 clicks of the micrometer adjuster). Sufficient adjustment will normally be found available using the distributor micrometer adjuster. When this has been achieved, the engine is statically timed.

10.   Difficulty is sometimes experienced in determining exactly when the contact breaker points open. This can be ascertained most accurately by connecting a 12-volt bulb in parallel with the contact breaker points (one lead to earth and the other from the distributor low tension terminal). Switch on the ignition, and turn the advance and retard adjuster until the bulb lights up indicating that the points have just opened.

11.   If a stroboscopic timing light is being used, attach one lead to No. 1 sparking plug, and attach the other lead into the free end of No. 1 plug ignition cable leading from the distributor. Start the engine and shine the light on the crankshaft pulley and timing indicators. If the engine idles at more than 600 r. p. m. then the correct static timing will not be obtained as the centrifugal weights will have started to advance.

12.   If the light shows the dimple in the pulley wheel to be to the right of the timing marks, then the ignition is too far advanced. If the dimple appears to the left of the timing marks, then the ignition is too far retarded. Turn the distributor body or micrometer adjuster until the timing dimple appears in just the right position in relation to the timing marks.

13.   Tighten the clamp bolt and recheck that the timing is still correct, making any small correction necessary with the micrometer adjuster.

14.   A better result can sometimes be obtained

by making slight readjustments under running conditions.

15. First start the engine and allow to warm up to normal temperature, and then accelerate in top gear from 30 to 50 m.p.h., listening for heavy pinking of the engine. If this occurs, the ignition needs to be retarded slightly until just the faintest trace of pinking can be heard under these operating conditions.

16. Since the ignition advance adjustment enables the firing point to be related correctly in relation to the grade of fuel used, the fullest advantage of any change of fuel will only be attained by re-adjustment of the ignition settings.

17. This is done by varying the setting of the index scale on the vacuum advance mechanism one or two divisions, checking to make sure that the best all-round result is attained.

11. SPARKING PLUGS AND LEADS

1. The correct functioning of the sparking plugs are vital for the correct running and efficiency of the engine.

2. At intervals of 5,000 miles the plugs should be removed, examined, cleaned, and if worn excessively, replaced. The condition of the sparking plug will also tell much about the overall condition of the engine.

3. If the insulator nose of the sparking plug is clean and white, with no deposits, this is indicative of a weak mixture, or too hot a plug. (A hot plug transfers heat away from the electrode slowly - a cold plug transfers it away quickly).

4. The plugs fitted as standard are the Champion N5 14 mm. type. If the top and insulator nose is covered with hard black-looking deposits, then this is indicative that the mixture is too rich. Should the plug be black and oily, then it is likely that the engine is fairly worn, as well as the mixture being too rich.

5. If the insulator nose is covered with light tan to greyish brown deposits, then the mixture is correct and it is likely that the engine is in good condition.

6. If there are any traces of long brown tapering stains on the outside of the white portion of the plug, then the plug will have to be renewed, as this shows that there is a faulty joint between the plug body and the insulator, and compression is being allowed to leak away.

7. Plugs should be cleaned by a sand blasting machine, which will free them from carbon more thoroughly then cleaning by hand. The machine will also test the condition of the plugs under compression. Any plug that fails to spark at the recommended pressure should be renewed.

8. The sparking plug gap is of considerable importance, as, if it is too large or too small, the size of the spark and its efficiency will be seriously impaired. The sparking plug gap should be set to 0.025 in. for the best results.

9. To set it, measure the gap with a feeler gauge, and then bend open, or close, the outer plug electrode until the correct gap is achieved. The centre electrode should never be bent as this may crack the insulation and cause plug failure if nothing worse.

10. When replacing the plugs, remember to use new plug washers, and replace the leads from the distributor in the correct firing order, which is 1, 3, 4, 2, No. 1 cylinder being the one nearest the radiator.

11. The plug leads require no routine attention other than being kept clean and wiped over regularly. At intervals of 5,000 miles, however, pull each lead off the plug in turn and remove them from the distributor by unscrewing the knurled moulded terminal knobs. Water can seep down into these joints giving rise to a white corrosive deposit which must be carefully removed from the brass washer at the end of each cable, through which the ignition wires pass.

12. IGNITION SYSTEM FAULT-FINDING

By far the majority of breakdown and running troubles are caused by faults in the ignition system either in the low tension or high tension circuits.

13. IGNITION SYSTEM FAULT SYMPTOMS

There are two main symptoms indicating ignition faults. Either the engine will not start or fire, or the engine is difficult to start and misfires. If it is a regular misfire, i.e., the engine is only running on two or three cylinders the fault is almost sure to be in the secondary, or high tension, circuit. If the misfiring is intermittant, the fault could be in either the high or low tension circuits. If the car stops suddenly, or will not start at all, it is likely that the fault is in the low tension circuit. Loss of power and overheating, apart from faulty carburation settings, are normally due to faults in the distributor or incorrect ignition timing.

14. FAULT DIAGNOSIS - ENGINE FAILS TO START

1. If the engine fails to start and the car was running normally when it was last used, first check there is fuel in the petrol tank. If the engine turns over normally on the starter motor and the battery is evidently well charged, then the fault may be in either the high or low tension circuits. First check the H.T. circuit. NOTE. If the battery is known to be fully charged; the

ignition light comes on, and the starter motor fails to turn the engine CHECK THE TIGHTNESS OF THE LEADS ON THE BATTERY TERMINALS and also the secureness of the earth lead to its CONNECTION TO THE BODY. It is quite common for the leads to have worked loose, even if they look and feel secure. If one of the battery terminal posts gets very hot when trying to work the starter motor this is a sure indication of a faulty connection to that terminal.

2 One of the commonest reasons for bad starting is wet or damp sparking plug leads and distributor. Remove the distributor cap. If condensation is visible internally dry the cap with a rag and also wipe over the leads. Replace the cap.

3 If the engine still fails to start, check that current is reaching the plugs, by disconnecting each plug lead in turn at the sparking plug end, and hold the end of the cable about 3/16 in. away from the cylinder block. Spin the engine on the starter motor by pressing the rubber button on the starter motor solenoid switch (under the bonnet).

4 Sparking between the end of the cable and the block should be fairly strong with a regular blue spark. (Hold the lead with rubber to avoid electric shocks). If current is reaching the plugs, then remove them and clean and regap them to 0.025 in. The engine should now start.

5 If the engine still fails to start (having eliminated the spark plugs and their leads as possible culprits) the fault may lie in the HT circuit between the coil and distributor. Detach the HT lead from the centre of the distributor cap, and hold the end of it about 3/16 inch from the cylinder block.

6 Spin the engine as before, when a rapid succession of blue sparks between the end of the lead and the block indicate that the coil is in order, and that either the distributor cap is cracked; the carbon brush is stuck or worn; the rotor arm is faulty, or that the contact points are burnt, pitted or dirty. If the points are in bad shape, clean and reset them as described in section 3. o8

8 If there are no sparks from the end of the lead from the coil, then check the connections of the lead to the coil and distributor head, and if they are in order, check out the low tension circuit starting with the battery.

9 Switch on the ignition and turn the crankshaft so the contact breaker points have fully opened. Then with either a 20-volt voltmeter or bulb and length or wire check that current from the battery is reaching the starter solenoid switch. No reading indicates that there is a fault in the cable to the switch, or in the connections at the switch or at the battery terminals. Alternatively, the battery earth lead may not be properly earthed to the body.

10 If in order, check that current is reaching terminal 'A' (the one with the brown lead) in the control box, by connecting the voltmeter between 'A' and an earth. If there is no reading this indicates a faulty cable or loose connections between the solenoid switch and the 'A' terminal. Remedy and the car will start.

11 Check with the voltmeter between the control box terminal A1 and an earth. No reading means a fault in the control box. Fit a new control box and start the car.

12 If in order, then check that current is reaching the ignition switch by connecting the voltmeter to the ignition switch input terminal (the one connected to the brown/blue lead) and earth. No reading indicates a break in the wire or a faulty connection at the switch or A1 terminals.

13 If the correct reading (approx. 12 volts) is obtained check the output terminal on the ignition switch (the terminal connected to the white lead). No reading means that the ignition switch is broken. Replace with a new unit and start the car.

14 If current is reaching the ignition switch output terminal, then check the A3 terminal on the fuse unit with the voltmeter. No reading indicates a break or short in the wire or loose connections between the ignition switch and the A3 terminal. Even if the A3 - A4 fuse is broken current should still be reaching the coil as it does not pass through the fuse. Remedy and the car should now start.

15 Check the SW terminal on the coil (it is marked 'SW' and a switch lead connects to it). No reading indicates loose connections or a broken wire from the A3 terminal on the fuse unit. If this proves to be the fault, remedy and start the car.

16 Check the CB terminal on the coil (it is marked 'CB') and if no reading is recorded on the voltmeter then the coil is broken and must be replaced. The car should start when a new coil has been fitted.17

17 If a reading is obtained at the CB terminal then check the low tension terminal on the side of the distributor. If no reading then check the wire for loose connections etc. If a reading is obtained then the final check on the low tension is across the braker points. No reading means a broken condenser which when replaced will enable the car to finally start.

15 FAULT DIAGNOSIS - ENGINE MISFIRES

1 If the engine misfires regularly, run it at a fast idling speed, and short out each of the plugs in turn by placing a short screwdriver across from the plug terminal to the cylinder. Ensure that the screwdriver has a WOODEN or PLASTIC INSULATED HANDLE.

2 No difference in engine running will be noticed when the plug in the defective cylinder is

short circuited. Short circuiting the working plugs will accentuate the misfire.

3. Remove the plug lead from the end of the defective plug and hold it about $^3/_{16}$ in. away from the block. Restart the engine. If the sparking is fairly strong and regular the fault must lie in the sparking plug.

4. The plug may be loose, the insulation may be cracked, or the points may have burnt away giving too wide a gap for the spark to jump. Worse still, one of the points may have broken off. Either renew the plug, or clean it, reset the gap, and then test it.

5. If there is no spark at the end of the plug lead, or if it is weak and intermittent, check the ignition lead from the distributor to the plug. If the insulation is cracked or perished, renew the lead. Check the connections at the distributor cap.

6. If there is still no spark, examine the dis-

tributor cap carefully for tracking. This can be recognised by a very thin black line running between two or more electrodes, or between an electrode and some other part of the distributor. These lines are paths which now conduct electricity across the cap thus letting it run to earth. The only answer is a new distributor cap.

7. Apart from the ignition timing being incorrect, other causes of misfiring have already been dealt with under the section dealing with the failure of the engine to start. (Section 14).

8. If the ignition timing is too far retarded, it should be noted that the engine will tend to overheat, and there will be a quite noticeable drop in power. If the engine is overheating and the power is down, and the ignition timing is correct, then the carburetters should be checked, as it is likely that this is where the fault lies. See Chapter 3 for details on this.

Badly burnt electrode

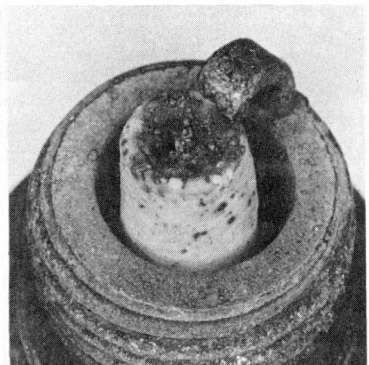
Pre-ignition damage

Chipped electrode

Too cold - dry, black fuel deposits

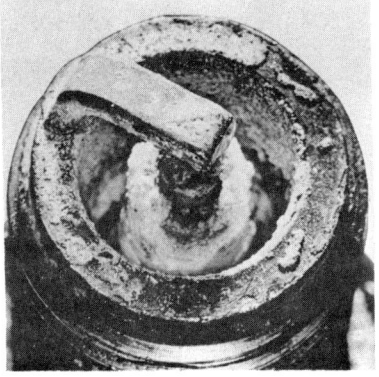
Too hot - white deposits

A normal clean plug with light deposits

CHAPTER FIVE

CLUTCH AND ACTUATING MECHANISM

CONTENTS

SPECIFICATIONS

Make	Borg & Beck
Type	A6 – G Single dry plate
Diameter	8 in. (20.32 cm.)
Clutch facing material	Spun yarn
No. of damper springs	6
No. of pressure springs	6
Damper springs identification colour	Black and light green
Pressure springs identification colour	Black and yellow
Clutch release bearing	Graphite
Clutch fluid	Castrol Girling Brake & Clutch Fluid – Amber
Torque wrench setting – Clutch to Flywheel bolts	25 lb/ft. (3.4 kg.m.)
Release lever ratio	4.6 to 1

1. GENERAL DESCRIPTION

All models are fitted with a Borg & Beck single dry plate clutch of 8 in. diameter which is hydraulically actuated and adjusts automatically for wear.

The clutch assembly comprises a steel cover which is bolted and doweled to the rear face of the flywheel and contains the pressure plate, pressure plate springs, release levers, and clutch disc or driven plate.

The pressure plate, pressure springs, and release levers are all attached to the clutch assembly cover. The clutch disc is free to slide along the splined first motion shaft and is held in position between the flywheel and the pressure plate by the pressure of the pressure plate springs.

Friction lining material is riveted to the clutch disc and it has a spring cushioned hub to absorb transmission shocks and to help ensure a smooth take off.

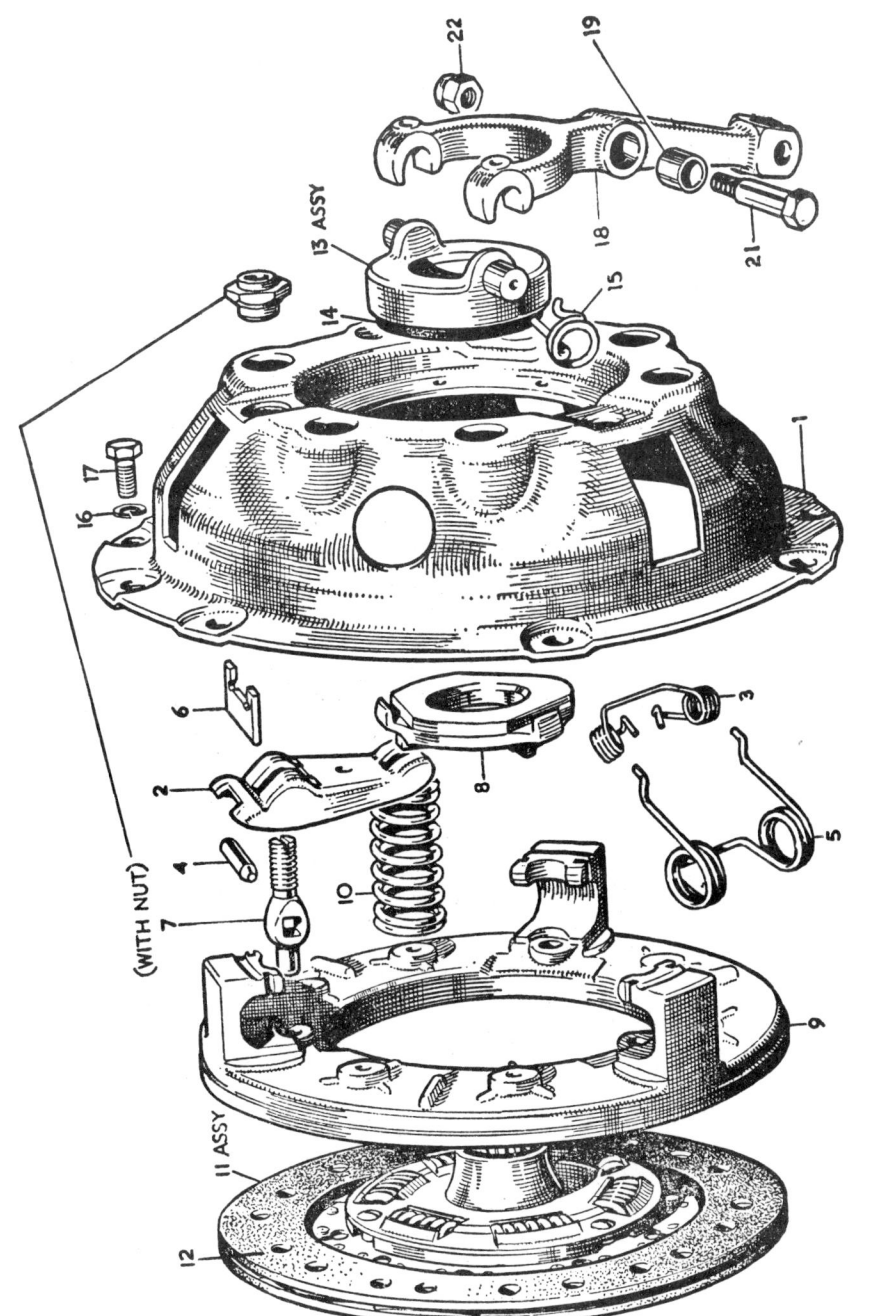

Fig. 5.1 EXPLODED VIEW OF THE CLUTCH ASSEMBLY

1 Cover—clutch. 2 Lever—release. 3 Retainer—lever. 4 Pin—lever. 5 Spring—anti-rattle. 6 Strut. 7 Eyebolt with nut. 8 Plate—bearing thrust. 9 Plate—pressure. 10 Spring—pressure plate. 11 Plate assembly—driven. 12 Lining. 13 Ring assembly—thrust. 14 Ring—carbon. 15 Retainer. 16 Washer—spring—cover screw. 17 Screw—cover to flywheel. 18 Lever—withdrawal. 19 Bushes. 21 Bolt for lever. 22 Nut for bolt.

97

The clutch is actuated hydraulically. The pendant clutch pedal is connected to the clutch master cylinder and hydraulic fluid reservoir by a short pushrod. The master cylinder and hydraulic reservoir are mounted on the engine side of the bulkhead in front of the driver.

Depressing the clutch pedal moves the piston in the master cylinder forwards, so forcing hydraulic fluid through the clutch hydraulic pipe to the slave cylinder.

The piston in the slave cylinder moves forward on the entry of the fluid and actuates the clutch release arm by means of a short pushrod. The opposite end of the release arm is forked and is located behind the release bearing.

As this pivoted clutch release arm moves backwards it bears against the release bearing pushing it forwards to bear against the release bearing thrust plate and three clutch release levers. These levers are also pivoted so as to move the pressure plate backwards against the pressure of the pressure plate springs, in this way disengaging the pressure plate from the clutch disc.

When the clutch pedal is released, the pressure plate springs force the pressure plate into contact with the high friction linings on the clutch disc, at the same time forcing the clutch disc against the flywheel and so taking the drive up.

As the friction linings on the clutch disc wear, the pressure plate automatically moves closer to the disc to compensate. This makes the inner ends of the release levers travel further towards the gearbox which decreases the release bearing clearance but not the clutch free pedal travel, as unless the master cylinder has been disturbed this is automatically compensated for.

2. MAINTENANCE

1. Routine maintenance consists of checking the level of the hydraulic fluid in the master cylinder every 1,000 miles and topping up with Girling Amber brake fluid if the level has fallen.
2. If it is noted that the level of the liquid has fallen then an immediate check should be made to determine the source of the leak.
3. Before checking the level of the fluid in the master cylinder reservoir, carefully clean the cap and body of the reservoir unit with clean rag so as to ensure that no dirt enters the system when the cap is removed. On no account should paraffin or any other cleaning solvent be used in case the hydraulic fluid becomes contaminated.
4. Check that the level of the hydraulic fluid is up to within $\frac{1}{4}$ in. of the filler neck and that the vent hole in the cap is clear. Do not overfill.

CLUTCH SYSTEM - BLEEDING

1. Gather together a clean jam jar, a 9 in. length of rubber tubing which fits tightly over the bleed nipple in the slave cylinder, a tin of hydraulic brake fluid, and a friend to help.
2. Check that the master cylinder is full and if not fill it, and cover the bottom two inches of the jar with hydraulic fluid.
3. Remove the rubber dust cap from the bleed nipple on the slave cylinder and with a suitable spanner open the bleed nipple one turn.
4. Place one end of the tube securely over the nipple and insert the other end in the jam jar so that the tube orifice is below the level of the fluid.
5. The assistant should now pump the clutch pedal up and down slowly until air bubbles cease to emerge from the end of the tubing. He should also check the reservoir frequently to ensure that the hydraulic fluid does not disappear so letting air into the system.
6. When no more air bubbles appear, tighten the bleed nipple on the downstroke.
7. Replace the rubber dust cap over the bleed nipple. Allow the hydraulic fluid in the jar to stand for at least 24 hours before using it, to allow all the minute air bubbles to escape.

4. CLUTCH PEDAL - REMOVAL & REPLACEMENT

1. Pull out the split pin from the clevis pin to separate the clutch pedal from the push rod and pull off the return spring. Undo the nut from the fulcrum pin bolt and pull out the fulcrum pin, washer and spacer, the pedal can now be pulled down. Replacement is a direct reversal.

5. CLUTCH REMOVAL

1. The clutch can be removed after removing the gearbox or, if preferred, after removing the engine.
2. Removal of the engine is described in Chapter 1/6 and removal of the gearbox in Chapter 6/3. The easiest way to gain access to the clutch is to just remove the gearbox.
3. Remove the clutch assembly by unscrewing the six bolts holding the cover to the rear face of the flywheel. Unscrew the bolts diagonally half a turn at a time to prevent distortion to the cover flange.
4. With all the bolts and spring washers removed lift the clutch assembly off the locating dowels. The driven plate or clutch disc will fall out at this stage as it is not attached to either the clutch cover assembly or the flywheel.

6. CLUTCH REPLACEMENT

1. It is important that no oil or grease gets on the clutch disc friction linings, or the pressure plate and flywheel faces. It is advisable to replace the clutch with clean hands and to wipe down the pressure plate and flywheel faces with a clean dry rag before assembly begins.

2. Place the clutch disc against the flywheel with the shorter end of the hub, which is the end with the chamfered splines, facing the flywheel. On no account should the clutch disc be replaced with the longer end of the centre hub facing the flywheel as on reassembly it will be found quite impossible to operate the clutch in this position.

3. Replace the clutch cover assembly loosely on the dowels. Replace the six bolts and spring washers and tighten them finger tight so that the clutch disc is gripped but can still be moved.

4. The clutch disc must now be centralised so that when the engine and gearbox are mated, the gearbox input shaft splines will pass through the splines in the centre of the driven plate hub.

5. Centralisation can be carried out quite easily by inserting a round bar or long screw-driver through the hole in the centre of the clutch, so that the end of the bar rests in the small hole in the end of the crankshaft containing the input shaft bearing bush. Ideally an input shaft should be used.

6. Using the input shaft bearing bush as a fulcrum, moving the bar sideways or up and down will move the clutch disc in whichever direction is necessary to achieve centralisation.

7. Centralisation is easily judged by removing the bar and viewing the driven plate hub in relation to the hole in the release bearing. When the hub appears exactly in the centre of the release bearing hole all is correct.

8. Tighten the clutch bolts to a final torque of 25 lb/ft., in a diagonal sequence to ensure that the cover plate is pulled down evenly, and without distortion of the flange.

9. Mate the engine and gearbox, and check that the clutch is operating properly.

7. CLUTCH DISMANTLING

1. It is not very often that it is necessary to dismantle the clutch cover assembly, and in the normal course of events clutch replacement is the term used for simply fitting a new clutch disc.

2. If a new clutch disc is being fitted it is a false economy not to renew the release bearing at the same time. This will preclude having to replace it at a later date when wear on the clutch linings is still very small.

3. It should be noted here that it is preferable to purchase an exchange clutch cover assembly

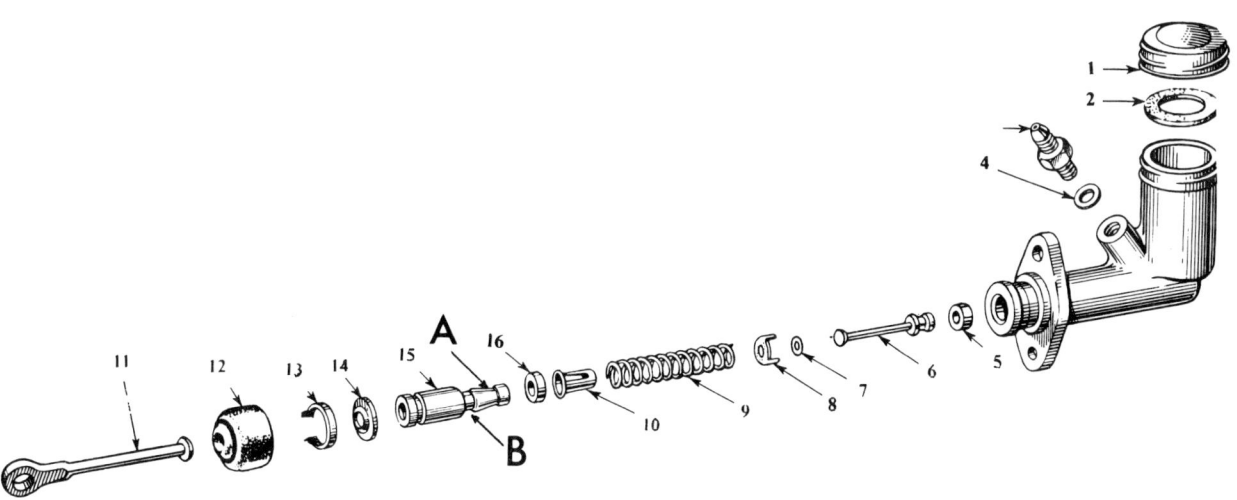

Fig. 5:2 EXPLODED VIEW OF THE CLUTCH MASTER CYLINDER.

1 Master cylinder cap.	9 Piston return spring.	13 Circlip.
2 Sealing ring.	10 Piston return spring retainer.	14 Washer.
3 Adaptor for hydraulic pipe.	11 Pushrod.	15 Piston.
4 Sealing washer.	12 Rubber boot.	16 Inner seal.
5 Valve seal.		
6 Valve stem.		
7 Valve seal spring washer.		
8 Seat spacer.		

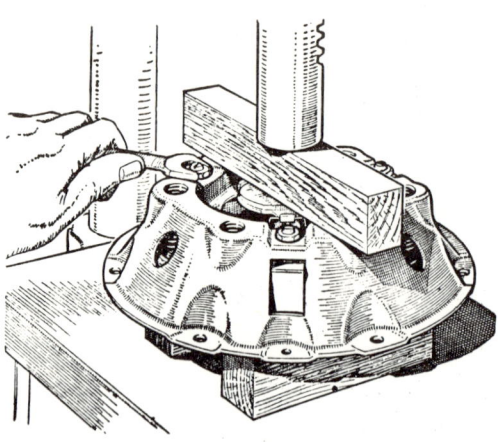

Fig. 5.3 Compressing the clutch springs with the aid of a hydraulic press and three wood blocks.

unit, which will have been properly balanced rather than to dismantle and repair the existing cover.

4. Before beginning work ensure that either the clutch assembly gauging tool 18G 99A or a press and a block of wood is available for compressing the clutch springs so that the three adjusting nuts can be freed.

5. Presuming that it is possible to borrow from your local BMC agent, clutch assembly tool 18G 99A, proceed as follows:-

6. Mark the clutch cover, release levers, and pressure plate lugs so that they can be refitted in the same relative positions.

7. Unhook the springs from the release bearing thrust plate and remove the plate and spring.

8. Place the three correctly sized spacing washers provided with the clutch assembly tool on the tool base plate in the positions indicated by the chart (found inside the lid of the assembly tool container).

9. Place the clutch face down on the three spacing washers so that the washers are as close as possible to the release levers, with the six holes in the cover flange in line with the six holes in the base plate.

10. Insert the six bolts provided with the assembly tool through the six holes in the cover flange, and tighten the cover down diagonally onto the base plate.

11. With a suitable punch, tap back the three tab washers and then remove the three adjusting nuts and bearing plates from the pressure plate bolts on early models, and just unscrew the three adjusting nuts on later models.

12. Unscrew the six bolts holding the clutch cover to the base plate, diagonally, and a turn at a time, so as to release the cover evenly. Lift the cover off and extract the six pressure springs and the spring retaining cups.

8. CLUTCH INSPECTION

1. Examine the clutch disc friction linings for wear and loose rivets and the disc for rim distortion, cracks, broken hub springs, and worn splines.

2. It is always best to renew the clutch driven plate as an assembly to preclude further trouble, but, if it is wished to merely renew the linings, the rivets should be drilled out and not knocked out with a punch. The manufacturers do not advise that only the linings are renewed and personal experience dictates that it is far more satisfactory to renew the driven plate complete than to try and economise by only fitting new friction linings.

3. Check the machined faces of the flywheel and the pressure plate. If either are badly grooved they should be machined until smooth. If the pressure plate is cracked or split it must be renewed, also if the portion on the other side of the plate in contact with the three release lever tips are grooved.

4. Check the release bearing thrust plate for cracks and renew it if any are found.

5. Examine the tips of the release levers which bear against the thrust plate, and renew the levers if more than a small flat has been worn on them.

6. Renew any clutch pressure springs that are broken or shorter than standard.

7. Examine the depressions in the release levers which fit over the knife edge fulcrums and renew the levers if the metal appears badly worn.

8. Examine the clutch release bearing in the gearbox bellhousing and if it is worn to within $1/16$ in. of the rim of the metal cup, or if it is cracked or pitted, it must be removed and replaced.

9. Removal of the clutch release bearing is easily accomplished by pulling off the two retaining springs.

10. Also check the clutch withdrawal lever for slackness. If this is evident, withdraw the lever and renew the bush.

9. CLUTCH REASSEMBLY

1. During clutch reassembly ensure that the marked components are placed in their correct relative positions.

2. Place the three spacing washers on the clutch assembly tool base in the same position as for dismantling the clutch.

CLUTCH AND ACTUATING MECHANISM

3. Place the clutch pressure plate face down on the three spacing washers.

4. Position the three release levers on the knife edge fulcrums (or release lever floating pins in the later clutches) and ensure that the anti-rattle springs are in place over the inner end of the levers.

5. Position the pressure springs on the pressure plate bosses.

6. Fit the flanged cups to the clutch cover and fit the cover over the pressure plate in the same relative position as it was originally.

7. Insert the six assembly tool bolts through the six holes in the clutch cover flange and tighten the cover down, diagonally, a turn at a time.

8. Replace the three bearing plates, tag washers, and adjusting nuts over the pressure plate studs in the early units, and just screw the adjusting nuts into the eyebolts in the later models.

9. To correctly adjust the clutch release levers use the clutch assembly tool as detailed below:-

a) Screw the actuater into the base plate and settle the clutch mechanism by pumping the actuater handle up and down a dozen times. Unscrew the actuater.

b) Screw the tool pillar into the base plate and slide the correctly sized distance piece (as indicated in the chart in the tool's box) recessed side downwards, over the pillar.

c) Slip the height finger over the centre pillar and turn the release lever adjusting nuts, until the height fingers, when rotated and held firmly down, just contact the highest part of the clutch release lever tips.

d) Remove the pillar, replace the actuater, and settle the clutch mechanism as in (a).

e) Refit the centre pillar and height finger and recheck the clutch release lever clearance, and adjust if not correct.

10. With the centre pillar removed, lock the adjusting nuts found on early clutches by bending up the tab washers.

11. Replace the release bearing thrust plate and fit the retaining springs over the thrust plate hooks.

12. Unscrew the six bolts holding the clutch cover to the base plate, diagonally, a turn at a time and assembly is now complete.

10. CLUTCH SLAVE CYLINDER - REMOVAL, DISMANTLING, EXAMINATION & REASSEMBLY

1. The clutch slave cylinder is located on the right-hand side of the bellhousing. The cylinder is held in place by two bolts and spring washers.

2. To remove the slave cylinder, completely disconnect the hydraulic pipe at the cylinder; catch the hydraulic fluid that will spill in a jam jar or other suitable container; undo the two retaining bolts and pull the cylinder away from the push rod which is left attached to the clutch release fork.

3. If it is wished to remove the cylinder because the gearbox is being removed, there is no need to disconnect the hydraulic pipe; the slave cylinder can be tied back out of the way. always blank off the open end of the hydraulic pipe.

4. Clean the outside of the cylinder before dismantling. Remove the rubber dust cap and shake the piston, seal, seal filler, and spring out of the cylinder. Clean all the components thoroughly with hydraulic fluid or alcohol and then dry them off.

5. Carefully examine the rubber components for signs of swelling, distortion, splitting or other wear, and check the piston and cylinder wall for wear and score marks. Replace any parts that are found faulty.

6. Reassembly is a straight reversal of the dismantling procedure, but NOTE the following points:-

a) As the component parts are refitted to the slave cylinder barrel, smear them with hydraulic fluid.

b) When reassembling the operating cylinder, locate the piston seal at the end of the piston so that the sealing lip is away from the body of the piston.

c) On completion of reassembly, top up the reservoir tank with the correct grade of hydraulic fluid and bleed the system.

11. CLUTCH MASTER CYLINDER - REMOVAL, DISMANTLING, EXAMINATION & REASSEMBLY

1. Free the master cylinder pushrod from the clutch pedal after undoing and removing the nut and bolt which hold them together. The numbers in the text refer to Fig. 5.2.

2. Place a rag under the master cylinder to catch any hydraulic fluid which may be spilt. Unscrew the union nut from the end of the hydraulic pipe where it enters the clutch master cylinder and gently pull the pipe clear.

3. Unscrew the two bolts and spring washers holding the clutch cylinder mounting flange to the mounting bracket.

4. Remove the master cylinder and reservoir unscrew the filler cap 1, and drain the hydraulic fluid into a clean container.

5. Pull off the rubber boot 12, which exposes the circlip 13 which must be removed so the pushrod complete with metal retaining washer

14 can be pulled out of the master cylinder.

6. Pull the piston 15 and valve assembly 6 as one unit from the master cylinder.

7. The next step is to separate the piston and valve assemblies. With the aid of a small screwdriver prise up the inner leg of the piston return spring retainer 10 which engages under a shoulder in the front of the piston and holds the retainer 10 in place.

8. The retainer 10, spring 9, and valve assembly 5-8, can then be separated from the piston.

9. To dismantle the valve assembly compress the spring 9, and move the retainer 10 (which has an offset hole) to one side in order to release the valve stem 6 from the retainer 10.

10. With the seat spacer 8 and valve seal washer 7 removed, the rubber seals can be taken off and inspected.

11. Clean and carefully examine all the parts, especially the piston cup and rubber washers, for signs of distortion, swelling, splitting, or other wear and check the piston and cylinder for wear and scoring. Replace any parts that are faulty.

During the inspection of the piston seal it has been found advisable to maintain the shape of this seal as regular as possible and for this reason do not turn it inside out as slight distortion may be caused.

12. Rebuild the piston and valve assembly in the following sequence:-

a) Fit the piston seal 16 to the piston 15 so the larger circumference of the rubber lip will enter the cylinder bore first. The seal sits in the groove 'B'.

b) Then fit the valve seal 5 to the valve 6 in the same way.

c) Place the valve spring seal washer 7 so its convex face abuts the valve stem flange 6 and then fit the seat spacer 8 and spring 9.

d) Fit the spring retainer 10 to the spring 9 which must then be compressed so the valve stem 6 can be reinserted in the retainer 10.

e) Replace the front of the piston 15 in the retainer 10, and then press down the retaining leg so it locates under the shoulder 'A' at the front of the piston 15.

f) Generously lubricate the assembly with hydraulic fluid and carefully replace it in the master cylinder taking great care not to damage the rubber seals as they are inserted into the cylinder bore.

g) Fit the pushrod 11 and washer 14 in place and secure with the circlip 13. Replace the rubber boot 12.

13. Replacement of the unit in the car is a straightforward reversal of the removal seq-

uence. Finally, bleed the system as described earlier in section 3.

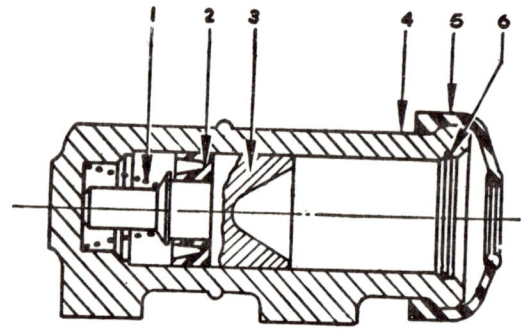

Fig. 5.4. Sectioned view of the clutch slave cylinder
1 Spring. 2 Seal. 3 Piston. 4 Body. 5 Dust cover. 6 Circlip

12 CLUTCH FORK & RELEASE BEARING - REMOVAL & REPLACEMENT

1. With the gearbox and engine separated to provide access to the clutch, attention can be given to the clutch operating fork and the release bearing located in the bellhousing.

2. The carbon release bearing is a relatively inexpensive but important component and unless it is nearly new it is a mistake not to replace it during an overhaul of the clutch. Shown in the photograph is a well worn release bearing.

3. To remove the old bearing from the clutch

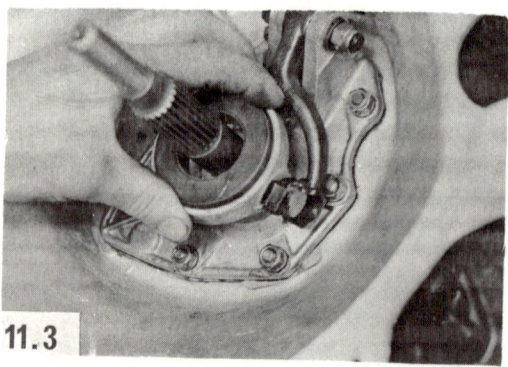

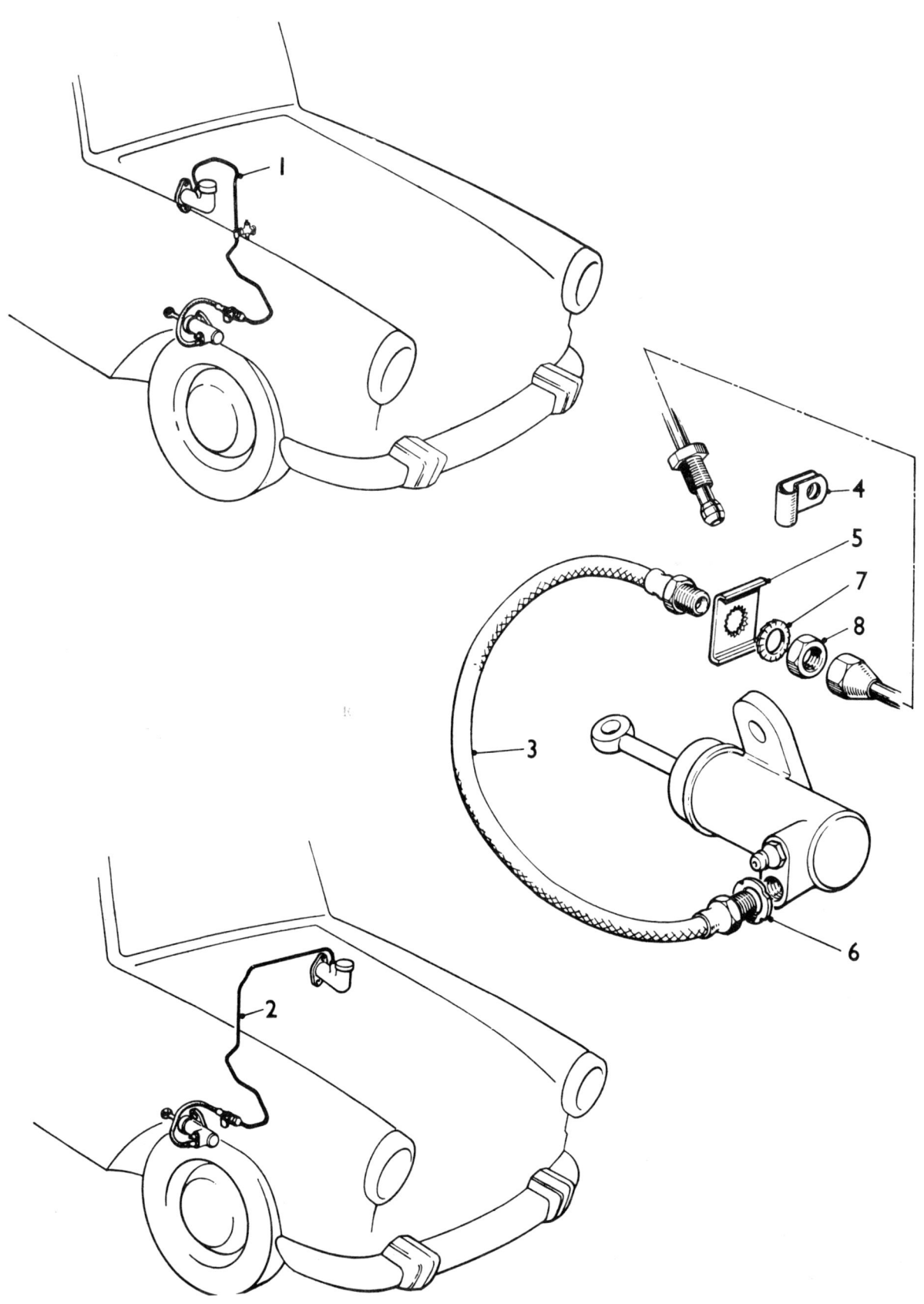

Fig. 5.5 EXPLODED VIEW OF THE SLAVE CYLINDER ASSOCIATED COMPONENTS
Pipe from master cylinder to slave cylinder. 2 Pipe from master cylinder to slave cylinder L. H. D.
3 Flexible hose. 4 Clip. 5 Flexible pipe to bracket locking plate.
6 Joint washer. 7 Shakeproof washer. 8 Nut.

operating fork simply turn the spring retaining clips through 90º and remove them. The bearing can be lifted out as shown.

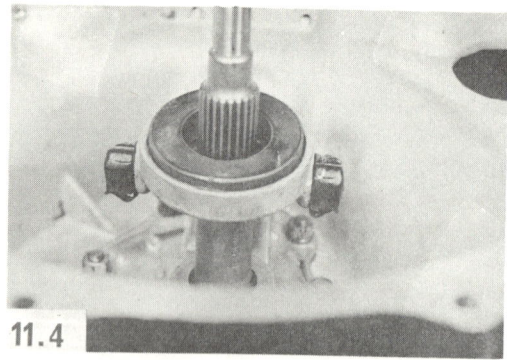

11.4

4. Replacement is a straightforward reversal of the removal sequence. Compare the height of the unworn carbon ring shown with that of the worn ring in photograph 11.2.

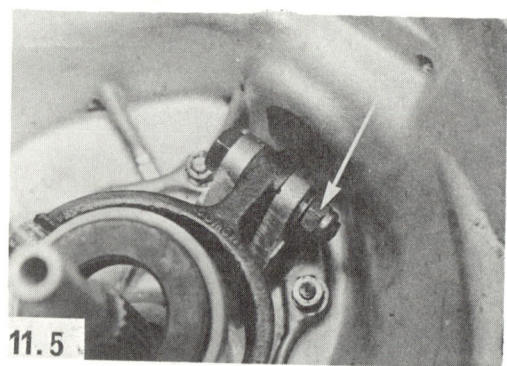

11.5

5. Check the clutch withdrawal lever for free play where it is held to the bellhousing. If very loose undo the locknut (arrowed) and remove the washer and bolt.
6. Take the lever from the bellhousing and if the clutch withdrawal lever bushes are worn they must be renewed at your local BMC garage or engineering works. Replacement is a straightforward reversal of the removal procedure.

13 CLUTCH FAULTS

There are four main faults which the clutch and release mechanism are prone to. They may occur by themselves or in conjunction with any of the other faults. They are clutch squeal, slip, spin, and judder.

14. CLUTCH SQUEAL - DIAGNOSIS & CURE

1 If on taking up the drive or when changing gear, the clutch squeals, this is a sure indication of a badly worn clutch release bearing.
2. As well as regular wear due to normal use, wear of the clutch release bearing is much accentuated if the clutch is ridden, or held down for long periods in gear, with the engine running. To minimise wear of this component the car should always be taken out of gear at traffic lights and for similar hold-ups.
3. The clutch release bearing is not an expensive item.

15. CLUTCH SLIP - DIAGNOSIS & CURE

1. Clutch slip is a self-evident condition which occurs when the clutch friction plate is badly worn, the release arm free travel is insufficient oil or grease have got onto the flywheel or pressure plate faces, or the pressure plate itself is faulty.
2. The reason for clutch slip is that, due to one of the faults listed above, there is either insufficient pressure from the pressure plate, or insufficient friction from the friction plate to ensure solid drive.
3. If small amounts of oil get onto the clutch, they will be burnt off under the heat of clutch engagement, in the process gradually darkening the linings. Excessive oil on the clutch will burn off leaving a carbon deposit which can cause quite bad slip, or fierceness, spin and judder.
4. If clutch slip is suspected, and confirmation of this condition is required, there are several tests which can be made.
5. With the engine in second or third gear and pulling lightly up a moderate incline, sudden depression of the accelerator pedal may cause the engine to increase its speed without any increase in road speed. Easing off on the accelerator will then give a definite drop in engine speed without the car slowing.
6. In extreme cases of clutch slip the engine will race under normal acceleration conditions.
7. If slip is due to oil or grease on the linings a temporary cure can sometimes be effected by squirting carbon tetrochloride into the clutch. The permanent cure is, of course, to renew the clutch driven plate and trace and rectify the oil leak.

16. CLUTCH SPIN - DIAGNOSIS & CURE

1. Clutch spin is a condition which occurs when there is a leak in the clutch hydraulic actuating mechanism where this system of actuation is used, the release arm free travel is excessive, there is an obstruction in the clutch either on the primary gear splines, or in the operating lever itself, or the oil may have partially burnt off the clutch linings and have left a resinous deposit which is causing the clutch disc to stick to the pressure plate or flywheel.
2. The reason for clutch spin is that due to any, or a combination of, the faults just listed, the clutch pressure plate is not completely freeing from the centre plate even with the clutch pedal fully depressed.

3. If clutch spin is suspected, the condition can be confirmed by extreme difficulty in engaging first gear from rest, difficulty in changing gear, and very sudden take-up of the clutch drive at the fully depressed end of the clutch pedal travel as the clutch is released.

4. Check the operating lever free travel. If this is correct examine the clutch master and slave cylinders and the connecting hydraulic pipe for leaks. Fluid in one of the rubber boots fitted over the end of either the master or slave cylinders, where fitted, is a sure sign of a leaking piston seal.

5. If these points are checked and found to be in order then the fault lies internally in the clutch, and it will be necessary to remove the clutch for examination.

17 CLUTCH JUDDER - DIAGNOSIS & CURE

1. Clutch judder is a self-evident condition which occurs when the gearbox or engine mountings are loose or too flexible, when there is oil on the faces of the clutch friction plate, or when the clutch pressure plate has been incorrectly adjusted.

2. The reason for clutch judder is that due to one of the faults just listed, the clutch pressure plate is not freeing smoothly from the friction disc, and is snatching.

3. Clutch judder normally occurs when the clutch pedal is released in first or reverse gears, and the whole car shudders as it moves backwards or forwards.

CHAPTER SIX

GEARBOX

CONTENTS

SPECIFICATIONS

Gearbox

No. of gears	4 forward, 1 reverse
Type of gears	Helical constant mesh
Synchromesh	2nd, 3rd, 4th
Top gear speed per 1,000 r.p.m.	16.6 m.p.h. saloon cars. 15.6 m.p.h. estate cars
Laygear end float	.002 to .003 in. (.051 to .076 mm.)
Mainshaft second & third gear end float	.004 to .006 in. (.102 to .152 mm.)
Speedometer gear ratio	9/28
Oil capacity	4½ pints (2.56 litres, 5.6 U.S. pints)

Gearbox Ratios

First	3.637 to 1
Second	2.215 to 1
Third	1.373 to 1
Fourth	1.000 to 1
Reverse	4.755 to 1

Overall Ratios	Estate Cars (pre 1961) – (after 1961) (also saloons to 1961)	Saloons (after 1961)	
First	17.74 to 1	16.55 to 1	15.64 to 1
Second	10.79 to 1	10.08 to 1	9.52 to 1
Third	6.690 to 1	6.25 to 1	5.91 to 1
Fourth	4.875 to 1	4.55 to 1	4.3 to 1
Reverse	23.20 to 1	21.64 to 1	20.45 to 1

Synchromesh Hub Springs

Free length	½ in. (12.7 mm.)
Fitted length	5/16 in. (7.9 mm.)
Load at Fitted length...	4 to 5 lb. (1.8 to 2.2 kg.)

Selector shaft detent springs

Free length	1 3/16 in. (30.16 mm.)
Fitted length	¾ in. (19.0 mm.)
Load at Fitted length...	18 to 20 lb. (8.16 to 9.07 kg.)

Reverse Plunger Springs

Free length	1 in.
Fitted length	1 3/16 in. (20.63 mm.)
Load at fitted length	91½ to 92½ lb. (41.4 to 41.9 kg.)

GEARBOX

1. GENERAL DESCRIPTION

The gearbox fitted to all models contains four forward and one reverse gear. Synchromesh is fitted between second and third, and between third and fourth gears. The aluminium alloy bellhousing and gearbox casing are a combined casting. Attached to the rear of the gearbox casing is an extension which houses the selector mechanism.

2. ROUTINE MAINTENANCE

1. Once every 6,000 miles remove the combined dipstick and filler from the top of the gearbox and check the level of the engine oil. Replenish as necessary. Change the oil at 12,000 miles; see pages 8 - 12.

3. GEARBOX REMOVAL & REPLACEMENT

1. The gearbox can be removed in unit with the engine through the engine compartment as described in Chapter 1/7. Alternatively, the gearbox can be separated from the engine end plate and lowered from the car. The latter is the best method to adopt.

2. Drain the gearbox oil and place the car on ramps (rear wheels only if necessary), over a pit, or on a hoist.

3. Release the exhaust pipe at the manifold by undoing the securing clamp and, on floor mounted gearlevers, lift off the dust excluder from the gear lever base after removing the gear lever knob. Compress and remove the circlip (118) (all numbers in brackets refer to Fig. 6.2) and withdraw the cover (117), spring (116) and gearlever (112).

4. On models with a steering column gearchange, disconnect the operating rods from the levers on the side of the 'gearbox.

5. The slave cylinder must now be separated from the gearbox casing. To do this, remove the clevis pin from the slave cylinder pushrod and undo the two bolts which hold the cylinder in place. DO NOT disconnect the hydraulic pipe and tie the slave cylinder safely out of the way.

6. Undo the round knurled nut which holds the speedometer cable in place on the pinion (131) protruding through the side of the gearbox and separate the cable from the pinion.

7. Scratch a mating mark on the flanges of the rear universal joint and undo and remove the four nuts and bolts which hold the rear U.J. flange to the rear axle flange. Separate the propeller shaft at the rear flanges and remove the shaft from the car by pulling it out rearwards.

8. Now support the underneath of the rear of the engine with a hydraulic jack or similar,

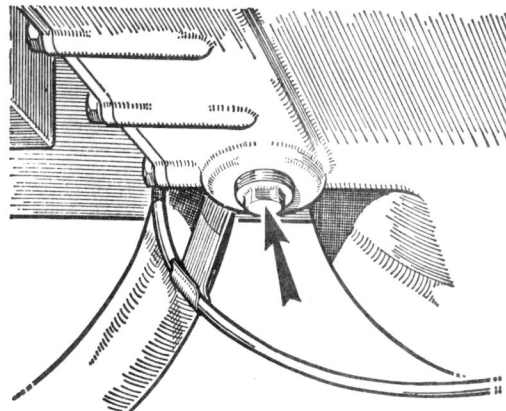

Fig. 6.1. The gearbox drain plug (arrowed)

and undo the six bolts which hold the rear cross member to the body. Disconnect the cross member from the gearbox rear mounting and remove the rear cross member from under the car.

9. Undo the bellhousing flange nuts and bolts and carefully pull off the gearbox from the rear of the engine. NOTE. It may be necessary to lower the jack under the rear end of the sump so the top of the bellhousing clears the car floor.

10. Replacement of the gearbox is a straightforward reversal of the removal sequence. Take great care when mating the gearbox to the engine that the gearbox primary shaft passes through the clutch centre. On no account should the gearbox be allowed to hang on the primary shaft. Support the gearbox while refitting the six nuts and bolts. Then fit the gearbox support and cross member, the propeller shaft (make sure the marks on the flanges coincide), the slave cylinder, speedometer drive and gearlever.

4. GEARBOX DISMANTLING

1. All numbers in brackets refer to Fig. 6.2. Pull out the dipstick and undo the two bolts and spring washers (153, 154), which hold the speedometer pinion bush (132) in place. Remove the bush (132), gasket (135) and speedometer pinion (131).

2. Examine the pinion for wear and replace it if necessary.

3. Undo the bolts holding the remote control tower (31) in place and remove the extension or tower.

4. Undo the bolts and washers which hold the extension side cover (26) in place and remove the cover and its joint washer (26, 27).

5. Lift out the interlock plate (109) and bracket and then undo the bolt and spring washer (121,

122) from the front selector lever (120). Undo the nuts, bolts, and spring washers which hold the extension (18) to the gearbox (1) and pull the extension off. Note that the selector lever (120) will fall free as the extension is pulled back.

6. Take off the side cover and gasket (11, 12) from the gearbox after undoing the three countersunk retaining screws, and seven bolts. Note the fibre washer (15) and the plain washer (14) under the head of the top rear bolt (13). It is vital these washers are replaced in the correct order on reassembly, as otherwise a severe oil leak will develop after a short time.

7. If it is wished to remove the three selectors (98, 100, 101) located outside the end face of the gearbox, from off the ends of the selector rods, cut through the locking wire, undo the retaining bolts (99) and pull the selectors away. It is not necessary to do this unless the selectors are to be renewed.

8. The three selector rods can be removed together with the selector rod block (95) as an assembly, or the selector rods can be removed one at a time. The latter course is easier unless a ring or socket spanner with very narrow walls is at hand to undo the two bolts (96) which are partially countersunk and hold the block to its dowels (2) on the end of the gearbox casing. With the bolts removed and after having removed the selector forks the block complete with selector rods can be lifted off.

9. To remove the three selector forks (83, 87, 89) release the locknuts (86) and loosen the fork locating bolts (84). As the selector rods (88, 90, 92) are pulled rearwards the forks can be slid off the forward ends of the rods and placed on one side.

10. It is important to remove the rods in the following order : Reverse rod (92), fourth and third gear rod (90), first and second gear rod (88). Place a rag round the block (95) as the selector rods are removed to catch the locating balls and springs (93, 94) which are liable to spring out. NOTE the distance tube over the third and fourth gear selector rod on some models. If the selector rods are difficult to remove, take off the front cover (6) and tap them out gently.

11. Undo and remove the bolt (52) which holds the reverse gear shaft (50) in position.

12. Undo the nuts and lockwashers (9, 10) which hold the front cover (6) in place, and remove the cover together with its gasket (8). Do not remove the bearing shims from the cover. Remove the reverse gear shaft.

13. Measure the end float of the laygear (44) with a feeler gauge. If the end float exceeds .003 in. then new thrust washers must be fitted

Fig. 6.2 EXPLODED VIEW OF THE GEARBOX

1 Casing assembly. 2 Dowel locating block to gearbox. 3 Stud for front cover. 4 Stud for rear extension. 5 Plug—drain. 6 Cover assembly (front). 7 Oil seal. 8 Joint washer— cover to casing. 9 Washer for stud (spring). 10 Nut for front cover stud. 11 Cover—gearbox side. 12 Joint washer—cover to casing. 13 Screw—gearbox side cover. 14 Washer— for screw (plain). 15 Washer for screw (fibre). 16 Screw—countersunk. 17 Washer for screw. 18 Extension (rear). 19 Bush—rear extension. 20 Oil seal—rear extension. 21 Plug—taper. 22 Joint washer—extension to casing. 23 Washer for screw and stud (spring). 24 Screw—extension to casing. 25 Nut for stud. 26 Cover—side—rear extension. 27 Joint washer for side cover. 28 Screw for screw (spring). 29 Screw—slide cover to extension. 30 Breather assembly. 31 Remote control tower. 32 Dowel for tower. 33 Joint washer—tower to extension. 34 Screw—tower to extension. 35 Washer for screw (spring). 36 Shaft—first motion. 37 Bearing. 38 Spring ring—bearing. 39 Shim for first motion shaft. 40 Washer for first motion shaft nut. 41 Nut for first motion shaft. 42 Needle rollers. 43 Layshaft. 44 Laygear. 45 Washer—thrust (front). 46 Washer—thrust (rear). 47 Rollers—needle bearing. 48 Tube—distance—laygear bearing. 49 Spring ring—laygear. 50 Shaft—reverse. 51 Washer for screw—locking. 52 Screw—reverse. shaft locking. 53 Gear assembly—reverse. 54 Bush—reverse gear. 55 Shaft—third motion. 56 Restrictor—oil. 57 Washer—thrust (front). 58 Washer—thrust (rear). 59 Peg for front thrust washer. 60 Spring for peg. 61 Wheel and synchronizer assembly. 62 Ball for synchronizer. 63 Spring for synchronizer ball. 64 Baulk ring for second gear. 65 Gear—second speed. 66 Bush—second gear. 67 Ring—interlocking. 68 Gear—third speed. 69 Bush for third speed gear. 70 Baulk ring—third and fourth gear. 71 Synchronizer—third and fourth gear. 72 Spring for synchronizer. 73 Ball for synchronizer. 74 Coupling—sliding. 75 Distance piece—main shaft. 76 Washer (locking). 77 Nut for main shaft. 78 Gear—speedometer. 79 Key for speedometer gear. 80 Housing—rear bearing. 81 Peg—locating. 82 Bearing—rear ball. 83 Fork—reverse. 84 Bolt for reverse fork (locating). 85 Washer for screw (shakeproof). 86 Locknut. 87 Fork—first and second speed. 88 Rod—first and second speed fork. 89 Fork—third and fourth speed. 90 Rod—third and fourth speed fork. 91 Distance piece. 92 Rod—reverse fork. 93 Ball for fork—locating. 94 Spring for locating ball. 95 Block—sliding shaft locating. 96 Screw—locating block to casing. 97 Washer for screw (spring). 98 Selector—first and second gear. 99 Screw—selector locating. 100 Selector—third and fourth gear. 101 Selector—reverse gear. 102 Plunger—reverse selector. 103 Spring—reverse plunger. 104 Screw—reverse plunger spring. 105 Washer for screw (spring). 106 Spring— detent. 107 Dowel—reverse plunger. 108 Ball for plunger. 109 Arm assembly—interlocking. 110 Switch—reverse light. 111 Washer (joint). 112 Gearlever. 113 Knob for lever. 114 Pin—change speed lever. 115 Washer for pin (spring). 116 Spring—change speed lever. 117 Cover for spring. 118 Circlip for cover. 119 Shaft—remote control. 120 Lever—selector (front). 121 Screw for selector lever. 122 Washer for screw (shakeproof). 123 Key—lever to shaft. 124 Lever—selector (rear). 125 Screw for selector lever. 126 Washer for screw (spring). 127 Bush for change speed lever. 128 Circlip for bush. 129 Cap for control shaft boss. 130 Joint washer for cap. 131 Pinion—speedometer. 132 Bush for pinion. 133 Seal—oil—pinion. 134 Ring—oil seal retaining. 135 Joint washer—speedometer bush. 136 Lever—clutch withdrawal. 137 Bush—withdrawal lever. 138 Bolt—clutch withdrawal lever. 139 Washer for bolt. 140 Nut for bolt (stiff). 141 Cover for clutch lever. 142 Oil level indicator. 143 Cover—starter pinion. 144 Washer for screw (spring). 145 Washer—cover to casing. 146 Turret—gearbox cover. 147 Gaiter—gear lever. 148 Retainer—gaiter. 149 Screw—gaiter to turret. 150 Screw. 151 Washer for screw. 152 Nut for screw. 153 Spring washer. 154 Bolt—speedometer pinion bush. 155 Button—speedometer pinion.

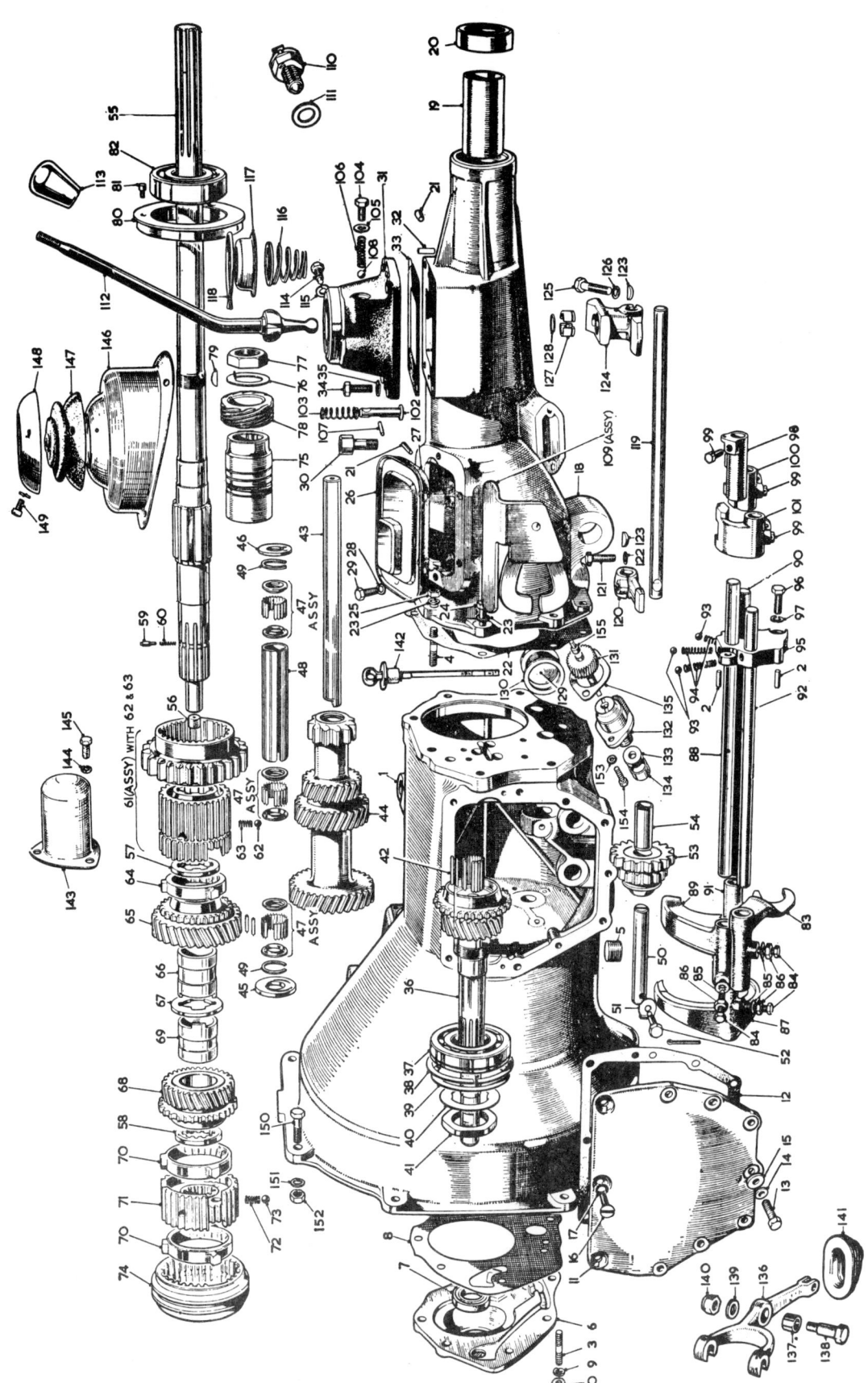

109

on reassembly. If the reading is in excess of .003 in. write it down so that the correctly sized washers can be obtained at a later stage.

14. With a suitable metal rod, drift the layshaft (43) out. The laygear cluster (44) and the two thrust washers (45, 46) will drop to the bottom of the gearbox casing as the drift used to push out the layshaft is withdrawn.

15. The mainshaft (55) is removed from the rear of the gearbox casing with the large ball bearing (82) and the bearing housing (80) complete as one assembly. Make a small scratch mark between the bearing housing and the gearbox casing so that the housing can be replaced in exactly the same position on reassembly. Freeing the bearing housing from the gearbox casing is sometimes difficult. Try gently tapping the bearing housing at alternate, diagonally opposite, points from inside the casing. Alternatively, remove the distance piece and speedometer gear drive (78, 75). Replace the nut (77) and tap vigorously against its underside. The housing will gradually emerge from the gearbox casing and as soon as it is sufficiently far out, place a puller or levers under the lip of the bearing housing to accelerate the complete removal of the mainshaft assembly from the gearbox. Take great care not to damage the bearing housing or the gearbox casing during this operation.

16. Insert a metal rod through the large hole in the gearbox casing left by the main shaft bearing housing, and locate the end of the rod in the hole in the end of the first motion shaft (36). Tap the first motion shaft complete with bearing into the bellhousing. Lift out the laygear.

17. The gearbox is now completely stripped. The component parts should now be examined for wear as detailed later, and the layshaft. first motion shaft, and main shaft broken down further, as shown in the next section.

5. GEARBOX EXAMINATION & RENOVATION
   1. Carefully clean and then examine all the component parts starting with the baulk ring synchronisers, for general wear, distortion, and damage to machined faces and threads.
   2. Examine the gearwheels for excessive wear and chipping of the teeth and renew them as necessary. If the laygear endfloat is above the permitted tolerance of .002 to .003 in. the thrust washers must be renewed. These are available from your local BMC agent in varying thicknesses to compensate for laygear wear. Compare the old thrust washers with new standard units as the wear may be in the thrust washers. New thrust washers are available in the follow-

ing thicknesses:- .154 to .156 in. (3.81 to 3.96 mm.), .157 to .159 in. (3.95 to 4.03 mm.), .160 to .161 in. (4.06 to 4.08 mm.), .163 to .164 in. (4.13 to 4.16 mm.).

3. Needle roller bearings are fitted at each end of the laygear. Unless the car has only done a very small mileage they invariably need renewing. To examine them, pull out the spring rings (49) and with a finger pull out the rollers (47) and the distance tube (48). Renew the roller bearings and races if worn. On early cars the rollers are loose but on later models they are caged. The later type are very much easier to deal with.

4. On early cars to reassemble the roller bearings inside the laygear, start by assembling them to the layshaft. Fit the stepped end of the layshaft in a vice, grease the shaft generously and fit the bottom rollers, distance tube and top two sets of rollers to the shaft. Slip the spring retaining ring into its groove in the front end of the laygear and carefully slide the laygear over the layshaft, taking great care not to dislodge any of the rollers. Remove the laygear and layshaft from the vice and fit the remaining spring retaining ring.

5. On later cars to assemble the caged roller bearings to the laygear, oil all the parts generously and then slip the distance tube and two bearings in at the small end followed by the remaining two bearings at the larger end of the laygear.

6. Examine the condition of the main ball bearings, one on the first motion shaft, and the other on the main shaft. If there is looseness between the inner and outer races the bearings must be pulled off and renewed.

7. On the first motion shaft it is necessary to remove the retaining nut and lockwasher before the bearing is pulled. NOTE. The locknut has a LEFT-HAND THREAD, and the position of the spring ring. On refitting a new bearing to the first motion shaft position the tag on the lockwasher in the shaft keyway so that it faces towards the nut.

8. On the mainshaft first check the end float on third gear as shown in Fig. 6.3 and note the measurement so the correct thrust washer can be fitted on reassembly. Then place the shaft (55) in a vice with padded jaws, release the speedometer gear (78), the half-moon shaped woodruff key (79), and distance piece (75), if this has not already been done, and then pull the bearing housing (80) and bearing (82) off the shaft. The bearing can then be drifted away from its housing.

9. Examine the first motion shaft needle roller bearings and renew them if worn.

10. If it is wished to renew the synchronisers or to examine the second and third gear bushes (66, 69) the mainshaft must be dismantled as described in the following paragraphs.

11. Slide the third and fourth gear synchroniser (71) complete with baulk rings (70) and the coupling sleeve (74) as one assembly off the end of the mainshaft. Take care not to pull accidently the coupling sleeve (74) off the gear synchroniser hub (71) as the springs and balls (72, 73) will jump out and may become lost.

12. With a thin electrical screwdriver, or thick piece of wire, depress the front thrust washer retaining peg (59) (see Fig. 6.4) through the hole in the front of third gear so the peg is flush with the mainshaft surface. Rotate the splined thrust washer (58), so that one of the spline protruberences holds the plunger down and the washer can be slid off the end of the shaft.

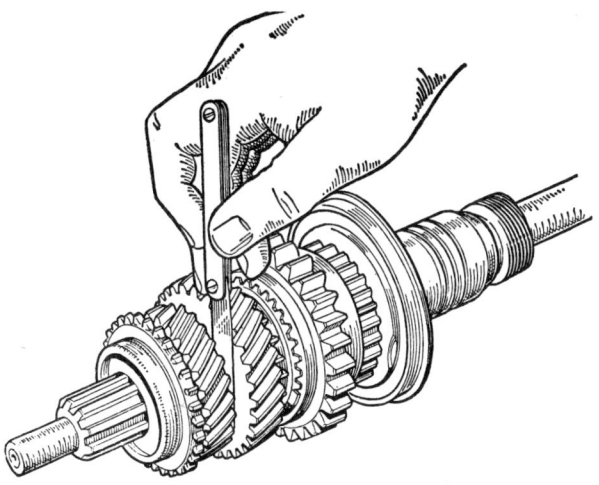

Fig. 6.3 Checking the endfloat on third gear with a feeler gauge.

13. The retaining peg and spring (59, 60) can now be removed and then third gear (68), the third gear bush (69), the interlock ring (67), second gear (65), the second gear bush (66), the synchroniser ring (64), and the thrust washer (57) can be slid off.

14. Finally slide off the first and second gear synchroniser the first gear (61), ensuring that first gear does not slide off the synchroniser hub because of the possibility of loosing the synchroniser balls and springs (62, 63).

15. Examine the second and third gear bushes and the reverse gear internal bush for wear, and renew them if suspect. If fitting new bushes to the mainshaft, heat them first to between 180° and 200°C (356° and 392°F) and make sure the locating tongues on the bushes are in line with the splines on the shaft and also that the oil holes are in line. When fitting a new bush to reverse gear press it in from the small end of the gear until the end of the bush is flush with the end face of the gear.

16. To exclude the possibility of oil leaks developing at the front or the rear of the gearbox the first motion shaft and mainshaft rear extension oil seals should be renewed as a matter of course. The seal (20) in the rear extension is most easily removed with the aid of BMC Service Tool 18G389 and 389B, and replaced with the aid of tools 18G134 and 18G134N. If the tools are not available then carefully prise the old oil seal out and drift the new one, equally carefully, into position.

17. The seal in the front cover can be removed fairly easily by gentle prising, and the new seal can be fitted by hand but make sure the lip faces towards the gearbox. If available tools 18G134 and 134N will make the job a little easier.

18. Renew the clutch release fork and gear-

lever rubber gaiters if they are split or have deteriorated. Examine the split nylon bush on the selector lever and renew it if it is damaged or worn. Thoroughly clean out the gearbox casing lubrication channels and oilways. The gearbox should be spotlessly clean as shown in the photograph.

19. Check the free length of the synchromesh hub springs which should be ½ in; the reverse plunger spring which should be 1 in; and the shaft and reverse plunger detent springs whose free length should be $1\frac{3}{16}$ in. Renew any springs which do not meet the required standard and reassemble the first speed gear and synchroniser, and the third and fourth gear synchroniser and coupling sleeve using Service Tools 18G222 and 18G223 if available to facilitate the rapid fitting of the springs and bolts.

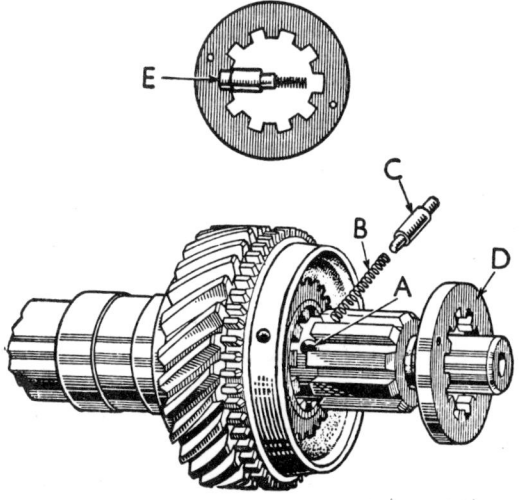

Fig. 6.4 The mainshaft gears are held in place by the locking washer 'D' which is retained by the peg 'C'. 'E' shows how the peg locates in the washer. 'A' is the hole for the spring and peg and 'B' is the spring.

6. MAINSHAFT & GEARBOX - REASSEMBLY

1. If the mainshaft has been dismantled, gearbox reassembly starts by rebuilding the former, Use new washers, gaskets and joint washers throughout during reassembly.

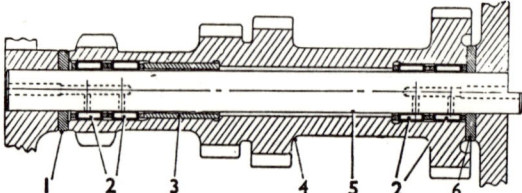

Fig. 6.5 THE LAYGEAR ASSEMBLY FITTED TO LATER MODELS. 1 Thrust washer —small. 2 Needle-roller bearing (pair). 3 Distance tube. 4 Laygear. 5 Layshaft. 6 Thrust washer—large.

2. Generously lubricate all the gears, bushes, and bearings with oil as they are assembled. Start by pressing the rear mainshaft bearing into its housing, and the combined bearing and housing onto the tail end of the mainshaft. Then fit the first gear and the second gear synchromesh assembly together with the rear thrust washer from the opposite end of the mainshaft. The completed assembly is shown in the photograph.

3. Then fit the distance piece to the rear end of the mainshaft with the machined end next to the bearing as shown.

4. Next fit the distance tube (arrowed), the lockwasher, and the mainshaft securing nut.

Note the slot for the speedometer drive just behind the distance tube.

5. Tighten the securing nut and gently tap over the lip of the retaining washer as shown to lock the nut in place.

6. Next slide the second to third gear baulk ring synchroniser into place as shown.

7. Fit the second gear mainshaft bush as shown with the oil holes in alignment and with the bush lugs facing the forward splined end of the mainshaft.

8. In the photograph the second gear mainshaft bush is shown in its correct position relative to the mainshaft oil holes.

9. The next step is to generously lubricate the bush as shown.

10. Slide on second gear with its conical face abuting the baulk ring synchroniser (see Photograph).

11. Then fit the interlocking ring for second and third gear bushes making sure the ring engages the lugs on the bush.

12. Slide the third gear mainshaft bush lug end first into place with its oil hole over the corresponding hole in the mainshaft as shown. If the bushes are very tight do not force them into place. Heat them gently so they will slide on easily.

13. Push the third gear bush into place so its lugs engage the two remaining slots in the interlocking ring. The semi-circular cut-out in the bush (arrowed) should now be abuting the hole in the mainshaft into which the retaining pin will fit.

14. Fit the retaining pin and the retaining pin spring to the mainshaft as shown.

15. Slide on third gear as shown, so the flat face lies next to second gear and the cone portion faces forward.

16. Rotate third gear so that the hole in the cone portion is over the pin and depress the pin with the aid of a thin stiff piece of wire. Fit the thrust washer over the splines and push it up over the head of the depressed pin. (See photograph).

17. Rotate the thrust washer as shown so the pin is able to rise and lock the washer in position.

18. In this photograph the thrust washer and pin are shown correctly assembled inside the cone of third gear. With the aid of a feeler gauge check the endfloat between second and third gear and adjust it so it is between .004 and .006 in. This is achieved by fitting the correct

thickness of thrust washer. The following three thicknesses are available : -

.1565 to .1575 in. (3.96 to 3.98 mm.)
.1585 to .1595 in. (4.01 to 4.03 mm.)
.1605 to .1615 in. (4.06 to 4.08 mm.)

6.19

19. Mainshaft reassembly is completed with the fitting of the third and fourth gear rear baulk ring, the third and fourth gear synchroniser and coupling sleeve, and the front baulk ring.

6.20

20. To assemble the component parts into the gearbox, begin by placing the laygear as shown and thrust washers in the bottom of the casing. The endfloat should have been measured as described in Section 5 para. 2, before the laygear was removed so thrust washers of the correct thickness should be to hand.

21. Note the cut-out (arrowed) on the inner face of the mainshaft bearing housing. This is to clear reverse gear.

22. Carefully fit the built up mainshaft from the rear of the gearbox as shown.

23. Make certain the marks on the gearbox casing and the bearing housing are in alignment as shown. Otherwise it will prove impossible to fit the rear extension. If no marks were made, place the gearbox extension gasket in position to align the dowel which mates with the rear extension. Gently tap down the flat portion of the mainshaft main bearing until it is flush with the end of the gearbox case.

24. Shown here is the bearing housing correct-

ly fitted with the dowel (arrowed) in its proper location.

25. Grease the orifice in the centre of the inner end of the first motion shaft and fit the needle rollers into position as shown. This is much better than fitting the rollers to the spigot on the end of the mainshaft as it is all too easy to dislodge a roller as the mainshaft and primary or first motion shaft are mated.

26. Fit the first motion shaft to the bellhousing end of the gearbox as shown.

27. Push and tap the first motion shaft fully home and ensure none of the needle rollers are dislodged. The mainshaft and first motion shaft are shown here correctly assembled.

28. Use a dummy shaft or rod to pick up the laygear and thrust washers and keep the shaft and rod pressed together until the layshaft is fully inserted. Make sure the cutaway end of the shaft faces forwards. The layshaft is shown here entering the gearcase.

29. Generously lubricate the gears and bearings throughout the assembly sequence.

30. Next fit the reverse gear and shaft into the gearbox as shown.

31. Note that the cut-out (arrowed) in the reverse gear shaft must line up under the threaded hole (arrowed) in the gear casing lug.

32. Replace the locating bolt (arrowed) and tab washer and lock the bolt head with the washer.

33. To ensure the gearbox front cover oil seal performs correctly it is important that the front cover (see photograph) 'floats' on its locating studs. The cover should be free to move on its studs very slightly in all directions, so allowing the oil seal to centralise over the first motion shaft.

34. Temporarily fit the front cover to the gearbox as shown.

35. In this way it is possible to line up the step on the end of the layshaft with the cut-out in the cover. The correct position of the layshaft step relative to the gearbox is shown in the photograph.

36. Fit the rubber gaskets to the recess in the flange of the cover as shown.

37. Oil the seal and fit the front cover and gasket over its studs pushing the cover firmly home. Secure the spring washers and nuts finger tight, and then tighten them down half a turn at a time in a diagonal sequence.

38. Next fit the first and second gear selector fork in position as shown.

39. Then fit the reverse selector fork to the gearbox as shown in the photograph.

40. The last selector fork to be fitted is that for third and fourth gears and is fitted over the front coupling as shown.

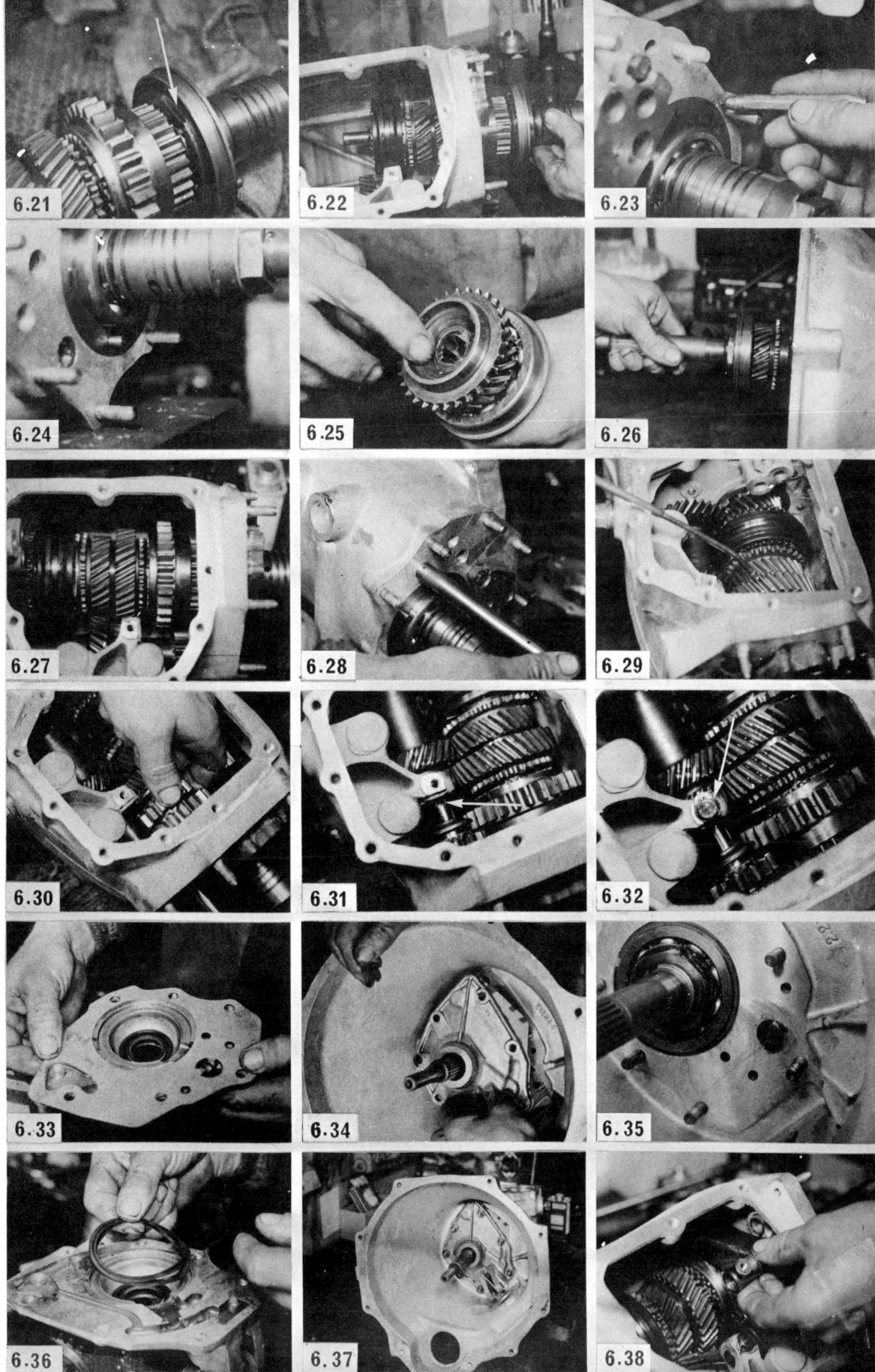

6.39

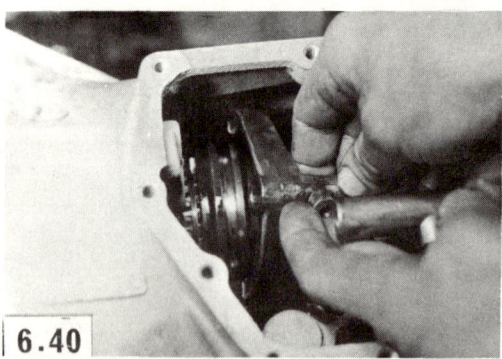

6.40

6.41

41. In this photograph all three selector forks are shown correctly assembled in the gearbox.

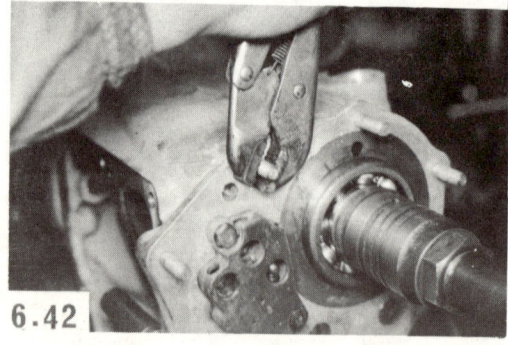

6.42

42. Before the selector rods can be replaced it is necessary to assemble and depress the locking balls and springs. To gain access to the block undo the stud directly above it as shown.

43. Fit the first spring into place and follow this with one of the locking balls. Press down on the ball with a screwdriver.

44. Then slide in the third and fourth gear selector rod as shown, taking great care that the locking ball does not spring out before it is covered by the rod.

45. Slide the distance tube over the third and fourth gear selector rod as it is fed into the gearbox. (See photograph).

46. Feed the third and fourth gear selector rod into the appropriate selector fork as shown.

47. Slide the first and second gear selector rod into the gearbox as shown after fitting the locking ball and spring with the end of a screwdriver.

48. Push the first and second gear selector rod into the first and second gear selector fork as shown and then into its orifice at the front end of the gearbox casing.

49. Finally fit the reverse gear selector rod to the reverse gear selector fork in the same manner and align the holes in the forks and shafts and fit the fork locating bolts and locknuts and tighten the bolts down firmly as shown.

50. With the bolts securely tightened, do up the locknuts as shown.

51. If removed, assemble the selectors to the exposed ends of the selector rods and secure them with their locating bolts. Lock the heads of the bolts to the selectors with locking wire. When correctly assembled the cut-outs in the selectors should line up as shown.

52. Thoroughly clean the end face of the gearbox casing and fit the rear extension gasket in place as shown.

53. Coat the face of the rear extension with jointing compound in order to help make an oil proof joint when the rear extension is mated to the endface of the gearbox casing.

54. Carefully fit the extension in place as shown in the photograph.

55. Fit the spring washers and nuts to the studs on the end of the gearbox casing and tighten them down securely as shown.

56. Next fit the interlock plate to the selectors in the rear extension as shown.

57. When correctly fitted the arms of the interlock plate will rest in the cut-out of the selectors as shown, and the side plate will rest in its recess in the housing.

58. Fit the intermediate selector lever as shown, to the arms of the interlock plate.

59. Position the intermediate selector lever orifice so it points outwards.

60. Slide the intermediate selector lever shaft into the extension from the rear and through the hole in the selector lever.

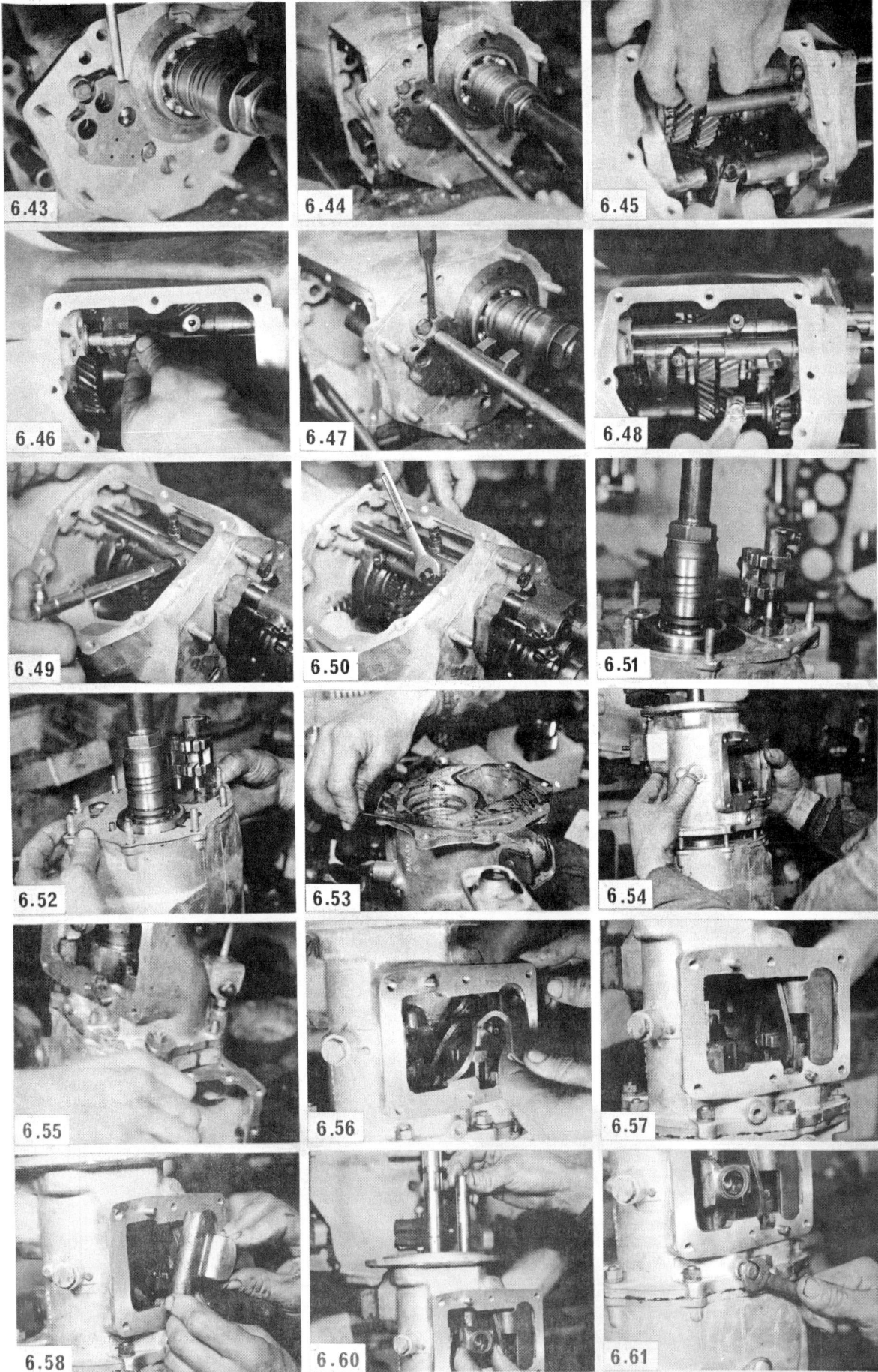

61. Insert and tighten up the bolt and locknut which holds the shaft in position as shown.

62. When correctly assembled, the components inside the extension will appear as in the photograph.

63. Thoroughly clean the gearbox side cover flange and fit a new gasket as shown.

64. Replace the cover on the side flange and ensure the felt washer lies under the plain washer, which must be under the head of the top right-hand bolt as shown. Failure to replace the felt washer in this position will lead to a serious oil leak.

65. Replace and do up the remaining six bolts and spring washers and the three screws.

66. The rebuilt gearbox is now ready for mating with the engine and replacement in the car, and should give thousands of miles of satisfactory motoring (see photograph).

67. Before fitting the gearbox to the engine smear the end of the first motion shaft, which engages with the small bush in the centre of the rear flange of the crankshaft, with grease as shown.

68. Mate engine and gearbox and then fit them to the car.

7. COLUMN GEAR CHANGE - ADJUSTMENT

1. Under normal running conditions no adjustment of the steering column gear change is necessary. If a replacement gearbox or new gearchange parts are fitted it will probably be necessary to reset the linkage to make all the gears easily selectable. The objective is to adjust the link rods to the right length with the correct positions of levers on the gearbox and the column mounted gearchange lever.

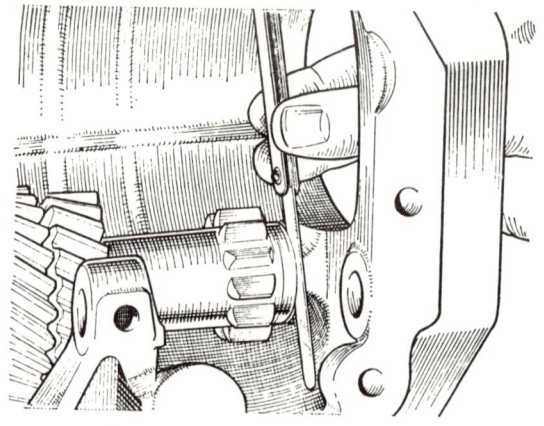

Fig. 6.6 Measuring the laygear end float with the aid of a feeler gauge.

2. Shift rods operated by the column change mechanism move two levers on the side of the gearbox (Fig. 6.7); the shifter lever (A), and the selector lever (B).

3. Free the shift rods from the two levers and put the gears into neutral. Move the selector

6.62   6.63   6.64

6.65   6.66   6.67

lever (B) backwards and forwards fully and position it so it is at the midpoint of its travel. In this position the gears selected would be first and second.

4. Obtain first gear by moving the shifter lever (A) as far forwards as possible. It may be necessary to move the car slightly forwards so the gears mesh. The selector lever will now be locked in mid-position but there will be a certain amount of free play present on either side.

5. Move the steering column gearchange lever into the first gear position, and position the selector lever so there is an equal amount of free play on either side of it.

6. Line up the selector rod ball joint with the adjacent hole in the selector lever. To do this it will probably be necessary to loosen the joint locknut and to change the position of the joint until the threaded portion will enter the hole in the selector lever (B). Tighten the locknut.

7. Adjust the length of the shift rod so the yoke of the rod aligns with the hole in the shifter lever (A). The length of the rod is altered by the adjuster nut at the other end of the rod.

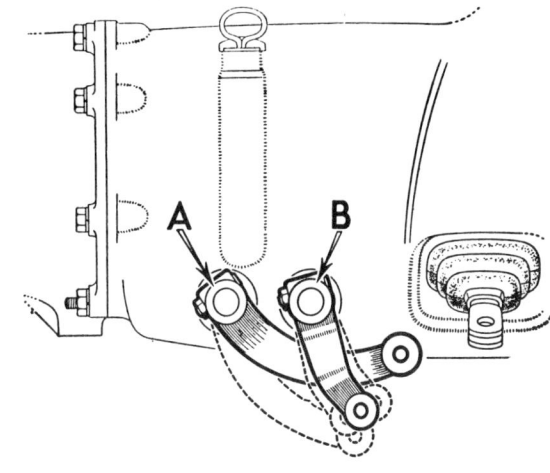

Fig. 6.7. With the gearbox in first gear the shifter lever 'A' and the selector lever 'B' should be in the positions shown.

8. When these two adjustments are finalised the selector mechanism will be correctly set for first gear; which ensures that all the other positions are also correct.

FAULT FINDING CHART

Cause	Trouble	Remedy
SYMPTOM:	WEAK OR INEFFECTIVE SYNCHROMESH	
General wear	Synchronising cones worn, split or damaged. Baulk ring synchromesh dogs worn, or damaged	Dismantle and overhaul gearbox. Fit new gear wheels and synchronising cones. Dismantle and overhaul gearbox. Fit new baulk ring synchromesh.
SYMPTOM:	JUMPS OUT OF GEAR	
General wear or damage	Broken gearchange fork rod spring Gearbox coupling dogs badly worn Selector fork rod groove badly worn Selector fork rod securing screw and locknut loose	Dismantle and replace spring. Dismantle gearbox. Fit new coupling dogs. Fit new selector fork rod. Remove side cover, tighten securing screw and locknut.
SYMPTOM:	EXCESSIVE NOISE	
Lack of maintenance General wear	Incorrect grade of oil in gearbox or oil level too low Bush or needle roller bearings worn or damaged Gearteeth excessively worn or damaged Laygear thrust washers worn allowing excessive end play	Drain, refill, or top up gearbox with correct grade of oil. Dismantle and overhaul gearbox. Renew bearings. Dismantle, overhaul gearbox. Renew gearwheels. Dismantle and overhaul gearbox. Renew thrust washers.
SYMPTOM:	EXCESSIVE DIFFICULTY IN ENGAGING GEAR	
Clutch not fully disengaging	Clutch pedal adjustment incorrect	Adjust clutch pedal correctly.

CHAPTER SEVEN

PROPELLER SHAFT AND UNIVERSAL JOINTS

CONTENTS

1. GENERAL DESCRIPTION

Drive is transmitted from the gearbox to the rear axle by means of a finely balanced Hardy Spicer tubular propeller shaft.

Fitted at each end of the shaft is a universal joint which allows for vertical movement of the rear axle. Each universal joint comprises a four-legged centre spider, four needle roller bearings and two yokes.

Fore and aft movement of the rear axle is absorbed by a sliding spline in the front of the propeller shaft which slides over a mating spline on the rear of the gearbox mainshaft. A supply of oil through very small holes from the gearbox lubricates the splines, and a grease nipple is fitted to each universal joint so that the needle roller bearings can be lubricated. NOTE. Most later models are fitted with the sealed type of universal joint which requires no maintenance.

The propeller shaft is a relatively simple component and to overhaul and repair it is fairly easy.

2. ROUTINE MAINTENANCE

1. At intervals of 3,000 miles fill a grease gun with Castrolease L.M. or a similar recommended multi-purpose grease and thoroughly lubricate the following, through the 2 appropriate grease nipples which should first be wiped clean.

Give 3–4 strokes of the grease gun:-
a) On the rear universal joint (non-sealed type).
b) On the front universal joint (non-sealed type).

3. PROPELLER SHAFT - REMOVAL & REPLACEMENT

1. Jack up the rear of the car, or position the rear of the car over a pit or on a ramp.

2. If the rear of the car is jacked up supplement the jack with support blocks so that danger is minimised should the jack collapse.

3. If the rear wheels are off the ground place the car in gear or put the handbrake on to ensure that the propeller shaft does not turn when an attempt is made to loosen the four nuts on each flange.

4. The propeller shaft is carefully balanced to fine limits and it is important that it is replaced in exactly the same position it was in prior to its removal. Scratch a mark on the propeller shaft and rear axle flanges to ensure accurate mating when the time comes for reassembly.

5. Unscrew and remove the four self-locking nuts, bolts, and securing washers which hold the flange on the propeller shaft to the flange on the rear axle. Lower the propeller shaft to the ground.

6. Replacement of the propeller shaft is a reversal of the above procedure. Ensure that the mating marks scratched on the sides of the propeller shaft flange line up with those on the rear axle flange.

4. UNIVERSAL JOINTS - INSPECTION & REPAIR

1. Wear in the needle roller bearings is characterised by vibration in the transmission, 'clonks' on taking up the drive, and in extreme cases of lack of lubrication, metallic squeaking, and ultimately grating and shrieking sounds as the bearings break up.

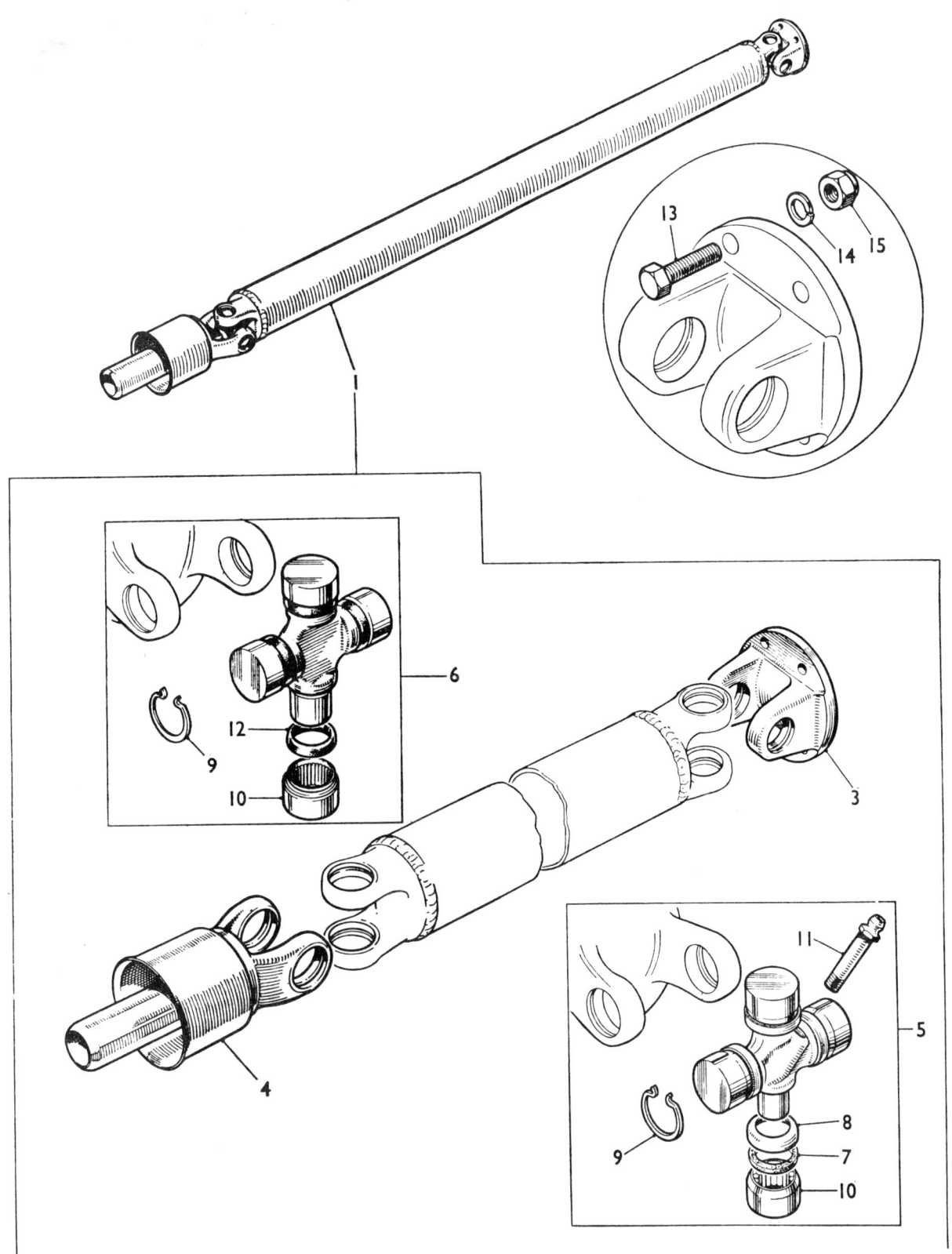

Fig. 7.   EXPLODED VIEW OF THE PROPELLER SHAFT

1 Complete propeller shaft assembly.   3 Yoke flange.   4 Yoke sleeve.   5 Journal replacement kit components.   6 Sealed journal assembly.   7 Journal gasket.   8 Gasket retainer.   9 Circlip.   10 Needle bearing.   11 Lubricating nipple.   12 Lip seal.   13 Bolt. 14 Spring washer. 15 Nut.

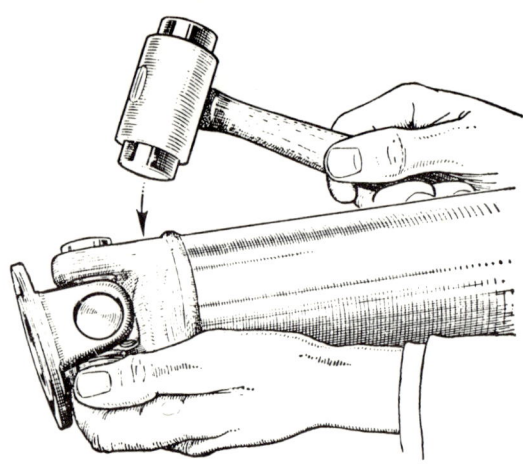

Fig. 7.2 Tap the yoke lightly as shown after removing the retaining circlip to free the bearing.

2. It is easy to check if the needle roller bearings are worn with the propeller shaft in position, by trying to turn the shaft with one hand, the other hand holding the rear axle flange when the rear universal is being checked, and the front gearbox coupling when the front universal is being checked. Any movement between the propeller shaft and the front and the rear half couplings is indicative of considerable wear.

3. If worn, the old bearings and spiders will

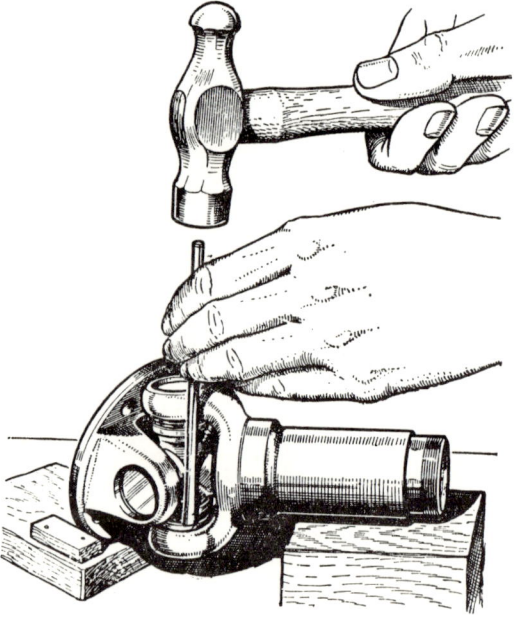

Fig. 7.3 If the bearings are difficult to remove tap them out (after removing the retaining circlip) from the inside with a thin drift as shown.

have to be discarded and a repair kit, comprising new universal joint spiders, bearings, oil seals, and retainers purchased. Check also by trying to lift the shaft and noticing any movement in the joints.

4. Examine the propeller shaft splines for wear. If worn it will be necessary to purchase a new front half coupling, or if the yokes are badly worn, an exchange propeller shaft.

5. It is not possible to fit oversize bearings and journals to the trunnion bearing holes.

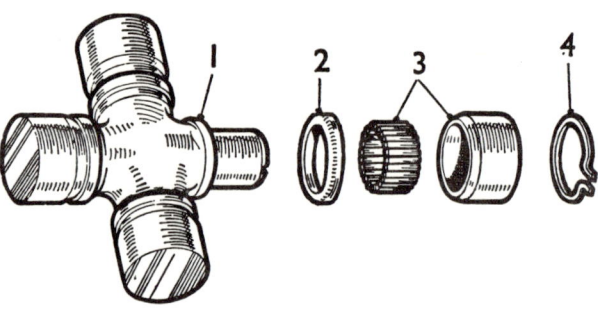

Fig. 7.4 COMPONENT PARTS OF THE SEALED TYPE OF UNIVERSAL JOINT.
1 Journal spider. 2 Rubber seal. 3 Needle rollers and bearing.
4 Circlip.

4. Examine the propeller shaft splines for wear. To do this unscrew the dust cap from the sleeve, and then slide the sleeve from the shaft. Take off the steel washer and the cork washer. With the sleeve separated from the shaft assembly the splines can be inspected. If worn it will be necessary to purchase a new front sleeve assembly, or if the yokes are badly worn an exchange propeller shaft. It is not possible to fit oversize bearings and journals to the trunnion bearing holes.

5. UNIVERSAL JOINTS - DISMANTLING

1. Clean away all traces of dirt and grease from the circlips located on the ends of the spiders, and remove the clips by pressing their open ends together with a pair of pliers and lever them out with a screwdriver. NOTE If they are difficult to remove tap the bearing face resting on top of the spider with a mallet which will ease the pressure on the circlip.

2. Hold the propeller shaft in one hand and remove the bearing cups and needle rollers by tapping the yoke at each bearing with a copper or hide faced hammer. As soon as the bearings start to emerge they can be drawn out with your fingers. If the bearing cup refuses to move then place a thin bar against the inside of the bearing and tap it gently until the cup starts to emerge.

3. With the bearings removed it is relatively easy to extract the spiders from their yokes.

If the bearings and spider journals are thought to be badly worn this can easily be ascertained visually with the universal joints dismantled.

6. UNIVERSAL JOINTS - REASSEMBLY

1. Thoroughly clean out the yokes and journals. Make certain that the grease passages are quite clear.

2. Fit new cork oil seals and retainers on the spider journals, place the spider on the propeller shaft yoke, and assemble the needle rollers in the bearing races with the assistance of some thin grease. NOTE It is essential to fit the spiders in the yoke flanges so the lubricating nipples are facing the propeller shaft and not the yoke flanges. If fitted the wrong way round it will be impossible to lubricate the universal joints.

3. Refit the bearing cups on the spider and tap the bearings home so that they lie squarely in position.

4. Replace the circlips and lubricate the bearings well with a lithium based grease.

7. UNIVERSAL JOINTS - SEALED TYPES - REMOVAL & REPLACEMENT

1. From June 1965 sealed type universal joints were introduced which require no maintenance. NOTE. Not all models may have them. These are removed in exactly the same way as the ordinary universal joints; see section 5 for details. The sealed type joints make use of a rubber seal instead of the gasket and retainer, and have no lubricating nipples.

2. On replacement great care must be taken to ensure the journals and associated parts are absolutely clean. Fill the grease holes in the journal spider with the recommended lubricant such as Castrolease LM making sure all air bubbles are eliminated. Fill each bearing assembly to a depth of approx. $1/8$ in. (3 mm.).

3. Fit new rubber seals to the spiders and then replace the spiders and bearings in the yokes. Refit the circlips.

CHAPTER EIGHT

REAR AXLE

CONTENTS

SPECIFICATIONS

Type	Hypoid - Three-quarter - Floating
Ratios - Estate Cars (pre 1961)	4. 875 to 1
Estate Cars (after 1961)	4. 55 to 1
Saloons (pre 1961)	4. 55 to 1
Saloons (after 1961)	4. 30 to 1
Differential carrier bearing preload	. 002 in. (. 05 mm.) 'nip' per bearing
Pinion bearing preload...	13 to 15 lb/in. (. 15 to . 17 kg. m.)
Crown wheel and pinion backlash	Etched on crown wheel
Backlash adjustment: Crown wheel	Shims
Backlash adjustment: Pinion	Head washer
Rear axle oil capacity	2¼ pints of S. A. E. 90 E. P. gear oil

TORQUE WRENCH SETTINGS

Crown wheel to differential carrier bolts	55 to 60 lb/ft. (7. 6 to 8. 3 kg. m.)
Differential bearing cap nuts	60 to 65 lb/ft. (8. 3 to 8. 9 kg. m.)
Pinion bearing nut	135 to 140 lb/ft. (18. 6 to 19. 3 kg. m.)
Rear brake adjuster securing nuts	5 to 7 lb/ft. (. 69 to . 97 kg. m.)
Bearing retaining nut	180 lb/ft. (24. 8 kg. m.)

1. GENERAL DESCRIPTION

The rear axle is of the three-quarter-floating type, and is held in place by semi-elliptic springs which are constructed from a number of individual leaves, of different lengths and are held together by a long bolt and clips. The semi-elliptic springs provide all the necessary lateral and longitudinal location of the axle. The rear axle incorporates a hypoid crown wheel and pinion, and a two pinion differential. All repairs can be carried out to the component parts of the rear axle without removing the axle casing from the car.

The crown wheel and pinion together with the differential gears are mounted in the differential unit which is bolted to the front face of the banjo-type axle casing.

Adjustments are provided for the crown wheel and pinion backlash; pinion depth of mesh; pinion shaft bearing pre-load; and backlash between the differential gears. All these adjustments may be made by varying the thickness of the various shims and thrust washers.

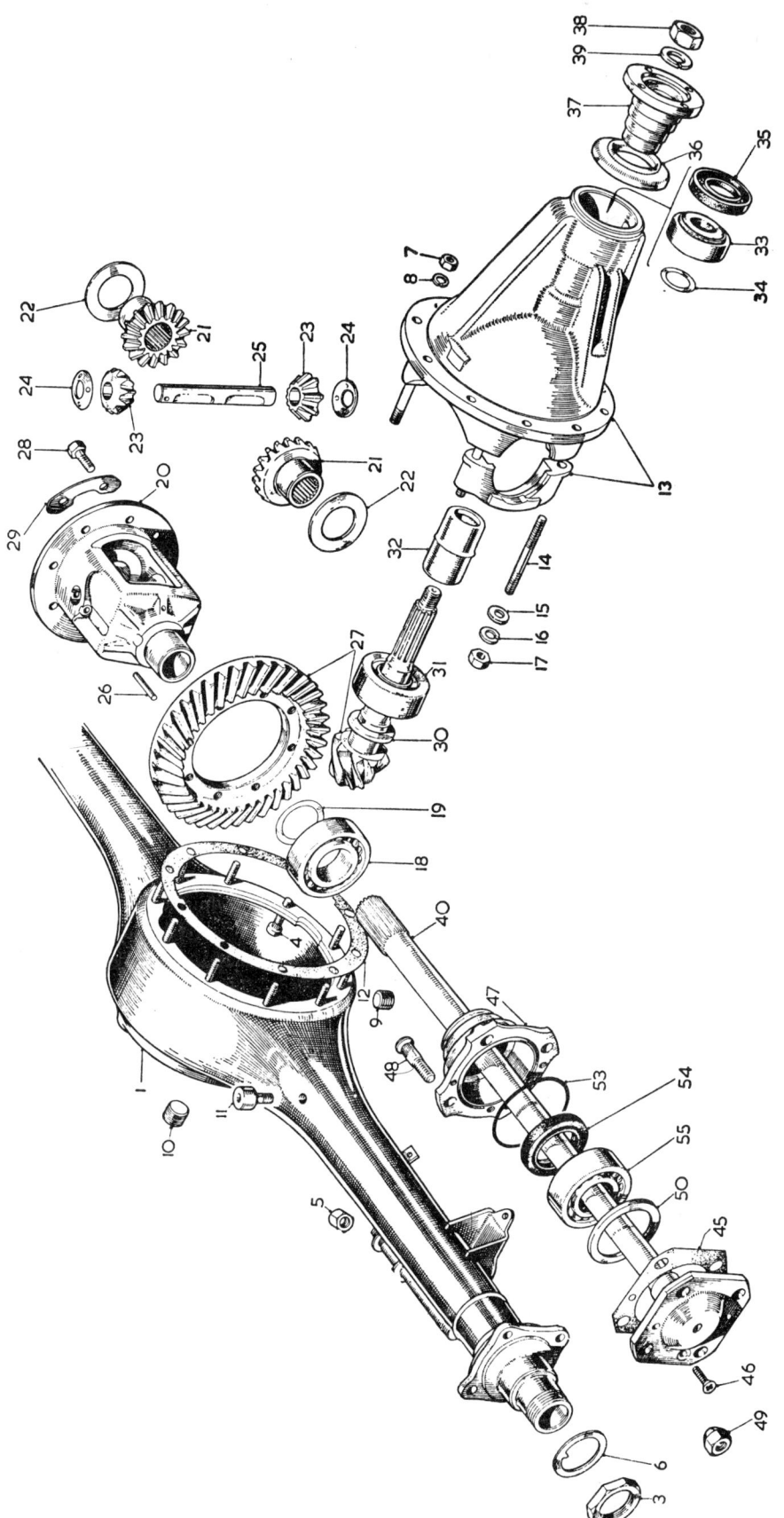

Fig. 8.1 EXPLODED VIEW OF THE REAR AXLE FITTED TO ALL MODELS

1 Case assembly. 3 Bearing retaining nut—L.H.T. 4 Gear carrier stud. 5 Rebound spindle nut. 7 Nut—gear carrier to axle case (not shown). 8 Washer—spring—nut (not shown). 9 Drain plug. 10 Filler plug. 11 Breather assembly. 12 Joint—gear carrier to axle case. 13 Differential carrier and bearing cap. 14 Stud—bearing cap. 15 Washer —plain—bearing cap. 16 Washer—spring—bearing cap. 17 Nut—stud. 18 Differential bearing. 19 Washer—bearing—packing—.002 to .010 in. (.051 to .254 mm.). 20 Differential cage. 21 Differential wheel. 22 Washer—thrust—differential wheel. 23 Differential pinion. 24 Washer—thrust—differential pinion. 25 Pinion shaft. 26 Pinion peg. 27 Crown wheel and pinion—11/43. 28 Bolt—crown wheel to differential cage. 29 Lock washer—bolt. 30 Pinion—thrust washer—.112 to .126 in. (2.85 to 3.20 mm.). 31 Rear pinion bearing. 32 Bearing spacer. 33 Front pinion bearing. 34 Shim—outer bearing—.004 to .030 in. (.102 to .762 mm.). 35 Oil seal. 36 Dust cover. 37 Universal joint flange. 38 Pinion nut. 39 Spring washer. 40 Half shaft (disc wheels). 45 Joint—shaft to hub. 46 Screw—countersunk—shaft to hub. 47 Hub assembly. 48 Stud—wheel. 49 Nut—wheel stud. 50 Spacer—bearing. 54 Seal—hub. 55 Bearing—hub.

The axle or half shafts are easily withdrawn and are splined at their inner ends to fit into the splines in the differential wheels. The inner wheel bearing races are mounted on the outer ends of the axle casing and are secured by nuts and lockwashers. The rear wheel bearing outer races are located in the hubs.

2. REAR AXLE - ROUTINE MAINTENANCE

1. Every 6,000 miles remove the filler plug in the rear axle casing and top up with an S.A.E. 90 E.P. gear oil such as Castrol Hypoy. After topping up the axle do not replace the plug for five minutes to allow any excess to run out. If the axle is overfilled it is likely that oil will leak out of the ends of the axle casing and ruin the rear brake linings.

2. Every 12,000 miles drain the oil when hot, clean the drain plug, and refill the axle with 2¼ pints of S.A.E. 90 E.P. gear oil.

3. REAR AXLE - REMOVAL & REPLACEMENT

1. Remove the rear wheel knave plates and loosen the wheel nuts.

2. Raise and support the rear of the body and the differential casing with chocks or jacks so that the rear wheels are clear of the ground. This is most easily done by placing a jack under the centre of the differential, jacking up the axle and fitting suitable chocks to support the body under the chassis frame just in front of the rear springs.

3. Remove both rear wheels and place the wheel nuts in the knave plates for safe-keeping.

4. Ensure that the handbrake is off and free the brake cable from the relay lever.

5. Undo the flexible hydraulic brake hose from the union located on the right-hand chassis side-member.

6. Undo the nuts and locknuts from the four 'U' bolts and remove the spring clamp and damper bracket plates.

7. Undo the nuts and remove them together with the spring washers from the propeller shaft flange bolts. Remove the bolts after having marked the propeller shaft and differential drive flanges to ensure replacement in the same relative positions.

8. Free the rear ends of the semi-elliptic springs by removing the rear shackle nuts and plates, and then lower the ends of the springs to the ground.

9. The axle will now be resting on the jack and can be lowered and removed from under the car. Replacement is a straightforward reversal of the removal sequence.

4. HALF SHAFT - REMOVAL & REPLACEMENT

1. Follow the sequence detailed in paras. 1, 2, and 3, of the preceeding section. (Rear Axle Removal and Replacement). NOTE that if the axle shaft is removed with the car on an even keel it is likely that oil will run out from the differential and contaminate the brake linings. If only one shaft is being removed then jack up that side of the car only. If both shafts are being removed drain the oil from the differential before proceeding further.

2. Release the handbrake and slacken the brake adjusters right off.

3. Unscrew the two Phillips-headed countersunk brake drum retaining screws and pull off the brake drum. If necessary tap the brake drums off with a wooden or hide hammer. Under no circumstances use a steel headed hammer directly on the drum. If using a steel headed hammer then interpose a piece of wood between the hammer head and the drum.

4. Unscrew the single shaft flange locating screw and pull the half shaft by its flange out from the axle casing. If the shaft appears to be stuck a little judicious levering with a tyre wrench will start the shaft moving. Once loose it will pull out quite easily.

5. Replacement of the half shafts is a reversal of the above process. Always renew the paper washers to ensure that no oil leaks will develop.

5. REAR HUB - REMOVAL & REPLACEMENT

1. Remove the brake drum and axle shaft as detailed in the preceeding section (Half Shaft Removal and Replacement). Take off the bearing spacer.

2. Knock back the tab of the locking washer and unscrew the hub retaining nut. NOTE that the left-hand hub bearing nut has a left-hand thread so must be turned clockwise to unscrew. The right-hand hub nut has a right-hand thread.

3. Remove the lock washer from the axle casing end by lifting the washer so its key is freed from the locating groove.

4. With a hub puller pull off the hub complete with bearing and oil seal.

5. Replacement is a reversal of the above process but the following points should be noted:

a) If fitting a new oil seal, carefully drift it into position before the bearing and ensure that it is placed with the lip facing outwards towards the wheel.

b) Before replacing the rear bearings lubricate them with high melting-point grease.

c) Always renew the washer between the hub assembly and the half shaft flange and if making

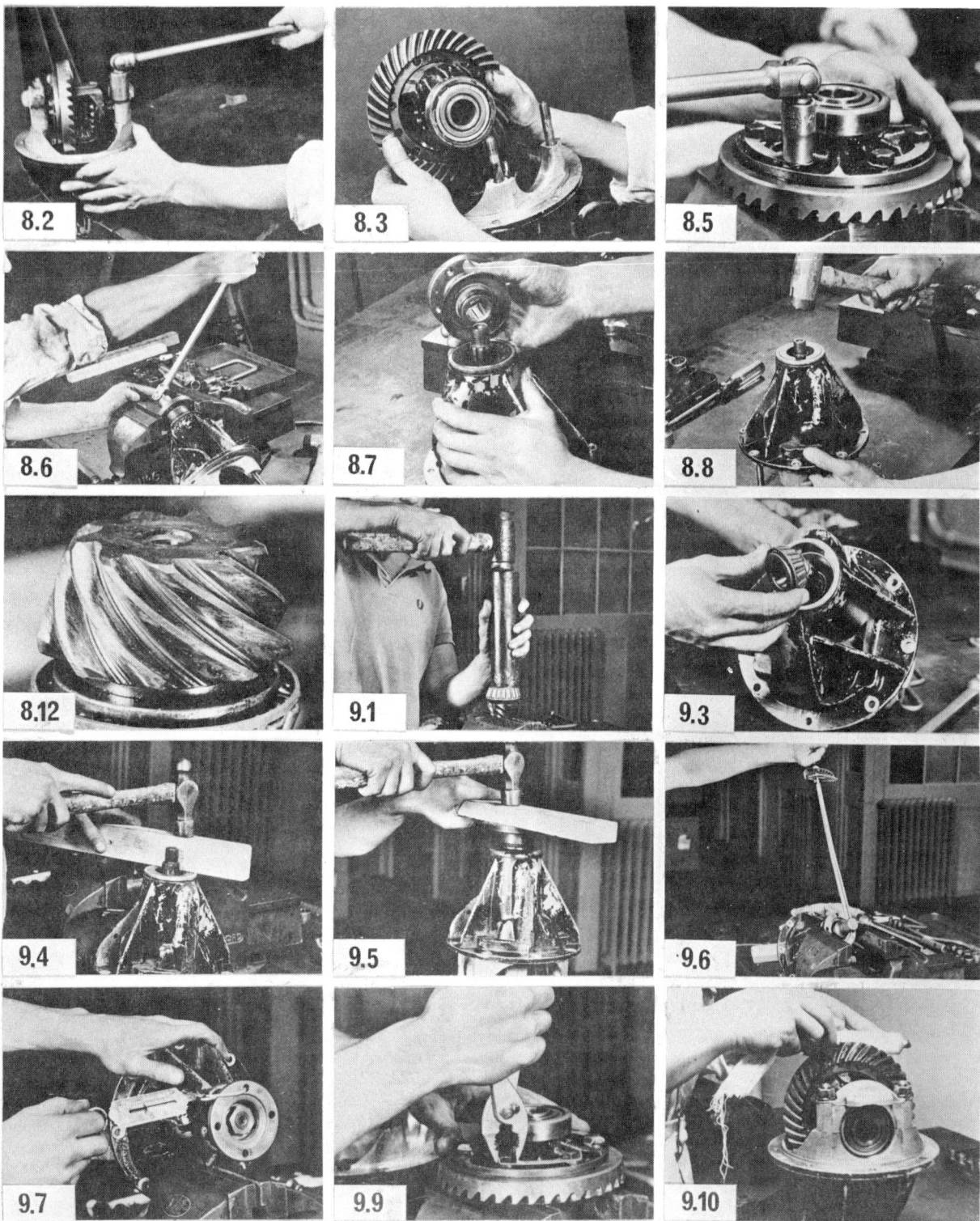

one up ensure that it is cut from paper at least .2 mm. thick.

d) Ensure that the outer face of the bearing spacer protrudes between .001 in. and .004 in. from the outer face of the hub after the bearing has been pressed into place. This is because the bearing must be held by the axle shaft driving flange and the abutment shoulder in the hub.

e) Remember to knock back the locking tab of the locking washer.

6. PINION OIL SEAL - REMOVAL & RE-PLACEMENT

If oil is leaking from the front of the differention nose piece it will be necessary to renew the pinion oil seal. If a pit is not available, jack and chock up the rear of the car. It is much easier to do this job over a pit, or with the car on a ramp.

1. Mark the propeller shaft and pinion drive flanges to ensure their replacement in the same relative positions.

2. Unscrew the nuts from the four bolts holding the flanges together, remove the bolts and separate the flanges.

3. If the oil seal is being renewed with the differential nose piece in position, drain the oil and check that the handbrake is firmly on to prevent the pinion flange moving.

4. Unscrew the nut in the centre of the pinion drive flange. Although it is tightened down to a torque of 140 lb/ft. it can be removed fairly easily with a long extension arm fitted to the appropriate socket spanner. Remove the nut and spring washer.

5. Pull off the splined drive flange, which may be a little stubborn, in which case it should be tapped with a hide mallet from the rear; the pressed steel end cover; and prise out the oil seal with a screwdriver taking care not to damage the lip of its seating.

6. Replacement is a reversal of the above procedure. NOTE that the new seal must be pushed into the differential nose piece with the edge of the sealing ring facing inwards, and take great care not to damage the edge of the oil seal when replacing the end cover and drive flange. Smear the face of the flange which bears against the oil seal lightly with oil before driving the flange onto its splines. Tighten the nut to 140 lb/ft.

7. DIFFERENTIAL ASSEMBLY - REMOVAL & REPLACEMENT

If it is wished to renew the differential carrier assembly or to exchange it for a factory reconditioned unit, first remove the axle shafts as detailed in Section 4.

1. Mark the propeller shaft and pinion flanges to ensure their replacement in the same relative position.

2. Unscrew the nuts from the four bolts holding the flanges together, remove the bolts and separate the flanges.

3. Remove the ring of nuts and spring washers which join the differential nose piece to the axle casing, and pull the nose piece complete with differential assembly out of the casing.

4. Carefully clean down the inside of the axle casing, fit a new nose piece to casing joint, and then fit the exchange or rebuilt differential assembly. Replacement being a reversal of the removal proceedure.

5. Refill the differential with the correct grade of oil and run the axle in slowly for the first 500 miles, and then change the oil when it is hot.

8. DIFFERENTIAL ASSEMBLY - DISMANTLING & EXAMINATION

Most professional garages will prefer to renew the complete differential carrier assembly as a unit if it is worn, rather than to dismantle the unit to renew any damaged or worn parts. To do the job 'according to the book' requires the use of special and expensive tools which the majority of garages do not have, and also, probably, do not have the skilled mechanics who know how these tools should be used.

The primary object of these special tools is to ensure that noise is kept to a minimum. If any increase in noise cannot be tolerated (providing that the rear axle is not already noisy due to a defective part) then it is best to purchase an exchange, built-up differential unit.

If the possibility of a slight increase in noise can be tolerated then it is quite possible to successfully recondition the rear axle without these special tools. The differential assembly should be stripped and examined in the following fashion:

1. Remove the differential assembly from the rear axle as detailed in the preceeding section. NOTE that all numbers in brackets refer to Fig. 8.1.

2. With the differential assembly on the bench begin dismantling the unit by unscrewing the nuts and washers (15, 16, 17) holding the differential bearing caps (13) in place. Ensure that the caps are marked to ensure correct replacement. (See photo).

3. Pull off the caps and then lever out the differential unit complete with crown wheel and differential gears. (See photo).

4. Check the differential bearings (18) for side play and if present draw them off from the differential cage (20) together with any shims (19)

fitted between the inner ring of each bearing and the cage.

5. Eight high tensile steel bolts (28) hold the crown wheel (27) to the differential cage (20). Knock back the tabs of the locking washers (29) and undo and remove the bolts as shown.

6. Professional fitters at BMC garages use a special tool for holding the pinion flange (37) stationary while the nut (38) in the centre of the flange is unscrewed. As it is tightened to a torque of 140 lb/ft. it will require considerable force to move it. As the average owner will not have the use of this tool use the following alternative method. Clamp the pinion flange in a vice and then undo the nut. Any damage caused to the edge of the flange by the vice should be carefully filed smooth as shown.

7. With the nut and spring washer removed, pull off the splined pinion flange (37), (tap the end of the pinion shaft (27) if the flange appears stuck), and remove the pressed end cover and oil seal as illustrated.

8. Drift the pinion shaft rearwards out of the nose piece. With it will come the inner race and rollers of the rear bearing (31), the bearing spacer (32), and shims. The outer race and front bearing (33) will be left in the nose piece. With the pinion shaft removed the rear outer race can be quite easily extracted. (See photo).

9. The inner race of the front bearing can now be tapped out and then the outer race extracted.

10. The inner race of the rear bearing is a press fit on the pinion shaft, and must be drifted off carefully. If the BMC special tool 18G47C is available this will help the removal of the inner race considerably. Remove the thrust washer (30) under the pinion gear head, and retain for future use.

11. Check the rollers and races for general wear, score marks, and pitting and renew these components as necessary

12. Examine the teeth of the crown wheel and pinion for pitting, score marks, chipping, and general wear. If a new crown wheel and pinion is required a mated crown wheel and pinion must be fitted. It is asking for trouble to renew one without the other. (See photo).

13. Tap out the pinion peg (26) from the crown wheel side of the differential cage (20) to free the pinion shaft (25) which is then driven out. NOTE that the hole into which the peg fits is slightly tapered, and the opposite end may be lightly peened over and should be cleared with a 3/16 in. (4.8 mm.) drill.

14. Extract the pinions, wheels, and thrust washers (23, 21, 22, 24) from the differential cage. Check them for wear and renew as necessary. Replacement of the pinion is a

reversal of the above process. NOTE that, after the peg has been inserted, the larger end of the hole should be lightly peened over to retain the pin in position.

9. DIFFERENTIAL ASSEMBLY - REASSEMBLY

1. Replace the thrust washer (30) on the pinion shaft and then fit the inner race of the rear bearing. If the special BMC bearing removal and replacement tool 18G47C is not available, it is quite satisfactory to drift the rear bearing on with a piece of steel electrical piping 12 to 14 in. long with sufficient internal diameter to just fit over the pinion shaft. With one end of the tube bearing against the race, tap the top end of the tube with a hammer, so driving the bearing squarely down the shaft and hard up against the underside of the thrust washer.

2. Slip the bearing spacer (32) over the pinion shaft and fit the outer race of the front and rear bearings to the differential nose piece (13).

3. Insert the pinion shaft (27) forwards into the differential nose piece from inside the casing and then drop the front inner bearing race and rollers (33) into place, as illustrated.

4. Lubricate the bearings with the correct grade of rear axle oil. Fit a new oil seal (35) with the edge of the sealing ring facing inwards. A block of wood is useful for ensuring the seal is driven on squarely. (See photo).

5. With the seal in position, replace the dust cover (36), lubricate the underside of the pinion flange (37) which bears against the oil seal and drive the flange onto the splines with a rawhide hammer as shown.

6. Replace the spring washer (39) and with the flange held securely in a vice tighten the flange nut (38) down to 140 lb/ft. (See photo).

7. To obtain the correct pinion bearing pre-load, slowly tighten the nut, taking frequent readings. The correct pre-load should be 13 to 15 lb/in. Measure this with a spring balance hooked into one of the drive flange holes. As these holes are 1½ in. from the shaft axis a pull of 9 lb/in. is the correct pre-load figure using this method. If the pre-load is too great use a thinner thrust washer. If too high, use a thicker thrust washer. (Illustrated).

8. Refit the shims (19) and differential bearings (18) to the differential cage (20).

9. Ensure that the crown wheel and cage are scrupulously clean and then bolt the crown wheel (27) to the differential cage flange, tightening the eight high tensile steel bolts down to a torque of 65 lb/ft. Turn up the tabs on the locking washers as shown.

10. Measure the backlash at the edge of the pinion flange. The reading should be between

1/32 in. to 1/8 in. Also check the meshing of the crown wheel and pinion by smearing engineers blue on the crown wheel and then turning the pinion. The contact mark should appear right in the middle of the crown wheel teeth. If the mark appears on the toe or the heel of the crown wheel teeth then shims must be removed from one side of the differential bearings to the other until the marks are in the correct position. (See photo).

11. The differential unit can now be refitted to the axle casing.

CHAPTER NINE

BRAKING SYSTEM

CONTENTS

SPECIFICATIONS

Make & Type ... ... Girling drum internal expanding
   Footbrake ... ... Hydraulic on all 4 wheels
   Handbrake ... ... Mechanical - to rear wheels only
   Brake Fluid ... ... Castrol Girling Brake Fluid Amber (S.A.E. 70R3)

Front Brakes - Type ... ... Twin leading shoe
   Drum diameter ... ... 9 in. (22.8 cm.)
   Lining material ... ... Ferodo AM3
   Lining area... ... ... 86.25 sq. in. (556.3 cm^2.)
   Lining dimensions ... ... 8.625 in. x 2.5 in. (21.91 cm. x 6.35 cm.)

Rear Brakes - Type ... ... Single leading shoe
   Drum diameter ... ... 9 in. (22.8 cm.)
   Lining material ... ... Ferodo AM3
   Lining area... ... ... 60.4 sq. in. (389.6 cm^2.)
   Lining dimensions ... ... 8.625 in. x 1.75 in. (21.91 cm. x 4.445 cm.)

1. DRUM BRAKES - GENERAL DESCRIPTION

The four wheel drum brakes fitted are of the internal expanding type and are operated hydraulically by means of the brake pedal which is coupled to the brake master cylinder and hydraulic fluid reservoir mounted on the front bulkhead.

The front brakes are of the two leading shoe type with a separate cylinder for each shoe. Both cylinders are fixed to the backplate and the trailing end of each shoe is free to slide laterally in a small groove in the closed end of the brake cylinders, so ensuring automatic centralisation when the brakes are applied.

The rear brakes are of the single leading shoe type, with one brake cylinder per wheel for both shoes. The cylinder is free to float on the backplate. Attached to each of the rear wheel operating cylinders is a mechanical expander operated by the handbrake lever through a cable which runs from the brake lever to a compensator on the rear axle and thence to the wheel operating levers.

Drum brakes have to be adjusted periodically to compensate for wear in the linings. It is unusual to have to adjust the handbrake system as the efficiency of this system is largely dependent on the condition of the brake linings and the adjustment of the brake shoes. The handbrake can, however, be adjusted separately to the footbrake operated hydraulic system.

The hydraulic brake system functions in the following manner: On application of the brake pedal, hydraulic fluid under pressure is pushed from the master cylinder to the brake operating cylinders at each wheel, by means of a four way union and steel pipe lines and flexible hoses.

The hydraulic fluid moves the pistons out so pushing the brake shoes into contact with the brake drums. This provides an equal degree of retardation on all four wheels in direct proportion to the pressure applied to the brake pedal. Return springs between each pair of brake shoes draw the shoes together when the brake pedal is released.

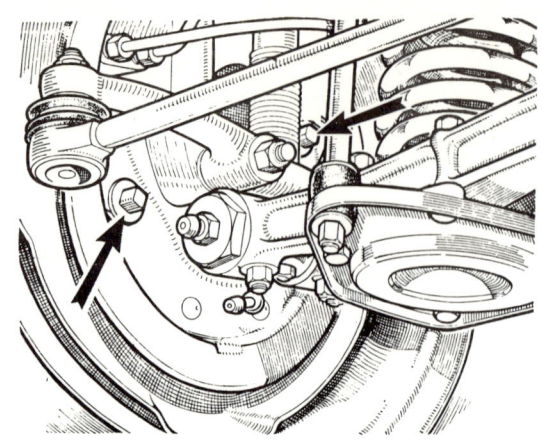

Fig. 9.1 The square-headed adjusters (arrowed) for the front brakes

2. BRAKES - MAINTENANCE

1. Every 3,000 miles, carefully clean the top of the brake master cylinder reservoir, remove the cap, and inspect the level of the fluid which should be 1/4 in. below the bottom of the filler neck. Check that the breathing holes in the cap are clear.

2. If the fluid is below this level, top up the reservoir with Castrol Girling Amber Brake Fluid, or a fluid which conforms to specification SAE 70 R3. It is vital that no other type of brake fluid is used. Use of a non-standard fluid will result in brake failure caused by the perishing of the special seals in the master and brake cylinders. If topping up becomes frequent then check the metal piping and flexible hosing for leaks, and check for worn brake or master cylinders which will also cause loss of fluid.

3. At intervals of 3,000 miles, or more frequently if pedal travel becomes excessive, adjust the brake shoes to compensate for wear of the brake linings.

4. At the same time lubricate all joints in the handbrake mechanism with an oil can filled with Castrolite or similar.

3. BRAKES - ADJUSTMENT

1. Jack up one side of the car to attend to the brakes on that side.

2. The brakes on all models are taken up by turning square headed adjusters on the rear of each backplate. The edges of the adjuster are easily burred if an ordinary spanner is used. Use a square headed brake adjusting spanner if possible (BMC part no. 18G 619). NOTE. When adjusting the rear brakes make sure the handbrake is off.

3. Two adjusters are fitted to each of the front

wheels (See Fig. 9.1) and one adjuster on the rear wheel backplate.

4. Turn the adjuster a quarter of a turn at a time until the wheel is locked. Then turn back the adjuster one notch so the wheel will rotate without binding.

5. Spin the wheel and apply the brakes hard to centralize the shoes. Recheck that it is not possible to turn the adjusting screw further without locking the shoe. NOTE. A rubbing noise when the wheel is spun is usually due to dust in the brake drum. If there is no obvious slowing of the wheel due to brake binding there is no need to slacken off the adjusters until the noise disappears. Better to remove the drum and blow out the dust.

6. Repeat this process to the other three brake drums. A good tip is to paint the head of the adjusting screws white which will facilitate future adjustment by making the adjuster heads easier to see.

4. BLEEDING THE HYDRAULIC SYSTEM

1. Removal of all the air from the hydraulic system is essential to the working of the braking system, and before undertaking this examine the fluid reservoir cap to ensure that both vent holes, one on top and the second underneath but not in line, are clear; check the level of fluid and top up if required.

2. Check all brake line unions and connections for possible seepage, and at the same time check the condition of the rubber hoses, which may be perished.

3. If the condition of the wheel cylinders is in doubt, check for possible signs of fluid leakage.

4. If there is any possibility of incorrect fluid having been put into the system, drain all the fluid out and flush through with methylated

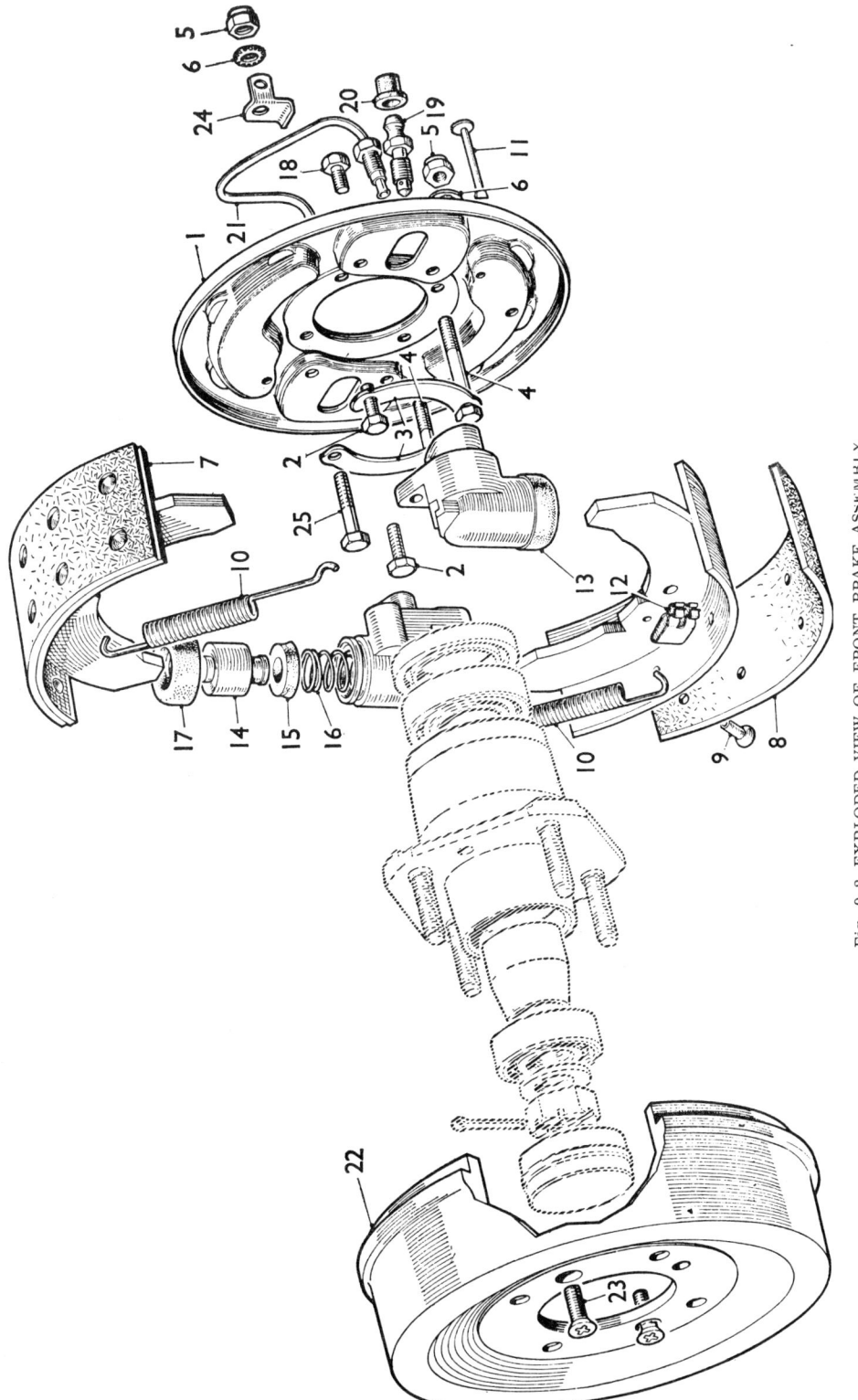

Fig. 9.2 EXPLODED VIEW OF FRONT BRAKE ASSEMBLY

1 Plate—brake—R.H. 2 Screw—brake-plate to swivel axle. 3 Washer for screw (lock). 4 Bolt—brake-plate and steering lever to swivel axle. 5 Nut for bolt. 6 Washer for nut (shakeproof). 7 Shoe assembly—brake. 8 Liner (with rivets). 9 Rivets. 10 Spring —brake-shoe return. 11 Pin—brake-shoe steady. 12 Spring for steady pin. 13 Cylinder assembly—wheel—R.H. 14 Piston. 15 Seal. 16 Spring. 17 Cover—dust. 18 Screw—wheel cylinder to brake-plate. 19 Screw—bleed. 20 Cover for bleed screw—dust. 21 Pipe—brake—R.H. 22 Drum—brake. 23 Screw—drum to hub. 24 Bracket brake hose (later models). 25 Bolt—brake-plate and steering lever to swivel axle (later models).

133

spirits. Renew all piston seals and cups since these will be affected and could possibly fail under pressure.

5. Gather together a clean jam jar, a 9 in. length of tubing which fits tightly over the bleed nipples, and a tin of the correct brake fluid. (Girling Amber brake fluid).

6. To bleed the system clean the areas around the bleed valves, and start on the rear brakes first by removing the rubber cup over the bleed valve and fitting a rubber tube in position.

7. Place the end of the tube in a clean glass jar containing sufficient fluid to keep the end of the tube underneath during the operation.

8. Open the bleed valve with a spanner and quickly press down the brake pedal. After slowly releasing the pedal, pause for a moment to allow the fluid to recoup in the master cylinder and then depress again. This will force air from the system, and should continue until no more air bubbles can be seen coming from the tube. At intervals make certain that the reservoir is kept topped up, otherwise air will enter at this point again.

9. Repeat this operation on all four brakes, and when completed, check the level of the fluid in the reservoir and then check the feel of the brake pedal, which should be firm and free from any 'spongy' action, which is normally associated with air in the system.

5. DRUM BRAKE SHOE - INSPECTION, REMOVAL & REPLACEMENT

After high mileages it will be necessary to fit replacement brake shoes with new linings. Refitting new brake linings to old shoes is not always satisfactory, but if the services of a local garage or workshop with brake lining equipment are available, then there is no reason why your own shoes should not be successfully relined.

1. Remove the hub cap, loosen off the wheel nuts, securely jack up the car, and remove the road wheel. Ensure the handbrake is off if the rear brake shoes are being removed.

2. Completely slacken off the brake adjustment and take out the two set screws, which hold the drum in place. Remove the brake drum. If it proves obstinate tap the rim gently with a soft-headed hammer. The shoes are now exposed for inspection.

3. The brake linings should be renewed if they are so worn that the rivet heads are flush with the surface of the lining. If bonded linings are fitted they must be removed when the material has worn down to $1/32$ in. at its thinnest point.

4. Press in each brake shoe steady pin securing

washer against the pressure of its spring. Turn the head of the washer so it will clear the securing bar on the steady pin and remove the spring and washer.

5. Detach the shoes and return springs by pulling one end of the shoes away from the slot in the closed end of one of the brake cylinders and pull the ends of both shoes out. Allow the return spring to pull the free end of the brake shoe down the side of the brake cylinder. Lift both brake shoes away.

6. Thoroughly clean all traces of dust from the shoes, backplates, and brake drums with a dry paint brush and compressed air, if available. Brake dust can cause squeal and judder and it is therefore important to clean out the brakes thoroughly.

7. Check that the pistons are free in their cylinders and that the rubber dust covers are undamaged and in position and that there are no hydraulic fluid leaks. Secure the pistons with wire or string.

8. Prior to reassembly smear a trace of white brake grease to all sliding surfaces. The shoes should be quite free to slide on the closed end of the cylinder and the piston anchorage point. It is vital that no grease or oil comes in contact with the brake drums or the brake linings.

9. Replacement is a straight reversal of the removal procedure, but note the following points:

a) Check that when the micram adjusters are replaced they are backed right off.

b) Ensure that the return springs are in their correct holes in the shoes and lie between them and the backplate.

6 FLEXIBLE HOSE - INSPECTION, REMOVAL & REPLACEMENT

Inspect the condition of the flexible hydraulic hoses leading from the chassis mounted metal pipes to the brake backplates. If any are swollen, damaged, cut, or chafed, they must be renewed.

1. Unscrew the metal pipe union nuts from its connection to the hose, and then holding the hexagon on the hose with a spanner, unscrew the attachment nut and washer.

2. The chassis end of the hose can now be pulled from the chassis mounting bracket and will be quite free.

3. Disconnect the flexible hydraulic hose at the backplate by unscrewing it from the brake cylinder. NOTE when releasing the hose from the backplate, the chassis end must always be freed first.

4. Replacement is a straight reversal of the above proceedure.

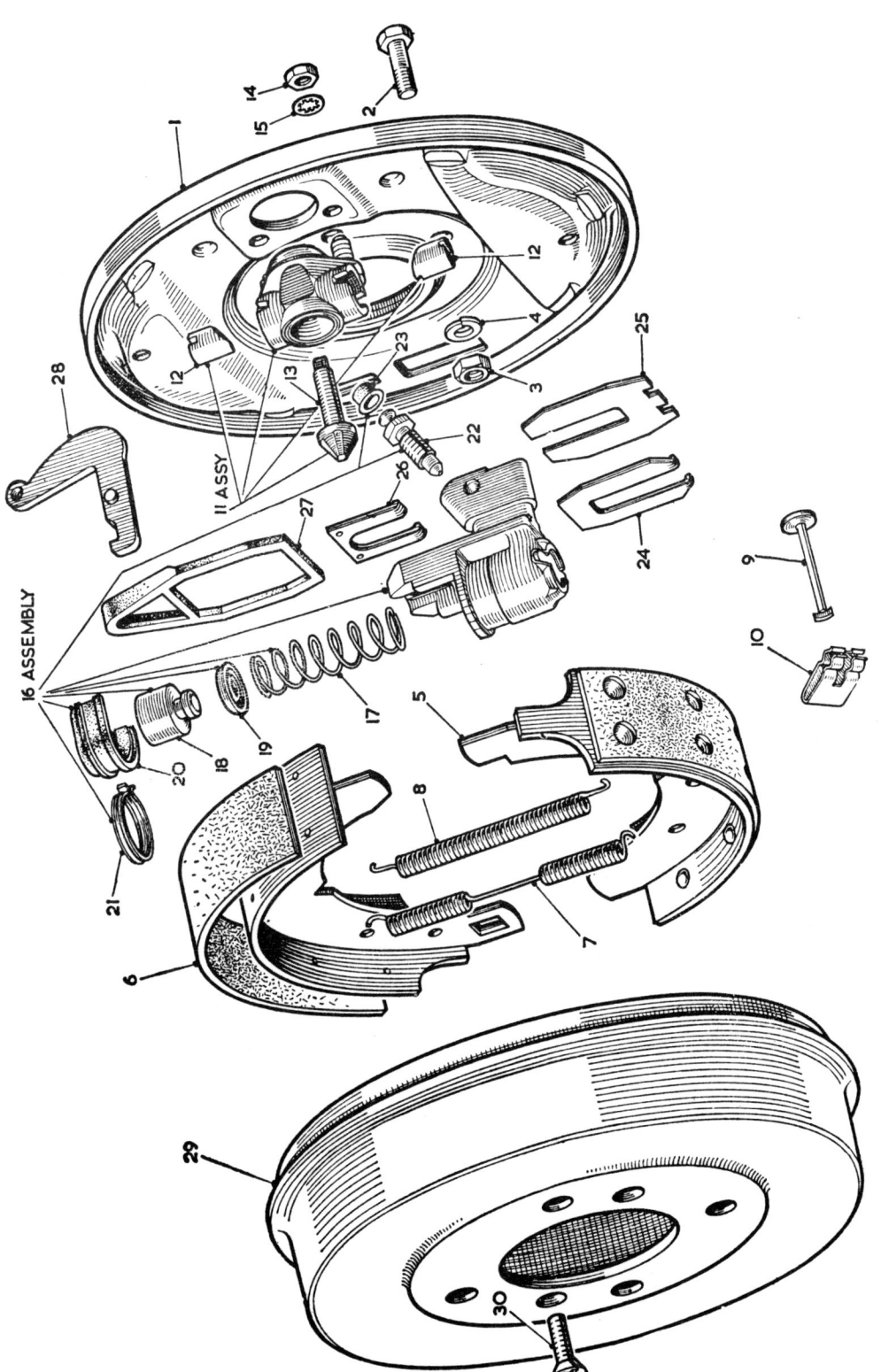

Fig. 9.3 EXPLODED VIEW OF THE REAR BRAKE ASSEMBLY

1 Plate—brake—R.H. 2 Bolt—backplate to axle case. 3 Nut for bolt. 4 Washer for bolt. 5 Brake-shoe assembly. 6 Liner. 7 Spring—shoe return—cylinder end. 8 Spring—shoe return—adjuster end. 9 Pin—brake-shoe steady. 10 Spring—brake-shoe steady (later type). 11 Adjuster assembly. 12 Tappet. 13 Wedge. 14 Nut—adjuster to backplate. 15 Washer for nut (shakeproof). 16 Cylinder assembly—wheel. 17 Spring. 18 Piston. 19 Seal for piston. 20 Cover for piston—dust. 21 Retainer for dust cover. 22 Screw—bleeder. 23 Cover for bleed screw—dust. 24 Spring—retaining—wheel cylinder. 25 Plate—locking. 26 Washer—distance. 27 Cover—dust—wheel cylinder to backplate. 28 Lever assembly—handbrake. 29 Drum—brake. 30 Screw—drum to hub.

135

7. BRAKE SEALS - INSPECTION & OVERHAUL

If hydraulic fluid is leaking from one of the brake cylinders it will be necessary to dismantle the cylinder and replace the dust cover and piston sealing rubber. If brake fluid is found running down the side of the wheel, or it is noticed that a pool of liquid forms alongside one wheel and the level in the master cylinder has dropped, and the hoses are all in good order, proceed as follows:

1. Remove the brake drums and brake shoes as described in Section 5.

2. Ensure that all the other wheels, and all the other brake drums are in place. Remove piston piston sealing rubber and the spring from the leaking cylinder by applying gentle pressure to the foot brake. Place a quantity of rag under the backplate or a tray to catch the hydraulic fluid as it pours out of the cylinder.

3. Inspect the inside of the cylinder for score marks caused by impurities in the hydraulic fluid. If any are found the cylinder and piston will require renewal together as an exchange assembly.

4. If the cylinder is sound thoroughly clean it out with fresh hydraulic fluid.

5. The old rubbers will probably be swollen and visibly worn. Smear the new rubbers with hydraulic fluid and reassemble in the cylinder the spring, seal and piston, and then the rubber boot.

6. Replenish the brake fluid, replace the brake shoes and brake drum, and bleed the hydraulic system as previously described.

8. FRONT WHEEL CYLINDERS - REMOVAL & REPLACEMENT

1. Remove the appropriate front brake drum and brake shoes as described in Section 5.

2. Undo the bridge pipe unions from the cylinders and also the flexible pipe if this is fitted to the cylinder being removed.

3. Undo the two nuts and washers which hold each wheel cylinder in place and remove the cylinder.

4. Replacement is a straightforward reversal of the dismantling process. Tighten the wheel cylinder nuts to between 5 and 7.5 lb/ft. (.7 to 1.0 kg.m.) and when assembled bleed the brakes.

9. REAR WHEEL CYLINDERS - REMOVAL & REPLACEMENT

1. Remove the left or right-hand brake drum and brake shoes as required, as described in Section 5. All numbers in brackets refer to Fig. 9.3.

2. Free the hydraulic pipe from the wheel cylinder (16) at the union; disconnect the hand-brake cable from the lever (28), and take off the protective rubber boot from the rear of the backplate.

3. Carefully prise the retaining spring (24) apart from the wheel cylinder locking plate (25) with a screwdriver and tap the plate (25) off the neck of the wheel cylinder (16).

4. Take off the lever (28) from between the wheel cylinder and the backplate and slide off the distance piece (26) and retaining spring (24).

5. The cylinder is now free and can be removed from the backplate.

6. On replacement smear the slot in the backplate and the cylinder neck with Girling white brake grease. Fit the cylinder neck into the backplate slot followed by the distance piece (26), spring (24) and lever (28). Tap the retaining plate (25) into position so the cranked ends of the spring (24) lock into the cut outs in the plate (25).

7. The rest of the replacement process is a straightforward reversal of the dismantling sequence. Bleed the brakes on completion of reassembly.

10. BRAKE MASTER CYLINDER - REMOVAL & REPLACEMENT

1. To remove the Girling type C.V. brake master cylinder first undo the union from the brake pipe outlet and pull the pipe clear.

2. Free the clevis pin from the yoke on the end of the pushrod and then undo the two nuts and spring washers from the studs passing through the master cylinder mounting flange.

3. The master cylinder can now be pulled off its studs and dismantled further if required. Replacement is a straightforward reversal of the removal sequence.

11. BRAKE MASTER CYLINDER - DISMANTLING & REASSEMBLY

1. First detach the fluid line, using a blanking plug in the pipe to prevent dirt from entering the system.

2. Note that when a replacement cylinder is to be fitted, the working surfaces are protected and it is essential to lubricate the seals before fitting.

3. Remove the blanking plugs from the pipe line, together with the pushrod dust cover so that clean brake fluid can be injected at these locations. By operating the piston several times the fluid will spread over the surfaces.

4. If the master cylinder is to be dismantled after removal, first pull back the pushrod cover and remove the circlip so that the pushrod and a dished washer can be pulled out. This will expose the plunger with a seal attached, and

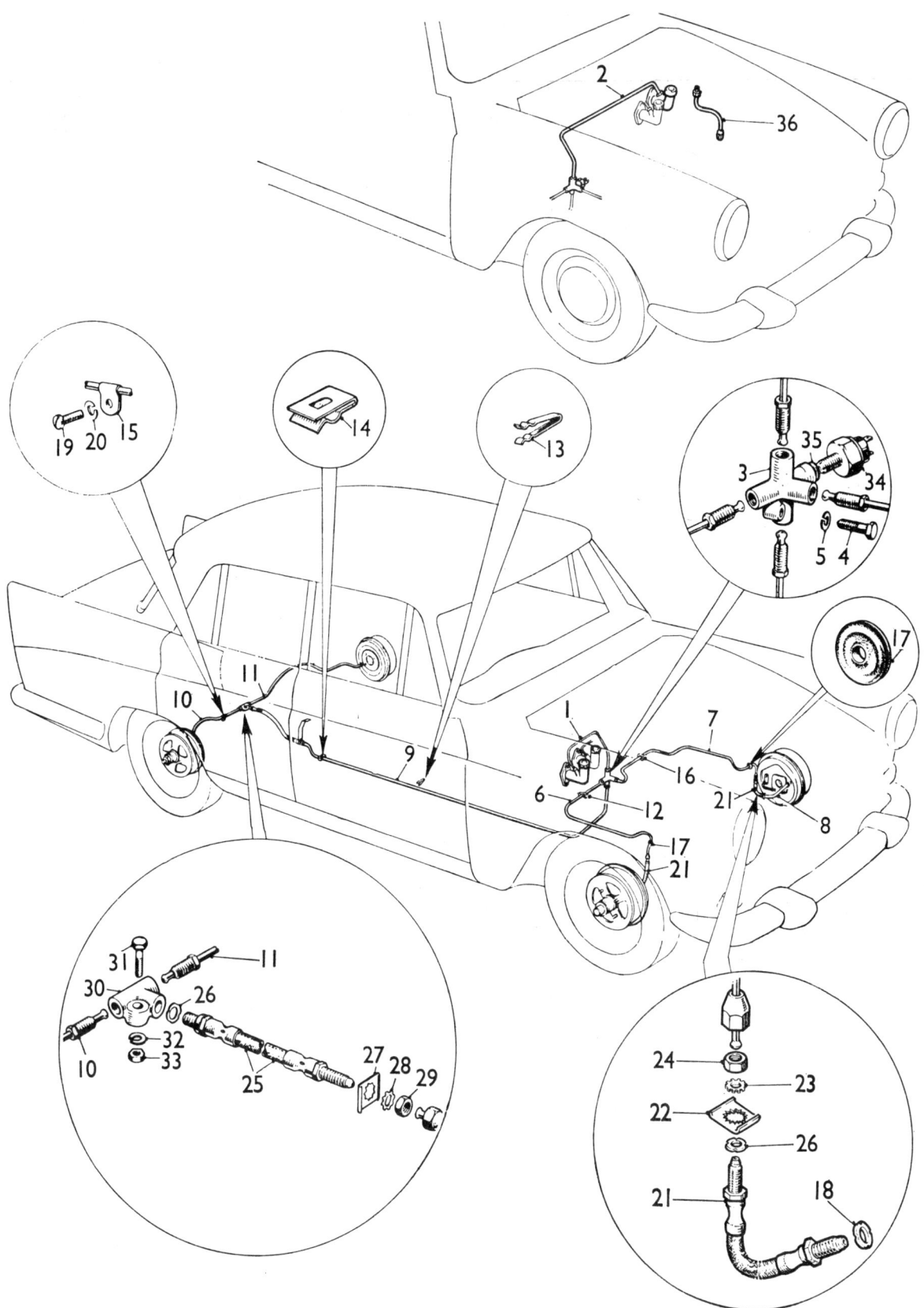

Fig. 9.4 EXPLODED VIEW OF THE LAYOUT OF THE HYDRAULIC BRAKE CIRCUIT

1 15 inch pipe to 4 way connection. **2** 26 inch pipe to 4 way connection fitted to L. H. D. cars. **3** 4 way connection. **4** Bolt. **5** Spring washer. **6** Pipe to R. H. front brake hose. **7** Pipe to L. H. front brake hose. **8** Flexible hose to front brake cylinder. **9** Pipe to rear hose 92½ in. long. **10** Pipe to rear R.H. brakes. **11** Pipe to rear L. H. brakes. **12** Pipe clip—valance and dash. **13** Pipe clip—side-member. **14** Pipe clip—floor. **15** Pipe clip to axle. **16** Pipe clip—dash. **17** Pipe grommet. **18** Gasket. **19** Screw. **20** Spring washer. **21** Flexible hose to front brakes. **22** Locking plate. **23** Shakeproof washer. **24** Nut. **25** Flexible hose—rear brakes. **26** Gasket. **27** Locking plate. **28** Shakeproof washer. **29** Nut. **30** 3 way connection. **31** Screw. **32** Spring washer. **33** Nut. **34 Stop lamp switch. 35 Packing washer.**

this must be removed as a unit. The assembly is separated by lifting the thimble leaf over the shouldered end of the plunger. The seal is then eased off.

5. Depress the plunger return spring allowing the valve stem to slide through the keyhole in the thimble, thus releasing the tension in the spring.

6. Detach the valve spacer taking care of the spacer spring washer which will be found located under the valve head.

7. Examine the bore of the cylinder carefully for any scores or ridges, and if this is found to be smooth all over, new seals can be fitted. If there is any doubt of the condition of the bore then a new cylinder must be fitted.

8. If examination of the seals shows them to be apparently oversize, or very loose on the plunger, suspect oil contamination in the system. Oil will swell these rubber seals, and if one is found to be swollen, it is reasonable to assume that all seals in the braking system will need attention.

9. To reassemble the master cylinder, replace the old valve seal as shown, and then replace the spring washer with its domed side against the underside of the valve head.

10. Replace the plunger return spring centrally on the spacer, insert the thimble into the spring and depress until the valve stem engages in the keyhole of the thimble.

11. Check that the spring is central on the spacer before refitting a new plunger seal onto the plunger with the flat face against the face

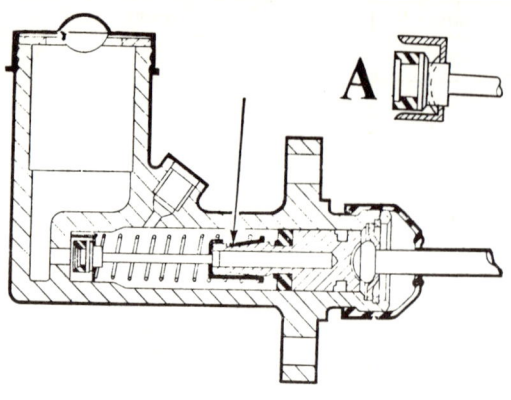

Fig. 9.6 Sectioned view of the master cylinder. The arrow shows the thimble leaf pressed into place. 'A' shows the correct way round to fit the centre valve

of the plunger, and a new back seal if required.

12. Insert the reduced end of the plunger into the thimble until the thimble engages under the shoulder of the plunger and press home the the thimble leaf as shown.

13. Make sure that the bore is clean, smear the plunger with brake fluid and insert the assembly into the bore valve end first, easing the lips of the plunger seal carefully into the bore.

14. Replace the pushrod and refit the circlip into the groove in the cylinder body, and replace the rubber cover.

12. HANDBRAKE ADJUSTMENT

1. After high mileages it is possible that the handbrake cables will have stretched and will need to be adjusted.

2. First adjust the rear brakes as described in Section 3.

3. With the rear wheels free off the ground and chocks under the front wheels to prevent any forward movement pull the handbrake on three notches.

4. Note that a cable adjusting nut and a locknut are fitted at the front end of the brake cable assembly. Hold the flats on the end of the cable assembly with a mole wrench or similar and slacken the locknut, taking the greatest care not to twist the cables.

5. Turn the adjusting nut until the rear brakes are firmly on and then release the handbrake. Check that the rear wheels turn freely, and then tighten the adjuster locknut.

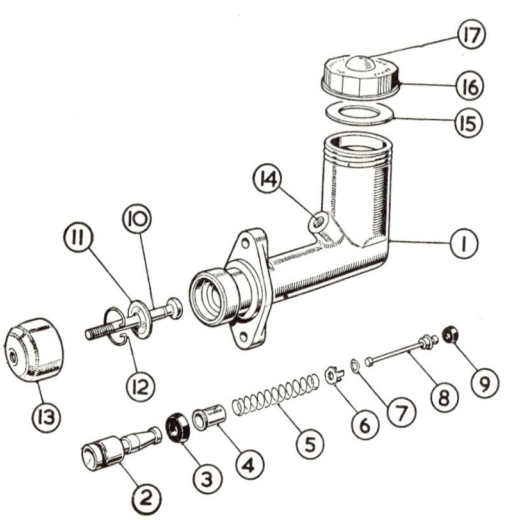

Fig. 9.5 Exploded view of the brake master cylinder. 1 Master cylinder body. 2 Piston. 3 Inner seal. 4 Piston return spring retainer. 5 Piston return spring. 6 Seat spacer. 7 Valve seal spring washer. 8 Valve stem. 9 Valve seal. 10 Pushrod. 11 Washer. 12 Circlip. 13 Rubber boot. 14 Outlet to pipe. 15 Seal. 16 Cap. 17 Vent hole.

BRAKING SYSTEM
FAULT FINDING CHART

Cause	Trouble	Remedy
SYMPTOM:	PEDAL TRAVELS ALMOST TO FLOORBOARDS BEFORE BRAKES OPERATE	
Leaks and air bubbles in hydraulic system	Brake fluid level too low	Top up master cylinder reservoir. Check for leaks.
	Wheel cylinder leaking	Dismantle wheel cylinder, clean, fit new rubbers and bleed brakes.
	Master cylinder leaking (Bubbles in master cylinder fluid)	Dismantle master cylinder, clean, and fit new rubbers. Bleed brakes.
	Brake flexible hose leaking	Examine and fit new hose if old hose leaking. Bleed brakes.
	Brake line fractured	Replace with new brake pipe. Bleed brakes.
	Brake system unions loose	Check all unions in brake system and tighten as necessary. Bleed brakes.
Normal wear	Linings over 75% worn	Fit replacement shoes and brake linings.
Incorrect adjustment	Brakes badly out of adjustment	Jack up car and adjust brakes.
	Master cylinder push rod out or adjustment causing too much pedal free movement	Reset to manufacturer's specification.
SYMPTOM:	BRAKE PEDAL FEELS SPRINGY	
Brake lining renewal	New linings not yet bedded-in	Use brakes gently until springy pedal feeling leaves.
Excessive wear or damage	Brake drums badly worn and weak or cracked	Fit new brake drums.
Lack of maintenance	Master cylinder securing nuts loose	Tighten master cylinder securing nuts. Ensure spring washers are fitted.
SYMPTOM:	BRAKE PEDAL FEELS SPONGY & SOGGY	
Leaks or bubbles in hydraulic system	Wheel cylinder leaking	Dismantle wheel cylinder, clean, fit new rubbers, and bleed brakes.
	Master cylinder leaking (Bubbles in master cylinder reservoir)	Dismantle master cylinder, clean, and fit new rubbers and bleed brakes. Replace cylinder if internal walls scored.
	Brake pipe line or flexible hose leaking	Fit new pipeline or hose.
	Unions in brake system loose	Examine for leaks, tighten as necessary.
SYMPTOM:	EXCESSIVE EFFORT REQUIRED TO BRAKE CAR	
Lining type or condition	Linings badly worn	Fit replacement brake shoes and linings.
	New linings recently fitted - not yet bedded-in	Use brakes gently until braking effort normal.
	Harder linings fitted than standard causing increase in pedal pressure	Remove linings and replace with normal units.
Oil or grease leaks	Linings and brake drums contaminated with oil, grease, or hydraulic fluid	Rectify source of leak, clean brake drums, fit new linings.
SYMPTOM:	BRAKES UNEVEN & PULLING TO ONE SIDE	
Oil or grease leaks	Linings and brake drums contaminated with oil, grease, or hydraulic fluid	Ascertain and rectify source of leak, clean brake drums, fit new linings.
Lack of maintenance	Tyre pressures unequal	Check and inflate as necessary.
	Radial ply tyres fitted at one end of car only	Fit radial ply tyres of the same make to all four wheels.
	Brake backplate loose	Tighten backplate securing nuts and bolts.
	Brake shoes fitted incorrectly	Remove and fit shoes correct way round.
	Different type of linings fitted at each wheel	Fit the linings specified by the manufacturers all round.
	Anchorages for front suspension or rear axle loose	Tighten front and rear suspension pick-up points including spring anchorage.
	Brake drums badly worn, cracked or distorted	Fit new brake drums.

Cause	Trouble	Remedy
SYMPTOM:	BRAKES TEND TO BIND, DRAG, OR LOCK-ON	
Incorrect adjustment	Brake shoes adjusted too tightly Handbrake cable over-tightened Master cylinder push rod out of adjustment giving too little brake pedal free movement	Slacken off brake shoe adjusters two clicks. Slacken off handbrake cable adjustment. Reset to manufacturer's specifications.
Wear or dirt in hydraulic system or incorrect fluid	Reservoir vent hole in cap blocked with dirt Master cylinder by-pass port restricted - brakes seize in 'on' position Wheel cylinder seizes in 'on' position	Clean and blow through hole. Dismantle, clean, and overhaul master cylinder. Bleed brakes. Dismantle, clean, and overhaul wheel cylinder. Bleed brakes.
Mechanical wear	Brake shoe pull off springs broken, stretched or loose	Examine springs and replace if worn or loose.
Incorrect brake assembly	Brake shoe pull off springs fitted wrong way round, omitted, or wrong type used	Examine, and rectify as appropriate.
Neglect	Handbrake system rusted or seized in the 'on' position	Apply 'Plus Gas' to free, clean and lubricate.

CHAPTER TEN

ELECTRICAL SYSTEM

CONTENTS

SPECIFICATIONS

Battery	Lead/Acid
Type	12-volt Lucas BT7A, BTZ7A, BT9A, or BTZ9A
Earthed terminal	Positive "+"
Capacity of 20-hr. rate	43 amp-hr. BT7A, BTZ7A models
Capacity at 20-hr. rate	58 amp-hr. BT9A, BTZ9A models
Electrolyte to fill one cell	3/4 pint (430 c.c.) BT7A, BTZ7A models
Electrolyte to fill one cell	1 pint (570 c.c.) BT9A, BTZ9A models
Level above separators	0.25 in.
Specific gravity reading below 27°C (80°F)	1.270 to 1.290 cell fully charged
No. of plates - BT7A, BTZ7A	7 plates
No. of plates - BT9A, BTZ9A	9 plates

| Dynamo ... ... | Lucas C39PC2 early models |
| | Lucas C40/1 later models |

	C39PC2	C40/1
Maximum output	19 amps	22 amps
No. of brushes	Two	Two
Minimum permissible brush length	11/32 in.	9/32 in.
Brush spring tension	22 to 25 oz.	30 to 33 oz.
Field resistance	6. 0 ohms	6. 0 ohms

Starter Motor	Lucas M35G/1 Four brush
Minimum permissible brush length	5/16 in. (7. 93 mm.)
Brush spring tension: Maximum...	30 to 34 oz. (850. 4 to 963. 8 gm.)
Minimum	25 oz. (709 gm.)

Regulator/Control Box	Lucas RB106/2 or modified RB106/2
Cut in voltage	12.˙7 to 13. 3 volts
Drop-off voltage ... ...˙.	8. 5 to 11. 0 volts
Reverse current	3. 0 to 5. 0 volts
Voltage setting at 3, 000 r. p. m.(...	10°C (50°F) 16. 1 to 16. 7 volts
Regulator RB106/2 (...	20°C (68°F) 16. 0 to 16. 6 volts
(modified) (...	30°C (86°F) 15. 9 to 16. 5 volts
(...	40°C (104°F) 15. 8 to 16. 4 volts
(...	10°C (50°F) 15. 5 to 16. 5 volts
Regulator RB106/2 (...	20°C (68°F) 15. 4 to 16. 4 volts
(...	30°C (86°F) 15. 3 to 16. 3 volts
(...	40°C (104°F) 15. 2 to 16. 2 volts

Windscreen Wiper	Lucas DR. 3A single speed
Normal running current	2. 7 to 3. 4 amps
Drive to wheelboxes	Rack and cable
Armature endfloat	. 008 to . 012 in. (. 20 to . 30 mm.)
Armature resistance	. 28 to . 35 ohms
Field resistance	8 to 9. 5 ohms
Wiping speed	45 to 50 cycles per minute

Horns...	Lucas 9H 12 volt
Maximum current consumption	3 1/2 amps

Fuse Unit	Adjacent to control box
No. of fuses	2 - 1 by 35 amps, 1 by 50 amps.
No. of spare fuses in holder	2 - 1 by 35 amps, 1 by 50 amps.

Bulbs...	Volts	Watts	BMC Part No.
Headlamps (R. H. D. except Sweden)	12	50/40	BFS 414
Headlamps (L. H. D. Europe except France – dip right)	12	45/40	BFS 410
Headlamps (L. H. D. France only – dip vertical)	12	45/40	BFS 411
Side lamps	12	6	BFS 989
Direction Indicators	12	21	BFS 382
Tail and stop lamps	12	6/21	BFS 380
Number plate illumination lamp	12	6	BFS 989
Panel and warning lamps	12	2. 2	BFS 987
Interior and luggage compartment	12	6	BFS 254
Direction indicator warning (lilliput bulb) ...	12	1. 5	BFS 280
Clock and automatic transmission	12	2	BFS 281

1. GENERAL DESCRIPTION

The electrical system is of the 12-volt type and the major components comprise: A twelve volt battery with the positive terminal earthed, a voltage regulator and cut-out; a Lucas dynamo which is fitted to the front right-hand side of the engine and is driven by the fan belt from the crankshaft pulley wheel; and a starter motor which is fitted to the end plate and gearbox bellhousing on the right-hand side of the engine.

The nine plate 12-volt battery supplies a steady supply of current for the ignition, lighting, and other electrical circuits, and provides a reserve of electricity when the current consumed by the electrical equipment exceeds that being produced by the dynamo.

The dynamo is of the two bush type and works in conjunction with the voltage regulator and cut-out. The dynamo is cooled by a multi-bladed fan mounted behind the dynamo pulley, and blows air through cooling holes in the dynamo end brackets. The output from the dynamo is controlled by the voltage regulator which ensures a high output if the battery is in a low state of charge or the demands from the electrical equipment high, and a low output if the battery is fully charged and there is little demand from the electrical equipment.

The C40/1 Dynamo fitted to later models differs little from the C39 type but has a higher output. The physical differences between the two dynamos are that the C40/1 unit has a smaller fan pulley wheel; an improved output fan; no oil retainer ring on the front bracket; differently rated springs and brushes; and some C40 commutators are of the moulded type. A modified RB106/2 control box is used in conjunction with the later type of dynamo.

2. BATTERY - REMOVAL & REPLACEMENT
   1. Disconnect the positive and then the negative leads from the battery terminals by slackening the retaining nuts and bolts, or by unscrewing the retaining screws if these are fitted.
   2. Remove the battery clamp and carefully lift the battery out of its compartment. Hold the battery vertical to ensure that none of the electrolyte is spilled.
   3. Replacement is a direct reversal of this procedure. NOTE. Replace the negative lead before the earth (positive) lead and smear the terminals with petroleum jelly (vaseline) to prevent corrosion. NEVER use an ordinary grease as applied to other parts of the car.

3. BATTERY - MAINTENANCE & INSPECTION
   1. Normal weekly battery maintenance consists of checking the electrolyte level of each cell to ensure that the separators are covered by $1/4$ in. of electrolyte. If the level has fallen top up the battery using distilled water only. Do not overfill. If a battery is overfilled or any electrolyte spilled, immediately wipe away the excess as electrolyte attacks and corrodes any metal it comes into contact with very rapidly.
   2. As well as keeping the terminals clean and covered with petroleum jelly, the top of the battery, and especially the top of the cells,

should be kept clean and dry. This helps prevent corrosion and ensures that the battery does not become partially discharged by leakage through dampness and dirt.

3. Once every three months remove the battery and inspect the battery securing bolts, the battery clamp plate, tray, and battery leads for corrosion (white fluffy deposits on the metal which are brittle to touch). If any corrosion is found, clean off the deposits with ammonia and paint over the clean metal with an anti-rust/anti-acid paint.

4. At the same time inspect the battery case for cracks. If a crack is found, clean and plug it with one of the proprietary compounds marketed by firms such as Holts for this purpose. If leakage through the crack has been excessive then it will be necessary to refill the appropriate cell with fresh electrolyte as detailed later. Cracks are frequently caused to the top of the battery cases by pouring in distilled water in the middle of winter AFTER instead of BEFORE a run. This gives the water no chance to mix with the electrolyte and so the former freezes and splits the battery case.

5. If topping up the battery becomes excessive and the case has been inspected for cracks that could cause leakage, but none are found, the battery is being overcharged and the voltage regulator will have to be checked and reset.

6. With the battery on the bench at the three monthly interval check, measure its specific gravity with a hydrometer to determine the state of charge and condition of the electrolyte. There should be very little variation between the different cells and if a variation in excess of 0.025 is present it will be due to either:
   a) Loss of electrolyte from the battery at some time caused by spillage or a leak resulting in a drop in the specific gravity of the electrolyte, when the deficiency was replaced with distilled water instead of fresh electrolyte.
   b) An internal short circuit caused by buckling of the plates or a similar malady pointing to the liklihood of total battery failure in the near future.

7. The specific gravity of the electrolyte for fully charged conditions at the electrolyte temperature indicated, is listed in Table A. The specific gravity of a fully discharged battery at different temperatures of the electrolyte is given at Table B.

TABLE A

Specific Gravity - Battery fully charged

1.268 at 100°F or 38°C electrolyte temperature
1.272 at 90°F or 32°C   "   "

1.276 at 80°F or 27°C "   "
1.280 at 70°F or 21°C "   "
1.284 at 60°F or 16°C "   "
1.288 at 50°F or 10°C "   "
1.292 at 40°F or 4°C "   "
1.296 at 30°F or -1.5°C "   "

TABLE B

Specific Gravity - Battery fully discharged

1.098 at 100°F or 38°C electrolyte temperature
1.102 at 90°F or 32°C "   "
1.106 at 80°F or 27°C "   "
1.110 at 70°F or 21°C "   "
1.114 at 60°F or 16°C "   "
1.118 at 50°F or 10°C "   "
1.122 at 40°F or 4°C "   "
1.126 at 30°F or -1.5°C "   "

4. ELECTROLYTE REPLENISHMENT

1. If the battery is in a fully charged state and one of the cells maintains a specific gravity reading which is 0.025 or more lower than the others, and a check of each cell has been made with a voltage meter to check for short circuits (a four to seven second test should give a steady reading of between 1.2 to 1.8 volts), then it is likely that electrolyte has been lost from the cell with the low reading at some time.

2. Top the cell up with a solution of 1 part sulphuric acid to 2.5 parts of water. If the cell is already fully topped up draw some electrolyte out of it with a pipette.

3. When mixing the sulphuric acid and water NEVER ADD WATER TO SULPHURIC ACID - always pour the acid slowly onto the water in a glass container. IF WATER IS ADDED TO SULPHURIC ACID IT WILL EXPLODE.

4. Continue to top up the cell with the freshly made electrolyte and then recharge the battery and check the hydrometer readings.

5. BATTERY CHARGING

1. In winter time when heavy demand is placed upon the battery, such as when starting from cold, and much electrical equipment is continually in use, it is a good idea to occasionally have the battery fully charged from an external source at the rate of 3.5 to 4 amps.

2. Continue to charge the battery at this rate until no further rise in specific gravity is noted over a four hour period.

3. Alternatively, a trickle charger charging at the rate of 1.5 amps can be safely used overnight.

4. Specially rapid 'boost' charges which are claimed to restore the power of the battery in 1 to 2 hours are most dangerous as they can cause serious damage to the battery plates through over-heating.

5. While charging the battery note that the temperature of the electrolyte should never exceed 100°F.

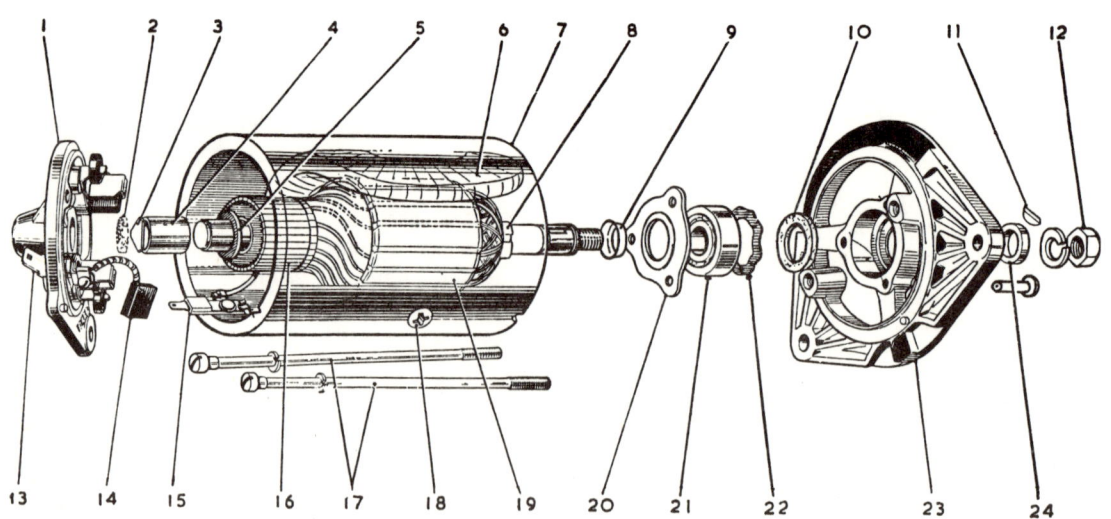

Fig. 10.1 EXPLODED VIEW OF THE DYNAMO

1 Commutator end bracket. 2 Felt ring. 3 Felt ring retainer. 4 Bronze bush. 5 Thrust washer. 6 Field coils. 7 Yoke.
8 Shaft collar. 9 Shaft collar retaining cup. 10 Felt ring. 11 Shaft key. 12 Shaft nut. 13 Output terminal 'D'. 14 Brushes.
15 Field terminal 'F'. 16 Commutator. 17 Through-bolts. 18 Pole-shoe securing screws. 19 Armature. 20 Bearing retaining
plate. 21 Ball bearing. 22 Corrugated washer. 23 Driving end bracket. 24 Pulley spacer.

6. DYNAMO - ROUTINE MAINTENANCE

1. Routine maintenance consists of checking the tension of the fan belt, and lubricating the dynamo rear bearing once every 6,000 miles.

2. The fan belt should be tight enough to ensure no slip between the belt and the dynamo pulley. If a shrieking noise comes from the engine when the unit is accelerated rapidly, it is likely that it is the fan belt slipping. On the other hand, the belt must not be too taut or the bearings will wear rapidly and cause dynamo failure or bearing seizure. Ideally $\frac{1}{2}$ in. of total free movement should be available at the fan belt midway between the fan and the dynamo pulley.

3. To adjust the fan belt tension slightly slacken the three dynamo retaining bolts, and swing the dynamo on the upper two bolts outwards to increase the tension, and inwards to lower it.

4. It is best to leave the bolts fairly tight so that considerable effort has to be used to move the dynamo; otherwise it is difficult to get the correct setting. If the dynamo is being moved outwards to increase the tension and the bolts have only been slackened a little, a long spanner acting as a lever placed behind the dynamo with the lower end resting against the block works very well in moving the dynamo outwards. Retighten the dynamo bolts and check that the dynamo pulley is correctly aligned with the fan belt.

5. Lubrication on the dynamo consists of inserting three drops of S.A.E. 30 engine oil in the small oil hole in the centre of the commutator end bracket. This lubricates the rear bearing. The front bearing is pre-packed with grease and requires no attention.

7. DYNAMO - TESTING IN POSITION

1. If, with the engine running no charge comes from the dynamo, or the charge is very low, first check that the fan belt is in place and is not slipping. Then check that the leads from the control box to the dynamo are firmly attached and that one has not come loose from its terminal.

2. The lead from the 'D' terminal on the dynamo should be connected to the 'D' terminal on the control box, and similarly the 'F' terminals on the dynamo and control box should also be connected together. Check that this is so and that the leads have not been incorrectly fitted.

3. Make sure none of the electrical equipment (such as the lights or radio) is on and then pull the leads off the dynamo terminals marked 'D' and 'F', join the terminals together with a short length of wire.

4. Attach to the centre of this length of wire the negative clip of a 0-20 volts voltmeter and run the other clip to earth on the dynamo yoke. Start the engine and allow it to idle at approximately 750 r.p.m. At this speed the dynamo should give a reading of about 15 volts on the voltmeter. There is no point in raising the engine speed above a fast idle as the reading will then be inaccurate.

5. If no reading is recorded then check the brushes and brush connections. If a very low reading of approximately 1 volt is observed then the field winding may be suspect.

6. If a reading of between 4 to 6 amps is recorded it is likely that the armature winding is at fault.

7. On early dynamos it was possible to remove the dynamo cover band and check the dynamo and brushes in position. With the Lucas C40 - 1 windowless yoke dynamo it must be removed and dismantled before the brushes and commutator can be attended to.

8. If the voltmeter shows a good reading then with the temporary link still in position connect both leads from the control box to 'D' and 'F' on the dynamo ('D' to 'D' and 'F' to 'F'). Release the lead from the 'D' terminal at the control box end and clip one lead from the voltmeter to the end of the cable, and the other lead to a good earth. With the engine running at the same speed as previously, an identical voltage to that recorded at the dynamo should be noted on the voltmeter. If no voltage is recorded then there is a break in the wire. If the voltage is the same as recorded at the dynamo then check the 'F' lead in similar fashion. If both readings are the same as at the dynamo then it will be necessary to test the control box.

8. DYNAMO - REMOVAL & REPLACEMENT

1. Slacken the two dynamo retaining bolts, and the nut on the sliding link, and move the dynamo in towards the engine so that the fan belt can be removed.

2. Disconnect the two leads from the dynamo terminals.

3. Remove the nut from the sliding link bolt, and remove the two upper bolts. The dynamo is then free to be lifted away from the engine.

4. Replacement is a reversal of the above procedure. Do not finally tighten the retaining bolts and the nut on the sliding link until the fan belt has been tensioned correctly. See 10/6.2 for details.

9. DYNAMO - DISMANTLING & INSPECTION

1. Mount the dynamo in a vice and unscrew and remove the two through bolts from the commutator end bracket. (See photo).

9.1

9.2

2. Mark the commutator end bracket and the dynamo casing so the end bracket can be replaced in its original position. Pull the end bracket off the armature shaft. **NOTE** some

versions of the dynamo may have a raised pip on the end bracket which locates in a recess on the edge of the casing. If so, marking the end bracket and casing is not necessary. A pip may also be found on the drive end bracket at the opposite end of the casing. (See photo).

3. Lift the two **brush** springs and draw the brushes out of the brush holders (arrowed).

4. Measure the brushes and if worn down to 9/32 in. or less unscrew the screws holding the brush leads to the end bracket. Take off the brushes complete with leads. Old and new brushes are compared in the photograph.

5. If no locating pip can be found, mark the drive end bracket and the dynamo casing so the drive end bracket can be replaced in its original

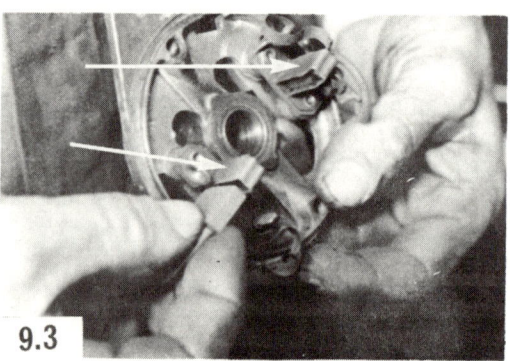

9.3

A

B

C

Fig. 10.2 METHOD OF FITTING THE COMMUTATOR END BRACKET AFTER RAISING AND TRAPPING THE BRUSHES BY THEIR SPRINGS.
A Brush trapped by spring in raised position. B Releasing the brush onto the commutator. C Normal position of brush.

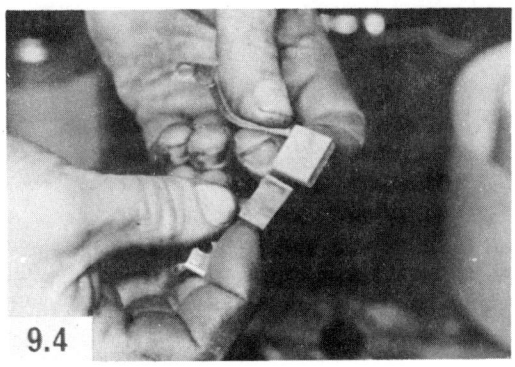

9.4

position. Then pull the drive end bracket complete with armature out of the casing.

6. Check the condition of the ball bearing in the drive end plate by firmly holding the plate and noting if there is visible side movement of the armature shaft in relation to the end plate. If play is present the armature assembly must be separated from the end plate. If the bearing is sound there is no need to carry out the work described in the following two paragraphs.

7. Hold the armature in one hand (mount it carefully in a vice if preferred) and undo the nut holding the pulley wheel and fan in place. Pull off the pulley wheel and fan.

8. Next remove the woodruff key (arrowed) from its slot in the armature shaft and also the bearing locating ring.

9. Place the drive end bracket across the open jaws of a vice with the armature downwards and gently tap the armature shaft from the bearing in the end plate with the aid of a suitable drift.

10. Carefully inspect the armature and check it for open or short circuited windings. It is a good indication of an open circuited armature when the commutator segments are burnt. If the armature has short circuited the commutator segments will be very badly burnt, and the overheated armature windings badly discoloured. If open or short circuits are suspected then test by substituting the suspect armature for a new one.

11. Check the resistance of the field coils. To do this, connect an ohmmeter between the field terminal and the yoke and note the reading on the ohmmeter which should be about 6 ohms. If the ohmmeter reading is infinity this indicates an open circuit in the field winding. If the ohmmeter reading is below 5 ohms this indicates that one of the field coils is faulty and must be replaced.

12. Field coil replacement involves the use of a wheel operated screwdriver, a soldering iron, caulking and riveting and this operation is considered to be beyond the scope of most owners. Therefore, if the field coils are at fault either

purchase a rebuilt dynamo, or take the casing to a BMC dealer or electrical engineering works for new field coils to be fitted.

13. Next check the condition of the commutator (arrowed). If it is dirty and blackened as shown clean it with a petrol damped rag. If the commutator is in good condition the surface will be smooth and quite free from pits or burnt areas, and the insulated segments clearly defined.

14. If, after the commutator has been cleaned pits and burnt spots are still present, wrap a strip of glass paper round the commutator taking great care to move the commutator $1/4$ of a turn every ten rubs till it is thoroughly clean.

15. In extreme cases of wear the commutator can be mounted in a lathe and with the lathe turning at high speed, a very fine cut may be taken off the commutator. Then polish the commutator with glass paper. If the commutator has worn so that the insulators between the segments are level with the top of the segments, then undercut the insulators to a depth of $1/32$ in. (.8 mm.). The best tool to use for this purpose is half a hacksaw blade ground to a thickness of the insulator, and with the handle end of the blade covered in insulating tape to make it comfortable to hold. This is the sort of finish the surface of the commutator should have when finished.

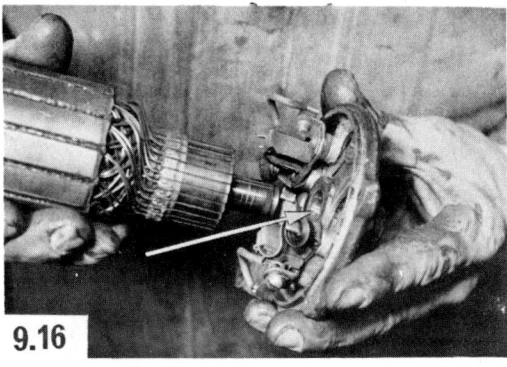

9.16

16. Check the bush bearing (arrowed) in the commutator end bracket for wear by noting if the armature spindle rocks when placed in it. If worn it must be renewed.

17. The bush bearing can be removed by a suitable extractor or by screwing a $5/8$ in. tap four or five times into the bush. The tap complete with bush is then pulled out of the end bracket.

18. NOTE before fitting the new bush bearing that it is of the porous bronze type, and it is essential that it is allowed to stand in S.A.E. 30 engine oil for at least 24 hours before fitment. In an emergency the bush can be immersed in hot oil (100°C) for 2 hours.

19. Carefully fit the new bush into the end plate, pressing it in until the end of the bearing is

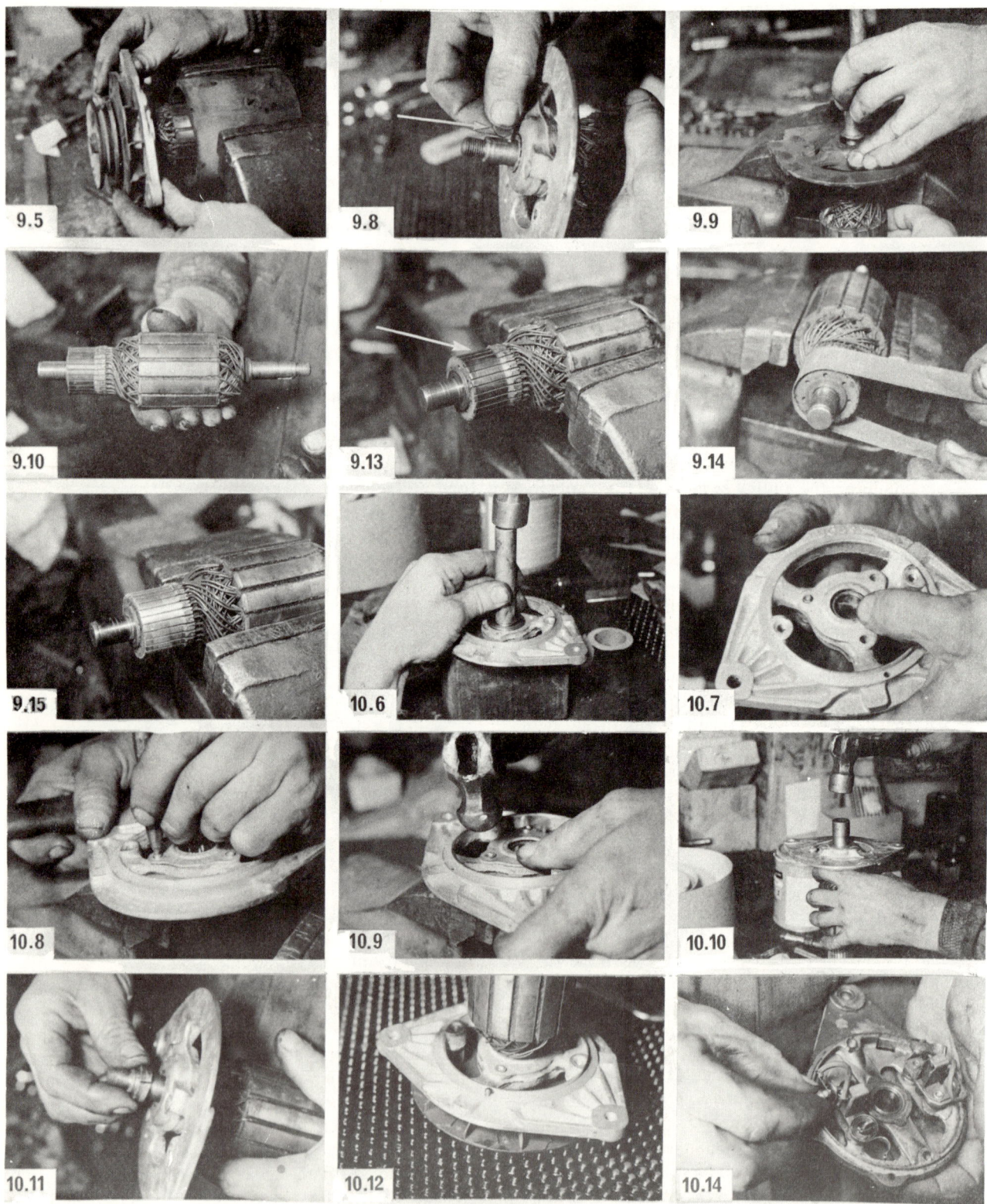

flush with the inner side of the end plate. If available press the bush in with a smooth shouldered mandrel the same diameter as the armature shaft.

10. DYNAMO - REPAIR & REASSEMBLY

1. To renew the ball bearing fitted to the drive end bracket drill out the rivets which hold the bearing retainer plate to the end bracket and lift off the plate.

2. Press out the bearing from the end bracket and remove the corrugated and felt washers from the bearing housing.

3. Thoroughly clean the bearing housing, and the new bearing and pack with high melting-point grease.

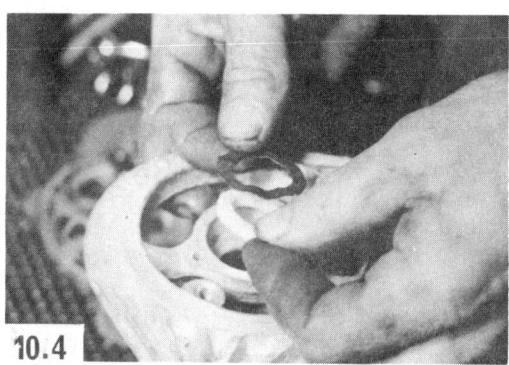

10.4

10.5

4. Place the felt washer and corrugated washer in that order in the end bracket bearing housing.

5. Then fit the new bearing as shown.

6. Gently tap the bearing into place with the aid of a suitable drift.

7. Replace the bearing plate and fit three new rivets.

8. Open up the rivets with the aid of a suitable cold chisel.

9. Finally peen over the open end of the rivets with the aid of a ball hammer as illustrated.

10. Refit the drive end bracket to the armature shaft. Do not try and force the bracket on but with the aid of a suitable socket abuting the bearing tap the bearing on gently, so pulling the end bracket down with it.

11. Slide the spacer up the shaft and refit the woodruff key.

12. Replace the fan and pulley wheel and then fit the spring washer and nut and tighten the latter. The drive bracket end of the dynamo is now fully assembled as shown.

13. If the brushes are little worn and are to be used again then ensure that they are placed in the same holders from which they were removed. When refitting brushes, either new or old, check that they move freely in their holders. If either brush sticks, clean with a petrol moistened rag and if still stiff, lightly polish the sides of the brush with a very fine file until the brush moves quite freely in its holder.

14. Tighten the two retaining screws and washers which hold the wire leads to the brushes in place.

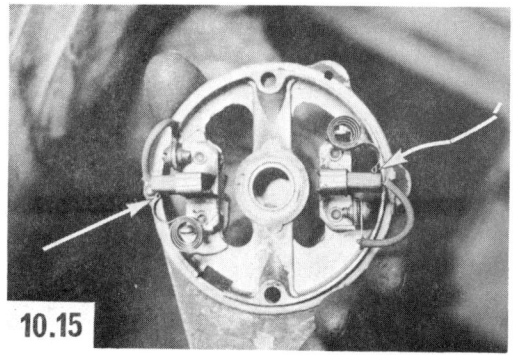

10.15

15. It is far easier to slip the end piece with brushes over the commutator if the brushes are raised in their holders as shown and held in this position by the pressure of the springs resting against their flanks (arrowed).

10.16

16. Refit the armature to the casing and then the commutator end plate and screw up the two through bolts.

17. Finally, hook the ends of the two springs off the flanks of the brushes and onto their heads so the brushes are forced down into contact with the armature.

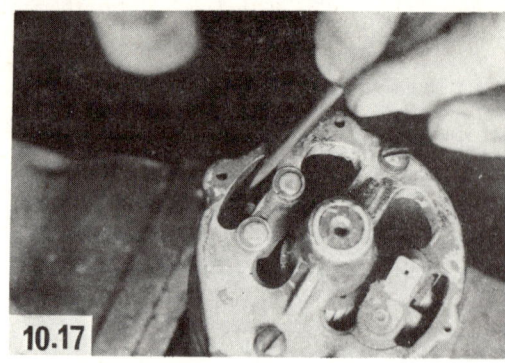
10.17

11. STARTER MOTOR - GENERAL DESCRIPTION

The starter motor is mounted on the right-hand lower side of the engine end plate, and is held in position by two bolts which also clamp the bellhousing flange. The motor is of the four field coil, four pole piece type, and utilises four spring-loaded commutator brushes. Two of these brushes are earthed, and the other two are insulated and attached to the field coil ends.

12. STARTER MOTOR - TESTING IN ENGINE

1. If the starter motor fails to operate then check the condition of the battery by turning on the headlamps. If they glow brightly for several seconds and then gradually dim, the battery is in an uncharged condition.

2. If the headlamps glow brightly and it is obvious that the battery is in good condition then check the tightness of the battery wiring connections (and in particular the earth lead from the battery terminal to its connection on the bodyframe). Check the tightness of the connections at the relay switch and at the starter motor. Check the wiring with a voltmeter for breaks or shorts.

3. If the wiring is in order then check that the starter motor switch is operating. To do this press the rubber covered button in the centre of the relay switch under the bonnet. If it is working the starter motor will be heard to 'click' as it tries to rotate. Alternatively check it with a voltmeter.

4. If the battery is fully charged, the wiring in order, and the switch working and the starter motor fails to operate then it will have to be removed from the car for examination. Before this is done, however, ensure that the starter pinion has not jammed in mesh with the flywheel. Check by turning the square end of armature shaft with a spanner. This will free the pinion if it is stuck in engagement with the flywheel teeth.

13. STARTER MOTOR - REMOVAL & REPLACEMENT

1. Disconnect the battery earth lead from the positive terminal.
2. Disconnect the starter motor cable from the terminal on the starter motor end plate.
3. Unscrew the two starter motor bolts.
4. Lift the starter motor out of engagement with the teeth on the flywheel ring and pull it forward towards the radiator until it can be lifted clear.
5. Replacement is a straight reversal of the removal procedure.

14. STARTER MOTOR - DISMANTLING & REASSEMBLY

1. With the starter motor on the bench, loosen the screw on the cover band and slip the cover band off. With a piece of wire bent into the shape of a hook, lift back each of the brush springs in turn and check the movement of the brushes in their holders by pulling on the flexible connectors. If the brushes are so worn that their faces do not rest against the commutator, or if the ends of the brush leads are exposed on their working face, they must be renewed.
2. If any of the brushes tend to stick in their holders then wash them with a petrol moistened cloth and, if necessary, lightly polish the sides of the brush with a very fine file, until the brushes move quite freely in their holders.
3. If the surface of the commutator is dirty or blackened, clean it with a petrol dampened rag. Secure the starter motor in a vice and check it by connecting a heavy gauge cable between the starter motor terminal and a 12-volt battery.
4. Connect the cable from the other battery terminal to earth in the starter motor body. If the motor turns at high speed it is in good order.
5. If the starter motor still fails to function or if it is wished to renew the brushes, then it is necessary to further dismantle the motor.
6. Lift the brush springs with the wire hook and lift all four brushes out of their holders one at a time.
7. Remove the terminal nuts and washers from the terminal post on the commutator end bracket.
8. Unscrew the two through bolts which hold the end plates together and pull off the commutator end bracket. Also remove the driving end bracket which will come away complete with the armature.
9. At this stage if the brushes are to be renewed, their flexible connectors must be un-

soldered and the connectors of new brushes soldered in their place. Check that the new brushes move freely in their holders as detailed above. If cleaning the commutator with petrol fails to remove all the burnt areas and spots, then wrap a piece of glass paper round the commutator and rotate the armature.

10. If the commutator is very badly worn, remove the drive gear as detailed in the following section. Then mount the armature in a lathe and with the lathe turning at high speed, take a very fine cut out of the commutator and finish the surface by polishing with glass paper. DO NOT UNDERCUT THE MICA INSULATORS BETWEEN THE COMMUTATOR SEGMENTS.

11. With the starter motor dismantled, test the four field coils for an open circuit. Connect a 12-volt battery with a 12-volt bulb in one of the leads between the field terminal post and the tapping point of the field coils to which the brushes are connected. An open circuit is proved by the bulb not lighting.

12. If the bulb lights, it does not necessarily mean that the field coils are in order, as there is a possibility that one of the coils will be earthing to the starter yoke or pole shoes. To check this, remove the lead from the brush connector and place it against a clean portion of the starter yoke. If the bulb lights the field coils are earthing. Replacement of the field coils calls for the use of a wheel operated screwdriver, a soldering iron, caulking and riveting operations and is beyond the scope of the majority of owners. The starter yoke should be taken to a reputable electrical engineering works for new field coils to be fitted. Alternatively, purchase an exchange Lucas starter motor.

13. If the armature is damaged this will be evident after visual inspection. Look for signs of burning, discolouration, and for conductors that have lifted away from the commutator. Reassembly is a straight reversal of the dismantling procedure.

15. STARTER MOTOR DRIVE - GENERAL DESCRIPTION

1. The starter motor drive is of the outboard type. When the starter motor is operated the pinion moves into contact with the flywheel gear ring by moving in towards the starter motor.

2. If the engine kicks back, or the pinion fails to engage with the flywheel gear ring when the starter motor is actuated no undue strain is placed on the armature shaft, as the pinion sleeve disengages from the pinion and turns independently.

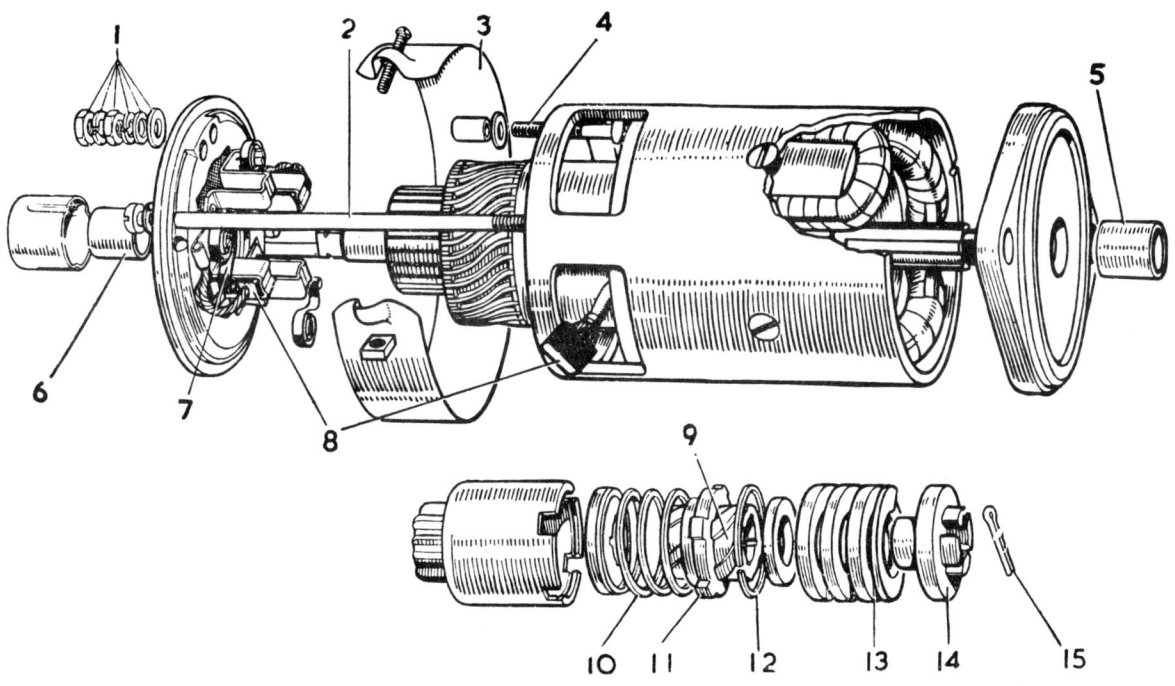

Fig. 10.3 EXPLODED VIEW OF THE STARTER AND DRIVE

1 Terminal nuts and washers. 2 Through-bolt. 3 Cover band. 4 Terminal post. 5 Bearing bush. 6 Bearing bush. 7 Brush spring. 8 Brushes. 9 Sleeve. 10 Restraining spring. 11 Control nut. 12 Retaining ring. 13 Main spring. 14 Shaft nut. 15 Cotter pin.

16. STARTER MOTOR DRIVE - REMOVAL & REPLACEMENT

1. Extract the split pin from the shaft nut on the end of the starter drive.

2. Holding the squared end of the armature shaft at the commutator end bracket with a suitable spanner, unscrew the shaft nut which has a right-hand thread, and pull off the main-spring.

3. Slide the remaining parts with a rotary action off the armature shaft.

4. Reassembly is a straight reversal of the above procedure. Ensure that the split pin is refitted. NOTE. It is most important that the drive gear is completely free from oil, grease and dirt. With the drive gear removed, clean all the parts thoroughly in paraffin. UNDER NO CIRCUMSTANCES OIL THE DRIVE COMPONENTS. Lubrication of the drive components could easily cause the pinion to stick.

17. STARTER MOTOR BUSHES - INSPECTION, REMOVAL & REPLACEMENT

1. With the starter motor stripped down check the condition of the bushes. They should be renewed when they are sufficiently worn to allow visible side movement of the armature shaft.

2. The old bushes are simply driven out with a suitable drift and the new bushes inserted by the same method. As the bearings are of the phospher bronze type it is essential that they are allowed to stand in S.A.E. 30 engine oil for at least 24 hours before fitment.

18. CONTROL BOX - GENERAL DESCRIPTION

The control box comprises the voltage regulator and the cut-out. The voltage regulator controls the output from the dynamo depending on the state of the battery and the demands of the electrical equipment and ensures that the battery is not overcharged. The cut-out is really an automatic switch and connects the dynamo to the battery when the dynamo is turning fast enough to produce a charge. Similarly it disconnects the battery from the dynamo when the engine is idling or stationary so that the battery does not discharge through the dynamo.

19. CUT-OUT & REGULATOR CONTACTS - MAINTENANCE

1. Every 12,000 miles check the cut-out and regulator contacts. If they are dirty or rough or burnt, place a piece of fine glass paper (DO NOT USE EMERY PAPER OR CARBORUNDUM PAPER) between the cut-out contacts, close them manually and draw the glass paper through several times.

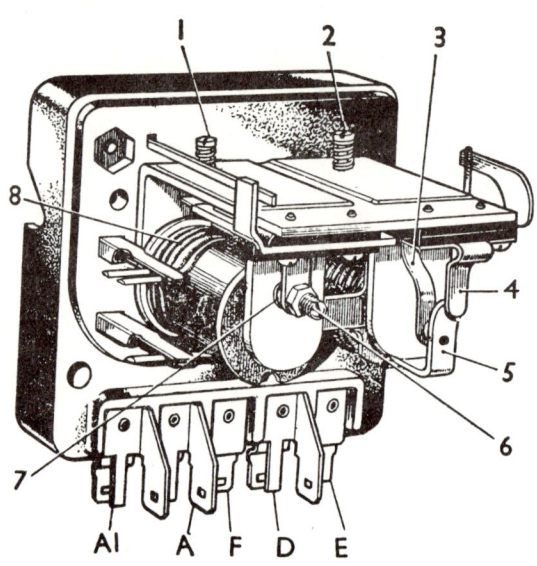

Fig. 10.4. VIEW OF THE REGULATOR & CONTROL BOX
1 Regulator adjusting screw. 2 Cut-out adjusting screw. 3 Fixed contact blade. 4 Stop arm. 5 Armature tongue and moving contact. 6 Regulator fixed contact screw. 7 Regulator moving contact. 8 Windings

2. Clean the regulator contacts in exactly the same way, but use emery or carborundum paper and not glass paper. Carefully clean both sets of contacts from all traces of dust with a rag moistened in methylated spirits.

20. VOLTAGE REGULATOR ADJUSTMENT

1. If the battery is in sound condition, but is not holding its charge, or is being continually overcharged and the dynamo is in sound condition, then the voltage regulator in the control box must be adjusted.

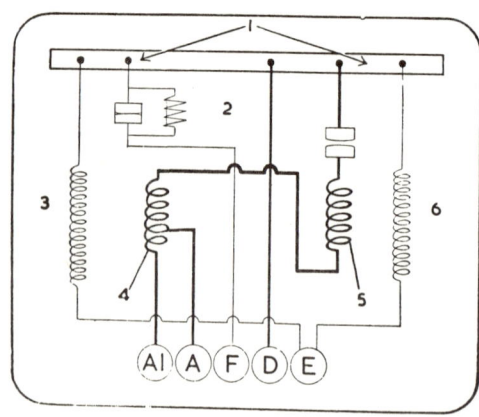

Fig. 10.5. PLAN OF THE REGULATOR & CUT-OUT. 1 Regulator and cut-out frame. 2 Field resistance. 3 Shunt coil. 4 Tapped series coil. 5 Series coil. 6 Shunt coil

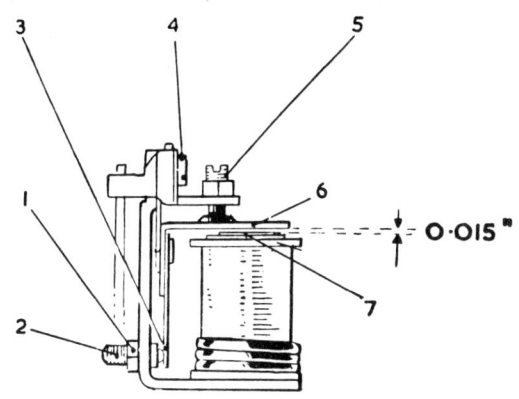

Fig. 10.6. SETTING THE REGULATOR MECHANICALLY
1 Locknut. 2 Voltage adjusting screw. 3 Armature tension spring.
4 Armature securing screws. 5 Fixed contact adjustment screw.
6 Armature. 7 Core face and shim

2. Check the regulator setting by removing and joining together the cables from the control box terminals A1 and A. Then connect the negative lead of a 20-volt voltmeter to the 'D' terminal on the dynamo and the positive lead to a good earth. Start the engine and increase its speed until the voltmeter needle flicks and then steadies. This should occur at about 2,000 r.p.m. If the voltage at which the needle steadies is outside the limits listed below, then remove the control box cover and turn the adjusting screw, (1) in Fig. 10.4, clockwise a quarter of a turn at a time to raise the setting and a similar amount, anti-clockwise, to lower it.

Air Temperature	Type RB 106/2 Open circuit voltage
10°C or 50°F	16.1 to 16.7
20°C or 68°F	16.0 to 16.6
30°C or 86°F	15.9 to 16.5
40°C or 104°F	15.8 to 16.4

3. It is vital that the adjustments be completed within 30 seconds of starting the engine as otherwise the heat from the shunt coil will affect the readings.

21. CUT-OUT ADJUSTMENT

1. Check the voltage required to operate the cut-out by connecting a voltmeter between the control box terminals 'D' and 'E'.
2. Remove the control box cover, start the engine and gradually increase its speed until the cut-outs close. This should occur when the reading is between 12.7 to 13.3 volts.
3. If the reading is outside these limits turn the cut-out adjusting screw, (2) in Fig. 10.4, a fraction at a time clockwise to raise the voltage, and anti-clockwise to lower it. To adjust

the drop off voltage bend the fixed contact blade carefully. The adjustment to the cut-out should be completed within 30 seconds of starting the engine as otherwise heat build-up from the shunt coil will affect the readings.
4. If the cut-out fails to work, clean the contacts, and, if there is still no response, renew the cut-out and regulator unit.

22. FUSES - GENERAL

1. Two fuses are fitted to a separate fuse holder positioned adjacent to the control box. The fuse marked A1 - A2 protects the electrical items such as the horn and lights, which function irrespective of whether the ignition is on or not.
2. The fuse marked A3 - A4 protects the ignition system and items which only operate when the ignition system is switched on, i.e., the stop lights, fuel gauge, flasher unit, and windscreen wiper motor.
3. If either of these fuses blow due to a short circuit or similar trouble, trace and rectify the cause before renewing the fuse.

23. FLASHER CIRCUIT - FAULT TRACING & RECTIFICATION

1. The actual flasher unit is enclosed in a small cylindrical metal container located in the engine compartment. The unit is actuated by the direction indicator switch.
2. If the flasher unit fails to operate, or works very slowly or very rapidly, check out the flasher indicator circuit as detailed below, before assuming there is a fault in the unit itself.
3. Examine the direction indicator bulbs front and rear for broken filaments.

Fig. 10.7. The two fuses are mounted in a block on the bulkhead. Two spare fuses are carried vertically in the block.

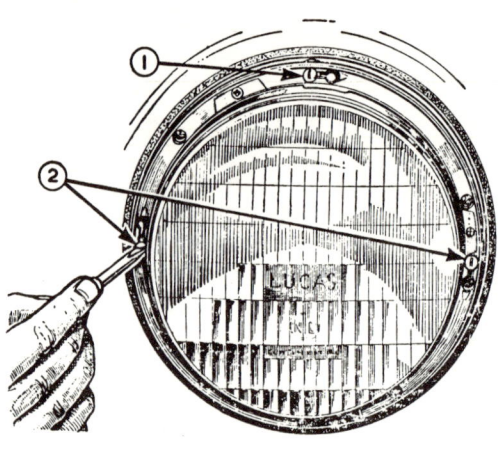

Fig. 10.8. THE SCREWS FOR ADJUSTING THE HEADLAMP BEAM. 1 Vertical adjustment screw. 2 Horizontal adjustment screws

the arms are in their normal parked position parallel with the bottom of the windscreen.

2. To remove an arm pivot the arm back and pull the wiper arm head off the splined drive.

3. When replacing an arm position it so it is in the correct relative parked position and then press the arm head onto the splined drive till the retaining clip clicks into place.

26. WINDSCREEN WIPER MECHANISM - FAULT DIAGNOSIS & RECTIFICATION

1. Should the windscreen wipers fail to park or park badly then check the limit switch on the gearbox cover.

2. Loosen the four screws which retain the gearbox cover and place the projection close to the rim of the limit switch in line with the groove in the gearbox cover.

3. Rotate the limit switch anti-clockwise 25° and tighten the four screws retaining the gear-

4. If the external flashers are working but the internal flasher warning light has ceased to function check the filament of the warning bulb and replace as necessary.

5. With the aid of the wiring diagram check all the flasher circuit connections if a flasher bulb is sound but does not work.

6. In the event of total direction indicator failure, check the A3 - A4 fuse.

7. With the ignition turned on check that current is reaching the flasher unit by connecting a voltmeter between the 'plus' or 'B' terminal and earth. If this test is positive connect the 'plus' or 'B' terminal and the 'L' terminal and operate the flasher switch. If the flasher bulb lights up the flasher unit itself is defective and must be replaced as it is not possible to dismantle and repair it.

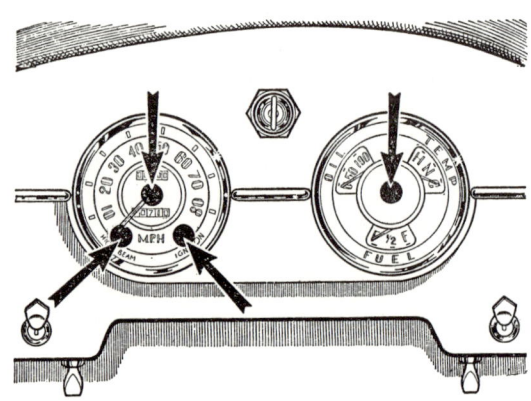

Fig. 10.9. THE POSITION OF THE INSTRUMENT BULBS ON THE AUSTIN A.55 Mk.II & AUSTIN A.60

24. WINDSCREEN WIPER MECHANISM - MAINTENANCE

1. Renew the windscreen wiper blades at intervals of 12,000 miles, or more frequently if necessary.

2. The cable which drives the wiper blades from the gearbox attached to the windscreen wiper motor is pre-packed with grease and requires no maintenance. The washer round the wheelbase spindle can be lubricated with several drops of glycerine every 6,000 miles.

25. WINDSCREEN WIPER ARMS - REMOVAL & REPLACEMENT

1. Before removing a wiper arm, turn the windscreen wiper switch on and off to ensure

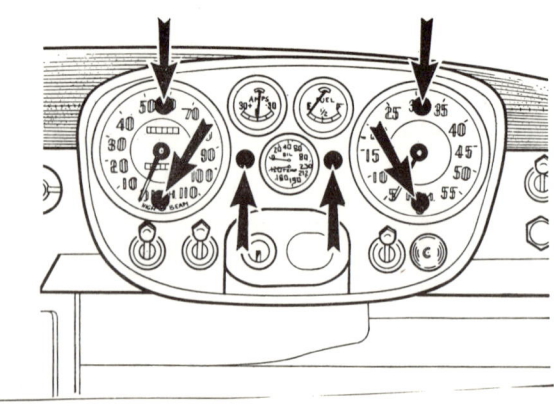

Fig. 10.10. THE POSITION OF THE INSTRUMENT BULBS ON THE RILEY 4/68 & 4/72

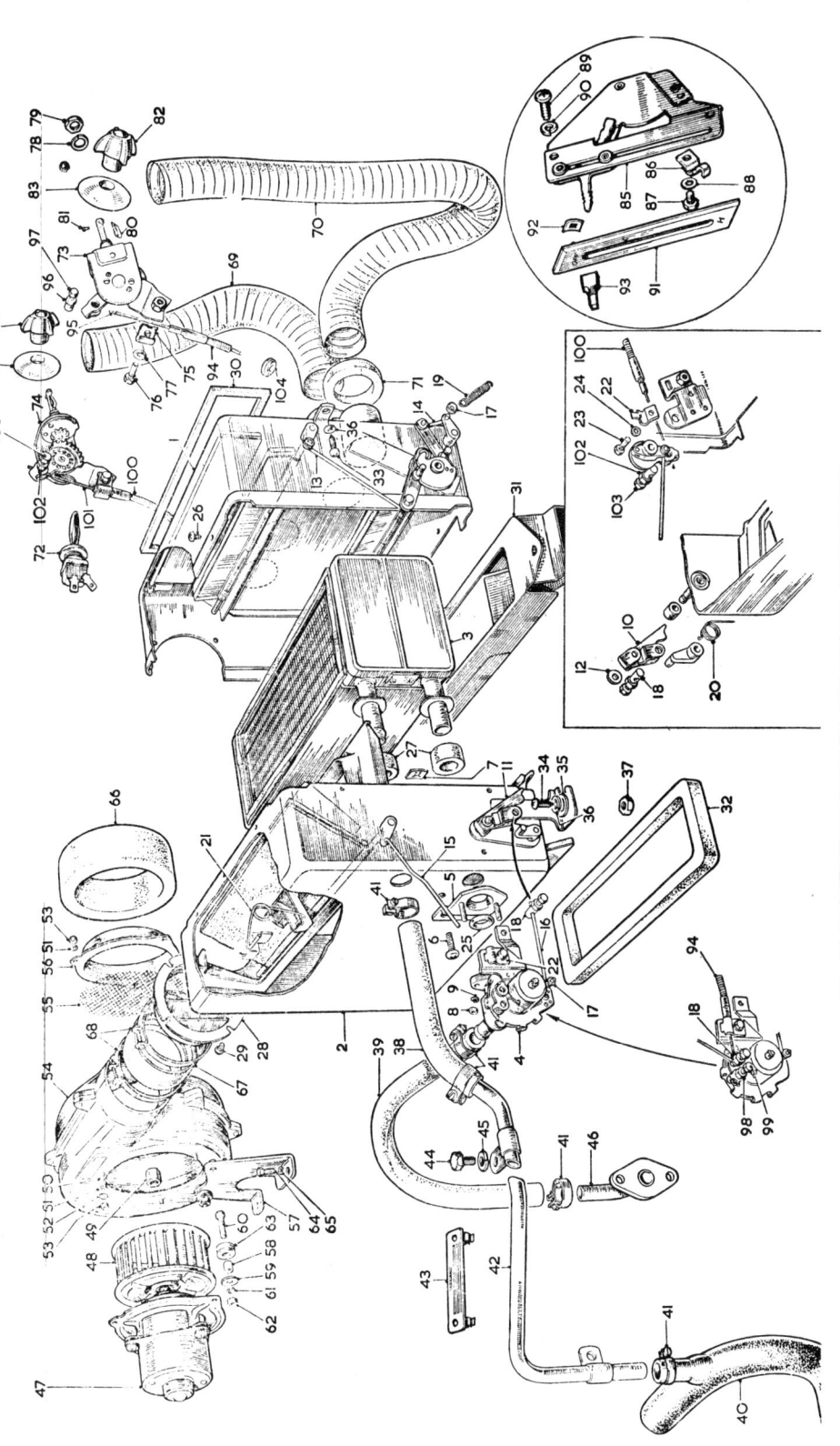

Fig. 10.11 EXPLODED VIEW OF THE HEATER COMPONENTS

1 Cover assembly—demist. 2 Cover assembly—heater. 3 Radiator assembly. 4 Valve assembly—water. 5 Bracket—water valve. 6 Screw—mounting bracket. 7 Nut—mounting bracket. 8 Nut—valve to bracket. 9 Washer. 10 Lever actuating—R.H. 11 Lever actuating—L.H. 12 Clip for lever. 13 Upper link—demist flap. 14 Lower link—demist flap. 15 Link—air mix flap. 16 Link—water valve. 17 Starlock washer—link. 18 Trunnion—water valve and lever. 19 Spring—coil—flap control. 20 Spring—outlet flap. 21 Spring—air mix flap. 22 Clamp—cable. 23 Screw—cable. 24 Washer. 25 Ring—sealing—radiator. 26 Screw—heating casing. 27 Washer—rubber. 28 Flange—inlet. 29 Screw for flange. 30 Seal—heater to bulkhead. 31 Heat deflector assembly. 32 Seal—heater base. 33 Screw—heater to dash. 34 Screw—heater to dash. 35 Washer for screw. 36 Washer for screw—spring. 37 Nut—screw. 38 Hose—heater outlet. 39 Hose—heater inlet. 40 Bottom radiator hose. 41 Clip—hose. 42 Pipe—water—heater to radiator. 43 Heater instruction plate. 44 Screw—water pipe to manifold. 45 Washer for screw—spring. 46 Elbow—heater. 47 Motor and runner assembly. 48 Runner. 49 Nut—runner. 50 Screw—motor to housing. 51 Washer for screw. 52 Washer for screw (curved). 53 Nut for screw. 54 Housing—blower. 55 Mesh—intake. 56 Flange—inlet. 57 Bracket—blower. 58 Spacer. 59 Screw. 60 Screw—bracket to housing. 61 Washer for screw. 62 Nut for screw. 63 Grommet—rubber. 64 Screw—blower to dash. 65 Washer for screw. 66 Seal—blower to heater. 68 Clip for sleeve. 69 Tube—demister—inner (12in. and 17 in.). 70 Tube—demister—outer (30 in.). 71 Seal—demist outlet. 72 Switch heater (A. 60 only). 73 Control assembly—heat. 74 Control assembly—demist. 75 Clamp—cable. 76 Screw for clamp. 77 Washer for screw. 78 Washer for screw. 79 Nut for spindle. 80 Clip—knob. 81 Pin—knob clip. 82 Knob—heat control. 83 Escutcheon—heat control. 84 Escutcheon—demist control. 85 Heat control assembly. 86 Clamp—cable. 87 Screw—clamp. 88 Washer for screw—shakeproof. 89 Screw—control to fascia. 90 Washer for screw—shakeproof. 91 Bezel—heat/demist control. 92 Clip—bezel to fascia. 93 Knob—heat/demist control. 94 Cable assembly—heat control. 95 Cable—inner. 96 Trunnion. 97 Screw for trunnion. 98 Trunnion—cable to water valve. 99 Screw for trunnion. 100 Cable assembly—demist control. 101 Cable—inner. 102 Trunnion. 103 Screw for trunnion. 104 Grommet.

box cover. If it is wished to park the windscreen wipers on the other side of the windscreen rotate the limit switch 180° clockwise.

4. Should the windscreen wipers fail, or work very slowly, then check the current the motor is taking by connecting up a 1-20 volt voltmeter in the circuit and turning on the wiper switch. Consumption should be between 2.7 to 3.4 amps.

5. If no current is passing through check the A3 - A4 fuse. If the fuse has blown replace it after having checked the wiring of the motor and other electrical circuits serviced by this fuse for short circuits.

6. If the fuse is in good condition check the wiper switch and the current operated thermostat by substitution.

7. If the wiper motor takes a very high current check the wiper blades for freedom of movement. If this is satisfactory check the gearbox cover and gear assembly for damage and measure the armature end float which should be between .008 to .012 in. (.20 to .30 mm.).

8. The end float is set by the adjusting screw. Check that excessive friction in the cable connecting tubes caused by too small a curvature is not the cause of the high current consumption.

9. If the motor takes a very low current ensure that the battery is fully charged. Check the brush gear after removing the commutator end bracket and ensure that the brushes are bearing on the commutator. If not, check the brushes for freedom of movement and if necessary renew the tension spring.

10. Check the armature by substitution if this unit is suspected.

27. WINDSCREEN WIPER MOTOR, GEARBOX & WHEELBOX - REMOVAL & REPLACEMENT

1. Remove the windscreen wiper arms by lifting the blades, carefully raising the retaining clip, and then pulling the arms off the splined drive shafts. Remove the air duct grille.

2. Disconnect the electrical cables from the wiper motor and release the outer cable from the gearbox housing.

3. Unscrew and remove the three screws which hold the bracket on which the combined wiper motor and gearbox is mounted.

4. Remove the motor, gearbox, bracket and cable rack from under the fascia panel. The cable rack is connected to the cross-head in the gearbox and passes through an outer casing which connects the gearbox on the wiper motor to the wheelbox on the passenger's side and then connects the wheelbox on the passenger's side to the wheelbox on the driver's side.

5. The windscreen wiper arm wheelboxes are located immediately underneath the splined drive shafts over which the wiper arms fit. To remove these wheelboxes release the cable rack outer casings by slackening the wheelbox cover screws. Remove the external nut, bush, and washer from the base of the splines and pull out the wheelboxes from under the fascia.

6. Replacement is a straight reversal of the above sequence but take care that the cable rack emerges properly and that the wheelboxes are correctly lined up.

28. WINDSCREEN WIPER MOTOR - DISMANTLING, INSPECTION & REASSEMBLY

1. Undo the four screws holding the gearbox cover in place and remove the cover.

2. Undo and remove the two through bolts from the commutator end bracket. Pull out the connector and free the end bracket from the yoke.

3. Carefully remove the brush gear as a unit from the commutator and then withdraw the yoke.

4. Clean the commutator and brush gear and if worn fit new brushes. The resistance between adjacent commutator segments should be .34 to .41 ohm.

5. Carefully examine the internal wiring for signs of chafing, breaks or charring which would lead to a short circuit. Insulate or replace any damaged wiring.

6. Measure the value of the field resistance which should be between 12.8 to 14 ohms. If a lower reading than this is obtained it is likely that there is a short circuit and a new field coil should be fitted.

7. Renew the gearbox gear teeth if they are damaged, chipped or worn.

8. Reassembly is a straightforward reversal of the dismantling sequence, but ensure the following items are lubricated:

a) Immerse the self aligning armature bearing in S.A.E. 20 engine oil for 24 hours before assembly.

b) Oil the armature bearings in S.A.E. 20 engine oil.

c) Soak the felt lubricator in the gearbox with S.A.E. 20 engine oil.

d) Grease generously the worm wheel bearings, cross head, guide channel, connecting rod, crankpin, worm, cable rack and wheelboxes and the final gear shaft.

29. HORN - FAULT TRACING & RECTIFICATION

1. Check the wiring for short circuits or loose connections and that the horn is secure and unobstructed. If all is sound externally check the contact breaker points which may be burnt or dirty. Clean with a fine file and dust away with a petrol moistened rag. Correct current consumption is $3-3\frac{1}{2}$ amps.

ELECTRICAL SYSTEM
FAULT FINDING CHART

Cause	Trouble	Remedy
SYMPTOM:	STARTER MOTOR FAILS TO TURN ENGINE	
No electricity at starter motor	Battery discharged Battery defective internally Battery terminal leads loose or earth lead not securely attached to body Loose or broken connections in starter motor circuit Starter motor switch or solenoid faulty	Charge battery. Fit new battery. Check and tighten leads. Check all connections and tighten any that are loose. Test and replace faulty components with new.
Electricity at starter motor: faulty motor	Starter motor pinion jammed in mesh with flywheel gear ring Starter brushes badly worn, sticking, or brush wires loose Commutator dirty, worn, or burnt Starter motor armature faulty Field coils earthed	Disengage pinion by turning squared end of armature shaft. Examine brushes, replace as necessary, tighten down brush wires. Clean commutator, recut if badly burnt. Overhaul starter motor, fit new armature. Overhaul starter motor.
SYMPTOM:	STARTER MOTOR TURNS ENGINE VERY SLOWLY	
Electrical defects	Battery in discharged condition Starter brushes badly worn, sticking, or brush wires loose Loose wires in starter motor circuit	Charge battery. Examine brushes, replace as necessary, tighten down brush wires. Check wiring and tighten as necessary.
SYMPTOM:	STARTER MOTOR OPERATES WITHOUT TURNING ENGINE	
Dirt or oil on drive gear	Starter motor pinion sticking on the screwed sleeve	Remove starter motor, clean starter motor drive.
Mechanical damage	Pinion or flywheel gear teeth broken or worn	Fit new gear ring to flywheel, and new pinion to starter motor drive.
SYMPTOMS:	STARTER MOTOR NOISY OR EXCESSIVELY ROUGH ENGAGEMENT	
Lack of attention or mechanical damage	Pinion or flywheel gear teeth broken or worn Starter drive main spring broken Starter motor retaining bolts loose	Fit new gear teeth to flywheel, or new pinion to starter motor drive. Dismantle and fit new main spring Tighten starter motor securing bolts. Fit new spring washer if necessary.
SYMPTOM:	BATTERY WILL NOT HOLD CHARGE FOR MORE THAN A FEW DAYS	
Wear or damage	Battery defective internally Electrolyte level too low or electrolyte too weak due to leakage Plate separators no longer fully effective Battery plates severely sulphated	Remove and fit new battery. Top up electrolyte level to just above plates Remove and fit new battery. Remove and fit new battery.
Insufficient current flow to keep battery charged	Fan/dynamo belt slipping Battery terminal connections loose or corroded Dynamo not charging properly Short in lighting circuit causing continual battery drain Regulator unit not working correctly	Check belt for wear, replace if necessary, and tighten. Check terminals for tightness, and remove all corrosion. Remove and overhaul dynamo. Trace and rectify. Check setting, clean, and replace if defective.
SYMPTOM:	IGNITION LIGHT FAILS TO GO OUT, BATTERY RUNS FLAT IN A FEW DAYS	
Dynamo not charging	Fan belt loose and slipping, or broken Brushes worn, sticking, broken, or dirty Brush springs weak or broken Commutator dirty, greasy, worn, or burnt	Check, replace, and tighten as necessary. Examine, clean, or replace brushes as necessary. Examine and test. Replace as necessary. Clean commutator and undercut segment separators.

ELECTRICAL SYSTEM

	Armature badly worn or armature shaft bent	Fit new or reconditioned armature.
	Commutator bars shorting	Undercut segment separations.
	Dynamo bearings badly worn	Overhaul dynamo, fit new bearings.
	Dynamo field coils burnt, open, or shorted.	Remove and fit rebuilt dynamo.
	Commutator no longer circular	Recut commutator and undercut segment separators.
	Pole pieces very loose	Strip and overhaul dynamo. Tighten pole pieces.
Regulator or cut-out fails to work correctly	Regulator incorrectly set	Adjust regulator correctly.
	Cut-out incorrectly set	Adjust cut-out correctly.
	Open circuit in wiring of cut-out and regulator unit	Remove, examine, and renew as necessary.

Failure of individual electrical equipment to function correctly is dealt with alphabetically, item by item, under the headings listed below:

FUEL GAUGE

Fuel gauge gives no reading	Fuel tank empty!	Fill fuel tank.
	Electric cable between tank sender unit and gauge earthed or loose	Check cable for earthing and joints for tightness.
	Fuel gauge case not earthed	Ensure case is well earthed.
	Fuel gauge supply cable interrupted	Check and replace cable if necessary.
	Fuel gauge unit broken	Replace fuel gauge.
Fuel gauge registers full all the time	Electric cable between tank unit and gauge broken or disconnected	Check over cable and repair as necessary.

HORN

Horn operates all the time	Horn push either earthed or stuck down	Disconnect battery earth. Check and rectify source of trouble.
	Horn cable to horn push earthed	Disconnect battery earth. Check and rectify source of trouble.
Horn fails to operate	Blown fuse	Check and renew if broken. Ascertain cause.
	Cable or cable connection loose, broken or disconnected	Check all connections for tightness and cables for breaks.
	Horn has an internal fault	Remove and overhaul horn.
Horn emits intermittent or unsatisfactory noise	Cable connections loose	Check and tighten all connections.
	Horn incorrectly adjusted	Adjust horn until best note obtained.

LIGHTS

Lights do not come on	If engine not running, battery discharged	Push-start car, charge battery.
	Light bulb filament burnt out or bulbs broken	Test bulbs in live bulb holder.
	Wire connections loose, disconnected or broken	Check all connections for tightness and wire cable for breaks.
	Light switch shorting or otherwise faulty	By-pass light switch to ascertain if fault is in switch and fit new switch as appropriate.
Lights come on but fade out	If engine not running battery discharged	Push-start car, and charge battery.
Lights give very poor illumination	Lamp glasses dirty	Clean glasses.
	Reflector tarnished or dirty	Fit new reflectors.
	Lamps badly out of adjustment	Adjust lamps correctly.
	Incorrect bulb with too low wattage fitted	Remove bulb and replace with correct grade
	Existing bulbs old and badly discoloured	Renew bulb units.
	Electrical wiring too thin not allowing full current to pass	Rewire lighting system.

ELECTRICAL SYSTEM

Cause	Trouble	Remedy
Lights work erratically - flashing on and off, especially over bumps	Battery terminals or earth connection loose Lights not earthing properly Contacts in light switch faulty	Tighten battery terminals and earth connection. Examine and rectify. By-pass light switch to ascertain if fault is in switch and fit new switch as appropriate.
WIPERS		
Wiper motor fails to work	Blown fuse Wire connections loose, disconnected, or broken Brushes badly worn Armature worn or faulty Field coils faulty	Check and replace fuse if necessary. Check wiper wiring. Tighten loose connections. Remove and fit new brushes. If electricity at wiper motor remove and overhaul and fit replacement armature. Purchase reconditioned wiper motor.
Wiper motor works very slowly and takes excessive current	Commutator dirty, greasy, or burnt Drive to wheelboxes too bent or un-lubricated Wheelbox spindle binding or damaged Armature bearings dry or unaligned Armature badly worn or faulty	Clean commutator thoroughly. Examine drive and straighten out severe curvature. Lubricate. Remove, overhaul, or fit replacement. Replace with new bearings correctly aligned. Remove, overhaul, or fit replacement armature.
Wiper motor works slowly and takes little current	Brushes badly worn Commutator dirty, greasy, or burnt Armature badly worn or faulty	Remove and fit new brushes. Clean commutator thoroughly. Remove and overhaul armature or fit replacement.
Wiper motor works but wiper blades remain static	Driving cable rack disengaged or faulty Wheelbox gear and spindle damaged or worn Wiper motor gearbox parts badly worn	Examine and if faulty, replace. Examine and if faulty, replace. Overhaul or fit new gearbox.

CHAPTER ELEVEN

SUSPENSION – DAMPERS – STEERING

CONTENTS

SPECIFICATIONS

Front Suspension ... ... Independent by coil springs and wishbones
   Coil spring diameter ... ... 4.187 in. (106.4 mm.)
   Free height ... ... 11.687 in. (297 mm.)
   No. of working coils ... ... $7\frac{1}{2}$
   Spring rate ... ... 300 lb. in. (3.45 kg.m.)
   Wheel camber angle ... ... $\frac{3}{4}$ to 1° positive
   Wheel castor angle ... ... $1\frac{1}{2}^{\circ}$ positive
                               ($\frac{1}{4}$ to 1° later models)
   King pin inclination ... ... $6\frac{1}{2}^{\circ}$ positive
   Mounting nuts torque ... ... 40 to 45 lb. ft. (5.5 to 6.2 kg.m.)

) Static
) unladen
) condition

Rear Suspension ... ... Semi-elliptic leaf springs
   No. of spring leaves 6
   Width of spring leaves ... ... $1\frac{3}{4}$ in. (44.45 mm.)
   Working load ... ... 625 lb. (283 kg.)
   Spring rate ... ... 167 lb. in. (1.9 kg.m.)
   Free camber ... ... 3 in. (76.2 mm.)

SUSPENSION – DAMPERS – STEERING

Steering	Cam and lever
No. of turns lock to lock	3 (early models), 2.9 (later models)
Steering wheel diameter	17 in. (43.2 cm.)
Turning circle	37 ft. (11.28 m.)
Toe in	$\frac{1}{16}$ to $\frac{1}{8}$ in. (1.59 to 3.18 mm.)
Ratio - early models	14-12-14 : 1
Ratio - later models	15-13$\frac{1}{2}$-15 : 1
Steering wheel nut torque	41 lb.ft. (5.76 kg.m.)
Steering box rocker shaft nut torque	75 lb.ft. (10.4 kg.m.)
Idler shaft nut torque	75 lb.ft. (10.4 kg.m.)
Steering box side cover set bolts torque ...	12 to 15 lb.ft. (1.8 to 2.1 kg.m.)
Dampers	Hydraulic - Front and rear
Front dampers	Lever arm type (Armstrong)
Rear dampers	Lever arm type (Armstrong)
Rear damper bolts torque	30 lb.ft. (4.1 kg.m.)
Damper fluid	Armstrong Super (Thin) Shock Absorber Fluid or a quality mineral oil to spec. S.A.E. 20/20W
Wheels & Tyres	Ventilated disc. 4 stud fixing
Size	4J x 14
Tyres - Saloons	5.90 by 14 or 165-14 SP
Tyres - Estates	5.90 by 14 or 6.40 by 14
Pressure - Front - Saloons	23 lb./sq.in. (1.62 kg./cm^2) all conditions
Pressure - Front - Normal - Estates	20 lb./sq.in. (1.41 kg./cm^2) 5.90 by 14
Pressure - Front - Normal - Estates	18 lb./sq.in. (1.27 kg./cm^2) 6.40 by 14
Pressure - Front - Laden - Estates	22 lb./sq.in. (1.55 kg./cm^2) 5.90 by 14
Pressure - Front - Laden - Estates	24 lb./sq.in. (1.69 kg./cm^2) 6.40 by 14
Pressure - Rear - Saloons	25 lb./sq.in. (1.76 kg./cm^2) all condition
Pressure - Rear - Normal - Estates	24 lb./sq.in. (1.69 kg./cm^2) 5.90 by 14
Pressure - Rear - Normal - Estates	22 lb./sq.in. (1.55 kg./cm^2) 6.40 by 14
Pressure - Rear - Laden - Estates	32 lb./sq.in. (2.25 kg./cm^2) 5.90 by 14
Pressure - Rear - Laden - Estates	30 lb./sq.in. (2.11 kg./cm^2) 6.40 by 14

GENERAL DESCRIPTION

The two independent front suspension units are attached to each end of a substantial crossmember which can be removed complete if required.

The crossmember is held in place on the underframe by four main bolts, and by four bolts on each side to the engine mounting plate. On early models flat rubber mountings fitted to the four main bolts insulate the body from road noise created by surface irregularities which are transmitted through the steering and suspension. Later models use rubber mountings and cups to hold the crossmember to the underframe; and the upper cups are welded to the body.

Each front suspension unit consists of a lower wishbone, coil spring, stub axle, kingpin and a double acting damper. The two arms of the latter serve to locate the top of the kingpin.

On 1622 c.c. models anti-roll bars are fitted front and rear in the interests of stability.

The lower wishbone arms are attached at their outer ends to the lower end of the kingpin by means of a double threaded fulcrum pin and two bushes. The inner ends of the arms are rubber bushed and secured to the crossmember by a spindle and two brackets.

The coil spring fits between a spigot on the underside of the crossmember and a special pan held in place between the two arms of the lower wishbone. Fitted to the top of the kingpin is a trunnion link to which is attached the outer ends of the damper arms which are held in place by a fulcrum pin and tapered rubber bushes.

The cam and lever steering gear is attached to the right-hand side of the chassis frame by four bolts. On the opposite side of the chassis is a steering idler box. The steering lever at the foot of the steering box connects to the idler lever by means of the track rod. Tie-rods from the steering and idler levers operate the steering arms via ball joints.

Double acting Armstrong dampers are fitted front and rear. The front dampers are bolted to the top of each end of the crossmember. The rear dampers are bolted to the bodyframe sidemembers and are connected to the rear axle by means of a link.

161

CHAPTER ELEVEN

The rear suspension is by semi-elliptic leaf springs which are rubber mounted. The spring shackles make use of rubber bushes. NOTE. Many of the suspension nuts and bolts will be rusted and very stiff on cars which have been on the road a number of years. On such models it is advisable to treat any nuts and bolts to be undone with a freeing agent such as 'Plus Gas' 24 hours before commencing work.

2. FRONT & REAR SUSPENSION - MAINTENANCE

1. The twelve nipples on the front suspension should be greased at intervals of 3,000 miles with a grease gun filled with Castrolease L.M. or a similar quality grease. Jack up the front of the car and remove the roadwheels. Nipples are positioned one on the top and one on the bottom of the kingpin bushes and one in the base of the kingpin. There are grease nipples on all the track rod and draglink ball joints (3 each side - 6 in all).

2. There are five further nipples which require attention. One is located on the rear of each rear spring shackle (total 2); one on the handbrake cable; and one at each end of the propeller shaft on the universal joints (total 2).

3. The securing nuts on the rear spring 'U' bolts should be checked for tightness at intervals of 6,000 miles. Check for broken leaves, loose shackles, and worn shackle bushes at the same time.

4. NOTE that rubber bushes are used throughout the suspension and the greatest care must be taken to keep them free of grease. If they become contaminated they will deteriorate rapidly. Note also that most 1622 c.c. models use sealed ball joints on the track rod and draglink, reducing the number of grease nipples on the front suspension from 12 to 6.

3. STEERING GEAR - MAINTENANCE

1. At intervals of 3,000 miles unscrew the large plug from the top of the steering box, and the square plug from the steering idler.

2. Check the level of the oil in the steering box and the steering idler and top up with Castrol Hypoy to bring the oil level up to the bottom of the plug threads.

4. FRONT & REAR DAMPERS - MAINTENANCE

1. At intervals of 6,000 miles thoroughly clean the area in the vicinity of the damper plugs (one on the top of each damper) and undo the plug. It is vital that this area is cleaned thoroughly as any dirt entering the damper will impair its efficiency.

2. Check the level of the oil which should be

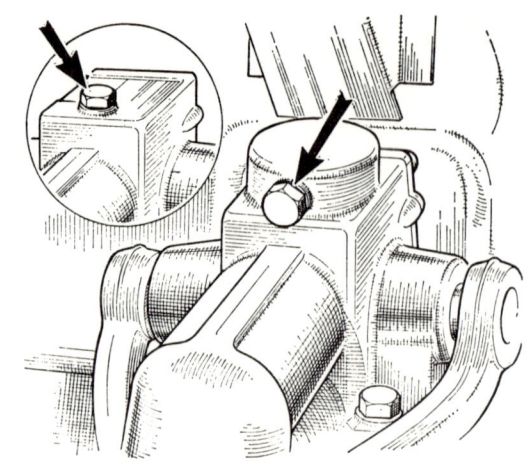

Fig. 11.1. Top up the front damper after removing the filler plug (arrowed). Shown inset is the position of the filler plug on early models

just below the filler plug threads. Top up the dampers as necessary with 'Armstrong Super (Thin) Shock Absorber Fluid No. 624'. Alternatively, if this is not available, use a quality mineral oil such as Castrol of an S.A.E. 20W rating.

3. Access to the filler plug on each of the rear dampers is gained after removing the dampers as described in section 12.

4. On no account omit to carry out this check at the mileage recommended as failure to do so could lead to the inoperation of the dampers due to air entering the pressure cylinders.

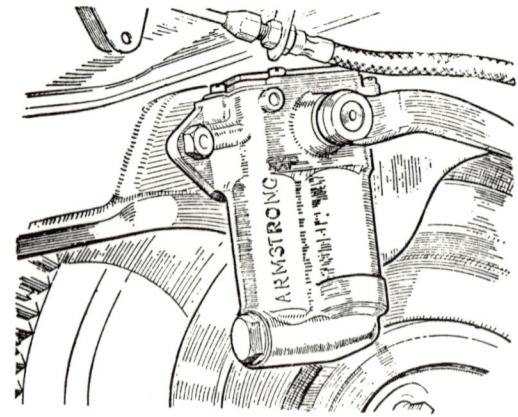

Fig. 11.2. To top up the rear damper it should first be removed from the chassis frame

SUSPENSION – DAMPERS – STEERING

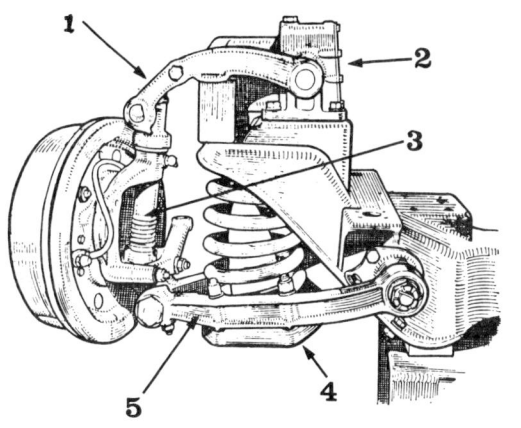

Fig. 11.3. 1 Damper arm (upper wishbone). 2 Damper. 3 King pin (or swivel pin). 4 Spring seat pan. 5 Lower wishbone

either the shock absorbers require topping up, or if they are already full, that the dampers are worn and must be replaced.

7. The dampers cannot be adjusted without special tools, and therefore must not be dismantled but exchanged with your local BMC agent for replacement units.

8. Excessive play in the steering gear will lead to wheel wobble, and can be confirmed by checking if there is any lost movement between the steering wheel and the steering lever at the base of the steering box. Provision is made for adjustment, but if all the adjustment has been taken up it will be necessary to fit a rebuilt steering box.

9. The ball joints are not prone to excessive wear providing they have been regularly greased and the rubber 'gaiters' renewed immediately if they split.

5. INSPECTING THE SUSPENSION, STEERING & DAMPERS FOR WEAR

1. To check for wear in the ball joints, place the car over a pit, or lie on the ground looking at the ball joints, and get a friend to rock the steering wheel from side to side. Wear is present if there is play in the joints.

2. To check for wear in the rubber and metal bushes, jack up the front of the car until the wheels are clear of the ground. Hold each wheel in turn, at the top and bottom, and try to rock it. If the wheel rocks continue the movement at the same time inspecting the upper trunnion link rubber bushes, and the rubber bushes at the inner ends of the wishbone for play.

3. If the wheel rocks and there is no side movement in the rubber bushes then the kinkpins and metal bushes will be worn. Alternatively, if the movement occurs between the wheel and the brake backplate, then the hub bearings require replacement.

4. The rubber bushes can be renewed by the owner, but, if there is play between the lower end of the kinkpin and the wishbone, then it will be necessary to renew the fulcrum pin.

5. Sideplay or vertical or horizontal movement of the upper link or damper arms relative to the damper body is best checked with the outer end of the damper arms freed from the upper trunnion link. If play is present the damper bearings are worn and a replacement damper should be purchased.

6. How well the dampers function can be checked by bouncing the car at each corner. After each bounce the car should return to its normal ride position within 1 to $1\frac{1}{4}$ up-and-down movements. If the car continues to move up-and-down in decreasing amounts it means that

6. FRONT ANTI-ROLL BAR - REMOVAL & REPLACEMENT

1. Jack up the front of the car and place support blocks under the wheels or run the front wheels up a pair of inspection ramps. Numbers in brackets refer to Fig. 11.7.

2. Undo the nut (48) from the lower end of each link (44) and remove the washers (46, 47) and rubber bushes (45).

3. Free the links (44) from their holes in the spring seats (32) and undo and remove the bolts and washers which hold the two lower front body stays in place.

4. Remove the bolts and spring washers (42, 43, 51, 52) which hold the bearing straps (41) to the bodyframe and also the locators (49, 50) and lower the anti-roll bar (39) to the ground.

5. If wished undo the nuts from the top end of each link (44) and separate the links from the anti-roll bar.

6. Replacement of the anti-roll bar is a straightforward reversal of the removal sequence. Renew the anti-roll bar rubber bearings (40) if worn.

7. REAR ANTI-ROLL BAR - REMOVAL & REPLACEMENT

1. Place the rear of the car over an inspection pit or on ramps.

2. The anti-roll bar is positioned slightly forward of the rear axle. Each end of the bar is attached to each of the damper arms by a 'U' bolt and an ordinary bolt.

3. Undo the three nuts and spring washers from the ends of the 'U' bolt and ordinary bolts on each side of the car, and remove the bar.

4. Replacement is a straightforward reversal of the removal sequence.

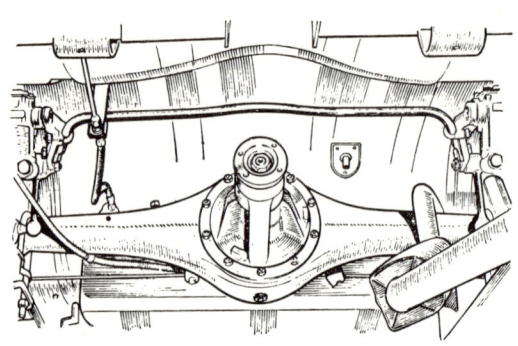

Fig. 11.4. THE POSITION OF THE REAR ANTI-ROLL BAR

8. COIL SPRINGS - REMOVAL & REPLACEMENT

1. Removal of one of the front springs is not difficult but it requires the use of a good jack (preferably hydraulic) in the absence of the proper BMC spring compressor (Service tool 18G693). All numbers in brackets refer to Fig. 11.7.

2. Loosen the front road wheel nuts, jack up the front of the car, place supports under each front side body member and remove the wheels. Where fitted remove the anti-roll bar as described in Section 6.

3. Place a jack under the front suspension pan (32, 36) with a piece of wood interposed between the spring retaining pan (19) and the head of the jack. Raise the jack to partially compress the coil spring (30). With the cars weight partially removed from the wishbone arms the four bolts, nuts and spring washers which hold the spring retaining pan to the wishbone arms can be removed and the jack slowly released. Take great care that the jack does not slip. As the jack is lowered, the coil spring and pan will come away.

4. Replacement is a straightforward reversal of the removal sequence. Measure the length of the spring and if less than 11.68 in. long it is best to renew it.

5. If the BMC spring compressor is available fit it in place on the lower wishbone arms and adjust it to take the weight of the spring. Remove the bolts securing the pan to the wishbone arms and unscrew the compressor to free the tension in the spring. Remove the pan and spring.

6. If a good jack is not available then use two $\frac{3}{8}$ in. bolts threaded their whole length which should be at least 4 in. Free two diagonally opposite nuts and bolts from the four which hold the lower wishbone arms to the spring retaining pan, and substitute the two 4 in. bolts.

Tighten the nuts on the 4 in. bolts down and then remove the two remaining small bolts. Unscrew the nuts from the 4 in. bolts equally until the spring is fully extended. The spring and retaining pan can now be removed.

9. REAR SEMI-ELLIPTIC SPRINGS - REMOVAL & DISMANTLING

1. Loosen the rear wheel securing nuts on the side from which the spring is to be removed. Jack up the rear of the car and place supports under the sidemembers. All numbers in brackets refer to Fig. 11.5. NOTE that the shackles on 1622 c.c. models differ slightly from earlier cars.

2. Remove the wheel and reposition the jack to take the weight of the axle casing. Undo the nut and washer holding the damper arm link to the bracket.

3. At the rear of the spring remove the nuts and spring washers (36, 37) or (29, 30, 31, 34, 35) which hold the shackle plate (24 or 25) to the shackle pin (33 or 28). With a suitable drift tap out the lower pin (28 or 33). On 1622 c.c. models remove the inner shackle plate (25) before attempting to drift out the lower pin (28).

4. At the front of the spring undo the nut and washers (39, 40, 41) which hold the eyebolt (38) in place and carefully pull out the bolt from the spring.

5. Undo the nuts (22) from the two 'U' bolts (21) and remove the plate clip (18), the locating plate (16) and the seating pad (17). With the 'U' bolts removed the spring can be lowered to the ground.

6. To dismantle the spring first place it in a vice so all the leaves are nipped but not the centre bolt and then remove the nuts, bolts, and washers (13, 14, 15) from the clips (9, 11). Straighten and remove the clips (9, 11) and the insulators (10, 12). Undo the nut (7) from the centre bolt (4), and tap the bolt out. Slowly open the jaws of the vice and then remove the spring leaves.

10. REAR SEMI-ELLIPTIC SPRINGS - INSPECTION, REASSEMBLY & REPLACEMENT

1. With a wire brush clean each leaf in turn and then inspect it for cracks. These are specially likely round the centre bolt holes.

2. To remove the silentbloc bushes (2) from the eyes in the main leaf (1) press them out with a tubular drift which MUST rest on the outer portion of the bushes. When fitting new bushes the same applies.

3. On 1622 c.c. models two rubber bushes are fitted to the rear main spring eye and these too should be removed and renewed.

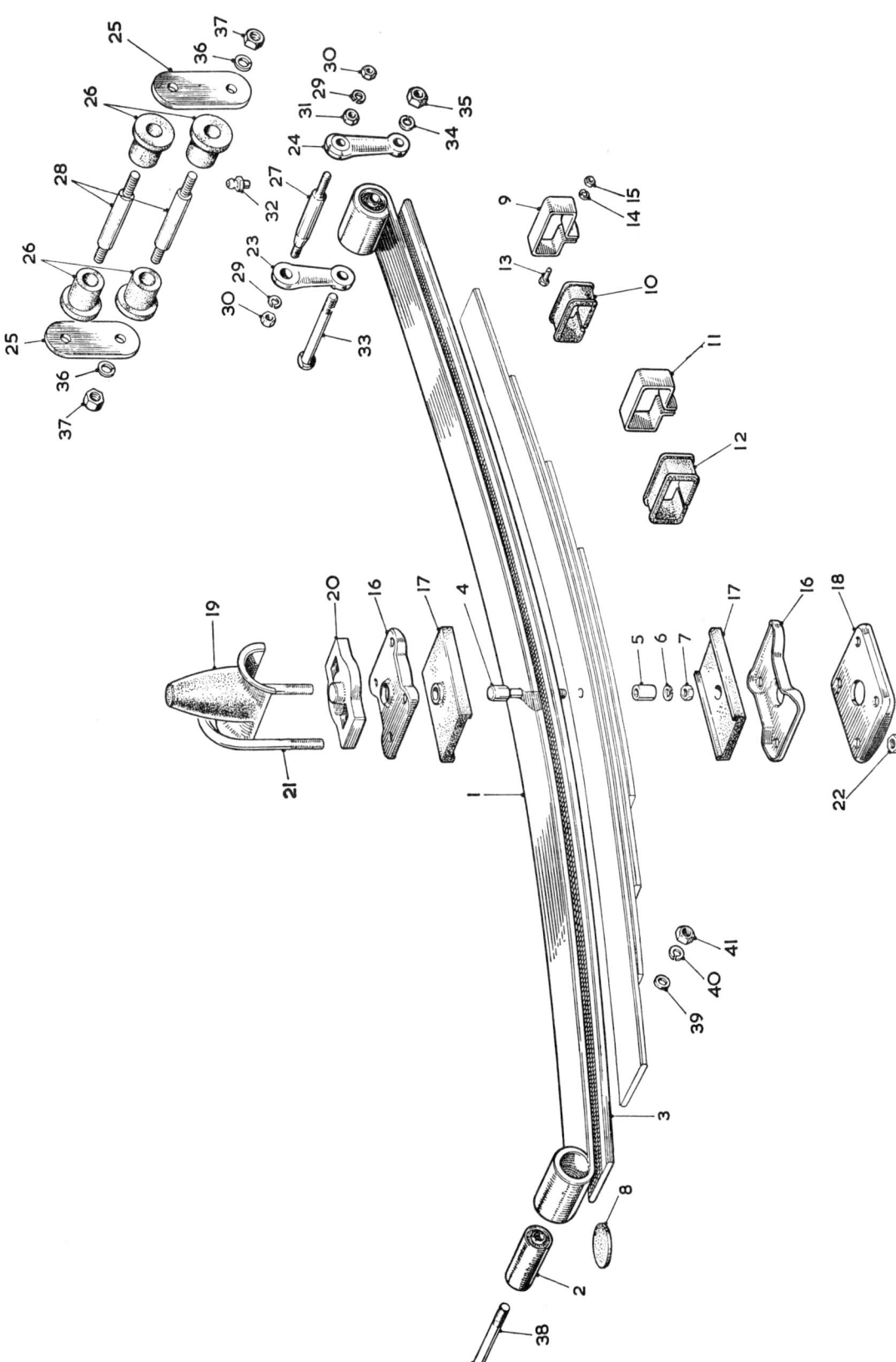

Fig. 11.5 EXPLODED VIEW OF THE REAR SPRING

1 Leaf—main. 2 Bush—main leaf. 3 Leaf—second. 4 Bolt—centre. 5 Distance piece—centre-bolt. 6 Washer for bolt (spring). 7 Nut for bolt. 8 Button (plastic). 9 Clip (short). 10 Insulator for clip. 11 Clip (long). 12 Insulator for clip. 13 Bolt for clips. 14 Washer for bolt (spring). 15 Nut for bolt. 16 Plate—locating. 17 Pad—seating. 18 Plate—clip. 19 Buffer—bump. 20 Packing piece—rear spring. 21 Clip—spring to axle. 22 Nut for clip. 23 Shackle (outer). 24 Shackle (inner). 25 Shackle—inner and outer. * 26 Bush—spring and shackle—rear end. * 27 Pin—shackle top. 28 Pin—shackle. * 29 Washer for pin (spring). 30 Nut for pin. 31 Nut for pin (lock). 32 Lubricator —top shackle pin. 33 Pin—shackle bottom. 34 Washer (spring). 35 Nut—inner shackle to bottom pin. 36 Washer for pin (spring). * 37 Nut for pin. * 38 Eyebolt. 39 Washer for pin (plain). 40 Washer for pin (spring). 41 Nut for pin.

* 1622 c. c. models only.

4. On early models phosphor-bronze bushes in two halves are fitted to the rear upper spring shackle. Before removing them undo the grease nipple. Each half of the bush can be driven out by placing a narrow drift through the opening in the shackle pin to rest against the inner end of the bush.

5. On reassembly grease the shackle pin and after assembling it to the bushes, tighten the nut and locknut just enough to eliminate end play. Make sure the shackle is still free to move backwards and forwards.

6. Fit the spring leaves together in the vice and with the aid of a long bolt or rod line up the holes in the centre of the spring. Fit the bolt (4), distance piece (5), spring washer (6), and the nut (7), and tighten firmly but not fully.

7. Fit the rubber insulators and clips (9, 10, 11, 12) and the nuts and bolts (13, 14, 15) but do NOT tighten fully until the spring is back in the car and in its normal laden position, i.e., taking the weight it will normally carry. Only in this position should all the bolts and nuts on the spring (excluding shackles) be finally tightened.

8. Refit the spring to the car connecting it to the bodybrackets at the front and rear before fitting the 'U' bolts. Ensure the head of the bolt (4) locates in the hole in the locating plate (16), and refer to Fig. 11.5 to ensure that the spring locating plates and pads are fitted the correct way round.

9. NOTE that on 1622 c.c. models the longest part of the spring measured from the hole for the securing bolt (4) must face the front of the car.

11. FRONT DAMPERS - REMOVAL & REPLACEMENT

1. Loosen the road wheel securing nuts, apply the handbrake and jack up the front of the car, placing the jack under the wishbone spring pan.

2. Remove the wheel (the numbers in brackets refer to Fig. 11.7) and pull out the split pin from the end of the top link to damper arm fulcrum pin (27). Undo and remove the castellated nut (29) and gently tap the fulcrum pin (27) out of the top suspension link.

3. Pull the hub unit and kingpin assembly away from the damper arms and then undo the four bolts and spring washers (25, 26) which hold the damper to the bodyframe crossmember. Lift away the damper unit. Keep the damper upright to prevent air getting into the operating chambers.

4. Replacement is a straightforward reversal of the removal sequence. Ensure the four damper retaining bolts are tightened to a torque of 45 lb/ft. (6.2 kg. m.).

12. REAR DAMPERS - REMOVAL & REPLACEMENT

1. It is not necessary to jack up the rear of the car for removal of the rear dampers if a pit or ramp is available. Otherwise jack up, and firmly support the rear of the car.

2. To remove a damper unscrew the nut and spring washer from the bolt which holds the damper link to the bracket on the spring; remove the rear anti-roll bar where fitted; remove the two nuts and spring washers from the damper securing bolts which hold the damper to the bodyframe sidemember and then remove the damper.

3. Keep the damper upright to prevent air getting into the operating chamber. Reassembly is a straight reversal of the removal procedure. Tighten the bolts to a torque of 45 lb/ft. (6.2 kg. m.)

13. FRONT HUBS - REMOVAL & REPLACEMENT

1. Should there be excessive slackness or unusual noises in the hubs, it is best to remove and examine them. To remove a hub, slacken the road wheel nuts, jack up the front of the car, support the underside of the car so there is no possibility of danger if the jack collapses and remove the wheel.

2. Undo the two countersunk screws holding the brake drum in position. Slacken the brake shoes right off and pull off the drum.

3. Prise off the grease retaining cap (37) (all numbers in brackets refer to Fig. 11.6.) and then remove the split pin which holds the castellated bearing retaining nut (36) in position. Undo and remove the nut (36) and flat washer (35).

4. The hub will normally pull off quite easily, but it may be necessary to use a couple of tyre levers or strong screwdrivers (in the absence of a proper hub puller), if the bearings are stuck to the stub axle.

5. From out of the hub pull the outer bearing (31), the bearing spacer or distance piece (32), the inner bearing (33) and the oil seal (34). It is not unusual for the latter two parts to be left behind on the stub axle when the hub is pulled off.

6. Thoroughly clean the bearings and the hub in paraffin, and then examine them for grooving flat spots, chips, pitting or other damage. Renew the bearing if worn.

7. Pack each bearing with a high melting point grease such as Castrolease L.M. Fit the inner bearing (33) to the hub (28) thrust side (the one with the part number on it) facing the centre of the hub. Grease the distance piece (32) and fit

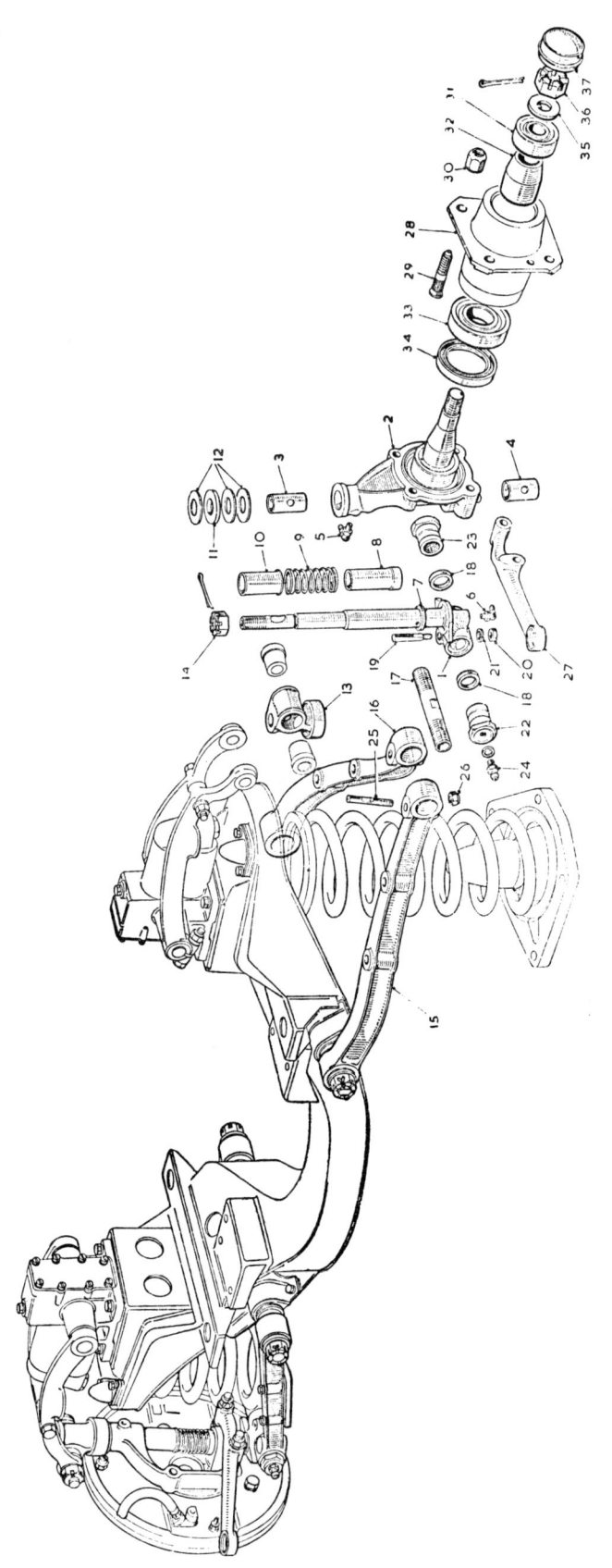

Fig. 11. 6. EXPLODED VIEW OF A FRONT HUB, KINGPIN & WISHBONES

1 Kingpin. 2 Stub axle. 3 Bush—top. 4 Bush—bottom. 5 Lubricator for swivel axle—upper. 6 Lubricator for swivel axle—lower. 7 Ring—cork. 8 Tube—dust excluder —bottom. 9 Spring for dust excluder. 10 Tube—dust excluder—top. 11 Washer—thrust. 12 Washer—floating thrust. 13 Trunnion—suspension link. 14 Nut—trunnion to swivelpin. 15 Arm—L.H. front and R.H. rear. 16 Arm—L.H. rear and R.H. front. 17 Pin—fulcrum—lower link. 18 Ring for fulcrum pin. 19 Pin—cotter—fulcrum pin to swivel pin. 20 Nut for cotter. 21 Washer for nut—spring. 22 Bushes (front)—swivel pin end. 23 Bushes (rear) for link—swivel pin end. 24 Lubricator. 25 Pin—cotter— link to bushes. 26 Nut for cotter. 27 Lever—steering—L.H. 28 Hub assembly. 29 Stud—wheel. 30 Nut for wheel stud. 31 Bearings for hub—outer. 32 Distance piece for bearing. 33 Bearings for hub—inner. 34 Seal—oil. 35 Washer—bearing retaining. 36 Nut for swivel axle. 37 Cup—grease retaining.

167

it in position so the domed portion faces the outer bearing (31).

8. Fit the oil seal over the inner bearing with the flat side facing the outside of the hub and fill the space between the oil seal and the race with grease.

9. Assemble the hub and bearings to the stub axle and carefully tap the assembly home by means of a metal tube bearing against the outer race of the outer bearing (31).

10. Fit the bearing retaining washer (35) and tighten the castellated nut (36), turning it on to line up the hole for the split pin with one of the cut-outs in the nut (36). The nut should be tightened to a torque of approximately 70 lb/ft. Check that the bearings turn freely, and replace the grease retaining cap (37).

14. **FRONT SUSPENSION - INSPECTION FOR WEAR**

1. To check the condition of the front suspension units (the steering gear and ball joints are dealt with in section 5) first jack up the front of the car.

2. Hold in turn each front wheel at the top and bottom and try rocking vertically. If there is no movement the suspension bushes are in good condition and will not require overhaul.

3. If the wheel rocks, get a friend to watch for movement between the wheel and the stub axle (worn hub bearings); for movement between the kingpin and the top and bottom links (worn kingpins and bushes); and for movement between the inner and outer ends of the wishbones and the fulcrum pins. (Worn pins and bushes).

4. If wear is evident in the kingpin bushes NOTE that the fitting of new bushes is a job for your local BLMC agent as it involves the use of special tools. In addition, after new bushes have been fitted to the top and bottom of the stub axle, they have to be line reamed. The kingpins should be checked for wear with a micrometer and replaced if worn.

5. Worn suspension rubbers can be renewed without too much difficulty. If the wishbone arm screwed bushes can be moved backwards or forwards on the fulcrum pin thread, then renew the bushes. If end play is then still evident it will be necessary to also renew the fulcrum pin.

6. If the front suspension has been accident damaged or is out of alignment, it should be checked by your local BLMC garage who will have the specialised alignment tools required.

15. **FRONT SUSPENSION - DISMANTLING & OVERHAUL**

1. Loosen the wheel nuts, jack up the car, and remove the road wheel.

2. Remove the brake drum and hub as described in section 13.

3. Remove the coil spring as described in section 8. Disconnect the anti-roll bar (where fitted) as described in section 6.

4. Remove the brake backplate and the steering lever.

5. Remove the Armstrong damper as described in section 11 and check the condition of the rubbers (28).

6. All numbers in brackets refer to Fig. 11.6. Pull out the split pin from the top of the kingpin (1) and undo the castellated nut (14). Lift off the suspension link trunnion (13) (note - it cannot be removed until the rubber bushes have been withdrawn from each side of the trunnion).

7. Remove the washers (11, 12) and then lift the stub axle (2) off the kingpin (1). Remove the cork ring (7) from the base of the kingpin.

8. Undo from the base of the two cotter pins (25), one on the outer end of each suspension arm (15, 16), the nut (26) and remove the two pins (25).

9. Unscrew the front and rear bushes (22, 23) from the fulcrum pin (17), and undo from the base of the cotter pin (19) in the centre of the bottom of the kingpin, the nut and spring washer (20, 21). Extract the cotter pin (19) upwards.

10. Slide out the fulcrum pin (17) and remove the two cork rings (18).

11. The stub axle and kingpin is now completely dismantled and must be carefully cleaned.

12. After cleaning the stub axle and kingpin examine them carefully for wear. Place the foot of the kingpin in a vice and fit the stub axle. The latter should turn easily on the kingpin without rocking. If play is present, then take the stub axle and kingpin to your local BMC garage for the old bushes to be pressed out and new bushes fitted and line reamered in position.

13. Examine the rubber bushes on the inner ends of the lower wishbone arms. If they are worn and slack, remove the split pin, castellated nut and washer from each end of the spindle, pull off the suspension arm and renew the rubbers.

FRONT SUSPENSION - REASSEMBLY

1. Fit the inner end of one of the suspension arms (15 or 16) onto its correct end on the spindle running through the crossmember and refit the washer and castellated nut loosely.

2. Slide the fulcrum pin (17) into its hole in the base of the kingpin (1) and align the flat on the fulcrum pin (17) with the cotter pin hole. Fit the cotter pin (19) and tighten the securing nut and washer (20, 21) down firmly.

3. Telescope together the two dust excluder

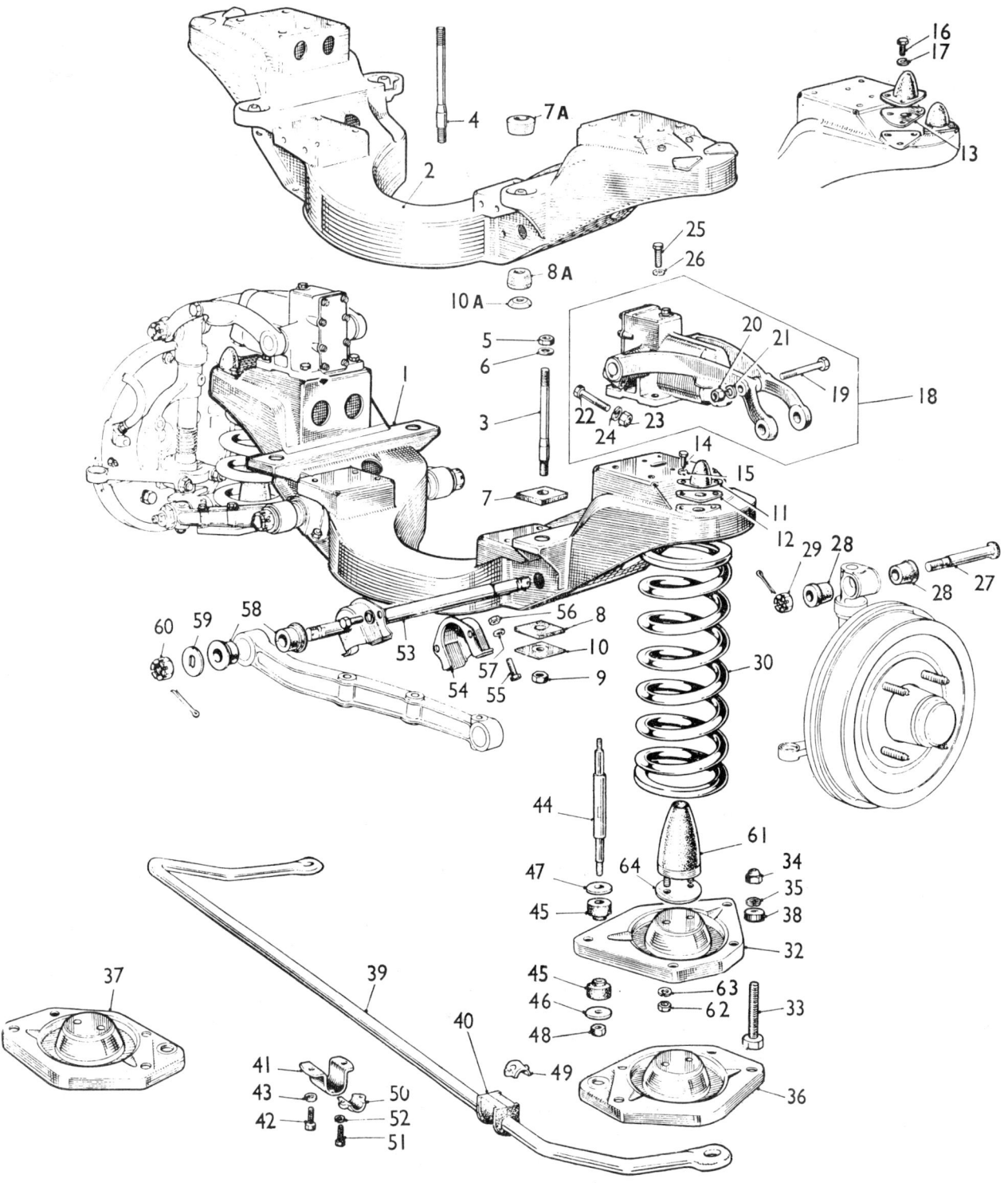

Fig. 11.7 EXPLODED VIEW OF THE FRONT SUSPENSION COMPONENTS

1 Early type crossmember. 2 Later type crossmember. 3 Early type crossmember to body underframe bolt (qty. 4). 4 Later type crossmember to body underframe bolt. 5 Nut. 6 Plain washer. 7 Rubber mounting (early type). 8 Rubber mounting (early type). 7A Rubber cup mounting (later type). 8A Rubber cup mounting (later type). 9 Nut. 10 Square special washer. 10A Special cup washer (later models). 11 Rebound buffer. 12 Spacer. 13 Packing piece. 14 Screw. 15 Spring washer. 16 Bolt. 17 Spring washer. 18 Armstrong damper unit—complete. 19 Bolt. 20 Nut. 21 Spring washer. 22 Clamp. 23 Nut. 24 Spring washer. 25 Damper mounting bolt. 26 Spring washer. 27 Fulcrum pin. 28 Top link bearings. 29 Castellated nut. 30 Coil spring. 31 Spring packing clip. 32 Spring seating. 33 Bolt. 34 Nut. 35 Spring washer. 36 Right-hand spring seating (later models). 37 Left-hand spring seating (later models). 38 Packing piece. 39 Anti-roll bar. 40 Anit-roll bar bearing. 41 Bearing strap. 42 Bolt. 43 Spring washer. 44 Link. 45 Bush. 46 Special washer. 47 Special washer. 48 Nut. 49 Upper locator. 50 Lower locator. 51 Screw. 52 Spring washer. 53 Lower link spindle. 54 Spindle bracket. 55 Screw. 56 Nut. 57 Spring washer. 58 Lower link bearing. 59 Washer. 60 Nut. 61 Buffer. 62 Nut. 63 Spring washer.

tubes and the spring (8, 9, 10) and fit them to the stub axle (2).

4. Slide the cork ring over the kingpin followed by the stub axle assembly.

5. Fit the thrust washer (11) between the floating thrust washers (12) on the top of the kingpin (1) and then fit the top trunnion (13). Replace and tighten the top castellated nut (14) and then measure the free lift of the stub axle on the kingpin which should not exceed .002 in. Different thickness floating thrust washers are available from your BMC stockist. Loosen the castellated nut (14) to make the remainder of the reassembly process easy.

6. Fit the cork rings (18) into the recess at each end of the trunnion hole in the base of the kingpin. The fulcrum pin (17) has already been fitted to the base of the kingpin, and the end of the former is now fitted to the hole in the outer end of the wishbone arm (15 or 16) already in position.

7. Fit the appropriate cotter pin (25) and bush (22 or 23) loosely to the end of the fulcrum pin (17) engaged in the hole suspension arm.

8. Refit the other suspension arm (15 or 16) to the spindle running through the crossmember and then fit the other cotter pin and bush loosely in position.

9. Replace the damper and refit the end of the damper arm to the top trunnion (13) using new rubber bushes.

10. Place a jack under the stub axle (2) and lift the suspension to its approximate working height.

11. Tighten the castellated nuts on the end of the spindle fully and replace the split pins. Temporarily refit the spring base plate and then screw the bushes (22, 23) in until a gap of .002 in. exists between the inside face of the hexagon head of each bush and the adjacent face of the suspension arm.

12. Remove the spring base plate and then refit the coil spring and base plate as described in section 8.

13. Refit the backplates, steering arm, hub, brake drum, and road wheel, and remove the supporting jacks to lower the front of the car to the ground. Then place a jack under the spring base plate, remove the road wheel, and lower the suspension the equivalent amount to simulate the correct height of the suspension unit when the wheel is fitted.

14. The top fulcrum pin retaining nut, and the trunnion nut can now be finally tightened and split pinned.

15. Grease the lubricating nipples generously.

170

17. FRONT SUSPENSION CROSSMEMBER - REMOVAL & REPLACEMENT

1. The front suspension units can be removed complete with the suspension crossmember. Loosen the front wheel nuts, jack up the front of the car, place supports under the side members (do not foul the crossmember securing nuts) and take off the wheels.

2. Support the engine by stands under the sump or hang it on an overhead sling.

3. Free the positive lead from the battery; separate the wires from the horn; empty the hydraulic fluid from the brake system by undoing one of the flexible hydraulic pipes from the brake backplate; and undo the remaining flexible hydraulic pipe from the opposite backplate.

4. Separate the drag link ball joints on the steering box arm, and the steering idler arm, by impact hammering after removing the split pin and castellated nuts.

5. Place a trolley jack under the centre of the suspension crossmember, undo the four engine bearer bolts on each side, and then the four chassis mounting nuts and bolts together with their spring washers and rubber packing pieces.

6. The crossmember can now be slightly lowered and removed from under the car.

7. Replacement is a straightforward reversal of the removal sequence. Renew the rubber mounting pads if worn or perished.

18. FRONT WHEEL ALIGNMENT

1. The front wheels are correctly aligned when they turn in at the front 1/16 in. to 1/8 in. Adjustment is effected by loosening the locknut on each end of the track rod, and turning the track rod until the adjustment is correct.

2. This is a job that your local BMC agent must do, as accurate alignment requires the use of expensive base bar or optical alignment equipment. On no account try to do this job yourself, using planks of wood or other makeshift implements.

3. If the wheels are not in alignment, tyre wear will be heavy and uneven, and the steering will be stiff and unresponsive.

19. STEERING WHEEL - REMOVAL & REPLACEMENT

1. Disconnect the battery leads and unscrew the three small grub screws from the steering wheel hub and prise off the horn button from the centre of the steering wheel.

2. On early 1489 c.c. models, undo the three bolts and spring washers which hold the steering wheel to the steering wheel hub. Lift off the steering wheel.

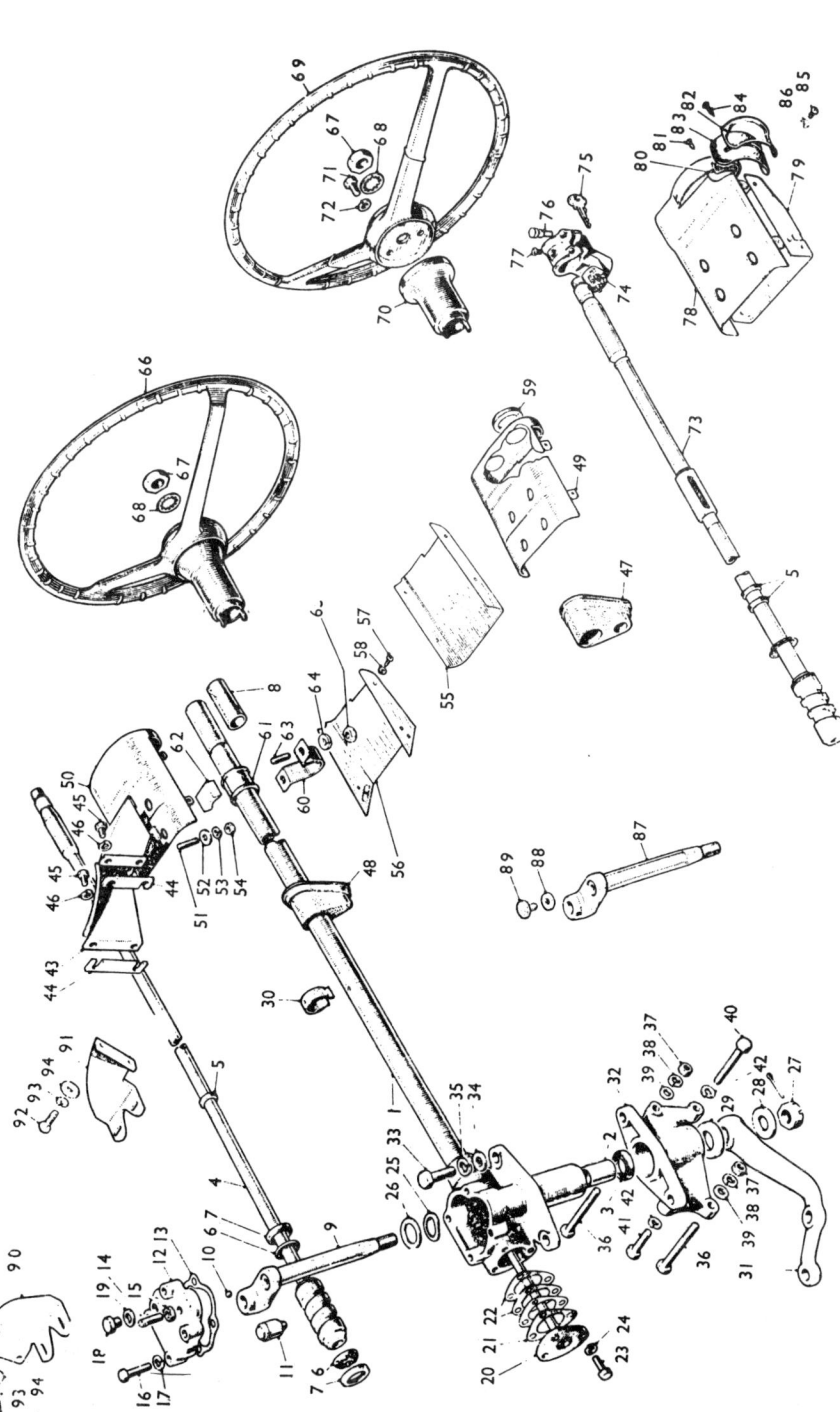

Fig. 11.8 EXPLODED VIEW OF THE STEERING GEAR, COLUMN AND WHEEL

1 Box and outer column. 2 Bush for rocker column. 2 Bush for rocker shaft. 3 Seal for rocker shaft. 4 Column with cam (inner). 5 Ring (rubber). 6 Cage assembly—ball. 7 Cup for ball cage. 8 B::h for side cover. 9 Shaft—rocker (with thrust disc). 10 Disc—thrust. 11 Roller assembly—cam. 12 Cover. 13 Joint for side cover. 14 Screw—thrust. 15 Nut for screw (lock). 16 Bolt for bolt (spring). 17 Washer for bolt (spring). 18 Plug—oil. 19 Washer for plug. 20 Cover—end (with stator tube). 21 Gasket. 22 Shim(s). 23 Bolt for end cover. 24 Wa:h change). 31 Lever—side. 32 Bracket—steering-box. 33 Bolt—steering-box to bracket. 34 Washer for bolt (plain). 35 Washer for bolt (spring). 36 Bolt—bracket to frame. 37 Nut for bolt. 38 Washer for bolt (spring). 39 Washer for bolt (plain). 40 Bolt—bracket to body. 41 Screw—bracket to body. 42 Washer for s:u.:::' (sprin:g) 43 Bracket support—steering-column. 44 Plate—distance (not Austin). 45 Screw—bracket. 46 Washer for screw (spring). 47 Grommet for steering-column (column gear change). 48 Grommet for steering-column (floor gear change). 49 Cover assembly—upper (column gear change). 50 Cover assembly—upper (floor gear change). 51 Stud—cover to bracket. 52 Washer for stud (plain). 53 Washer for stud (spring). 54 Nut for stud. 55 Cover assembly (lower)—Wolseley. 57 Screw—lower to upper cover. 59 Washer (spring). 59 Grommet—gear control lever. 60 Clip for steering-column. 61 Packing-piece. 62 Distance piece. 63 Stud—clip to column. 64 Washer for stud (spring). 65 Nut for stud. 66 Wheel—steering. 67 Nut for steering-wheel. 68 Washer for nut (shakeproof). 69 Wheel—steering. 70 Hub—steering-wheel. 71 Screw—wheel to hul.. 72 Washer for screw (spring). 73 Column (with cam)—inner. * 74 Lock assembly—steerin::. * 75 Key. * 76 Bolt—shear. * 77 Screw—location. * 78 Cover assembly—steeriu:. column—upper. ∤ 79 Cover assembly—steering-column—lower. ∤ 80 Distance piece—finisher. ∤ 81 Finisher. ∤ 82 Finisher. ∤ 83 Diaphragm—finish·:·· (rubber). ∤ 84 Screw—finisher to cover. ∤ 85 Screw—lower to upper cover. ∤ 86 Washer (spring). ∤ 87 Shaft—rocker. + 88 Disc—spring. + 89 Thrust pad. + 90 Support bracke... R.H.D. 91 Support bracket L.H.D. 92 Screw—bracket to valance. 93 Washer (spring). 94 Washer (plain).

* Ignition/steering lock. ∤ Automatic transmission. + Second type. Item Nos. 70 to 72 inclusive. Early-type steering-wheel only. Item Nos. 90 to 94 inclusive. Later models.

171

CHAPTER ELEVEN

3. On 1622 c.c. models, undo the nut in the centre of the hub with a socket spanner. Remove the nut and retaining washer under it and pull the wheel off the splines on the column.

4. Replacement is a simple reversal of this process. To ensure the wheel is correctly aligned on refitment it is helpful to mark the boss and a corresponding spline before pulling the wheel off.

20. STEERING GEAR - REMOVAL & REPLACEMENT

1. Remove the steering wheel as described in section 19. Also remove the hub after undoing the securing nut on 1489 c.c. models.

2. Underneath the steering box is the horn wire. Disconnect it at the snap connector.

3. Drain the cooling system and remove the radiator and windscreen washer bottle.

4. Undo and remove the four screws which hold the lower half of the steering column cowl in place and remove the cowl. Disconnect the Lucar connector from the direction indicator switch.

5. On models fitted with the steering column change undo the two nuts which hold the lower clamp bracket to the steering column and lift off the top half of the bracket.

6. Cut the locking wire from the square headed bolt at the bottom of the gear change shaft, loosen the bolt and free the gear change levers.

7. Loosen the lock screw in the top bracket and pull out the gear change lever and its column from inside the car.

8. Undo the four nuts which hold the upper half of the cowl in place and remove the cowl, packing plate, block and rubber strip. From off the steering column take the trafficator switch, wire clips, and the gear change shaft top bracket.

9. 1622 c.c. models make use of a steering support bracket which must now be separated from the valance.

10. The steering box is held in place by four bolts. Two are accessible from the top and two from below. Jack up the front of the car, free the ball joints from the steering box side lever by impact hammering and undo the four steering box bolts.

11. Remove the steering box and column from under the car.

12. Replacement is a straightforward reversal of the removal sequence but the following two points must be noted:

a) Ensure the steering column is correctly in place inside the car before tightening the steering box attachment bolts. In the case of later models this means that the support bracket

must be tightened firmly to the valance before tightening the steering box nuts.

b) Make certain that the direction indicator switch, the steering column cowl plate, and the steering wheel are so positioned that the self-cancelling direction indicators are in the correct position.

21. STEERING IDLER - REMOVAL & REPLACEMENT

1. Jack up and support the front of the car and disconnect the track rod, drag link, and side lever.

2. Undo the two nuts and bolts and the set bolt which holds the idler to the chassis and lift the idler off.

3. Replacement is a straightforward reversal of the removal sequence. Ensure the securing bolts are fully tightened.

22. STEERING GEAR - DISMANTLING & REASSEMBLY

1. To dismantle the steering gear, first remove the castellated nut and split pin and then pull off the side lever from its splines.

2. Empty the oil from the box by undoing the filler plug.

3. All numbers in brackets refer to Fig. 11.8. Undo the four bolts and soring washers (16,17) holding the cover (12) in place, and take off the cover (12) and then the rocker shaft (9).

4. Undo the three bolts and spring washers (23,24) which hold the end cover (20), gasket (21), and shims (22) in place and take off the latter.

5. Hold the assembly upright with the steering box at the top and tap the end of the inner column (4) with a soft drift to free the column. Pull out the inner column (4) and remove the ball bearings and cup assembly (6,7).

6. Remove the felt bush in the top of the column (8).

7. Examine all the component parts for wear and in particular the rocker shaft bush (2), the seal (3), the bearings (6), the grooves in the cam (4) and conical roller cam assembly (11).

8. Reassembly is a straightforward reversal of the dismantling procedure but the following points should be noted:

a) The purpose of the shims (22) under the end cover is to allow for adjustment to prevent end play in the inner column. Add or subtract shims as required but ensure the bearings (6) are not preloaded. Shims are available in three thicknesses; .0024 in. (.061 mm.), .005 in. (.127 mm.), and .010 in. (.254 mm.)

b) Always fit a new felt bush (8) to the top of the outer column (1) and dip it in Hypoid oil before fitment.

172

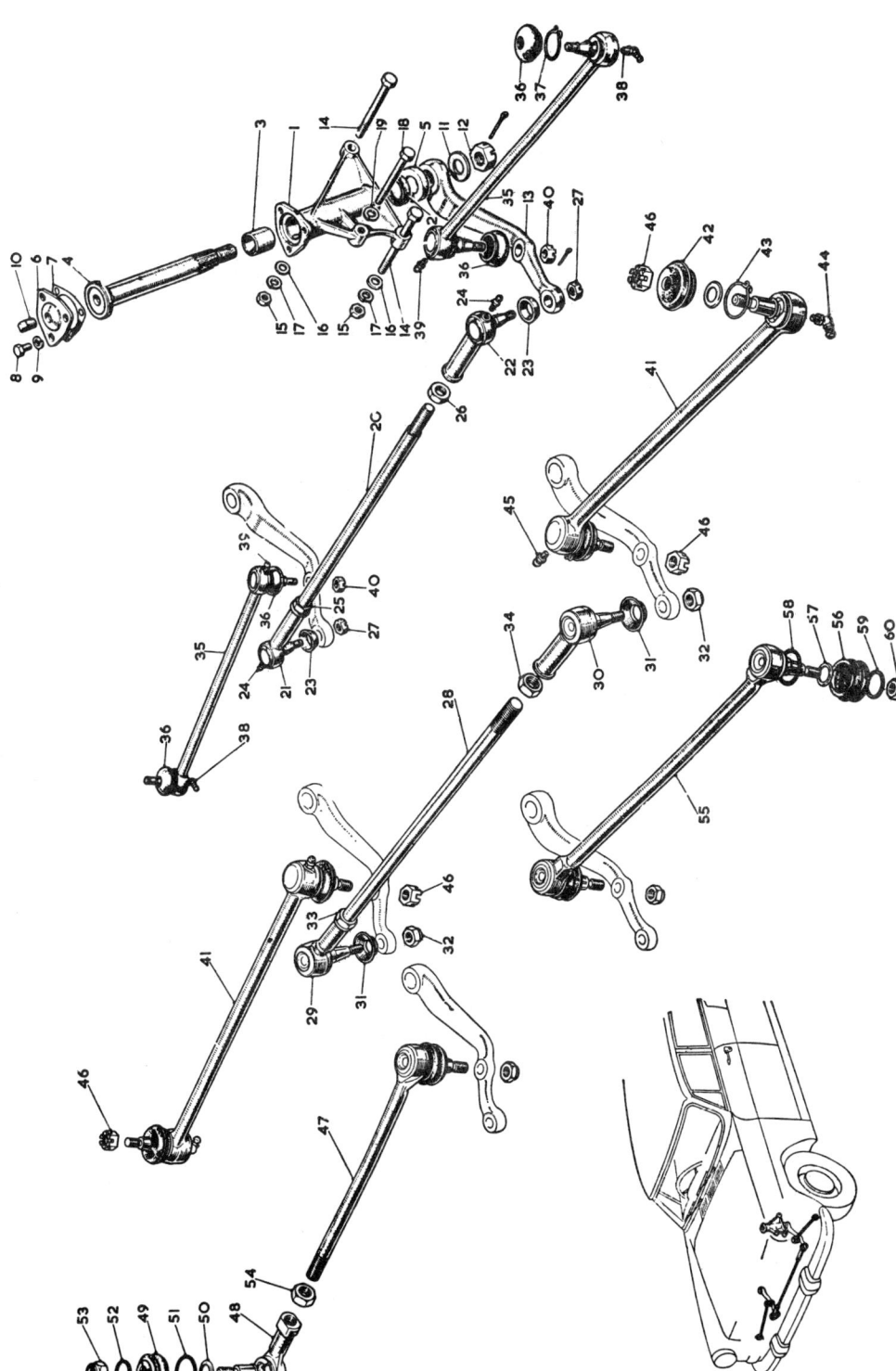

Fig. 11.9 EXPLODED VIEW OF THE TRACK ROD AND STEERING IDLER BOX

1 Body—idler. 2 Seal. 3 Bush. 4 Shaft—idler. 5 Seal—dust. 6 Cover—idler body. 7 Joint for cover. 8 Screw. 9 Washer. 10 Plug—oil filler. 11 Plain washer—shaft.*
12 Slotted nut—shaft * 1: Lever—side. 14 Bolt—idler to frame. 15 Nut for bolt. 16 Washer for bolt. 17 Washer for bolt (spring). 18 Bolt—idler to frame. 19 Washer.
20 Rod assembly. 21 End assembly (R.H.T.). 22 End assembly (L.H.T.). 23 Cover—ball joint. 24 Lubricator. 25 Cover—dust—ball joint. 26 Nut—lock (R.H.T.). 27 Nut for
ball pin. 28 Rod—cross. 29 End assembly (R.H.T.). 30 End assembly (L.H.T.). 31 Cover—ball joint. 32 Nut for ball pin. 33 Nut—lock (R.H.T.). 34 Nut—lock
(L.H.T.). 35 Rod assembly—side. 36 Cover—ball joint. 37 Retainer—dust cover. 38 Lubricator. 39 Lubricator. 40 Nut for ball pin. 41 Rod—assembly side. 42 Cover—
dust—ball joint. 43 Retainer—dust cover. 44 Lubricator (angular). 45 Lubricator (straight). 46 Nut for ball pin. 47 End assembly (male). 48 End assembly (female). 49 Cover
—dust—ball joint. 50 Retainer—dust cover. 51 Spring—garter. 52 Washer for dust cover. 53 Nut for ball pin. 54 Lockmut. 55 Rod assembly—side—steering idler. 56 Cover
—dust—ball joint. 57 Retainer—dust cover. 58 Spring—garter. 59 Washer for dust cover. 60 Nut for ball pin. From Car Nos. A-HS9-6507 A-HS6-70452 A-HW9-8461 M-HW6-8566.

*11 Tab washer. 12 Plain nut. (Replace with same type of washer and nut). A60, Oxford (Series VI) and 16/60.
N.B. Item Nos. 28 to 34 and 47 to 60 inclusive.

173

Fig. 11.10. THE ADJUSTING NUT (ARROWED) ON THE STEER-ING BOX

c) Undo the locknut (15), and unscrew the adjuster thrust screw (14) before refitting the cover (12).

d) Always use new gaskets to ensure oil tight joints are made.

e) Adjust the steering gear when it is refitted to the chassis as described in section 23. Remember to refill the steering box with Castrol Hypoy or similar.

23. STEERING GEAR - ADJUSTMENT

1. Provision is made for taking up the wear between the cam grooves and the connical roller cam peg, by means of an adjuster screw (14), which rests on a thrust pad (10) on the inner end of the rocker shaft (9). Tightening the adjuster forces the connical peg further into the cam grooves which have connical sides.

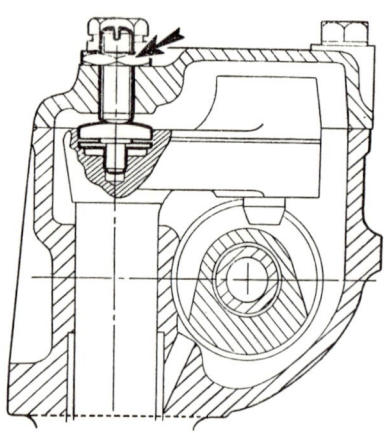

Fig. 11.11. Section view of the 2nd type of steering box with modified rocker shaft and spring loaded thrust pad

2. Wear in the cam grooves is naturally greatest when the steering is in the straight ahead position, rather than when it is on full lock. To prevent the steering becoming 'tight' when turned towards full lock slight end play is designed into the cam grooves when the steering wheel is turned hard right or hard left. It is therefore essential that the steering is adjusted when in the straight ahead position.

3. Jack up the front of the car and remove the roadwheels. Remove the steering wheel, adjust the inner column endfloat as described in Section 22.8(2) and then replace the steering wheel.

4. Release the locknut (15) and turn down the adjusting screw (14) until all play has been taken up in the straight ahead position and very slight resistance can be felt. Check the steering on full lock and if unduly tight slacken the adjuster screw a fraction.

5. When the correct adjustment has been made tighten down the locknut.

6. From cars numbered A-HS 10-176061, A-HW 10-176278, MHS6-167575, M-HW6-28649, W-HS3-58317, G-HS2-27144, R-HS3-20146 a spring-loaded thrust screw was fitted and adjustment slightly different.

7. Release the locknut (15) and turn down the adjusting screw (14) until the steering is locked solid. Then turn back the adjusting screw (14) a quarter of a turn. It is vital that the thrust screw is adjusted by turning in an anti-clockwise direction only. If the screw has been turned back too much then tighten down hard and re-adjust. Check that the loading is not excessive and retighten the locknut.

24. STEERING IDLER - DISMANTLING & RE-ASSEMBLY

1. With the idler out of the car (see section 21 for removal instructions) undo and remove the three top cover bolts and spring washers. Lift off the cover and gasket, and push the idler shaft out of the body. Only remove the oil seal if it is to be renewed.

2. Replacement is a straightforward reversal of the removal procedure but note the following points:

a) Take great care not to damage the oil seal when refitting the idler shaft.

b) Check that when fully assembled the idler shaft will turn freely without endfloat. If stiff, or if endfloat is present, add or subtract joint washers until the shaft fits correctly.

c) When refitted to the car remove the plug on top of the idler and fill up with Castrol Hypoy or similar.

25. BALL JOINTS - REMOVAL & REPLACEMENT

1. If any of the ball joints are worn it will be necessary to renew the whole joint assembly as they cannot be dismantled and repaired.

2. To remove a ball joint, slacken off the ball joint locknut (and where appropriate the ball joint locating locknut).

3. Do not loosen by more than three turns the nut on the ball joint shank. Hit the head of the nut with a soft-faced hammer to free the shank of the ball joint from its locating hole.

4. Remove the nut, pull the shank right out and where appropriate unscrew the complete ball assembly.

5. It is essential that no dirt gets into the ball joint. If the protecting rubber is damaged accidently while working on the suspension, it is satisfactory to renew just the rubber.

6. Later models make use of nylon seated ball joints which are sealed during manufacture. If it is ever necessary to renew the protecting rubber, cover the joint with Dextragrease Super G.P. before fitting the rubber in place.

CHAPTER TWELVE

BODYWORK AND UNDERFRAME

CONTENTS

1. GENERAL DESCRIPTION

The combined body and underframe is of all steel welded construction. This makes a very strong and torsionally rigid shell. Styled by Farina of Italy the most noticeable feature are the rear lights and flashing trafficators which are mounted on top of each other in the tail fins giving each side of the rear of the car a cathedral-like appearance when viewed from behind.

On standard models a heater and screen washer could be fitted as 'extras', but these items were included in the 'De Luxe' specification, as were twin horns.

Four doors are fitted with hinges at the front. Forward hinging quarter lights are fitted to the front doors and are held shut by catches. The windows in the doors wind down completely.

2. MAINTENANCE – BODYWORK & UNDER-FRAME

1. The condition of your car's bodywork is of considerable importance as it is on this that the secondhand value of the car will mainly depend. It is much more difficult to repair neglected bodywork than to renew mechanical assemblies. The hidden portions of the body, such as the wheel arches and the underframe and the engine compartment are equally important, though obviously not requiring such frequent attention as the immediately visible paintwork.

2. Once a year or every 12,000 miles, it is a sound scheme to visit your local main agent and have the underside of the body steam cleaned. This will take about $1\frac{1}{2}$ hours and cost about £4. All traces of dirt and oil will be removed and the underside can then be inspected carefully for rust, damaged hydraulic pipes, frayed electrical wiring and similar maladies. The car should be greased on completion of this job.

3. At the same time the engine compartment should be cleaned in the same manner. If steam cleaning facilities are not available then brush 'Gunk' or a similar cleanser over the whole engine and engine compartment with a stiff paint brush, working it well in where there is an accumulation of oil and dirt. Do not paint the ignition system and protect it with oily rags when the Gunk is washed off. As the Gunk is washed away it will take with it all traces of oil and dirt, leaving the engine looking clean and bright.

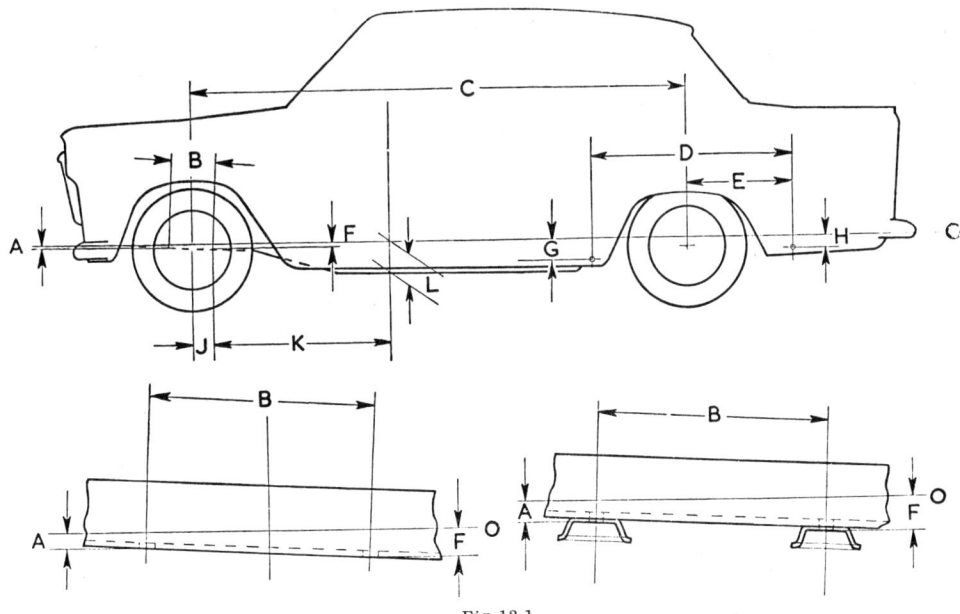

Fig. 12.1

Dimension	1489c.c. models		1622c.c. models		Location
O	—	—	—	—	Datum (body line)
A	$\frac{43}{64}$ in.	17·065 mm.	$\frac{47}{64}$ in.	18·65 mm.	Datum to front cross-member front mounting
B	$9\frac{1}{8}$ in.	232 mm.	$9\frac{7}{8}$ in.	251 mm.	Front cross-member, front to rear mountings
C	$99\frac{1}{4}$ in.	2521 mm.	$100\frac{1}{4}$ in.	2546 mm.	Wheelbase
D	$43\frac{5}{16}$ in.	1100 mm.	$43\frac{5}{16}$ in.	1100 mm.	Rear spring centres, eye to eye
E	$21\frac{5}{16}$ in.	541 mm.	$20\frac{5}{16}$ in.	516 mm.	Rear spring centre-bolt to rear spring rear shackle
F	$1\frac{5}{64}$ in.	27·38 mm.	$1\frac{11}{64}$ in.	29·76 mm.	Datum to front cross-member rear mounting
G	5 in.	127 mm.	5 in.	127 mm.	Datum to rear spring front shackle
H	$2\frac{1}{2}$ in.	63·5 mm.	$2\frac{1}{2}$ in.	63·5 mm.	Datum to rear spring rear shackle
J	$4\frac{19}{32}$ in.	116·68 mm.	$4\frac{31}{32}$ in.	126·2 mm.	Front suspension to front cross-member rear mounting
K	$27\frac{19}{32}$ in.	701 mm.	$27\frac{15}{64}$ in.	692 mm.	Front cross-member rear mounting to rear cross-member rear mounting
L	$5\frac{9}{16}$ in.	141·28 mm.	$5\frac{9}{16}$ in.	141·28 mm.	Datum to rear cross-member rear mounting hole

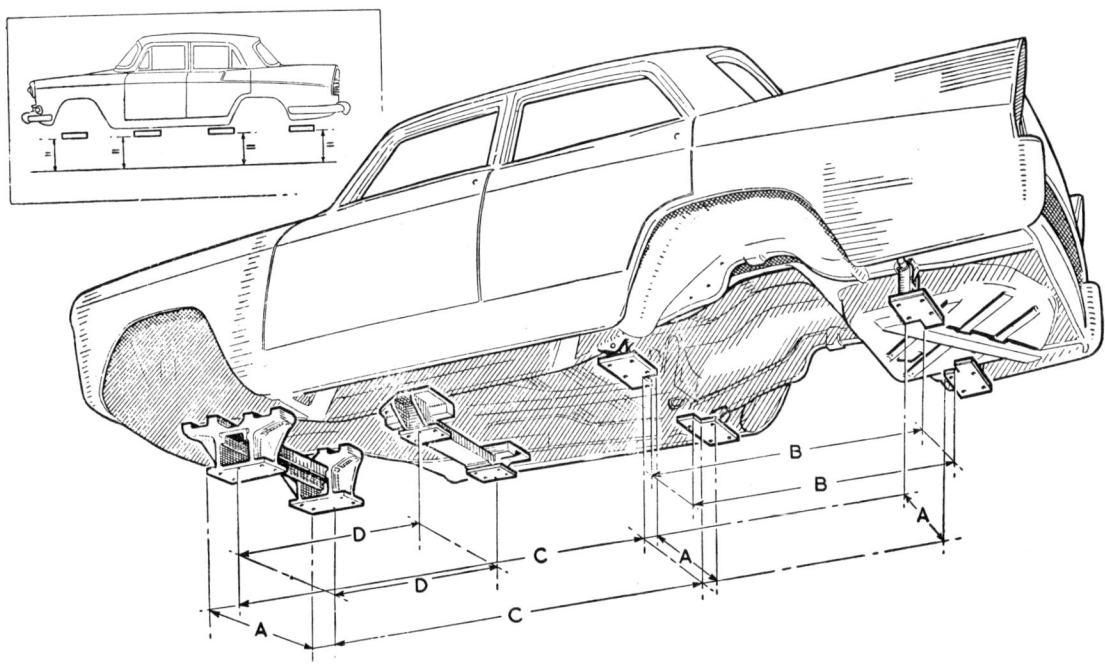

Fig. 12.2 The jig used by BMC garages for checking 1489 c.c. models

A. 26 in. (66·04 cm.).   C. 79 in. (200·66 cm.).
B. $43\frac{1}{4}$ to $43\frac{3}{8}$ in. (109·85 to 110·17 cm.).   D. $34\frac{1}{4}$ in. (86·48 cm.).

4. The wheel arches should be given particular attention as undersealing can easily come away here and stones and dirt thrown up from the road wheels can soon cause the paint to chip and flake, and so allow rust to set in. If rust is found, clean down to the bare metal with wet and dry paper, paint on an anti-corrosive coating such as Kurust, or if preferred, red lead, and renew the paintwork and undercoating.

5. The bodywork should be washed once a week or when dirty. Thoroughly wet the car to soften the dirt and then wash the car down with a soft sponge and plenty of clean water. If the surplus dirt is not washed off very gently, in time it will wear the paint down as surely as wet and dry paper. It is best to use a hose if this is available. Give the car a final washdown and then dry with a soft chamois leather to prevent the formation of spots.

6. Spots of tar and grease thrown up from the road can be removed with a rag dampened with petrol.

7. Once every six months, or every three months if wished, give the bodywork and chromium trim a thoroughly good wax polish. If a chromium cleaner is used to remove rust on any of the car's plated parts remember that the cleaner also removes part of the chromium so use sparingly.

3. MAINTENANCE - UPHOLSTERY & CARPETS
1. Remove the carpets and thoroughly vacuum clean the interior of the car every three months or more frequently if necessary.
2. Beat out the carpets and vacuum clean them if they are very dirty. If the headlining or upholstery is soiled apply an upholstery cleaner with a damp sponge and wipe off with a clean dry cloth.

4. MINOR BODY REPAIRS
1. At some time during your ownership of your car it is likely that it will be bumped or scraped in a mild way, causing some slight damage to the body.
2. Major damage must be repaired by your local BMC agent, but there is no reason why you cannot successfully beat out, repair, and respray minor damage yourself. The essential items which the owner should gather together to ensure a really professional job are:
a) A plastic filler such as Holts 'Cataloy'.
b) Paint whose colour matches exactly that of the bodywork, either in a can for application by a spray gun, or in an aerosol can.
c) Fine cutting paste.
d) Medium and fine grade wet and dry paper.

3. Never use a metal hammer to knock out small dents as the blows tend to scratch and distort the metal. Knock out the dent with a mallet or rawhide hammer and press on the underside of the dented surface a metal dolly or smooth wooden block roughly contoured to the normal shape of the damaged area.
4. After the worst of the damaged area has been knocked out, rub down the dent and surrounding area with medium wet and dry paper and thoroughly clean away all traces of dirt.
5. The plastic filler comprises a paste and a hardener which must be thoroughly mixed together. Mix only a small portion at a time as the paste sets hard within five to fifteen minutes depending on the amount of hardener used.
6. Smooth on the filler with a knife or stiff plastic to the shape of the damaged portion and allow to thoroughly dry - a process which takes about six hours. After the filler has dried it is likely that it will have contracted slightly so spread on a second layer of filler if necessary.
7. Smooth down the filler with fine wet and dry paper wrapped round a suitable block of wood and continue until the whole area is perfectly smooth and it is impossible to feel where the filler joins the rest of the paintwork.
8. Spray on from an aerosol can, or with a spray gun, an anti-rust undercoat, smooth down with wet and dry paper, and then spray on two coats of the final finishing using a circular motion.
9. When thoroughly dry polish the whole area with a fine cutting paste to smooth the resprayed area into the remainder of the wing and to remove the small particles of spray paint which will have settled round the area.
10. This will leave the wing looking perfect with not a trace of the previous unsightly dent.

5. MAJOR BODY REPAIRS
1. Because the body is built on the monocoque principle and is integral with the underframe, major damage must be repaired by competent mechanics with the necessary welding and hydraulic straightening equipment.
2. If the damage is serious it is vital that the bodyshell is in correct alignment, as otherwise the handling of the car will suffer and many other faults such as excessive tyre wear, and wear in the transmission and steering, may occur. The BMC produce a special alignment jig and to ensure that all is correct a repaired car should be checked on this jig.
3. Alternatively, with the bodyshell jacked up off a level floor a series of measurement checks can be carried out to determine whether mis-

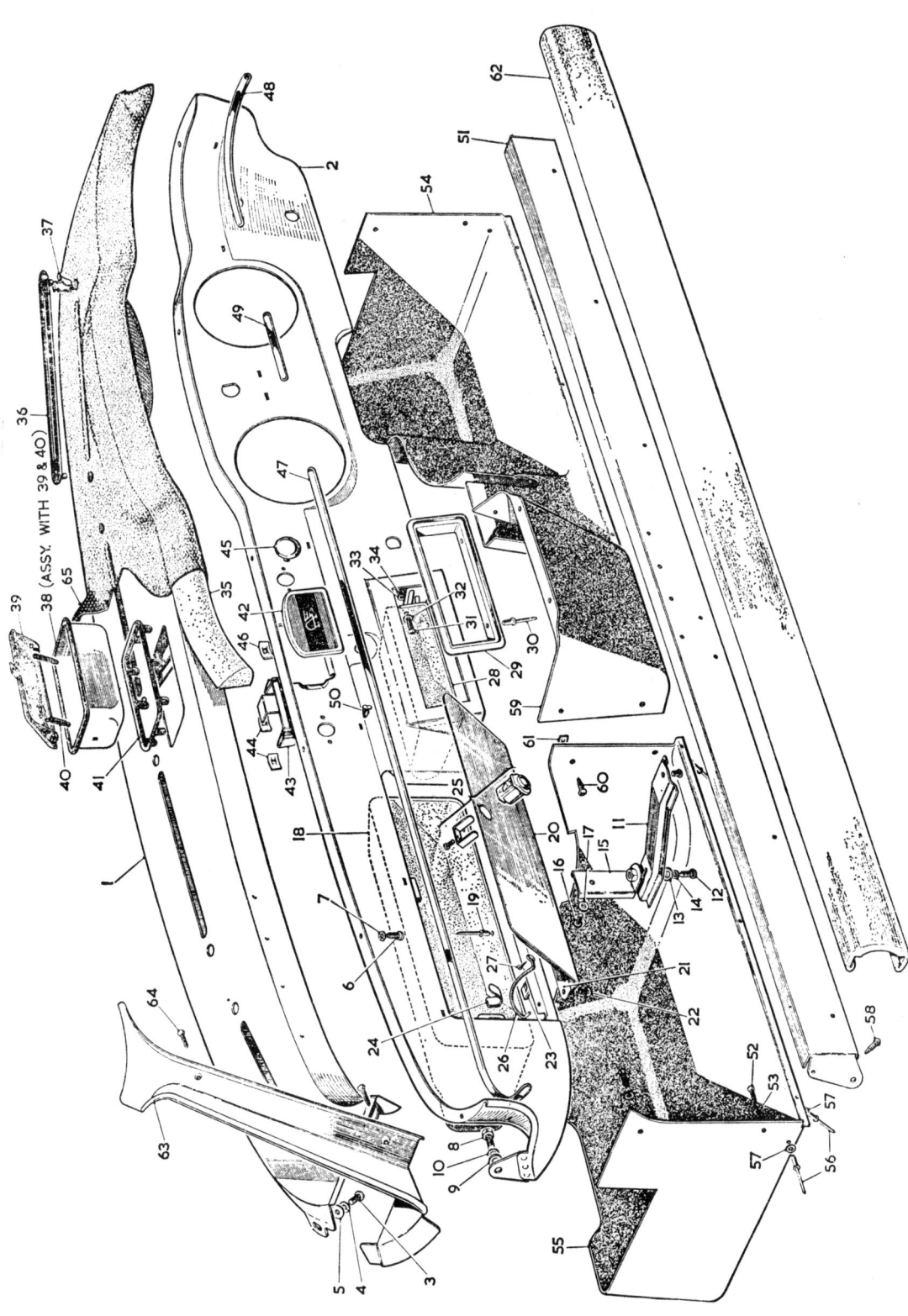

Fig. 12.3 EXPLODED VIEW OF THE AUSTIN A.55 MK.II FASCIA PANEL

1 Panel assembly—upper. 2 Panel assembly—lower. 3 Screw—panel to body. 4 Washer. 5 Washer. 6 Screw—lower to upper fascia. 7 Washer. 8 Screw—fascia to dash side. 9 Washer. 10 Washer. 11 Stiffener. 12 Screw—stiffener to bracket. 13 Washer. 14 Washer. 15 Bracket. 16 Screw—bracket. 17 Washer. 18 Glovebox. 19 Rivet. 20 Lid—glovebox. 21 Hinge—lid. 22 Screw. 23 Nut for screw. 24 Spring—glovebox lid. 25 Catch—glovebox lid. 26 Stay—glovebox lid. 27 Screw. 28 Box—oddment. 29 Bezel—oddment box. 30 Rivet. 31 Screw. 32 Washer. 33 Washer. 34 Nut. 35 Pad. 36 Escutcheon—demister. 37 Clip—escutcheon. 38 Ashtray. 39 Lid—ashtray. 40 Spring. 41 Bezel—ashtray. 42 Mask—clock aperture. 43 Retainer—mask. 44 Retainer—push-on fix. 45 Mask—demist control aperture. 46 Push-on fix for mask. 47 Beading—fascia. 48 Beading—fascia. 49 Beading—fascia. 50 Clip—beading. 51 Support—parcel tray. 52 Screw—support to dash. 53 Washer. 54 Tray—parcel—R. H. 55 Tray—parcel—L. H. 56 Rivet. 57 Washer. 58 Screw—parcel tray to dash. 59 Tray—parcel—centre. 60 Screw—parcel tray to fascia. 61 Nut. 62 Strip—protection. 63 Finisher—'A' post—L. H. 64 Screw. 65 Cover assembly—fascia top.

179

alignment is present or not. Start by dropping a plumb line from the centre of each of the front suspension crossmember holes to the floor and mark the spot. Repeat this from the rear spring shackle mounting points. Carefully determine the centre line by scribing two arcs on the floor between AA and DD as shown in Fig. 12.2. Further horizontal and vertical alignment checks can be made by referring to Figs. 12.1 and 12.2.

6. MAINTENANCE - HINGES & LOCKS

Once every six months or 6,000 miles the door, bonnet, and boot hinges should be oiled with a few drops of engine oil from an oil can. The door striker plates can be given a thin smear of grease to reduce wear and ensure free movement.

7. FRONT BUMPER - REMOVAL & REPLACEMENT

1. Undo the set bolts and spring washers together with the rubber packing pieces (one each side) which hold the ends of the bumper to the body. NOTE. Access to the various nuts and bolts is gained from under the bumper.
2. Undo and remove the nuts from the studs attached to the bumper and pull the bumper away from the two brackets mounted to the body.
3. If it is wished to remove the bumper brackets these can be pulled off after undoing the set bolts and spring washers.
4. To remove the over-riders (where fitted) undo and remove the nut and washer which secures each over-rider to the bumper bar.
5. Replacement is a straightforward reversal of the removal sequence.

8. REAR BUMPER - REMOVAL & REPLACEMENT

1. The method of removing the rear bumper is exactly the same as for the front bumper with one addition.
2. Before lifting the bumper off, disconnect the positive lead from the battery, and remove the number plate light from the bumper together with the lead. It is a good idea to place the light in the boot where it will not be prone to damage.

9. WINDSCREEN GLASS - REMOVAL & REPLACEMENT

1. If you are unfortunate enough to have a windscreen shatter fitting a replacement windscreen is one of the few jobs which the average owner is advised to leave to a professional mechanic. For the owner who wishes to do the job himself the following instructions are given:

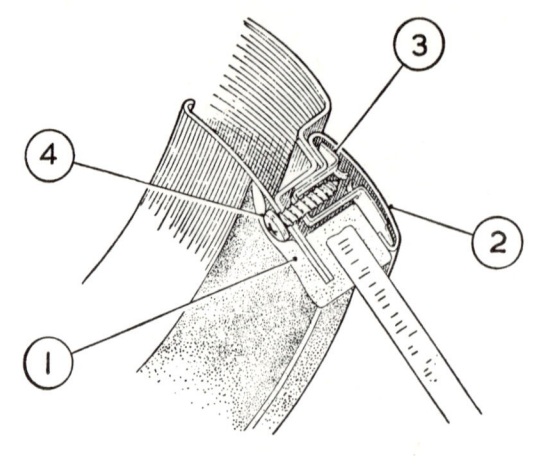

Fig. 12.4. SECTION VIEW OF 1489 c.c. WINDSCREEN SURROUNDS
1 Rubber channel. 2 Finisher. 3 Clip. 4 Phillips headed screw

2. Remove the cappings from the windscreen pillars after undoing the three screws which hold each capping in place. Remove the demister vent rail from the fascia top after undoing the five retaining screws. Undo the fascia top rear fixing screws and the six screws along the underneath of the front crash pad and remove the fascia top.
3. Lift back the inner flange of the rubber windscreen surround and undo the eighteen screws which hold the outer finishers in place. NOTE that these screws are not fitted to later 1622 c.c. models.
4. On early models slide the centre cappings sideways and remove the finishers. On later models this operation can be carried out when the windscreen has been removed.

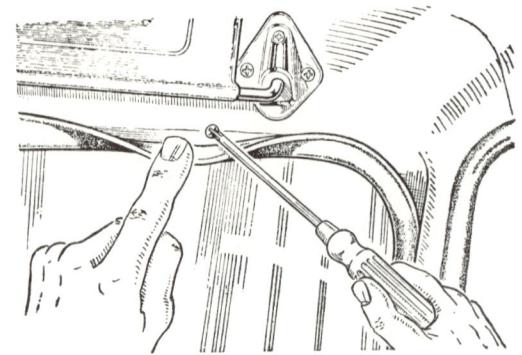

Fig. 12.5. Pull back the rubber lip of the channel to gain access to the Phillips headed screw

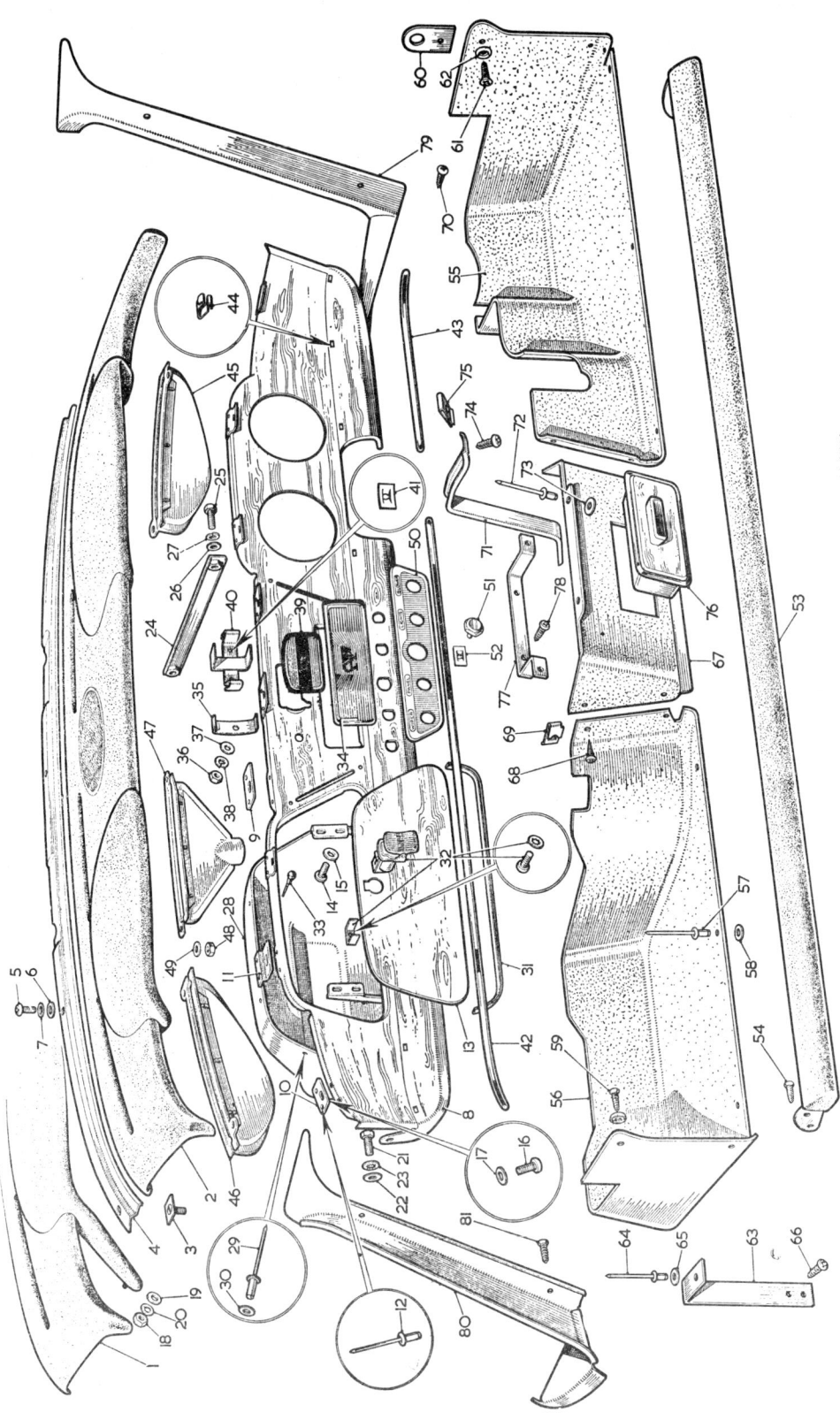

Fig. 12. 6. EXPLODED VIEW OF THE AUSTIN A. 60 FASCIA PANEL

1 Fascia panel—upper.* 2 Fascia panel—upper. 3 Stud plate. 4 Fascia support—upper. 5 Screw. 6 Plain washer. 7 Shakeproof washer. 8 Fascia panel—lower—R. H. D. 9 Bracket—fascia lower to fascia upper—outer. 11 Bracket—fascia lower to nacelles. 12 Rivet—bracket to fascia lower. 13 Glovebox lid. 14 Screw—glovebox lid hinge. 15 Plain washer. 16 Screw—fascia lower to fascia upper. 17 Plain washer. 18 Nut—nacelle extension to fascia lower.* 19 Plain washer.* 20 Shakeproof washer.* 21 Screw—fascia lower to body. 22 Plain washer. 23 Shakeproof washer. 24 Strap—fascia lower to dash. 25 Screw—strap to fascia and dash. 26 Plain washer. 27 Spring washer. 28 Glovebox. 29 Rivet—glovebox to fascia. 30 Plain washer. 31 Covering—glovebox flange. 32 Lock and pull assembly—glovebox lid. 33 Buffer—glovebox lid. 34 Radio aperture mask. 35 Retainer—mask. 36 Nut—mask to fascia. 37 Plain washer. 38 Spring washer. 39 Clock aperture mask. 40 Retainer —mask. 41 Push-on fix—retainer. 42 Fascia beading—long. 43 Fascia beading—short. 44 Clip—beading to fascia. 45 Demister duct—outer—R. H. 46 Demister duct— outer—L. H. 47 Demister duct—inner. 48 Nut—demister ducts to fascia upper. 49 Plain washer. 50 Bezel switches. 51 Plug—heater switch hole. 52 Push-on fix. 53 Support assembly—parcel tray. 54 Screw—support to dash side. 55 Parcel tray—R. H. 56 Parcel tray—L. H. 57 Rivet—tray to support. 58 Plain washer. 59 Screw—parcel tray to support. 60 Support plate—parcel tray—R. H. 61 Screw—support plate. 62 Cup washer. 63 Support bracket—parcel tray L. H. 64 Rivet—bracket to parcel tray. 65 Plain dash side. 66 Screw—bracket to dash. 67 Parcel tray—centre. 68 Screw—parcel tray to fascia. 69 Spire nut. 70 Screw—parcel tray to dash. 71 Stiffener—centre parcel tray. washer. 73 Plain washer. 74 Screw—stiffener to fascia. 75 Spire nut. 76 Ashtray—1st type. 77 Retainer—ashtray. 78 Screw—ashtray to retainer. 72 Rivet—stiffener to parcel tray. 79 Finisher—'A' post—R. H. 80 Finisher—'A' post—L. H. 81 Screw—finisher to 'A' post. Item Nos. 60 to 62 inclusive. R. H. D. Item Nos. 63 to 66 inclusive. L. H. D.

*Up to A/HS9 19529 (R. H. D.), A/HS9 24029 (L. H. D.), A/HW9 11181.

181

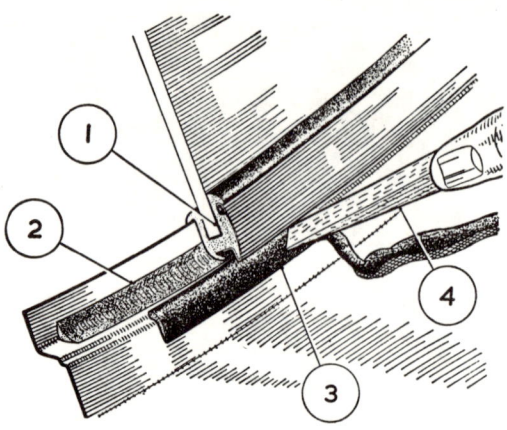

Fig. 12.7. To avoid leaks seal the windscreen as shown. 1 Seelastik
2 Caulking compound. 3 Seel-a-strip. 4 Wooden wedge

5.   The windscreen is removed on both early and later models complete with the rubber moulding.   Carefully slide a screwdriver or similar in under the inside lip of the rubber and pressing the glass out from inside the car, ease the rubber lip over the windscreen aperture flange.   It is easiest to start in a corner and work progressively round the windscreen.

6.   The windscreen is replaced after having smeared seelastik sealing compound on the outside edge of the glass where it is covered by the rubber surround.

7.   Before fitting the windscreen apply Glastikon Caulking compound all round the outside

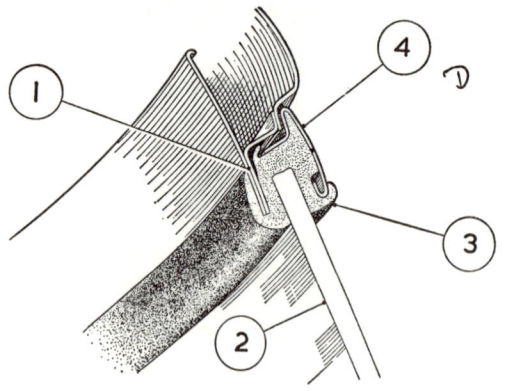

Fig. 12.8. SECTION VIEW OF THE 1622 c.c. WINDSCREEN &
SURROUNDS. 1 Body flange. 2 Glass. 3 Rubber moulding
4 Finisher

of the windscreen aperture flange, and $\frac{1}{2}$ in. Seel-a-strip $\frac{1}{16}$ in. thick all round the outside corner of the aperture flange.

8.   With the rubber surround and finisher fitted to the windscreen insert 16 ft. of cord all round the channel in the rubber which will sit over the windscreen aperture flange.   Allow the two free ends of the cord to overlap slightly.

9.   Fit the windscreen from outside the car and with an assistant pressing the rubber surround hard against the body flange, slowly pull one end of the cord out moving round the windscreen and so drawing the lip of the rubber over the windscreen flange on the body.

10.   The refitting of screws, cappings, etc. is now a straightforward reversal of the removal sequence.

10. DOOR RATTLES - TRACING & RECTIFICATION

1.   The commonest cause of door rattle is a misaligned, loose, or worn striker plate but other causes may be:

a) Loose door handles, window winder handles or door hinges.

b) Loose, worn or misaligned door lock components.

c) Loose or worn remote control mechanism.

2.   It is quite possible for door rattles to be the result of a combination of the above faults so a careful examination must be made to determine the causes of the fault.

3.   If the nose of the striker plate is worn and as a result the door rattles, renew and then adjust the plate as described in Section 11.

4.   Should the inner door handle rattle this is easily cured by fitting a rubber washer between the escutcheon and the handle.

5.   If the nose of the door lock wedge is badly worn and the door rattles as a result, then fit a new lock as described in section 12.

6.   Should the hinges be badly worn, then they must be replaced.

11. STRIKER PLATE - REMOVAL, REPLACEMENT & ADJUSTMENT

1.   If it is wished to renew a worn striker plate mark its position on the door pillar so a new plate can be fitted in the same position.

2.   To remove the plate simply undo the three Phillips screws which hold the plate in position. Replacement is equally straightforward.

3.   To adjust the striker plate close the door and then push it hard against its sealing rubber. The door edge furthest from the hinges should move in $\frac{3}{32}$ in.

4.   Loosen the door striker plate screws and

adjust the plate until the clearance is correct. Tighten the screws and check that the door closes properly without lifting or dropping, and that on the road it does not rattle.

12. DOOR LOCKS - REMOVAL & REPLACEMENT

1. Take off the door trim as described in section 13.

2. Refering to Fig. 12.9 pull off the circlip and washer which hold the remote control lever connecting link to a dowel on the lock lever (I).

3. Undo the three screws holding the remote control in place and remove the unit complete.

4. Undo the three screws which secure the lock unit to the door panel and remove the lock unit. Under normal circumstances it is not necessary to loosen the nut (L) or the Phillips screw (M) which hold the handle in position.

5. Thoroughly grease the moving components of a new lock and fit the unit in place ensuring that the pushbutton moves freely in the outside door handle. If necessary slacken the nut (L) and screw (M).

6. Tighten the three screws which hold the lock unit in place not omitting the washers.

7. The remote control unit can now be refitted and it is most important that it is fitted in the locked position. When new remote control units are supplied for the front doors they carry a small peg holding the unit in the locked position.

8. Place the end of the connecting link over the stud on the lock lever and lock it in position with the washer and circlip.

9. To align the assembly correctly slide the remote control (which makes use of elongated holes for this purpose) towards the lock unit until the lock lever (1) abuts the lock case as shown in Fig. 12.12. The three screws securing the remote control can now be tightened down fully.

10. Check the assembly for correct functioning and replace the trim.

13. DOOR TRIM PANELS - REMOVAL & RE-PLACEMENT

1. Remove the front door pull by undoing the two securing screws.

2. Remove the ashtray by pressing down the spring 'A' in Fig. 12.11 and then undo the two Phillips screws holding the ashtray holder in place.

3. To remove the door handle push in the escutcheon 'C' in Fig. 12.10 to expose the peg 'D' which is simply pushed out of the handle shank. Pull off the handle. Repeat this process with the window winder handle noting that two escutcheons are fitted with a light spring between

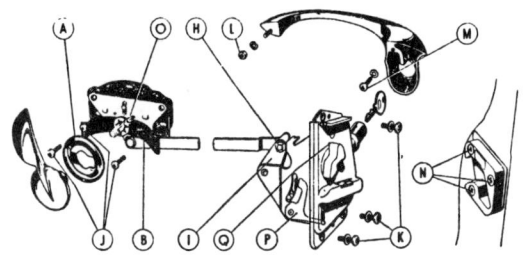

Fig. 12.9. COMPONENT PARTS OF THE DOOR HANDLE & LOCK referred to in the text

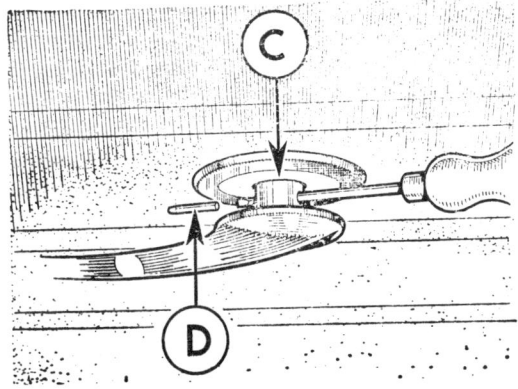

Fig. 12.10. PUSHING OUT THE INTERIOR DOOR HANDLE RE-TAINING PIN. C Door handle shank. D Pin.

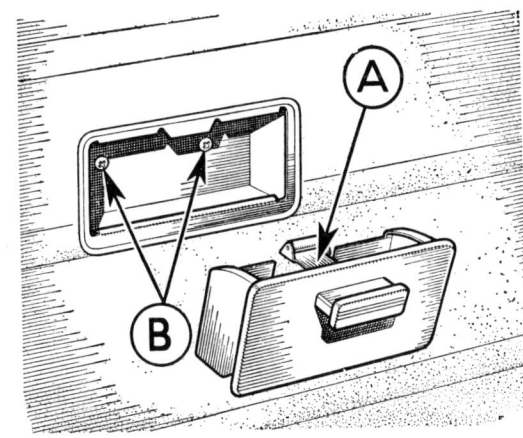

Fig. 12.11. TO REMOVE THE ASHTRAY depress the spring 'A'. Undo the screws 'B' to remove the ashtray surround

them. Push in the outer plastic one to expose the head of the pin.

4. As the trim panel is held in position by spring clips, with the aid of a broad screwdriver carefully prise away the panel from the door starting at the bottom edge and moving up each

183

side until the door capping is reached. Bump the top of the door capping carefully, all the while pulling up on the trim panel to release the clips holding the capping, which on its reverse side is fixed to the trim panel.

5. Take great care not to bend the trims as they are renewed. Replacement is a straightforward reversal of the removal sequence.

14. EXTERIOR DOOR HANDLES - REMOVAL & REPLACEMENT

1. To remove an outside door handle, first remove the door trim as described in section 13.
2. Then remove the door lock unit as described in section 12.
3. Referring to Fig. 12.9, undo the Phillips headed screw (M) and the nut and spring washer (L) from inside the door frame and pull away the handle from the outside of the door.
4. Replacement is a straightforward reversal of the removal sequence.

15. FRONT WINDOW WINDER MECHANISM - REMOVAL & REPLACEMENT

1. To remove the window winder mechanism first remove the front door trim as described in section 13.
2. Undo and remove the four set screws from the spindle plate and the four set screws which hold the window mechanism to the door shell.
3. Undo and remove the half bolt from the bottom of the window channel. Remove the mechanism through the cut-outs in the lower portion of the inside door panel.
4. Replacement is a straightforward reversal of the removal instructions.

16. REAR WINDOW WINDER MECHANISM - REMOVAL & REPLACEMENT

1. Remove the rear door trim as described in section 13.
2. Undo and remove the four set screws which hold the winder mechanism to the door shell. Slide the winder arm or regulator from its channel at the bottom of the window.
3. Remove the mechanism through the cut-outs in the lower portion of the inside door panel.
4. Replacement is a straightforward reversal of the removal sequence.

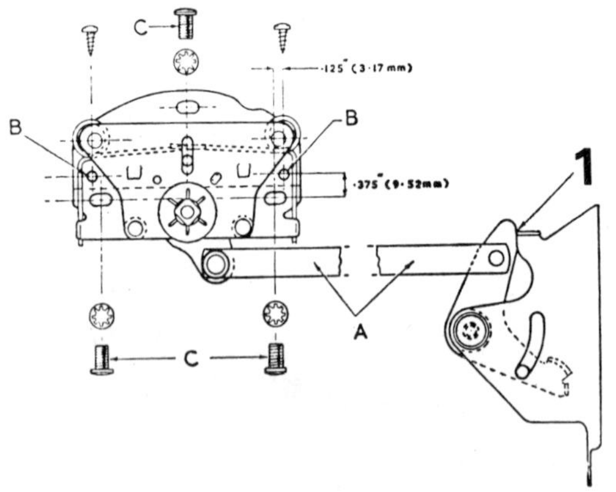

Fig. 12.12 The door lock remote control

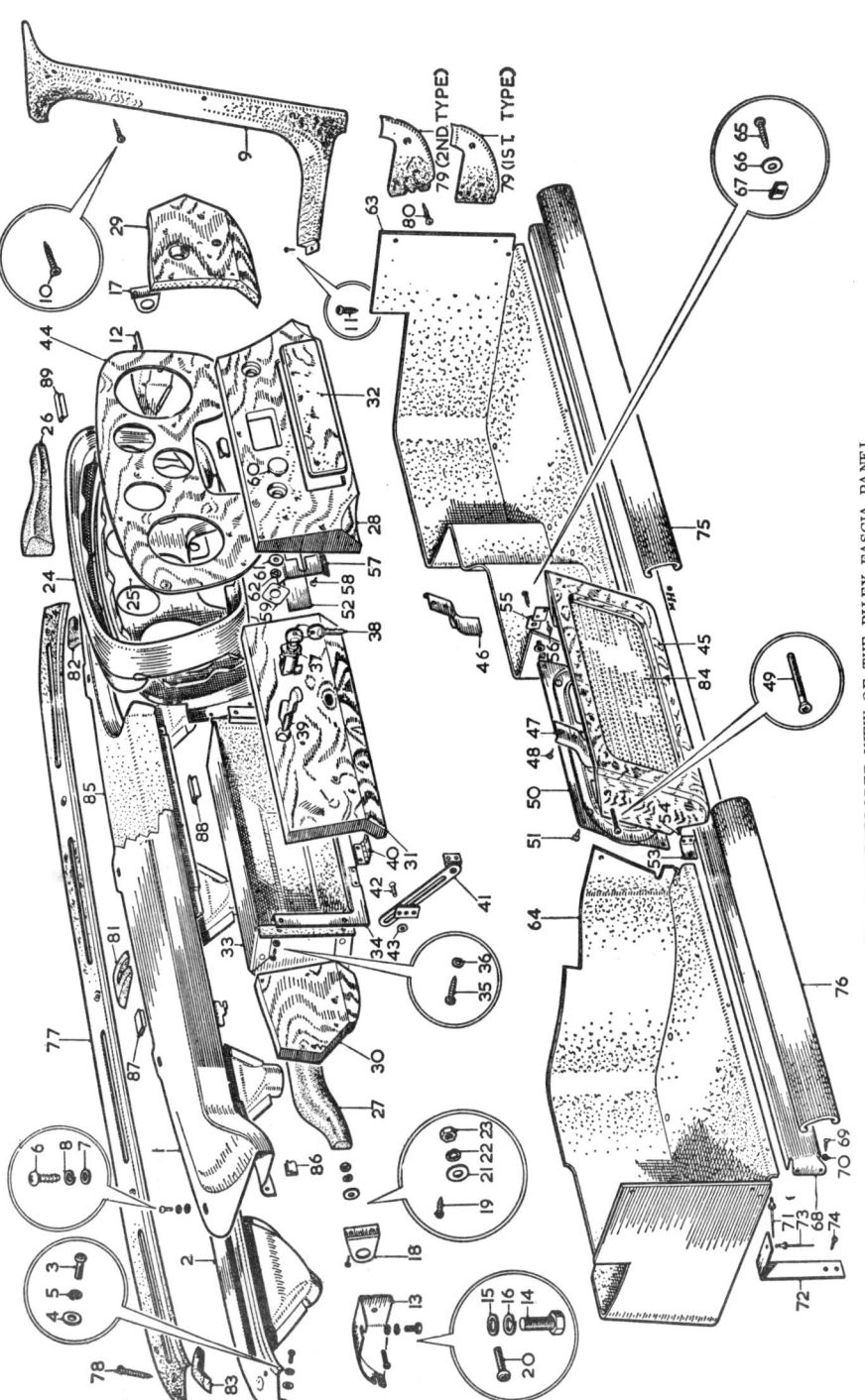

Fig. 12.13 EXPLODED VIEW OF THE RILEY FASCIA PANEL

1 Panel assembly—fascia top. 2 Support assembly—rail—fascia top. 3 Screw—support to body. 4 Washer for screw (plain). 5 Washer for screw (spring). 6 Screw—fascia top panel to support. 7 Washer for screw (plain). 8 Washer for screw (spring). 9 Finisher assembly—'A' post—R. H. 10 Screw—finisher to body. 11 Screw—finisher to body. 12 Bracket—fascia support—outer—R. H. 13 Bracket—fascia support—outer—L. H. 14 Screw—bracket to body. 15 Washer for screw (plain). 16 Washer for screw (spring). 17 Bracket—fascia to support—R. H. 18 Bracket—fascia to support—L. H. 19 Screw—bracket to fascia. 20 Screw—bracket to bracket. 21 Washer for screw (plain). 22 Washer for screw (spring). 23 Nut for screw. 24 Panel assembly—instrument cowl. 25 Panel assembly—instrument. 26 Rail protection—R. H. 27 Rail protection—L. H. 28 Board—centre. 29 Board—outer—R. H. 30 Board—outer—L. H. 31 Lid—glovebox. 32 Filler piece—radio aperture. 33 Glovebox. 34 Surround—glovebox. 35 Screw—glovebox to fascia. 36 Washer for screw (plain). 37 Catch—glovebox lid. 38 Key. 39 Finger pull—glovebox lid catch. 40 Hinge—glovebox lid. 41 Support—glovebox lid. 42 Rivet—support to fascia and lid. 43 Washer for rivet (plain). 44 Panel—instrument (front). 45 Surround—radio speaker. 46 Bracket—speaker surround—R. H. 47 Bracket—speaker surround —L. H. 48 Screw—bracket to fascia. 49 Screw—surround to bracket. 50 Plate—mounting plate to fascia. 51 Screw—mounting plate to fascia. 52 Plate—radio aperture mounting piece. 53 Bracket—lower—speaker surround. 54 Screw—bracket to surround. 55 Bracket—speaker to parcel tray. 56 Screw for bracket. 57 Plate—radio mounting —front. 58 Screw—plate to fascia. 59 Plate—locating—demister knob. 60 Plug—heater switch hole. 61 Washer for plug (plain). 62 Push-on fix for plug. 63 Tray—parcel —R. H. 64 Tray—parcel—L. H. 65 Screw—parcel tray to speaker. 66 Washer for screw (plain). 67 Nut for screw (spire). 68 Support—channel—parcel tray. 69 Screw— support to dash side. 70 Washer for screw (cup). 71 Rivet—parcel tray to support. 72 Bracket—support—parcel tray. 73 Rivet—bracket to parcel tray. 74 Screw—bracket to dash. 75 Strip—protection—parcel shelf—R. H. 76 Strip—protection—parcel shelf—L. H. 77 Finisher—parcel shelf. 78 Screw—finisher to fascia. 79 Finisher—fascia lower—R. H. 80 Screw—finisher to body. 81 Block—support—centre. 82 Block—support—side—R. H. 83 Block—support—side—L. H. 84 Material—speaker fret. 85 Vyweld material (black). 86 Clip—trim—fascia top—rear. 87 Clip—trim—fascia top. 88 Clip—trim—instrument cowl. 89 Clip—trim—instrument cowl.

185

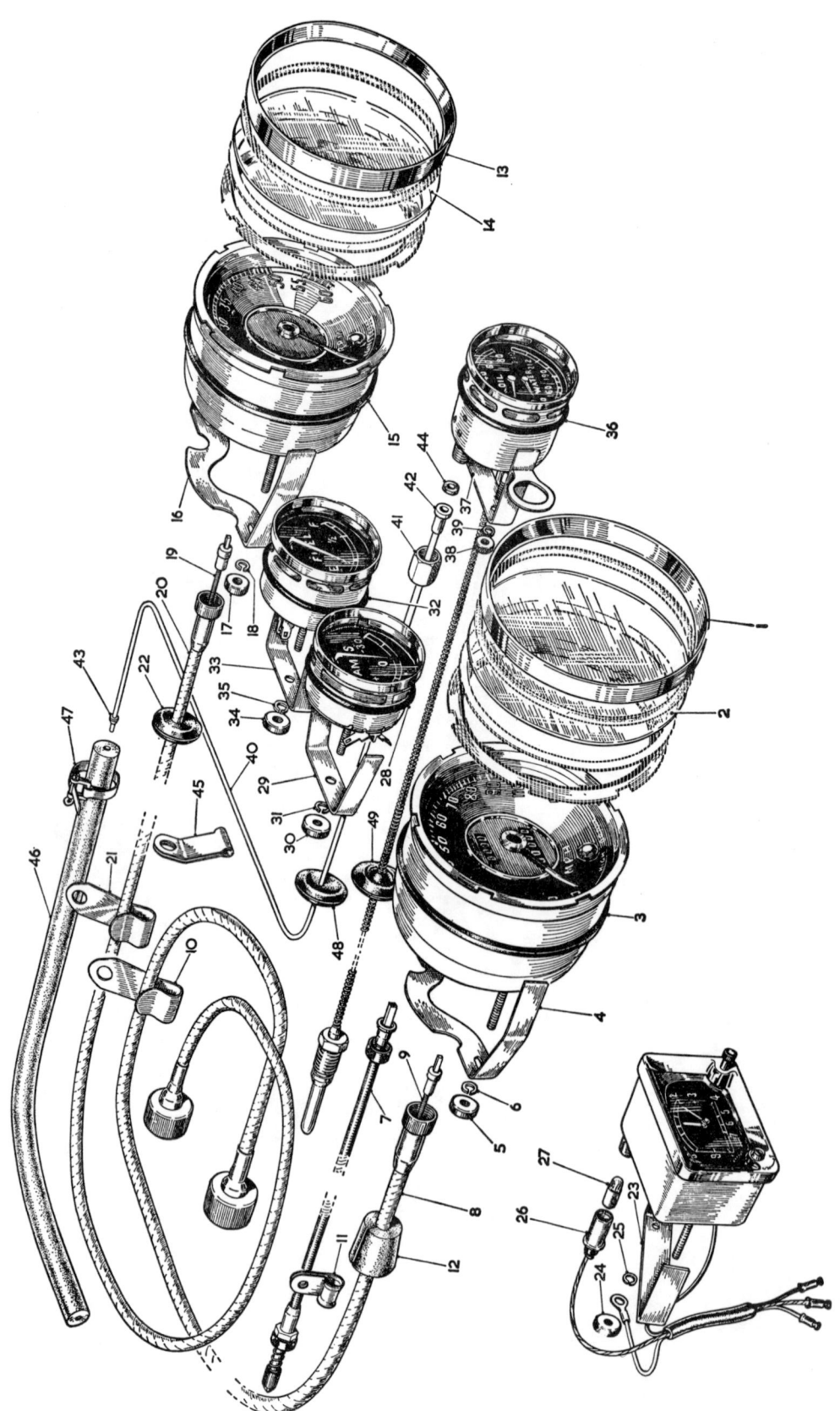

Fig. 12.14 EXPLODED VIEW OF THE INSTRUMENTS FITTED TO THE RILEY 4/68 AND 4/72

1 Bezel. 2 Glass. 3 Ring (rubber). 4 Strap—fixing. 5 Nut (thumb). 6 Washer for nut. 7 Control—trip reset. 8 Cable—outer. 9 Cable—inner. 10 Clip—cable to engine bolt. 11 Clip—cable to dash. 12 Plug—cable through dash. 13 Bezel. 14 Glass. 15 Ring (rubber). 16 Strap—fixing. 17 Nut (thumb). 18 Washer for nut. 19 Cable—inner. 20 Cable—outer. 21 Clip—cable to blower mounting. 22 Grommet—cable through dash. 23 Clamp. 24 Nut (thumb). 25 Washer for nut. 26 Bulb holder and cable. 27 Bulb. 28 Ring (rubber). 29 Strap—fixing. 30 Nut (thumb). 31 Washer for nut. 32 Ring (rubber). 33 Strap—fixing. 34 Nut (thumb). 35 Washer for nut. 36 Ring—rubber. 37 Strap —fixing. 38 Nut (thumb). 39 Washer for nut. 40 Pipe—oil gauge. 41 Nut. 42 Union. 43 Olive. 44 Washer—pipe to gauge. 45 Clip—oil gauge pipe. 46 Pipe—flexible. 47 Clip—flexible pipe. 48 Grommet. 49 Grommet.

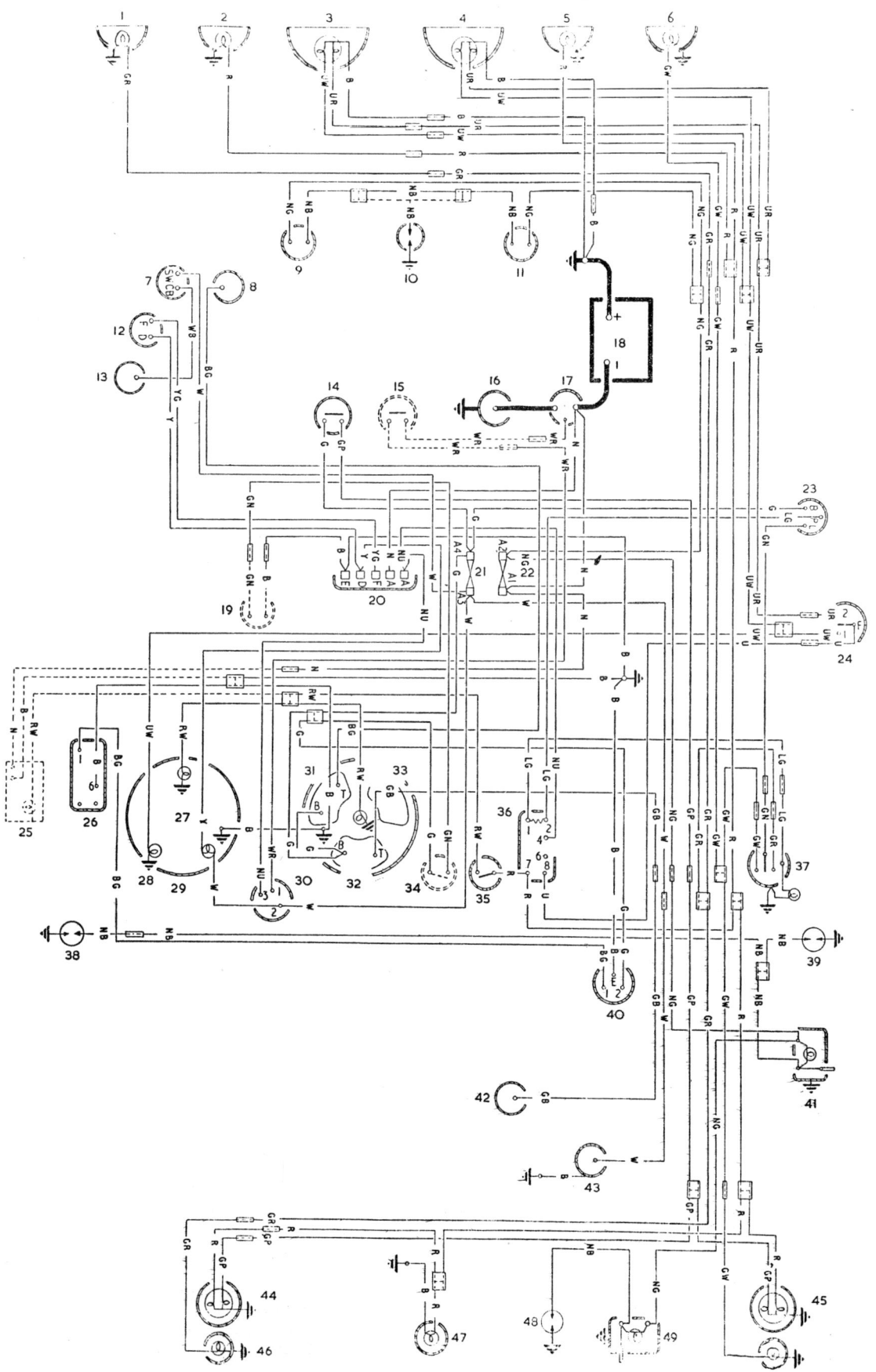

A.55 (Mk. II) Saloon & Countryman

1. L.H. flasher
2. L.H. sidelamp
3. L.H. headlamp
4. R.H. headlamp
5. R.H. sidelamp
6. R.H. flasher
7. Ignition coil
8. Thermo-element
9. L.H. horn
10. Horn-push
11. R.H. horn
12. Dynamo
13. Distributor
14. Stop lamp switch
15. Safety switch—automatic gearbox
16. Starter
17. Starter solenoid
18. Battery
19. Heater motor
20. Voltage regulator & cut-out
21. 35-amp fuse
22. 50-amp fuse
23. Flasher unit
24. Dip switch
25. Clock
26. Wiper switch
27. Ignition warning lamp
28. Main-beam warning lamp
29. Speedometer
30. Ignition/starter switch
31. Radiator thermometer gauge
32. Fuel gauge
33. Oil pressure gauge
34. Heater switch
35. Panel lamp switch
36. Lighting switch
37. Direction indicator switch
38. L.H. door switch
39. R.H. door switch
40. Wiper motor
41. Interior lamp
42. Tank unit
43. Petrol pump
44. L.H. stop/tail lamp
45. R.H. stop/tail lamp
46. L.H. flasher lamp
47. Number-plate lamp
48. Tail-gate switch   )
49. Rear interior lamp   ) Countryman only
50. R.H. flasher lamp

COLOUR CODE

B Black	G Green	S Slate	D Dark
U Blue	P Purple	W White	L Light
N Brown	R Red	Y Yellow	M Medium

When a cable has two colour code letters the first denotes the
main colour and the second denotes the tracer colour

A.60

1. Dynamo
2. Control box
3. Battery
4. Starter switch
5. Starter motor
6. Lighting switch
7. Headlamp dip switch
8. R.H. headlamp
9. L.H. headlamp
10. Main-beam warning lamp
11. R.H. sidelamp
12. L.H. sidelamp
13. Panel lamp switch
14. Panel lamps
15. Number-plate lamp
16. R.H. stop & tail lamp
17. L.H. stop & tail lamp
18. Stop lamp switch
19. Fuse unit
20. Interior lamp
21. R.H. door switch
22. L.H. door switch
23. Horns
24. Horn-push
25. Flasher unit
26. Direction indicator switch
27. Direction indicator warning lamp
28. R.H. front flasher lamp
29. L.H. front flasher lamp
30. R.H. rear flasher lamp
31. L.H. rear flasher lamp
32. Heater switch
33. Heater motor
34. Fuel gauge
35. Fuel gauge tank unit
36. Windscreen wiper switch
37. Windscreen wiper motor
38. Ignition/starter switch
39. Ignition coil
40. Distributor
41. Fuel pump
43. Oil pressure gauge
44. Ignition warning lamp
45. Speedometer
46. Coolant temperature gauge
47. Coolant temperature transmitter
56. Clock*
65. Boot/tail-gate lamp switch
66. Boot/tail-gate lamp
67. Line fuse
75. Starter inhibitor switch—automatic transmission*
76. Indicator lamp—automatic transmission*

Items marked thus * may be fitted as optional extras. Their
circuits are shown dotted on the Wiring Diagram.

COLOUR CODE

B Black	G Green	S Slate	D Dark
U Blue	P Purple	W White	L Light
N Brown	R Red	Y Yellow	M Medium

When a cable has two colour code letters the first denotes the
main colour and the second denotes the tracer colour

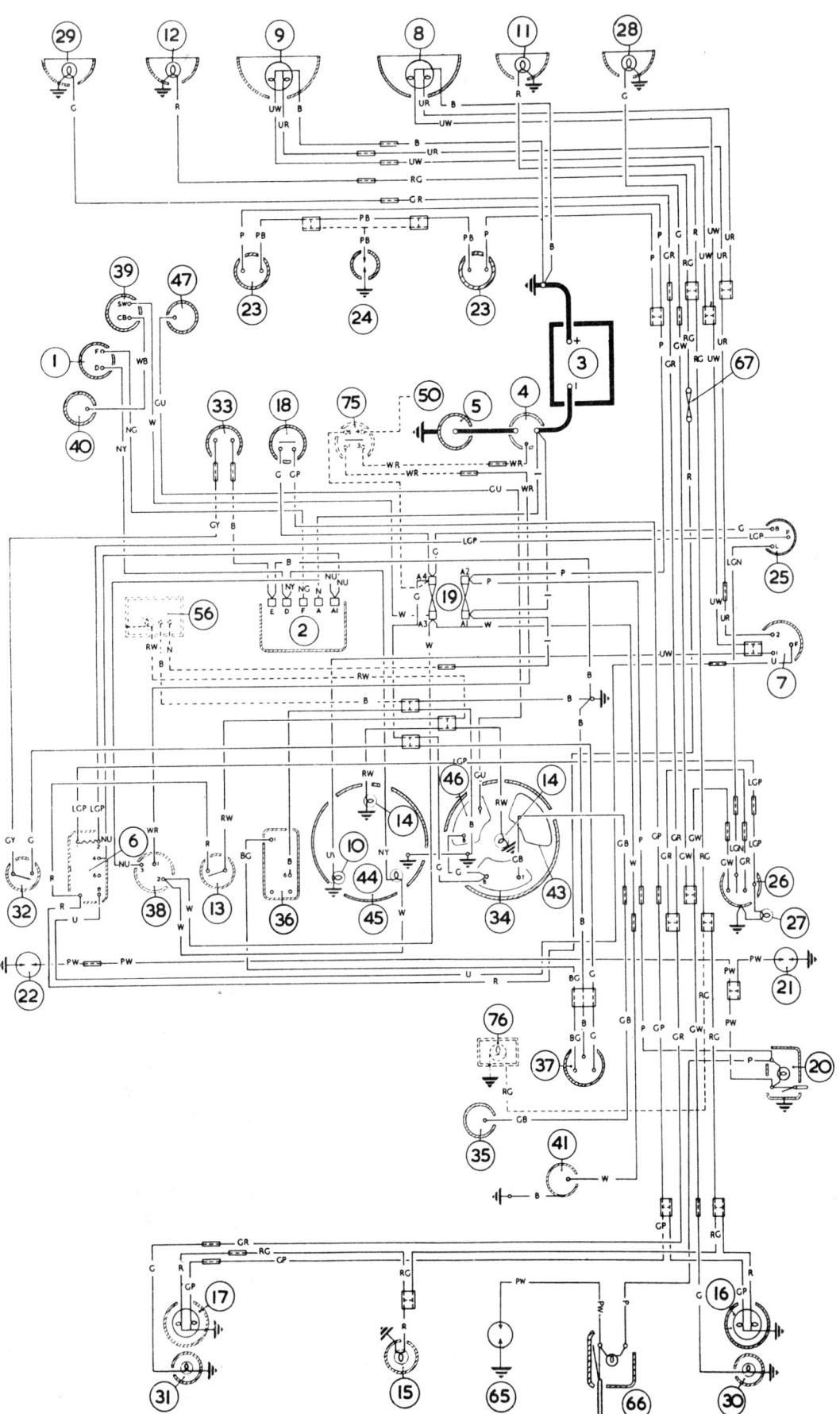

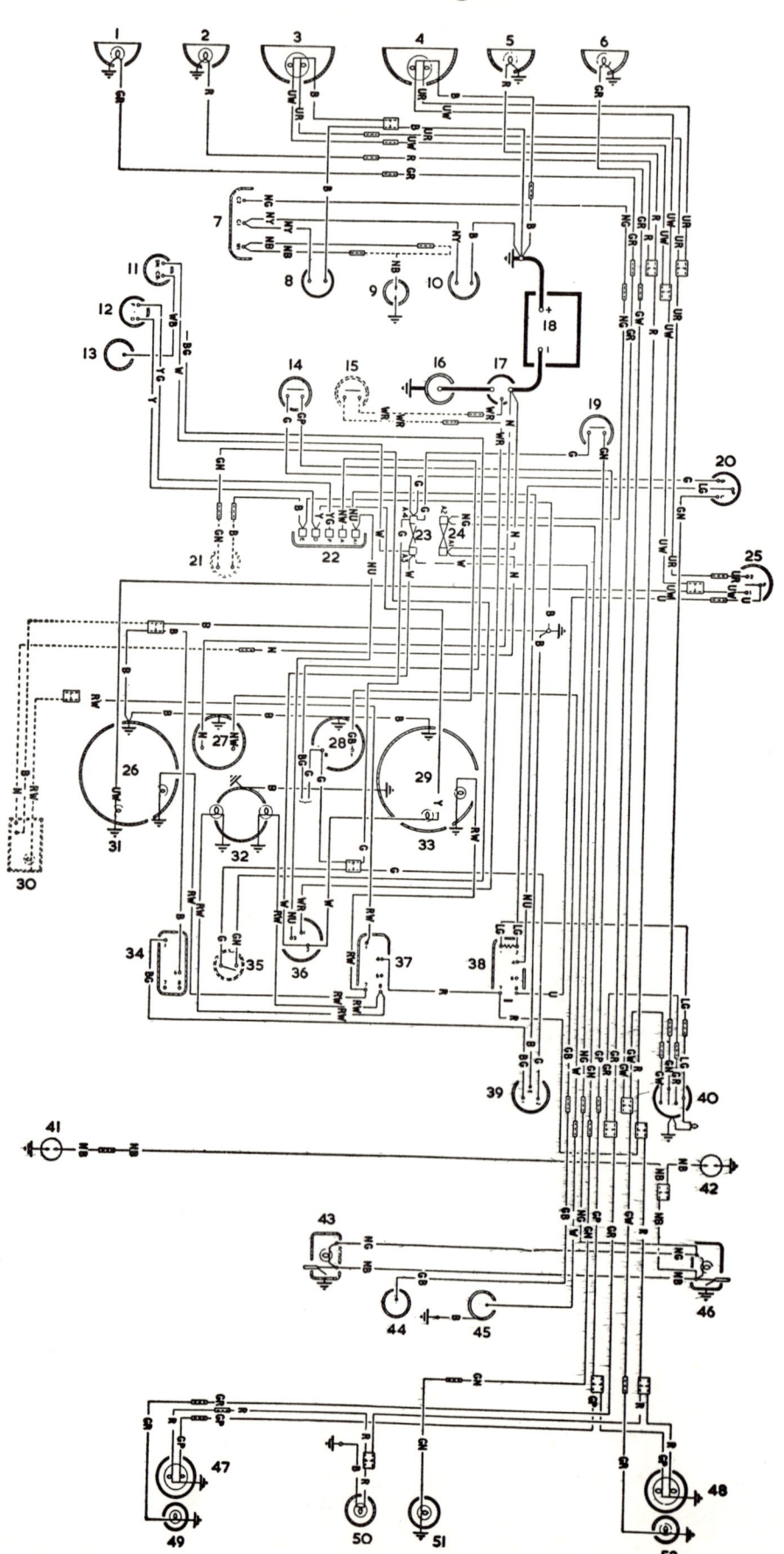

KEY TO WIRING DIAGRAM

4/68

1. L.H. flasher
2. L.H. sidelamp
3. L.H. headlamp
4. R.H. headlamp
5. R.H. sidelamp
6. R.H. flasher
7. Horn relay
8. L.H. horn
9. Horn-push
10. R.H. horn
11. Ignition coil
12. Dynamo
13. Distributor
14. Stop lamp switch
15. Safety switch—automatic gearbox
16. Starter
17. Starter solenoid
18. Battery
19. Reverse lamp switch
20. Flasher unit
21. Heater motor
22. Voltage regulator & cut-out
23. 35-amp. fuse
24. 50-amp. fuse
25. Dip switch
26. Revolution indicator
27. Ammeter
28. Fuel gauge
29. Speedometer
30. Clock
31. Main-beam warning lamp
32. Oil pressure & temperature gauge
33. Ignition warning lamp
34. Wiper switch
35. Heater switch
36. Ignition/starter switch
37. Panel lamp switch
38. Lighting switch
39. Wiper motor
40. Direction indicator switch
41. L.H. door switch
42. R.H. door switch
43. L.H. interior lamp
44. Tank unit
45. Petrol pump
46. R.H. interior lamp
47. L.H. stop/tail lamp
48. R.H. stop/tail lamp
49. L.H. flasher lamp
50. Number-plate lamp
51. Reverse lamp
52. R.H. flasher lamp

COLOUR CODE

B Black	N Brown	P Purple	W White	L Light
U Blue	G Green	R Red	Y Yellow	M Medium
	K Pink	S Slate	D Dark	

KEY TO WIRING DIAGRAM

Riley 4/72

1. Dynamo
2. Control box
3. Battery
4. Starter switch
5. Starter motor
6. Lighting switch
7. Headlamp dip switch
8. R.H. headlamp
9. L.H. headlamp
10. Main-beam warning light
11. R.H. sidelamp
12. L.H. sidelamp
13. Panel light switch
14. Panel lights
15. Number-plate lamp
16. R.H. stop/tail lamp
17. L.H. stop/tail lamp
18. Stop lamp switch
19. Fuse unit
20. Interior lamp
21. R.H. door switch
22. L.H. door switch
23. Horn
24. Horn-push
25. Flasher unit
26. Direction indicator switch
27. Indicator warning light
28. R.H. front flasher
29. L.H. front flasher
30. R.H. rear flasher
31. L.H. rear flasher
32. Heater switch
33. Heater motor
34. Fuel gauge
35. Fuel gauge tank unit
36. Windshield wiper switch
37. Windshield wiper motor
38. Ignition/starter switch
39. Ignition coil
40. Distributor
41. Fuel pump
43. Oil pressure gauge
44. Ignition warning light
45. Speedometer
46. Coolant temperature gauge
47. Coolant temperature gauge transmitter
48. Ammeter
49. Reversing lamp switch
50. Reversing lamp
56. Clock
65. Boot lamp switch
66. Boot lamp
67. Line fuse
75. Automatic gearbox—safety switch
76. Automatic gearbox—indicator lamp
95. Revolution indicator

COLOUR CODE

B Black	G Green	S Slate	D Dark
U Blue	P Purple	W White	L Light
N Brown	R Red	Y Yellow	M Medium

When a cable has two colour code letters the first denotes the main colour and the second denotes the tracer colour

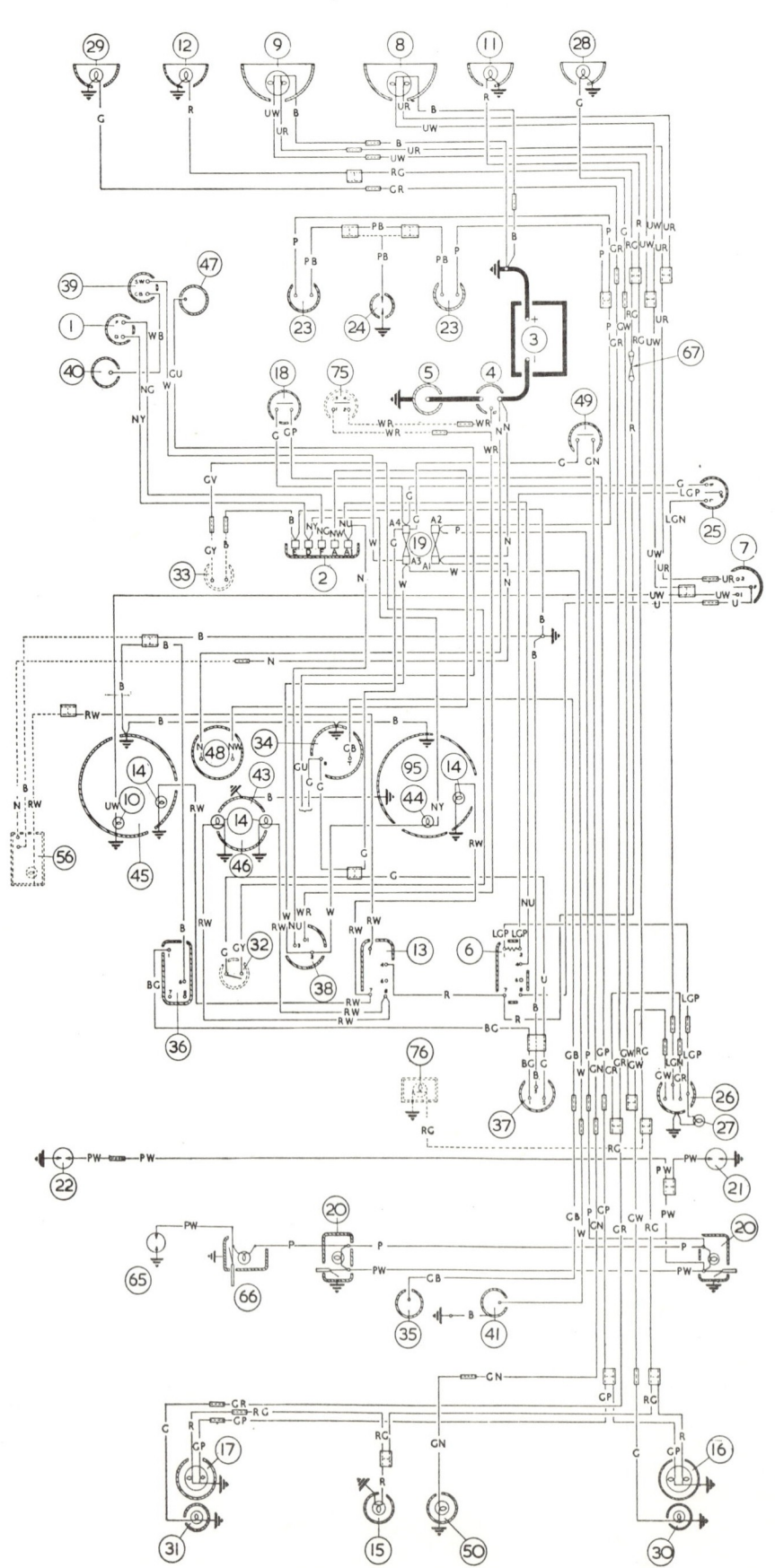

INDEX

INDEX

INDEX